# Alexander Korda
*The Man Who Could Work Miracles*

# Alexander Korda

*The Man Who Could Work Miracles*

### Karol Kulik

ARLINGTON HOUSE·PUBLISHERS
NEW ROCHELLE, N. Y.

PRINTED AND BOUND IN GREAT BRITAIN
BY RICHARD CLAY (THE CHAUCER PRESS) LTD

ISBN 0–87000–335–6

# Contents

ALEXANDER KORDA

To Thorold and Joanna

# Preface

WHEN I began to study the British cinema in 1969, I chose to concentrate my research on the so-called 'economics' of the British film industry. After six months, I came to the conclusion, shared by most of my colleagues in this field and indeed by almost everyone who has ever had the opportunity to work in British films, that any insights or proposals which I could make would have little value for an industry which was plagued by the same crises in the seventies that it had suffered throughout its history. On the suggestion of my tutor, I decided to focus my attention instead on a study of Alexander Korda, one of the men who had dared to offer Britain a potential solution to its film-making problems.

The thesis I wrote in 1971 has been greatly expanded for the purposes of this book. I was able to conduct much additional research in London, Hollywood, Paris, Budapest, and Vienna, seeing more of Korda's films and interviewing many people who had worked with or known Alex Korda. At all times my aim was to delve deeply into the subject in order to find the man behind the legend, to evaluate the merits of his films, and to assess the extent of his influence.

In this endeavour certain difficulties had to be faced. There were, for instance, no 'Korda papers' from which I could work, for these had been destroyed shortly after Korda's death, and I was to receive little assistance from Korda's remaining family or from his closest associates. The 'loss' of Korda's earliest films made a critical re-appraisal of his early work in the cinema impossible, and there were even problems in deciding exactly what constitutes a 'Korda' film. For example, many British films were 'serviced' by Korda's studios, but Korda had absolutely nothing to do with them. Some films which had been accredited to Korda elsewhere turned out, after research, to have been directed or produced by other men. I have chosen to exclude these films from my discussions, for my grounds for inclusion, both within the text and in the filmography, are that internal or external evidence can be found to prove that Korda played some creative role, however minor, in the initiation or production of the film. Despite these complications, I believe that this biography presents an objective and definitive account of Korda's life and career.

Some preparatory explanations are perhaps in order. With regard to names and accents—Hungarian names retain their proper accent marks in the two chapters set in Hungary. Thereafter I have changed to the anglicised spellings which were used by most of those who left Hungary. With respect to films—they are referred to by their original titles, and the dates after film titles represent the year of their first public showing in the country of origin. The words in parentheses after a title are only a translation, whereas those in square brackets are an alternate release title. The amount and nature of the discussion devoted to each film varies according to what I feel is most important about Korda's association with them. Plots of some of the more famous or least familiar films are retold, and in some cases more time is spent on the production history of the picture than on its critical merits, while sometimes the opposite holds true. Throughout I have made no attempt to presume that writing about a film replaces seeing it. If anything, this book is an attempt to encourage the viewing or re-viewing of Korda's films. Finally, regarding the use of material from fictional sources—while I accept that fiction can at times throw a too exaggerated light on biography, I tend to share Robert Browning's sentiments as expressed in *The Ring and the Book*:

> Well, now; there's nothing in nor out o' the world
> Good except truth: yet this, the something else,
> What's this then, which proves good yet seems untrue?
> This that I mixed with truth, motions of mine
> That quickened, made the inertness malleolable
> O' the gold was not mine,—what's your name for this?
> Are means to the end, themselves in part the end?
> Is fiction which makes fact alive, fact too?

London, February 1975                                    K.K.

# Acknowledgements

SINCE this book is the end result of a research project which I under-took at the Slade Film Unit, University College, London, in 1969, I am especially indebted to Professor Thorold Dickinson and the Slade staff who helped to guide my work in its early stages. Many of Korda's friends and associates gave generously of their time, either in personal interviews or in correspondence, and provided me with useful in-formation and welcome insights regarding Korda's life and career. I would particularly like to thank Sir Michael Balcon, John and Roy Boulting, Ian Dalrymple, Jeffrey Dell, Brian Desmond Hurst, June Duprez, Ivan Foxwell, Stanley Hall, John Justin, David Korda, Jesse Lasky, Jnr, Muir Mathieson, Leslie Mitchell, Victor Saville, R. C. Sherriff, Mischa Spoliansky, Mrs P. J. Steele, Diana Napier Tauber, Ann Todd, Lady Sarita Vansittart, Basil Wright, and Mrs Harold Young. I would also like to acknowledge Jeffrey Richards, Dr Rachael Low Whear, and Robert Vas, who, although not connected with Korda, were willing to discuss Korda and his work in the British cinema with me.

Several people have at different times read part or all of the manu-script, and their suggestions and corrections have been gratefully appreciated. For their time spent and assistance given, I owe special thanks to Kingsley Canham, Brenda Davies, Thorold and Joanna Dickinson, Kevin Gough-Yates, and Robert Vas.

Although little has been written about Korda, three works do stand out. Above all, I am indebted to the late Paul Tabori for having pieced together the facts of Korda's life in his biography, *Alexander Korda* (London, Oldbourne, 1959), and I wish to thank MacDonald and Janes for permission to quote from that work. David Lewin's series of *Daily Express* articles entitled 'The Man Who Made the Stars Shine' (26–31 January 1956) and Ian Dalrymple's article 'Alex', which first appeared in *The Journal of the British Film Academy* (Spring 1956), have both been extremely rewarding sources of information, and I am grateful to the *Daily Express*, Ian Dalrymple, and the Society of Film and Television Arts for allowing me to use material from these articles.

In addition, I should like to thank the following for permission to quote from their works: István Nemeskürty and Antisjus for the material from *Word and Image: History of the Hungarian Cinema* (Budapest, Corvina, 1968); Jeffrey Dell, A. D. Peters & Co., and William Heinemann Ltd for excerpts from Dell's novel *Nobody Ordered Wolves* (London, 1939); Dr Heinrich Fraenkel and his publisher Kindler Verlag for quotations from *Unsterblicher Film* (Munich, 1956); R. C. Sherriff and Victor Gollancz Ltd for extracts from *No Leading Lady* (London, 1968); Christopher Brunel and Forbes Robertson Ltd for excerpts from Adrian Brunel's autobiography *Nice Work* (London, 1949); Rodney Ackland and Elspeth Grant for the quotes from *The Celluloid Mistress* (London, Allan Wingate, 1954); Basil Dean and Hutchinson Publishing Group Ltd for the material from *Mind's Eye* (London, 1973); A. D. Peters & Co. and William Heinemann Ltd for the quotation from J. B. Priestley's novel *Bright Day* (London, 1946); Kevin Gough-Yates for the extracts from *Michael Powell in collaboration with Emeric Pressburger* (London, British Film Institute, 1971); and Sir Ralph Richardson and *Sight and Sound* for the quotes from 'Sir Alexander Korda', *Sight and Sound* (Spring 1956).

My special thanks go to the BBC for having produced two invaluable television documentaries: Robert Vas's *The Golden Years of Alexander Korda* (1968) and Bill Duncalf's *The Epic That Never Was* (1965). Sir John Clements has been kind enough to give me permission to quote from his interview with Robert Vas, conducted for, but not used in Vas's documentary.

My account of Korda's early career in Hungary and Austria would not have been possible without the assistance of Mrs C. Kristóf, Mrs L. Somogyi, and Mrs M. Szalai of Hungarofilm, Mr István Nemeskürty of the Budapest Film Studio, and Mr Peter Konlechner of the Österreichisches Filmmuseum, whose generosity and hospitality enabled me to visit Budapest and Vienna in October 1973. While in

ACKNOWLEDGEMENTS

Budapest I had the pleasure to work in the Magyar Filmtudományi Intézet és Filmarchivum (Hungarian Film Institute), and I would like to express my gratitude to Dr István Molnár, Mrs Garay, and Mrs Szathmáry for the help which they gave me and especially for the photographs which they kindly provided for this book. I am also grateful to Mrs Vera Surányi whose skill as an interpreter was warmly appreciated.

It would be impossible to write an acknowledgement in a book about the British cinema without praising the patient and perseverant staff of the British Film Institute's Information and Documentation Department. For their contributions to my bibliographical research, Gillian Barrett and Gillian Hartnoll deserve special mention, and my thanks go to Jeremy Boulton for arranging screenings. I am also indebted to friends like E. W. Harter who did additional research for me in Hollywood, Priscilla Murphy who ably translated several quotations, Kevin Gough-Yates who ferreted out many valuable sources and diligently checked and amended the filmography, Sarah Barker who helped to organise the manuscript, and Fred Zentner of the Cinema Bookshop who encouraged me in the project and found some of the rarer stills included in this book.

Finally, I want to thank the many close friends who listened with patience and never failed to give me support over the past years.

PART ONE

*Years of Preparation*

CHAPTER ONE

# Kellner to Korda

WILD-EYED men ran around the studio lot wondering whether heads were going to roll, and if so, whose. *The Thief of Bagdad* had been in production for several weeks; several thousand pounds had already been spent. Yet all this had happened in the absence of Alexander Korda, the film's producer, and now that he had returned everyone knew he was less than happy with the film's progress, although no one had quite figured out what was wrong. The crew probably held their breath as Korda walked from one stage to another surveying the newly constructed sets. In front of one particular scene he stopped. He turned to the art director, his brother Vincent, and in a rush of angry words heavily spiced with a Hungarian accent, Alex Korda pronounced judgement on the set and, indeed, on the film's production to date: 'Vincent, you are crazy! Go away, get a lot of men, build it four times as big and paint it all crimson. It stinks.'[1]

That was the quintessential Korda, the man whose life, whose films and aspirations were drawn on the largest canvas. In a lifetime that spanned seven decades, he spent over forty years in film-making. He directed or produced close to one hundred and fifty films which were made in all the film capitals of the world—Hollywood, Paris, Berlin, London. On three occasions he had to pick up the pieces of a shattered career and start over again. Twice he was able to create a film empire of enormous size and international influence, and for a time he was hailed as the biggest film producer and star-maker outside Hollywood. His personal charm and intellect and his flamboyant lifestyle became

3

legendary long before his death. He was a Master Showman, and as Sir Alexander Korda he also became the world's first film knight.

Yet underneath the film tycoon enshrined as Sir Alexander there was the man Sándor László Kellner, born in Puszta Turpásztó, a settlement on the outskirts of Túrkeve, Hungary on the 16th of September 1893.* Hungary is sliced from north to south by the wide Danube River, and east of the Danube stretch the vast Hungarian Plains where Korda grew up. Sparsely populated, isolated peasant settlements make up this Kunság region. Driving through the area today we feel that it can hardly have changed in the last eighty years—the same flat land, dark earth, broken only occasionally with a stately row of trees to afford protection from the wind. The white cottages with red tile or thatched roofs are still there, although newer, more colourful buildings now stand beside them. The bicycle may be the main mode of transportation for the Plains people of the Seventies, but the familiar horse and cart can be seen everywhere. The inhabitants of Túrkeve, which lies some eighty miles east of Budapest, have mostly forgotten the town's most famous 'son'; the acclaimed town 'expert' on Korda, as it turns out, never actually knew him, even though he does try every year to persuade the town officials to commission a commemorative Korda statue.

From the little information which is available, we can piece together a brief sketch of Korda's early life. He was the first of three sons born to Henrik and Ernesztina (née Weiss) Kellner: Zoltán was born in 1895, Vincent two years later. Thirty years old at the time of Sándor's birth, Henrik Kellner had been a soldier before becoming overseer of the Salgó family estate outside Túrkeve. During a period when the gentry owned almost all the land and peasant unrest was growing, Henrik's job provided both security and a degree of respectability. It guaranteed the Kellners a home, and husband and wife worked together to fulfil the various duties of an estate manager. The Kellner boys had a modest, yet happy childhood, and as with most Jewish families, the familial bonds were strongly felt.

The carefree peasant life did not satisfy the precocious Sándor for very long. At the age of five he persuaded his parents to send him to the Jewish school in Túrkeve where Zoltán later joined him. Zoltán would always follow in Sándor's footsteps (less so Vincent, who was that

* Some doubt about the accuracy of this birthdate has recently arisen as a consequence of information received from the present registrar of Jewish births in Túrkeve whose records apparently place Korda's birth three days earlier, on the 13th of September.

much younger), and Zoltán's son David believes that the closeness of the two elder brothers in their formative years explains why their temperaments were so alike—both were highly strung and volatile—and so dissimilar to Vincent's calmer disposition. Both Zoli and Vincent adored their elder brother, but when a quarrel broke out, as it often did, it was generally between Zoli and Sándor. Their arguments were intensified by the fact that the two carried more than a touch of stubbornness in their characters, and time would not change this.

With regard to their academic abilities, Alex later admitted: 'We neither ran away nor got expelled, were neither prodigies nor dunces.'[2] Even so, Sándor was the most academically inclined of the three. An astute and enthusiastic student, he won a secondary school scholarship at the age of nine. He studied first in Kisújszállás, a small settlement ten miles north of Túrkeve, and then in Mezőtúr, a larger town to the south. According to all reports, he was a voracious reader with an almost photographic memory. His taste in literature leaned towards the more popular areas of science fiction, thrillers, and adventure stories—literary genres which became staple subjects for his films. Unfortunately, as a youth, Sándor was improperly treated for an eye affliction and almost lost his sight in one eye. Afterwards he was forced to wear thick glasses (they became a personal trademark) although he still took them off for reading, an activity which he accomplished with his nose scarcely an inch from the printed page.

The stability of the family environment was disrupted in October 1906 when Henrik Kellner died from a ruptured appendix which the doctor had failed to diagnose or treat properly. Henrik's premature death left the family destitute, and for the next three years the Kellners had to depend on the generosity of relatives in order to survive. Together they moved to Kecskemét, a major agricultural centre, to live with Henrik's father Károly; but Sándor soon left for Budapest, where he stayed with cousins and attended a local secondary school. It was here that he came under the influence of Oscar Faber, a teacher who instilled in him a love of Hungarian history and literature and who introduced him to left-wing politics and philosophy. Aware of the Kellner's financial state, Faber must have been responsible for arranging for Sándor to tutor his less gifted classmates for a small, but welcome fee. Even more welcome, however, were the newspaper assignments which Faber was able to negotiate for him with a large Budapest daily paper, *Független Magyarország* (Independent Hungary).

The grandeur and sheer beauty of Budapest must have overwhelmed the teenage peasant boy more familiar with the monotony of the Plains. Previously two cities—Buda the older, hilly area and Pest the flat land on the other bank of the Danube—Budapest was not united until 1873. By the first decade of the twentieth century it was already one of the most exciting and physically beautiful capitals of Europe. The decorative architectural style of the city was exemplified in buildings like the Uránia Theatre, which rivals even Grauman's Chinese Theatre in Hollywood in ornamental embellishments.

During a visit to one such fabulous Budapest music hall, Sándor saw two words inscribed high on the wall, *Sursum Corda* ('Lift up your hearts'). He was impressed by these words, which he also found in the Roman Catholic mass he had become fascinated by, and when he began writing short stories and *feuilletons* at school and for the newspaper, he signed all his articles with this Latin phrase. A pseudonym was necessary since students were forbidden to work outside school hours, but to Sándor the words had a significance beyond their immediate usefulness. It is a measure of his condition and his expectations that he found solace and support in this simple Latin appeal. From it he would eventually take his name.

Early in 1909 the Kellner family was reunited in Budapest. They tried to make ends meet with Sándor's tutoring and newspaper work, Zoli's odd jobs, and the paying lodgers whom they took in. 'Poverty brings out the best and worst in a man,' Korda once said. 'It brought out both in me.'[3] The precarious family financial situation did weigh heavily on him. He took a night job in the editorial offices of *Független Magyarország*, but even this didn't provide enough money. Frustrated with trying to juggle his school life with his more gainful employment, Sándor left school in the winter of 1909, a few months before graduation. There is no evidence that he considered this a momentous decision. Years later he observed: 'I had a normal education, but the education that matters is what you acquire after leaving school, learning for the love of the thing.'[4]

Thus, at sixteen, Sándor became the family provider. As the eldest brother, he had already received some preparation for this new role, and he had a career which, at least for a time, would support a family. Without hesitation, and seemingly without regret, he accepted paternal responsibility for his mother and brothers; yet, as will be seen, it was a role which he would find it difficult to stop playing.

The year before, Sándor had stumbled across something which had really fired his imagination—the cinema. Paul Tabori colourfully describes the first initiation of Alex Korda into the magical world of motion pictures:

> Some time in 1908 one of his schoolmates took him to the Café Venice. Schoolboys weren't expected to frequent coffee-houses in Hungary; but there was a special attraction in this case. Three or four times a day the windows were darkened and a short show was put on for the customers. A movie show! It lasted only about half an hour and no film was longer than five or six minutes. Korda watched with absorbed interest. When they left the smoky café, he was unusually excited. 'This is the future!' he cried, grabbing his friend's arm. 'This is what I want to do!'*5

Sándor would have to wait three years before he could begin to pursue his new goal.

In the meantime he devoted all his energy to journalism. He started out as a cub reporter on the *Független Magyarország* staff, writing crime stories and reviews and occasionally conducting interviews. His most auspicious interview was with Lajos Biró, the celebrated Hungarian playwright and novelist who had also started his career in journalism. Although this initial encounter did nothing to cement their relationship, Biró was at least impressed with the young and spunky reporter. In ten years' time, a deep friendship and important working association was to develop between them.

By now, Kellner's by-lines came out under the name Sándor Korda. Exactly when he lifted the second half of his pseudonym *Sursum Corda* and changed the 'c' to 'k' is difficult to trace. Perhaps he did it when he became a full-time reporter in 1910. The reasons for the name change are equally elusive. We might assume that just as an actor takes on a stage name Sándor felt his new post deserved a special name which had no associations with the past and which provided a little flair, or perhaps

---

* We can only conjecture at the type of films which Sándor saw at his first screening. They were most likely newsreels or educational shorts produced by Projectograph, the film company which dominated the early industry in Hungary. Projectograph had been founded by Mór Ungerleider and József Neumann in 1898, and it carried on the business of film production, distribution, and exhibition, as well as equipment rental. Ungerleider himself owned the Café Velence (Venice) where the first films were shown. Cafés were already major entertainment centres in Budapest, and proprietors went to great lengths to attract and entertain their customers.

that Kellner was simply too ethnic. This does not, however, take into account the strong nationalist feelings which Korda shared with his fellow Hungarian Jews. As the noted Hungarian historian István Nemeskürty told me, the peasant Jews were incredibly chauvinistic, more 'Hungarian' than the rest of the population. During this period many of them changed their names, but not to disguise their Jewishness, rather to become more Hungarian. This same spirit may have motivated Korda to take on a new identity.

Korda's rise in journalism was steady, if not exciting. Promoted first to the status of 'special writer', he eventually became night editor for the paper. Journalism was a far from lucrative profession, however, and he never made much money from it. (Shortly before his death, Korda calculated that he had earned about £10 a month.) For eighteen months he plugged away at his job, but the restlessness which he had experienced during his last year at school soon reappeared. He hadn't completely forgotten the cinema, for he did try to persuade the newspaper's editors to allow him to write film criticism. They weren't, however, convinced that film warranted any space in their paper.

In 1911 Korda decided that he must go to Paris, then the self-acclaimed cultural centre of the world. He asked his superiors to send him as a correspondent, but they weren't interested in subsidising a trip to Paris for a seventeen year old. They might pay him for articles which he would send back, but no promises were made. With mounting frustration he appealed to others, to relatives, without success. By now, he had convinced himself that going to Paris was somehow the key to his future. He had two ambitions—to be a great writer and to do 'something' in films—and Paris seemed the best place for learning about both. In the end, his mother, who realised the extent of his determination, managed to scrape together enough money to send him off. He left Budapest for the French capital in June 1911.

In the first years of the twentieth century, Paris was like an enormous, powerful magnet attracting to itself all the brightest and most creative minds in Europe. The city had recently undergone an extensive face-lift, and the grand boulevards and cafés provided the perfect milieu for the artistic and intellectual ferment which went on night and day. The people were aware of the city's role as dictator of fashions, tastes and pleasures, and as pacesetter in the *avant-garde* art movements. As the writer Roger Shattuck put it, it was as if Paris were a large theatre stage where 'everyone wore a costume and displayed himself to best advantage'.[6] Shattuck pinpointed what was especially exciting about these years in his book *The Banquet Years*: 'To a greater extent than at any time since the Renaissance, painters, writers, and musicians lived and worked together and tried their hands at each other's arts in an atmosphere of perpetual collaboration. It was their task to contain and transform the teeming excitement, the corruption, and idealism of this stage-struck era.'[7] Thus, composers wrote musical scores which looked like graphic designs, and writers discoursed at length on the 'musicality of painting'. And everyone tried his hand at the cinema.

For the tall, slim, and fair-haired Hungarian youth who didn't even know the language, it was overpowering. But there was at least a large émigré community in Paris with which Korda could feel at home and share his innumerable experiences. His most fortuitous discovery was the Pathé Film Studio where he spent most of his waking hours, absorbing sponge-like all that he saw and at times lending a hand in the productions. The most advanced film-producing enterprise of its day, Pathé, between 1908 and 1912, was primarily involved in making spectacular historical and costume epics, heavily influenced by the then wildly popular Italian extravaganzas.

During the fourteen months that Korda spent at Pathé, he might have worked with, or at least observed the work of several already accomplished French film directors. Ferdinand Zecca was there directing a series of films which came out under the title *Scènes de la vie cruelle* (1912–14), and Albert Capellani, then at the peak of his Pathé career, was filming a version of *Les Misérables* (1911). It is even possible that Korda might have watched the great French film pioneer Georges Méliès at work on another fantasy, *La Conquête du Pôle*, for Pathé in 1912. No one could have asked for a better film apprenticeship.

But his money was running out. If he was being paid for articles sent to Hungary, the payments were far from reliable. Finally, in August 1912, the Hungarian Consulate in Paris was forced to pay his fare back to Budapest. Though penniless, he arrived back in a triumphant mood, ready at last to realise his dreams.

Although Korda went straight back to his job on the newspaper, he now supplemented his income by contributing film articles to other magazines and papers. Within a few weeks, he accepted employment as secretary and general 'go-fer' for Ungerleider's Projectograph company. He later told one reporter that he took this job 'not because he had any advanced perception of the cinema as an art form, but simply because the film people offered him more money'.[8] He needed it, not only to bolster the family income but also to accommodate his new, seemingly extravagant habits, which included cigar-smoking. In a description of this period in his life, he later explained to *Daily Express* reporter David Lewin why film men acquired a taste for cigars: 'I earned £60 a month. But films were considered something rather lowly —more lowly than newspapers. Cigars were large and cheap at the time. We smoked cigars to show we were important and to make up for our loss of position.'[9]

As company secretary Korda had several duties at Projectograph. His experience as a journalist came in handy, for he was put in charge of the company's weekly programme announcement sheets and its overall publicity machine. At this time the Hungarian Government passed an official order requiring all films shown in Hungary to be in Hungarian, so Sándor began translating the explanatory titles and dialogue of the silent foreign films which Projectograph imported and distributed throughout the country. He spent many long hours in the dark screening room, watching films, concentrating on the action and story, and composing appropriate Hungarian titles. Thus, at this early stage, Korda had the opportunity to become familiar with the different visual and narrative styles of numerous national cinemas and individual film directors. In addition, he was able to pick up the rudiments of several of the languages he would later speak fluently.

While at Projectograph he continued to write for the papers, but he now confined himself to writing about the cinema. His own assertion to the contrary, it is abundantly clear in Korda's writings that he did have a fairly advanced understanding of the inherent artistic possibilities of the medium. In an article for *Mozgófénykép Híradó* (Motion Picture News), the first film trade paper in Hungary, Korda advocated the practically revolutionary view of the film director as a creative artist. Korda even convinced the editorial staff of the large Budapest daily paper *Világ* (World) to print the first regular film column in Hungary. This was written by Korda himself, but only ran for three months, from August to November 1912.

It was a momentous autumn for the film industry in Hungary, and Korda sensed this and took advantage of it. He had been working as co-ordinator of film material for a weekly magazine covering all aspects of Hungarian entertainment called *Szinházi Élet* (Theatre Life), but he saw that there was a need for a film periodical designed for the general public. In October 1912, in the midst of this artistic flurry,

Korda and a fellow journalist, István Várnai, started their own film journal. Named *Pesti Mozi* (Budapest Cinema), it was a weekly magazine sold in the cinemas. There were no proper offices for the magazine staff, so all the editorial work was done either in cafés or in the editors' homes.

*Pesti Mozi* was primarily concerned with in-depth studies of particular films. In one of the first issues, Korda informed his readers that 'each week we will publish critiques, but only about one film'. He went on to assure them that this one film would be chosen by the editors on its merits; *Pesti Mozi* would not become a trade paper promoting the latest releases of the film companies. The magazine's focus was not, however, restricted to the area of film discussion and criticism. It was an idealistic, radically left-wing journal, in every sense a 'young man's' forum (Korda had just turned nineteen). It printed short stories, sketches, and political cartoons, contributed by well-known authors poets, and artists, including Frigyes Karinthy and Marcell Vértes—two men who later worked with Korda in film-making. As happened in France, the cinema in Hungary was embraced by the country's intellectuals and artists. There was no barrier between trained 'film' men and men from other disciplines who wanted to collaborate with the film industry; everyone exchanged ideas freely and enthusiastically. Mr Nemeskürty drew an interesting hypothetical parallel in his discussion with me when he said that this interplay between artists in Hungary with respect to the cinema was 'like saying that D. W. Griffith had John Dos Passos and Upton Sinclair as his best friends'.[10]

Under Korda's guidance *Pesti Mozi* struggled along for eight months before financial difficulties forced it to stop publication. The magazine reappeared for three months (September to November) in 1913 as *Mozi* (Cinema). In February 1915 Korda started up again with *Mozihét* (Ciné-Weekly); but already there was a difference, for *Mozihét* was the journal of a film 'producer', something which Korda had in the meantime become. Combining a talent for journalism and a love of the cinema had been one thing, but it was still a long way from actually making films. This was Korda's next step.

Film journalism was even further away from Korda's youthful intentions, if we are to believe a comment he made in 1953: 'My ambitions as a young man were literary. When I was eighteen I wanted to write a great big novel—a novel as great and as big as *War and Peace*. Or if that wouldn't go, a very slender volume of wonderful poetry, about a dozen sonnets in a lifetime. Nothing more.'[11] Biographers and readers alike tend to pounce too often on statements like this, constructing from a few words uttered late in life a false picture of lifelong frustration caused by unfulfilled ambitions. It is therefore necessary for us to keep some sense of proportion about Korda's brief reference to his own past. Korda may well have had these literary aspirations when he was young; but to think for a minute that failure to achieve them cast a pallor over Korda's subsequent career is a melodramatic distortion of what are, after all, the normal, healthy ambitions of anyone at all sensitive to literature. What is valuable, however, is to note how these early ambitions were transformed or integrated into the new aspirations which arose as Korda's career advanced.

1. Kevin Gough-Yates, 'Interview with Michael Powell', in *Michael Powell in collaboration with Emeric Pressburger*, London, British Film Institute, 1971.
2. Philip Johnson, 'The Creed of Korda', *The Star*, 9 March 1936.
3. Paul Holt, 'A Cabby Decided his Future', *Daily Herald*, 9 May 1953.
4. Jympson Harman, ' "Alex": a study of Korda', in *British Film Yearbook 1949–50*, ed. Peter Noble, London, Skelton Robinson, 1949, p. 107.
5. Paul Tabori, *Alexander Korda*, London, Oldbourne, 1959, p. 29.
6. Roger Shattuck, *The Banquet Years*, revised edition, London, Jonathan Cape, 1969, p. 6.
7. *Ibid*, p. 28.
8. E. M. Wood, 'Korda: Dreamer and Spellbinder', *Leader Magazine*, 24 May 1947, p. 17.
9. David Lewin, 'The Man Who Made the Stars Shine', Chapter Three, *Daily Express*, 28 January 1956.
10. Interview with István Nemeskürty conducted by the author, 22 October 1973.
11. Sir Alexander Korda, 'The First Talking Pictures', *Radio Times*, 25 December 1953, p. 5.

CHAPTER TWO

# Rise and Fall in Hungary

SÁNDOR KORDA was a strikingly handsome young man. A portrait photograph of the time reveals a magnificent head, full lips, high cheek bones, straight nose, and hypnotic, slanting eyes. It is a dramatic, evocative picture which suggests at the same time a powerful character and a sensitive nature, with a touch of mystery thrown in for good measure. This was the young man who lived at home but spent most of his days and nights in the Budapest cafés in heated debate with the rest of Budapest's young, idealistic community. In the cafés a cup of coffee and a glass of water could last all day, newspapers from all over the world could be studied, and it was easy to make valuable contacts, for everyone was a café regular. Korda thrived in this environment, and it was here that he met most of the men who would assist him in his film-making career.

The First World War turned Europe upside down, and Hungary, dragged unwillingly into the turmoil, was no exception. It was the worst possible time to enter film-making, for the primitive conditions under which everyone in the business already had to work became more primitive as the effects of wartime and wartime shortages were felt. Nevertheless, it was in 1914 that Korda's career as a film-maker began.* Since the films that Korda made in Hungary are apparently

* Korda had been exempted from military service either because of his bad eyesight or, as has been suggested but not verified, because of a 'weak' heart. His brothers, on the other hand, were both called up for active service. While in the Army Zoltán contracted tuberculosis, the disease which was to plague him for the next twenty years.

lost (the Budapest archives were destroyed by bombing during the Second World War), a critical re-evaluation of Korda's five, prolific film-making years in his native country is impossible. We do at least have some notion of what his films were like and how they were set up.

At 16 Kinizsi Street the city of Budapest owned a film studio where films were produced for showing in the schools. It was called the Pedagogical Film Studio, and in 1914 the Hungarian actor Gyula Zilahy went to the studio and offered to make films for them. Zilahy chose to produce these films under his own company name, Tricolor—after the three colours in the Hungarian flag—although the company as an operating concern never really existed. Béla Zsitkovszky, the head technician and cameraman at Pedagogical, worked on Tricolor's three films; but Zilahy, who planned to star in them, needed someone to help him with the direction. How he came to choose Korda is anybody's guess. All we do know is that at least two of the three films—*A becsapott újságíró* (The Duped Journalist—a suitably ironic title for Korda's first film) and *Tutyu és Totyó* (Tutyu and Totyo)—were co-directed by Korda. The third film, *Őrház a Kárpátokban* (Watch-house in the Carpathians), may have also been a collaboration between Zilahy and Korda, although there is no conclusive evidence to establish this. Since neither man had much practical experience, the films were undoubtedly rather amateur efforts. They were released in 1914 and 1915; but by the second year the Tricolor–Pedagogical connection had been severed, and Korda had to look elsewhere for his next film project.

In February 1915 Korda's third film journal, *Mozihét*, appeared. Through it Sándor met Móricz Miklós Pásztory, a florist and gardener who had ventured into film production and exhibition. Both men shared a special fascination with the cinema and its possibilities, and they became good friends. Pásztory had already achieved some success in films by exploiting a neglected market: films with rural settings and stories to be shown to peasant audiences at touring cinema screenings. In 1914 Pásztory had founded his own production company, Nemzeti (National); he now suggested a film collaboration to Korda. The film which they co-directed was a far cry from the peasant tales of Pásztory's previous film work. *Lyon Lea* (Lea Lyon—1915) was an adaptation of a popular stage play written by the celebrated Hungarian playwright Sándor Bródy. Although the early Pásztory–Korda association was confined to this one film, two years later their friendship developed into a more fruitful partnership.

Korda had still not directed a film of his own. In the middle of 1915 he was given the chance to do this for József Neumann's Korona Company. Neumann had once been Mór Ungerleider's partner at Projectograph, but the two men had quarrelled and parted company. Mainly a distributor, Neumann set up Korona in 1914 and decided to compete with Ungerleider by producing films as well. Neumann asked the young Sándor, whom he knew from his early days at Projectograph, to direct one Korona film. Korda acquiesced, but only on the condition that Neumann keep Korda's name off the credits in order to avoid hurting Ungerleider, with whom he had no quarrel. Thus, when *A tiszti kardbojt* (The Officer's Swordknot) was released in 1915, the directorial credit went to Neumann, not Korda.

The film, a traditional wartime romance, was written by Korda, photographed by Béla Zsitkovszky, and starred Gábor Rajnay, a leading Hungarian actor. It was shot in three days, the speed being made possible by Korda's resourceful use of actual military training grounds and training soldiers as extras for the 'action' scenes. The interiors were probably shot at the Pedagogical Studio. Korda himself later liked to tell journalists that his first film was shot in an old barn, perhaps an accurate description of Pedagogical. *A tiszti kardbojt* was a modest success and gave Korda the necessary encouragement to think of himself as a solo film director. His first four (or five) films had, however, been haphazard affairs, one-shot efforts which were not part of a coherent production programme. Korda's next films were just the opposite.

Jenő Janovics was the man who gave Korda his first major break. Director of the National Theatre of Kolozsvár in Transylvania, Janovics, like Korda, had been introduced to film by the Pathé Film Company. Pathé had made two films in Kolozsvár in 1913, utilising Janovics's company of National Theatre players in these productions. For Janovics, film-making was to be a useful device to keep his actors busy and to record for posterity his theatrical successes. He established his own film studio in the provincial city in 1914 and began producing film adaptations of the plays from the National Theatre repertoire, which were distributed by Projectograph as 'Proja' (Projectograph + Janovics) films.

At first Janovics left the direction of his films to others, notably

Mihály Kertész, the Hungarian actor who became one of the mainstays of the Hollywood cinema in the thirties and forties under the more familiar name of Michael Curtiz. After Kertész's departure, however, Janovics undertook to direct the films himself. In 1916 the distribution contract with Projectograph was dissolved, and Janovics changed the name of his company to Corvin, in honour of the Renaissance Hungarian King Matthias Corvinus. It was at this time that he started looking for someone to take on the directing chores at Corvin.

In 1936 Janovics described his first meeting with Sándor Korda, remembering the 'cold marble table' of the café and the 'warm ideas' of the 'young Korda boy'. Janovics decided to take a chance on Korda and offered him the job at the healthy salary of 18,000 kronen a year. The job meant, of course, that Korda would have to leave Budapest, temporarily suspending his editorship of *Mozihét* which had by now grown into an influential film periodical.

Examining issues of *Mozihét* today, we are struck by the artistic excellence of its presentation and the depth and range of its coverage of the film world both in Hungary and abroad. Each issue ran anywhere from forty to eighty pages, and most pages were decorated with a colourful scroll which framed the articles and reviews. Unlike *Pesti Mozi, Mozihét* was exclusively devoted to film. Programme announcements of current film showings in Budapest, descriptions of the works in progress at the various Hungarian studios, editorial tirades against uncultured Hungarian directors, unscrupulous exhibitors and distributors, and unresponsive Government officials, and reviews and analyses of specific films, directors, and artists*—all these were standard features included in each week's issue of the magazine.

Korda and co-editor István Várnai were responsible for most of the long editorials, which were usually a forum for some campaign (e.g. the founding of a film museum in Budapest), but contributors were obviously welcome. There were, for example, some lively, theoretical film articles written by Jenő Török, a forerunner of Hungary's greatest film aesthetician Béla Balázs. From the number of colour film advertisements contained in each issue, it is clear that Korda had no trouble getting studio support through advertising, perhaps one reason why *Mozihét* fared better financially than its predecessors. It was an enormous achievement on the part of the twenty-three-year-old Korda to

* In particular, the films of Danish actress Asta Nielsen, American director D. W. Griffith, and actor-director Charles Chaplin received special attention and promotion in *Mozihét*.

have put together such a magazine, but *Mozihét* had to be left behind when Korda moved to Kolozsvár in 1916.

If little is known about Korda's earliest films, not much more information is available about the half dozen films he directed for Corvin in Transylvania. Following the formula already established by Janovics, they were film adaptations of popular novels or plays, and Korda probably had no choice in the selection of film subjects. Korda learned much from Janovics about the handling of actors, even though Janovics, as Tabori reports, had to support his young director against an attempted mutiny of the actors who were insulted by Korda's presumptuousness in criticising their theatrical acting style. Janovics's confidence in Korda paid off in the end, for the films did well commercially and were highly praised by the press.

Korda's first Corvin film, *Fehér éjszakák* (White Nights—1916)—an adaptation of Victorien Sardou's *Fedora*—was a milestone in that it was one of the first films made by a Hungarian film company to be shown outside the country. This was an accomplishment in itself, since neither Korda nor Janovics was really concerned with gaining international distribution for Corvin's films.

> 'We did not think much about markets in those days,' Korda told an interviewer in 1933. 'The director was usually quite out of touch with commercial considerations and simply made his picture as he saw it. . . . We were Hungarians making Hungarian pictures for Hungarian people. But if we had made a notably good one—and if the world had been at peace—I believe it would have had an appeal anywhere. It would have been characteristically Hungarian and a good film—therefore it would have been international. But you must remember the times in which we were working then.'[1]

An emphasis on the international marketability of films later became the foundation of Korda's film-making policies, but for now he was pleased if his films satisfied the Hungarian market and in some way promoted the development of a healthy national cinema.

Sándor directed six more films for Corvin in 1916.* The films were

---

* *A nagymama* (The Grandmother) from the play by Gergely Csiky and starring Hungary's 'Sarah Bernhardt' Lujza Blaha and the young Hungarian actor Mihály Várkonyi, who became famous in Hollywood as Victor Varconi, was followed immediately by *Mesék az írógépről* (Tales of the Typewriter), an adaptation of István Szomaházy's novel. Janovics and Korda then co-wrote the

shot in no more than two weeks and were photographed by either Mihály Fekete or Árpád Virágh, Corvin's two resident cameramen. As the months passed, however, the relationship between employer Janovics and employee Korda deteriorated. Korda obviously felt responsible for the great success of the Corvin films and thought that Janovics's tight schedules and budgets impinged too much on his artistic rights. Korda wanted more autonomy, more control over the producing side of his films; his ambitions needed room to grow, and Janovics refused to give him enough freedom and space. It was a clash of egos which could not be resolved as long as Korda remained a hired director.

During the winter of 1916–17 Korda started to think about setting up his own company. In the spring he returned to Budapest to discuss the idea with Miklós Pásztory. They knew that a business venture of this size required a substantial financial backing, and they were luckily able to interest Richard Strasser, scion of a rich merchant family, in the project. In April 1917 the negotiations were completed. Korda and Pásztory now had their own film production company, and after buying the rights to the name from Janovics, they christened it 'Corvin'. (This was an especially shrewd move, for Korda's new company could capitalise on audience familiarity with the Corvin name.) The parting with Janovics, who stayed in Kolozsvár making films under the new 'Transylvania' banner, was certainly amicable. Korda never forgot the man who had been willing to take a risk on him when he was unknown and untested. Years later, when he was established in England, Korda brought Janovics to London on many occasions as his guest.

The first order of business of the Korda–Pásztory–Strasser trium-

---

script for *Az egymillió fontos bankó* (The One Million Pound Note), from Mark Twain's story of the same title. Two vehicles for the Hungarian actress Lili Berky—*A kétszívű férfi* (The Man with Two Hearts) and *Vergődő szívek* (Struggling Hearts)—came next; and lastly Korda directed husband-and-wife team Sándor and Ella Kertész Góth in *Ciklámen* (Cyclamen). There is some evidence that Korda also directed *Mágnás Miska* (Miska the Magnate—1916), a classic Hungarian musical comedy, with Lili Berky and Mihály Várkonyi, although whether or not the film was actually completed and released is unknown. Likewise, Korda may have made the crime story *A nevető Szaszkia* (The Laughing Saskia) for the Unió production company in 1916, perhaps during one of his visits to Budapest or soon after he left Janovics. (There is no information to be found on Unió; Mr Nemeskürty himself guesses that it was run by some 'grocer', his term for those fly-by-night producers who had a little money to spend on making films.)

virate was to build a studio. There was no question of keeping Corvin in Transylvania, for that part of the country was periodically occupied by Rumanian troops. So Korda began to search for a suitable location in the environs of Budapest. Korda finally discovered a likely site in the Zugló suburb at 39 Gyarmat Street; but while this studio was being built, Korda used a make-shift studio closer to the city centre, at the corner of what is today Gorkij Avenue and Dózsa György Street. Six months later, the studio in Zugló was ready, and Korda and Company moved in.

A few relics of Corvin Studios still exist. The premises now house the largest film studio complex in Hungary (Mafilm), but amidst the overgrown shrubbery at the unused Gyarmat Street entrance the small statue of a raven—which figures in King Matthias Corvinus's coat of arms and which became Korda's personal emblem—can still be found. The other remnants of the past are nearby: the small entryway, staircase, and garden which were part of the main building where Korda's offices were located. The wood panelling, gracefully curved stairs, and decorative glass doors are reminders of the grandiose physical structure of Korda's studio. There was nothing tatty or make-shift about Corvin: it was as impressive in its day as Denham Studios was to be twenty years later.

With the establishment of Corvin Korda was at last free to experiment with his film-making ideas. He made it clear from the start that Corvin stood for quality, prestige productions. A rival firm might produce forty-eight films a year; Corvin would settle for twelve, though the same amount of time and money might be spent on Korda's one dozen as would be spent on someone else's four. Korda considered this policy of films 'of quality' rather than 'in quantity' the secret of successful film-making. 'One good picture can make a company,' he was often quoted as saying, 'a dozen good pictures can make an industry.' Corvin gave him the chance to make his point.

The studio structure which Korda devised for Corvin set the pattern for all future Hungarian film studios. The key man in this structure was the literary editor or dramaturge, who:

> . . . should be well trained in film-making as well as in literature who, while representing the interests of the director and studio, guided the writers, who were not expert in films . . . at the same time guarding each author's individuality and ideas. The dramaturge of a motion picture studio acts as liaison between the worlds

of films and literature. It is his duty to contact eminent writers and persuade them to write for the screen.[2]

What inspired Korda to put literary considerations above all others? First, Korda's personal predilections: as we know, he had always been responsive to and respectful of literature. Second, Korda's past experiences: the success of the Korda–Janovics films, all taken from literary sources, convinced Korda that familiar or recognisable stories were what the public wanted. Third, the Hungarian people's particular obsession with their literary heritage: in Hungary at that time an 'artistic' film was equated with a 'literary' adaptation, the two words being synonymous. Korda's own leanings, then, could be profitably exploited in a country where ninety per cent of the films produced were literary adaptations.

At Corvin the position of dramaturge was shared by two men, both well known in the literary world: the writer Frigyes Karinthy, an early contributor to Korda's film journals, and the playwright László Vajda, famous for his later work with the German director G. W. Pabst.* Their job was to plan a series of screen adaptations from the best of Hungarian literature—including works by Ferenc Molnár, Sándor Bródy, Ferenc Herczeg, Jenő Heltai, and Kálmán Mikszáth—'but', to quote Mr Nemeskürty, 'no longer in order to perpetuate past literature, but to create films . . . [for] in Korda's eyes the task of film-makers was to interpret literature on a worthy level. Yet he was aware of the film as a medium having its own peculiar means by which the director could convey the writer's ideas in a specific cinematographic form.'[3] Korda discussed this in an article for *Szinházi Élet* in 1917, concluding that the old 'over-literary approach' to cinema was out-dated and that 'only action that can be expressed in images is suitable for the screen'.[4] In most of the Corvin films, however, Korda did not respect his own dictum. As he wrote much later: 'My approach to films was always from the literary rather than the pictorial side.'[5]

All this should not lead us to the conclusion that only writers were put under contract to Corvin. Gusztáv Kovács was hired to be Corvin's principal cameraman, and Korda employed László Márkus as head of the studio's art department. The list of actors and actresses under contract was impressive: Lili Berky, Márton Rátkai, Gábor Rajnay, Mihály Várkonyi, Oszkár Beregi, and a little later, an unknown named

* Fifteen years later Lajos Biró was employed by Korda in this same capacity in England.

Antónia Farkas. (The last two, like Várkonyi, had careers in Hollywood, as Oscar Beregi and Maria Corda.)

In his first year as production head of Corvin Korda produced and directed four films.* The company did not, of course, survive on Korda's films alone; both Miklós Pásztory and Sándor Antalffy directed films for Corvin release in 1917.† The small output meant that Korda was able to take much care with the preparations and filming of each project. He needed to spend extra time on the films, for towards the end of the war even basic materials were scarce and film-making became increasingly difficult. Korda complained: 'We have only the minimum of technical resources; sets, costumes, transport, and many other requirements present tremendous problems and one must give up many an idea which our foreign colleagues could easily realise. I was unable to get ten pounds of plaster of paris in the whole of Budapest.'[6] It was a time when Korda had to make the most of what was available, and the resourcefulness which he learned then was to be put to good use in later years.

In spite of these adverse conditions, Korda rose to become the top producer in Hungary, with no one except Michael Curtiz to touch his achievements. In the Christmas 1917 issue of *Mozihét*, one of the contributors attempted a prophecy about Korda's future career: 'I don't know where Sándor Korda's career will end, but I know that it will be one of richness, a life without work. He will grow old early, but will

---

* The first *Szent Péter esernyője* (St Peter's Umbrella—1917) was adapted from Kálmán Mikszáth's novel. Korda then pulled off quite a literary coup by gaining permission from the writer Mihály Babits to film a version of his most recent novel; *A gólyakalifa* (The Stork Caliph—1917) came out within a year of the book's first publication. These literary adaptations were followed by two films taken from original screenplays: *Mágia* (Magic—1917) written by Frigyes Karinthy and Kálmán Sztrókay and *Harrison és Barrison* (Harrison and Barrison—1917) co-scripted by Gyula Kőváry and Richárd Falk. The latter film was a 'wild burlesque' very much in the Mack Sennett comedy tradition, which depended heavily on visual humour and the comedy teamwork of the leads, Dezső Gyárfás and Márton Rátkai, two of Hungary's most popular comedians. Korda apparently considered *Harrison és Barrison* his best film of the period; it was made, rumour has it, with the intention that if Korda later went to Hollywood he would take a copy of the film with him to show the Hollywood producers his film-making talents. The success of these two 'non-literary' films did not, however, change Korda's basic view, for he quickly returned to what was for him the 'safer' territory of literary adaptation.

† Sándor Antalffy made *A testőr* (The Guardsman), and Pásztory directed *A riporterkirály* (The King of Reporters) and *A kétlelkű asszony* (The Woman with Two Souls).

have great, great cigars. . . . However, not so famous as Korda, the first man whom an express train will bring to fame is Mihály Kertész.'[7] It is an uncanny prediction of the fates of these two men who dominated the young Hungarian film industry. Although he had worked in films longer than Korda, Curtiz was, as the comment suggests, not as well known since he was exclusively a film director, owning neither a film studio nor a journal as Korda did. Even so, both men significantly affected the development of the Hungarian cinema; they fathered the country's two distinct film-making traditions: the literary adaptations and Pathé heritage derived from Korda, the original screenplays and Danish Nordisk Company influence from Curtiz. Their careers upon leaving Hungary followed the same path from Vienna to Hollywood. From then on, their careers had little in common. Curtiz, who was a far better director than Korda, was able to establish himself in the American cinema. Korda, as we shall see, was not so lucky.

While still in Hungary Korda did come to the attention of at least one Hollywood mogul. The journalist Philip Johnson narrates the story:

> Adolph Zukor, of Paramount (Pictures), Hollywood, California, heard of him, and wrote to him. Korda had never heard of Zukor, and didn't answer the letter. It was some years later, when he was working for Ufa in Berlin, that the young Korda first came into close touch with the might of the American film industry, and learned who Adolph Zukor was. He wrote to him—'a momentous decision', as he told me. This time it was Zukor who didn't answer.[8]

Although it seems hard to believe that Korda had never heard of Zukor, one of the major American film producers of that time,* it must be remembered that American films did not have a stranglehold on the Hungarian market, as they did in France and England for example. Hungarian screen time was dominated by a foreign country, but that country was Germany, not America.

Even though Corvin and film-making monopolised most of Korda's time, he still managed to continue his editorship of *Mozihét*. 'From a business point of view,' notes István Nemeskürty in *Word and Image: History of the Hungarian Cinema*, 'this was a clever move, for by an efficiently edited paper he could assume control over the whole

---

* In another version of this story, the Hollywood mogul is quoted as being Jesse Lasky, also with Paramount Pictures at the time.

country's film industry, which he actually did.'[9] Through *Mozihét* Korda became the spokesman for the film industry, as well as its number one producer. He spoke out against many bad practices in the industry and launched a virulent attack on the German domination of Hungarian screens (similar in many ways to his later campaign against Hollywood's control of the British cinema). At the height of these anti-German attacks, in December 1917, he wrote:

> I'm almost ashamed to say it again as I have done it so often before, but I have a deep faith in Hungarian films. . . . I do not expect Hungarian film production to vegetate among the many other national film industries; I believe unflinchingly and have been shouting it at the top of my voice for four or five years: we Hungarians will soon get to the top. The doubters I cannot convince. It would be better for them to wait. In a year's time I'll present them with the proofs.[10]

The 'doubters' may have been impressed by Korda's profession of faith in Hungarian films and his acceptance of personal responsibility for the future of the Hungarian cinema, but their scepticism was reinforced six months later when the news leaked out that Korda was himself thinking of leaving Hungary for greener pastures. He had received an invitation from Charles Magnusson to come to Sweden to direct films for the Svenska Company. Although Korda refused the offer, the possibility of a more international career must have appealed to him. As early as the summer of 1918, then, Korda was beginning to look beyond the borders of the small and insular Hungarian film industry which he had conquered by the age of twenty-four.

Soon after his return to Budapest in 1917 Korda had moved out of the family home and into a fashionable downtown hotel. As his fortune and reputation increased, so his lifestyle became more extravagant. Although he fraternised socially with most of the city's most influential people, he remained closely tied to his family. He found that the easiest way to keep the family together was to bring its members into his own professional life. This he did in 1918 when he employed his brother Zoltán at Corvin. Zoli, who immediately adopted the 'Korda' surname, directed one film in collaboration with Miklós Pásztory (*Károly-bakák* —1918). For the time being, Vincent pursued his own career. Vincent's artistic talents had been discovered quite early, and he was allowed to study painting and drawing, first at the College of Industrial Art and then as a student of Béla Grünwald, the celebrated Hungarian painter. Sometime in 1918 Korda also met a young Hungarian beauty named Maria Farkas.

Born in Déva, Hungary in 1898, Maria Farkas had moved while still in her teens to Budapest where she had become a dancer on the Budapest stage. She called herself Antónia Farkas, and under this stage name she came to Korda's attention, was put under contract to Corvin, and starred in four of Korda's last five Hungarian films. She was a tall, statuesque dark-blonde with a classical, almost Grecian face. A studio portrait taken at this time gives us a demure picture of the twenty-year-old girl who was destined to play the temptress, the vamp, the 'Delilah', or 'Helen of Troy', in films directed by the man who became her husband. In 1919 Sándor Korda and Maria Farkas were married.

As the First World War ended, Hungary entered one of the most intensely chaotic periods in the country's history. The changes in Korda's career reflected the political and economic crises which were gripping the country; his film-making output diminished in 1918 and 1919, and several projects had to be abandoned.* Nevertheless, Korda's actual position in the film industry remained unaffected—a tribute more to political adaptability than to stoical fortitude. Hungary's precarious situation led to the formation and collapse of two governments in less than a calendar year. Korda played a key role in both these governments.

In the autumn of 1918 Allied and Rumanian troops were poised on the Hungarian borders waiting to carve up the territory. On the 31st of October Count Mihály Károlyi, leader of a party of pacifistic liberals who championed the American democratic system, became head of a coalition government which declared the formation of a republic two weeks later. Hungarians were unified in their resentment of the war and their fear of losing territory now that the Central Powers had been defeated, but Károlyi's Government did not have the necessary muscle to deal with the fears and frustrations of the Hungarian people.

* During 1918 Korda directed only three films, but all of them were attempted on a scale which probably exhausted the Corvin facilities. *Faun* (1918) from Eduard Knoblauch's novel was a tale of magic which afforded Gábor Rajnay one of his most imaginative roles. Korda then planned a series of screen adaptations of the novels of popular nineteenth-century writer Mór Jókai. Only two were completed: *Az aranyember* (The Man with the Golden Touch—1918) and *Fehér rózsa* (White Rose—1919). Israel Zangwill's novel was the source for Korda's last production of the year, *Mary Ann* (1918).

Korda believed in Károlyi and the goals of his government; Károlyi considered Korda his 'film man' and appointed him 'commissioner of film production with authorisation to organise progressive bourgeois film production'.[11] Lajos Biró became Károlyi's Secretary of State for Foreign Affairs. Korda and Biró had just begun to fulfil their new duties when the Allied Army entered Hungary in January 1919 and offered Károlyi an unsatisfactory territorial settlement. Károlyi could not accept the offer, but neither was he prepared to continue military hostilities in order to secure a better settlement. He responded in the only way he could: he threatened to hand over the government to the Hungarian Communist Party which he knew would fight to regain the territories. In March Károlyi stepped down, and a Communist 'proletariat dictatorship' was established under the leadership of Béla Kun, a Hungarian Jew.

Like most of his fellow countrymen, Korda accepted the Communist regime not because he ideologically supported Marxist doctrine, but rather because he saw the Communists as guardians of Hungary's sovereignty and freedom. Both Biró and Korda—neither of whom were party members—were appointed to the Communist Directory for the Arts, and it was Korda who convinced Béla Kun to nationalise the film industry in April 1919.

Throughout 1918 Korda had waged a press campaign against the film 'middle men', the distributors, who were bleeding the industry and hindering the development of a truly artistic national cinema. Korda and his fellow film producers welcomed nationalisation as the best way to deal with the economic inequalities of a capitalist system. Centralised control of the industry was maintained through three directories, and Korda was a member of the directory which was concerned with the industry as a whole. From April to August 1919, for the first time in film history, nationalised, socialist film production was carried out in the Hungarian Councils' Republic.*

In those four months Korda made three films. One, *Fehér rózsa* (White Rose), was already in production when the Communist regime was set up. It is worthwhile quoting the plots of the other two films— *Ave Caesar!* and *Yamata*—for in them we can detect more than a tinge of party-line propaganda.

> *Yamata* is the story of a Negro slave's revolt. His master flogs him so cruelly that Yamata's body is covered with blood. His miserable

* The film industry in the USSR was not nationalised until August 1919.

plight arouses the pity of a marquis who buys him and treats him well, though he, too, exploits the man, but more subtly. . . . *Ave Caesar!* is the story of a profligate Hapsburg prince, actually a variation of *Le Roi s'amuse*. The prince gets his aide-de-camp to kidnap a gipsy girl who is branded for life by this adventure. Obviously the film was directed against the feudal class.[12]

Whether or not Korda approved of the content of these films scripted by Corvin's dramaturge László Vajda is immaterial; that he made them at all was enough to cause his victimisation after the Communists were overthrown.

On the first of August the Communist regime fell, and Béla Kun fled the country. For three months Rumanian troops occupied the capital until they were chased out by the counter-revolutionary army of Admiral Miklós Horthy. A full-scale purge, known as the White Terror, resulted. Directed against liberals and Communists in general and Jews and film-makers in particular, this systematic purge began even before Horthy was in complete control of the country. Anyone who had worked with the Communists was arrested and thrown in prison or persecuted and deprived of his property and livelihood. A Jew, a liberal, and a film-maker, Sándor Korda was, to put it mildly, a prime target.

Sometime in the last two weeks of October Korda was arrested by Horthy's henchmen. In his biography of Korda, Paul Tabori tells us that the arrest was a mistake, that they had picked up the wrong man, and that Korda was released as soon as the misunderstanding was cleared up. (They had been looking for an actor, a known Communist, with the same name.) It is an unnecessarily elaborate explanation, one which pales in comparison with István Nemeskürty's simple account:

'Admiral Horthy wanted to see [Korda's] films,' Mr Nemeskürty told me, 'and after seeing them said that the man who made these films must go to prison. Korda spent some days in prison, and nobody knows how he was able to get out of the country and flee to Vienna. Unlike so many other refugees, both at that time and even after 1956, Korda never again returned to Hungary. He was deeply hurt by the way he had been treated.'[13]

This version is far more plausible, even though it leaves unanswered the whole question of Korda's escape. A curious comment in an article on Korda in *The Observer* (22 April 1951) would have us believe that a

British official helped Korda to obtain his release from Horthy's men. How or why he might have done this must, however, be left to our imagination.

Before his arrest Korda had been invited to direct films for Count Kolowrat's Sascha Film Company in Vienna. Korda quickly finished the two films which he had been working on—*Se ki, se be* (Neither In Nor Out—1919) and *A 111-es* (Number 111—1919)—and in November 1919 Sándor and Maria left Budapest for the Austrian capital. Korda was never again to set foot in Hungary.

An ironic footnote to this whole episode is provided by a brief news item which appeared in the French film journal *Cinémagazine* in May 1921:

### THE JEWS IN HUNGARY

The Hungarian Government is undertaking a lively campaign against film directors of the Jewish religion. It proposes simply to expropriate them.

The Germans, having considerable interest in the affairs of the Hungarian cinema, are protesting vehemently.

Yet another conflict . . .[14]

1. Stephen Watts, 'Alexander Korda and the International Film', *Cinema Quarterly*, vol. 2, no. 1, Autumn 1933, p. 13.
2. István Nemeskürty, *Word and Image: History of the Hungarian Cinema*, Budapest, Corvina, 1968, p. 30.
3. *Ibid*, p. 31.
4. Translated from Korda article, Paul Tabori, *op cit*, p. 50.
5. Sir Alexander Korda, 'The First Talking Pictures', *loc cit*.
6. Translated from Korda article, Paul Tabori, *op cit.*, p. 53.
7. *Mozihét*, no. 51, 1917, translated for me by István Nemeskürty.
8. Philip Johnson, *loc cit*.
9. István Nemeskürty, *op cit*, p. 31.
10. Translated from *Mozihét* article, Paul Tabori, *op cit*, p. 51.
11. István Nemeskürty, *op cit*, p. 42.
12. *Ibid*, pp. 45–6.
13. Interview with István Nemeskürty conducted by the author, 22 October 1973.
14. *Cinémagazine*, May 1921, translation by the author.

# CHAPTER THREE

# Viennese Patronage

IT had taken Alexander Korda less than five years to rise through the ranks of the Hungarian film industry. In a few frenetic weeks his career had been shattered; he had lost his studio, his magazine, and, more importantly, his position at the top of an industry hierarchy. The next eleven years of his life were to be years of constant transition and re-adjustment, frustrating years during which he tried to re-establish the career, reputation, and life which he had been forced to leave behind in Hungary. Like a gypsy he moved from one country to another, never staying long enough to set up a permanent career. This transient existence was not motivated by a wanderlust spirit; Korda, like so many others, was simply reacting to the times. During the twenties the fluctuating economic situation on the Continent tended to thwart most individual or national efforts towards financial recovery and stability, and in this respect Korda's career reflected the common dilemma.

Although Korda was twenty-six when he and Maria arrived in Vienna, he looked much younger and compensated for his youthful appearance by growing a beard and, on occasion, wearing a monocle. At this time he also dropped 'Sándor' in favour of 'Alexander', its equivalent, while his wife began to experiment with different professional surnames in order to distinguish herself from her husband. Maria was a strong-willed and independent woman who planned to have a career in her own right. She was not, however, prepared to sever in a drastic way the professional connection with Alex, for the surname she settled on—'Corda'—represented a marginal distinction and was to lead to endless confusion in the press.

The move to Vienna provided an easy transition for Korda. Vienna and Budapest, both situated on the Danube and for years the principal cities of the same empire, were quite similar physically and culturally. As was the case in Budapest, Viennese social life revolved around the café society, and Alex felt at home in this environment. The Kordas affected a grandiose lifestyle which they could ill afford; they hired fancy, chauffeur-driven cars and lived in the best hotels. These affectations were all-important for a couple who wanted to impress potential employers or financiers. Rather than appear like the uprooted refugees they were, Alex and Maria presented the image of an ideal film-making team—film star married to film director—who had decided to grace the wider film world with their presence and their talent.

Many of Korda's employers during this period were not typical industry businessmen, but film 'patrons': men from other professions or wealthy families who were fascinated with cinema, eager to finance productions, but not, on the whole, interested in directing films themselves. Film patronage had existed before (even Hungary had had its 'grocers'), but it now played a vital role in Continental film production. Since traditional studio-organised film-making was prey to the changing economic conditions, the film-maker needed a financier who could afford to sink money into films without having to depend totally on box-office returns in order to continue a production programme. Korda's first sponsor in Vienna was the epitome of this type of film patron.

Count Alexander ('Sascha') Kolowrat-Krokowsky was an American-born, Austrian nobleman whose bank account more than matched his size (over twenty stone). His company, Sascha-Film, had been set up before the war and had produced series of silent comedies, such as the 'Cocl' and 'Pampulik' films directed by the stars of each series, Rudolf Walter and Max Pallenberg. During the First World War Sascha-Film branched out into newsreel production, but Kolowrat's company did not earn a reputation until after the war when the Count was able to attract German and Hungarian directors to Vienna. Michael Curtiz was just one of the film directors to precede Korda at Sascha-Film.

Korda had known about Kolowrat and his work prior to his flight to Vienna, for Kolowrat had contributed articles to *Mozihét*; and at least at the beginning the two men got along well together, enjoying as they did a similar flamboyant approach to life. It was not until June 1920, however, that Korda began his first Sascha project. Costume pictures were in vogue in Europe after the war, following on the successes of the earlier Italian and American costume epics. In Germany Ernst Lubitsch had just completed two period films, *Madame Dubarry* (1919) and *Anna Boleyn* (1920), the latter starring Emil Jannings, the great German actor, as King Henry VIII. Korda and Kolowrat decided to join the bandwagon with an adaptation of Mark Twain's novel *The Prince and the Pauper*.

Twain's story about Henry VIII's son Prince Edward, the young pauper Tom Canty who is Edward's physical double, and the confusion that results when the boys switch places was adapted by Lajos Biro, who had also been forced to flee Hungary with the arrival of Admiral Horthy. This was Korda's second adaptation from Twain, an author whose work obviously impressed him, and the film was to be the first of twenty-three collaborations between Korda and Biro. The art director Artur Berger and the costumer Lambert Hofer had the task of re-creating the Tudor atmosphere; the dual role of prince and pauper was played by Tibi Lubinsky, a famous child star (not without the aid of some effective trick photography), and Alfred Schreiber portrayed Henry VIII. When the film was shown in Britain in 1924, the British trade papers congratulated Schreiber on his performance: '. . . for once he departs from the stage tradition which makes that maligned monarch either a ruffianly Bluebeard or a vulgar buffoon'.[1] Biro and Korda, of course, were as responsible for this new interpretation of Henry as was the actor, and the film therefore provided a testing ground for a more important Korda–Biro collaboration in 1933.

The solid, all-too-solid narrative structure which became a feature of the Korda–Biro films was already evident in *The Prince and the Pauper*; the parallel action and continual visual contrast between the grandeur of the English Court and the squalor of the City of London apparently dominated the entire film. One English reviewer was carried away by the film's visual conception: 'The story of the little Prince and Tom Canty,' he wrote, 'as the central motive of a series of magnificent pictures has been used by the producer much in the same way as Turner used the legends of ancient mythology as the subject of some spacious and ideal landscapes.'[2] On a more down-to-earth level, some felt that the pageantry overwhelmed the intimate scenes (a criticism to be levelled on many Korda films), and the editing was condemned as 'jerky', a fault perhaps of later editing for the foreign versions.

Known mainly by its German title *Seine Majestät das Bettelkind*, the film was well received in Austria and Germany on its release in November 1920. American distribution, on the other hand, was held up by litigation between Sascha-Film and an American production company which had just completed its own version of the novel. In their zeal to make the film Korda and Kolowrat had forgotten that Twain's works were not yet in the public domain and that they should have negotiated for the screen rights. Sascha-Film eventually won the legal battle, the American film was withdrawn, and Korda's version was distributed with great success in the United States.

Korda later said that the American success of this film was 'the first thing to make me give conscious thought to the problem of international films'.[3] The great significance of the film to Korda's future development as a film producer must, therefore, be acknowledged. In addition, the unexpected legal dispute over film rights provided Korda with a lesson he was not soon to forget; in later years he insisted on buying the screen rights to any and everything on the market, in part as a protection against being 'caught out' again by a rival film company. And finally, this picture anticipated the film which was to launch Korda's British career thirteen years later, *The Private Life of Henry VIII*.

In the spring of 1920 Alex's mother and brother Zoltan joined him in Vienna, while Vincent remained in Hungary pursuing his art studies. For almost a year Alex waited for Kolowrat to approve his next project, and in the meantime he travelled back and forth from Vienna to Rome, where Maria was much in demand for film work, and planned several projects whose lifespans barely outlasted the train journey. Frustrated with the temporary halt in his career and perhaps disconcerted by the rise in Maria's fortunes, Korda began to feel isolated and unsure of his future. The Christmas 1920 issue of *Mozihét* contained a letter from Korda which reveals his uncertainty and confusion: 'Perhaps I'll stay in Vienna, perhaps I won't. I had offers to work in Rome and Berlin but it's a little difficult to get used to such a gipsy existence. For the time being I have no intention to come home. Not yet.'[4] In 1921, a Korda–Corda production of quite another sort undoubtedly raised Alex's spirits, for in that year Maria gave birth to a son, whom they named Peter Vincent. Not long after Peter's birth, however, Mrs Kellner died in a Viennese sanatorium after a prolonged illness. Alex was deeply depressed by her death, and the close bonds between the three brothers were further reinforced.

During the last half of 1921 Korda finally returned to the studio floor to direct two films for Sascha, *Herren der Meere* (Masters of the Sea— 1922) and *Eine Versunkene Welt* (A Vanished World—1922),* but Korda's relationship with Kolowrat steadily deteriorated as the Count insisted on interfering with the production side of Korda's work. By the time these two films were released, Korda had left Sascha-Film and formed his own company, Corda Film Consortium. It was called 'Corda' rather than 'Korda' perhaps because the financing came from Maria's earnings or because a screen star's name was considered a better box-office attraction. The first and only picture made by Corda-Film was a co-production with another company, Vita-Film, owned by a Hungarian film distributor named Szücs. Vita-Film had been in operation for two years, but its output, most of which were co-productions, was relatively small. Szücs's inexperience as a film producer became apparent during the making of Korda's last Viennese film, *Samson und Delila* (1923).

As its subtitle ('the story of an opera singer') indicates, *Samson und Delila* was not merely a reworking of the Biblical story. Korda and Ernest Vajda wrote an original screenplay for the film which described in a melodramatic fashion the tribulations of an opera singer (Maria Corda) who refuses to sing the role of Delilah opposite a new, young tenor. (The rapprochement is finally effected after the tenor rescues her from the clutches of a roguish Russian autocrat.) Interwoven with the contemporary scenes were episodes from the ancient tale of Samson and Delilah, which a Jewish scholar relates to the opera singer. Thus, Maria had a chance to play a dual role—the two Delilahs—while the two settings provided Korda with the opportunity to exploit the costume epic within the framework of a modern-day story, thereby attracting a wider audience.

* Both films were scripted by Hungarians (Ernest Vajda and Lajos Biro) from their own novels (*The Pirates* and *Serpoletto* respectively). Several Hungarians who had worked with or known Korda at Corvin were also employed on the films, including producer Arnold Pressburger, actors Mihály Várkonyi [Victor Varconi] and Gyula Szöreghy, and the art director Alexander Ferenczy. 'Maria Palma', the leading actress in both films, was almost certainly Maria Corda under one of her later-discarded pseudonyms. The films were romantic 'sea stories': *Herren der Meere* was about modern-day pirates and pirate treasure, and *Eine Versunkene Welt* told of a Hapsburg archduke who became a common sailor. The latter film won for Korda his first international prize, the Gold Medal for the Best Dramatic Film at the Milan International Cinema Concourse.

*Samson und Delila* was shot over the winter of 1921–2, and the actual production was apparently a series of expensive fiascos, including a temple set which only collapsed after the frustrated 'Samson' and crew had given up and the cameras were no longer filming. Four hundred extras, three cameramen, two art directors, and three costume designers worked on this ambitious project, and the shooting schedule ran to a hundred and sixty working days, an almost unheard of figure at that time. Even though Szücs was nominally the film's producer, it appears that he had no control over Korda's expenditures.* The scale of production was most enterprising, but then so were Korda's ambitions.

From the publicity stills and hand-outs for *Samson und Delila*, which concentrate on the big crowd scenes of the Biblical half of the story, we can see that Korda wanted to create a spectacle along the lines of the Babylon sequences in D. W. Griffith's *Intolerance* (1916). Korda had long admired the work of this American director, and he was only one of many European directors, Lubitsch and Curtiz among them, who tried to imitate the more grandiose aspects of *Intolerance* (and the Italian costume epics which preceded it) during the early twenties.† Korda's decision to mix a modern drama with an ancient one may have also derived from the similar mixture in Griffith's film, in which four stories taken from different periods in time are intercut. It must, of course, be remembered that *Intolerance* was Griffith's biggest commercial failure and that the imitators on the whole tried to improve their chances by imitating the scale, but not the message or length of the film. Even so, Korda and the others had little hope of matching, in size and technical and financial resources alone, the American film, which, for example, used in one scene forty times the number of extras (sixteen thousand) than Korda had had at his disposal.

Korda had therefore tried to accomplish too much with *Samson und Delila*; he had neither the talent nor the resources to pull off such a venture. It was inevitable that his attempt to deal with two very different genres with only the most tenuous link between them was not

* An Austrian reference book lists the following cost items from the *Samson und Delila* budget (in parentheses 1922 £ equivalent):

| | |
|---|---|
| 400 beards, 100 kilograms men's hair | 1,500 kronen (£62) |
| Masks | 275,000 kronen (£11,449) |
| 160 working days | 4,400,000 kronen (£183,181) |
| Total Cost | 12,333,750 kronen (£513,478)[5] |

† cf. Ernst Lubitsch's German film *Das Weib des Pharao* [*The Loves of Pharaoh*—1921] and Michael Curtiz's two-part Austrian epic *Sodom und Gomorrah* (1922–3).

to meet with success. When Stoll Film Company released the film in Britain in 1923, one reviewer remarked:

> The aim of the producer of this pretentious film is so indefinite that it is not quite obvious whether it should be accepted as modern comedy or classical drama. In either case the result cannot be regarded as entirely satisfactory. One would imagine that the object has been rather to exhaust the capabilities of a film studio than to adapt its means to the requirements of a story. . . . The incongruous combination of classical drama with crude comedy melodrama quite robs one portion of the film of a certain dignity and impressiveness which it should be entitled to from the scale on which it is attempted. With the modern portion omitted, the spectacular have an artistic interest which would make this film an undoubted showman's proposition.[6]

The film had, indeed, exhausted the capabilities and finances of both Vita-Film and Corda Film Consortium. Alex was forced to find another patron, but there weren't any left in Vienna, or at least none who would back him after his last film. In late 1922 or early 1923 Corda-Film was dissolved, and Alex and Maria moved on to Berlin.

For all its disappointments and frustrations, Korda's brief stay in Vienna represented an important advance in the development of his career. Estranged from the insular environment of the Hungarian film industry, Korda had to adapt quickly to the demands of a more international film-making arena and had to learn, often the hard way, the ground rules for this kind of film production. For the first time he directed a lavish spectacle in the Hollywood manner which was later associated with men like Cecil B. De Mille and David O. Selznick and for which Korda himself was to become famous. Korda had already, by 1922, attempted ambitious projects, assembled international casts and the best technical staff (mostly Hungarian), and spent vast sums of money, usually not his own, to achieve impressive visual effects. These were the foundations upon which the Korda pattern of film-making was to be built.

1. *The Bioscope*, 24 January 1924, p. 53.
2. *Ibid.*
3. Stephen Watts, *loc cit.*
4. Translated from Korda letter in *Mozihét*, Paul Tabori, *op cit*, p. 65.
5. Walter Fritz, *Die Österreichischen Spielfilme der Stummfilmzeit (1907–1930)*, Wien, Österreichischen Gesellschaft für Filmwissenschaft, 1967.
6. *The Bioscope*, 26 July 1923, p. 43.

# CHAPTER FOUR

# The Unknown To-morrow—Berlin

AS Alex Korda journeyed from Vienna to Berlin, he might well have wondered about the wisdom of his latest move. Certainly there was no point in staying in Vienna where he had exhausted his credit with the local film patrons, but in many respects Germany presented an even more uncertain working environment. Post-war reparations, or rather the failure to meet them, had put tremendous political and economic strains on the country. Uprisings and strikes, foreign occupation of the Ruhr, and spiralling inflation had helped to create an acutely tense and unstable atmosphere throughout Germany. In August 1922 the Deutsche Mark had fallen in value to 8,500 marks to the pound, and this was a good rate of exchange compared to what it was to become in the following months. German art, and in particular German cinema, strangely blossomed in this climate of chaos. It was as if the threat of impending gloom and the deterioration of human values, of morality, were the foods on which German artists not only survived but actually thrived. It was this frenzied artistic atmosphere which probably drew Korda on towards Berlin.

In a short paragraph in her fascinating book on the German cinema, *The Haunted Screen*, Lotte Eisner summed up the attraction, albeit morbid, of Germany in the early twenties:

> One can picture those excited minds. It was a period of inflation when everybody wanted to live at any cost, to drink the cup of pleasure to the dregs, to keep his balance somehow and anyhow

on the debris of normal life. But no one could free himself from the anguish of the morrow. The cost of pleasure went up from minute to minute, billions of marks becoming mere scraps of paper.[1]

Alex and Maria accepted the challenge of living in this milieu. Their extravagant tastes remained unchanged, even as the price of maintaining a polished veneer steadily climbed. Like so many others, they acted as if their lives were untouched by the crises around them. It is fitting, none the less, that the first film the two Kordas were to make in Berlin was entitled *The Unknown To-morrow*.

As had been the case in Vienna, Korda's German career was only made possible through the help of two patrons of the cinema, Hungarians both. In February 1923 Korda obtained Gabriel Schwarz's financial support for the incorporation of a new film production company, Korda-Film, Alex's third film-making concern in six years. Later in 1923 Korda also joined an international distribution organisation, FIHAG, in order to secure distribution for his company's films. The film which inaugurated the company was *Das unbekannte Morgen* [*The Unknown To-morrow*—1923]; and although the inflation crisis delayed production several times, the film was finally completed in October 1923 and released some time after that. Seen in the light of Korda's previous and subsequent work, it is an unusual film worthy of detailed examination, for in it Korda attempted to deal with German expressionist themes and techniques while following a narrative familiar to the Korda repertoire.

Korda and Ernest Vajda together wrote the script of *Das unbekannte Morgen*: a contemporary melodrama about a proud wife's struggle to redeem her reputation and regain her family after her husband, driven by a belief in his wife's infidelity, has disowned her. The adulterous act which the husband, famous astronomer Gordon Manners (Carl Ebert), discovers has, of course, been engineered with the aid of accomplices by Marc Muradock (Werner Krauss), who is in love with, but has been spurned by Manners's wife Stella (Maria Corda). The wife exposes Muradock's treachery and is reunited with her husband and child. The film leaves us with the moral that had Manners not devoted so much time to his work, thus neglecting his wife, the entire calamity would have been averted. What adds dimension to this otherwise banal plot is the way in which Stella is able to clear herself.

The film begins with Stella being thrown out of her home and being saved from a suicide attempt by a dark stranger swathed in a black cloak. 'You don't know what tomorrow will bring,' he assures her. 'Trust me I can foretell the morrow.' 'He' is Raorama Singh, a Hindu mystic who can see the future in his crystal ball. In flashbacks Stella recalls for Raorama, and for the audience, the events leading up to her disgrace. The mystic then leads her into his inner sanctum where, out of an inky blackness, a smoky crystal globe appears, floating in mid-air. As the sphere expands to fill the screen, and the two characters fade, we are transported to the 'future'. We see Stella's divorce from Manners and the coerced marriage with Muradock which follows. After a punch-up between Manners and one of Muradock's assistants in a Berlin night club (frequented by all the major characters), the accomplice tries to blackmail Muradock. Manners, by now convinced of his wife's innocence, arranges a rendezvous with Stella, during which the evil Muradock murders his accomplice in a hotel room, leaving behind evidence which incriminates Manners. As the police arrest Manners for murder, the scene returns to the present and to an hysterical Stella who has seen that the worst is yet in store for her. The mystic now plays his trump card: 'With this knowledge you've gained you can alter the future.' With legal counsel and police in tow she goes to the hotel room that she saw in the 'future' and apprehends the accomplice (and the maid who was in on it too). Cornered, Muradock flees, and as he chases after Stella, he falls to his death from the ledge of Manners's observatory.

In an explanation of the German preoccupations which dominated the classic German films of this period, Lotte Eisner has noted that 'the German is obsessed by the phantom of destruction and, in his intense fear of death, exhausts himself in seeking means of escaping Destiny'.[2] Through a rational application of mysticism, through 'cheating' the future, Stella is able to do just that, escape her destiny. In this respect the film is very close to Arthur Robison's Schatten [Warning Shadows—1922], which Korda may have seen, wherein six party guests are hypnotised so that they envisage what Siegfried Kracauer calls a 'collective nightmare', the future which will occur if the guests act out their passions. In Schatten, as in Das unbekannte Morgen, the inevitable disasters are thereby avoided; the horrors of the future are 'experienced', but never really played out.

In addition to this theme, Expressionist film buffs would be delighted by two other aspects of Korda's film: the acting of Werner Krauss and the camera lighting of certain scenes.

Krauss, who is perhaps most famous for his performance as Dr Caligari in Robert Wiene's *Das Kabinett des Dr Caligari* [*The Cabinet of Dr Caligari*—1919], here portrays the 'violinist-maniac' Marc Muradock using the whole alphabet of Expressionist gestures and looking much as he did in Wiene's film. It is by no means a great performance, but Krauss's emphatic acting is undermined by the non-Expressionist playing of the other key actors, notably Maria Corda whose best scenes are not the dramatic moments, but the quiet, understated sequences—mostly gratuitous to the story—where she has to appear subtly alluring and provocative.

There is no hint of Expressionist influence in the set designs created by Hungarian Alexander Ferenczy even though, like most German films of the time, the entire film was shot in the studio. The most impressive set is the Berlin night club, called, possibly with tongue in cheek, the 'Cabaret Macabre', which is reminiscent of many similar sets in other German films of the period. Typically Expressionistic, however, is the visual interplay of light and shadow in the film. Every scene is dimly lit—in contrast to Korda's startlingly bright Hollywood films—and the technique of using pools of light to illuminate action in an isolated part of the larger frame is fully explored. With the exception of the crystal ball sequence, there are few camera 'tricks', and the editing is straightforward, the complexity of action coming from the flashback, flashforward narrative requirements. The editor, Karl Hartl, did fashion an extraordinarily tense series of scenes by effective parallel cutting between the accomplice's murder and the reunion of Gordon and Stella, who remain blissfully unaware of the crime which is being perpetrated in order to further entrap them.

*Das unbekannte Morgen* is certainly not Korda's best film, although it is much better than many of the films for which he is acclaimed. Korda's blending of a lightweight morality tale with deeper, inherently Germanic themes demonstrates his adaptability, but often leaves us (as in *Samson und Delila*) with two parts to the whole, each of which tends to isolate the half rather than enhance the whole.

The profits from *Das unbekannte Morgen* helped Alex pay his way into the distribution company FIHAG. Unfortunately the stabilisation of the Deutsche Mark in 1924 threw FIHAG into liquidation, and Korda's financial position became rather shaky. The finances of his backer Schwarz were hardly better, and Schwarz was forced to discontinue his support of Korda's film-making ventures. Korda called on another Hungarian, Josef Somlo, then head of the foreign division of Germany's largest film concern, Ufa. Somlo made arrangements for Alex and Maria to make a film in Vienna for Ufa and Dreamland Studio: *Jedermanns Frau* (Everybody's Woman—1924).

The stay in Vienna over the winter of 1923–4 was a fruitful one for the couple. Maria's career received another boost when she starred as 'Merapi, known as Moon of Israel' in *Die Sklavenkönigin* [*Moon of Israel*—1924], an epic directed by Korda's compatriot Michael Curtiz. And Korda found yet another Hungarian patron, the Viennese banker Imre Gross. Korda's idea for his next project apparently appealed to Gross; it was to be a romantic re-enactment of the famous Hapsburg scandal involving Crown Prince Rudolf and his mistress Maria Vetsera. Given the go-ahead by Gross, Alex and Maria returned to Berlin where the interiors for *Tragödie im Hause Habsburg* (Tragedy in the House of Hapsburg—1924) were filmed. (Exteriors had already been shot in Vienna.) Maria Corda and Koloman Zatony played the tragic lovers, and Emperor Franz Josef was portrayed by Emil Fenyvessy, a Hungarian actor who had often worked at Corvin. The film was released by Ufa at the end of May 1924. According to Tabori, the film had cost $80,000 and only earned back half of this total. Imre Gross became another casualty to add to Korda's increasing list of depleted financial investors.

For the better part of the next year the Kordas remained away from the cameras. They took a pleasure trip to Italy with Zoltan, ran out of money frequently, and were saved numerous times by money wired to them from Josef Somlo. When they came back, Somlo had a concrete offer for them, a film to be made for his and Herman Fellner's production and distribution company, Felsom. In the post-war period German film companies promoted film subjects with a French or English setting in order to exploit those foreign markets and earn needed foreign currency. The Felsom picture which Korda directed in 1925 fell into this category, for it was a bubbly French comedy adapted by Korda and Adolf Lantz from a Parisian boulevard play by Armont and Bousquet.

*Der Tänzer meiner Frau*, released in Britain as *Dancing Mad*, was shot in three months in the late spring of 1925. Maria starred as a dance-crazy young wife who is only reconciled to her domestic duties after an old flame has kindled her husband's jealousy. It was the kind of light, petulant role at which Maria could excel. When the film was trade shown in London in February 1927, a British reviewer would say: 'Maria Corda has never been better suited nor so well directed and secures sympathy for a character which is by no means made up of perfection.'[3] By now Maria's reputation on the Continent and abroad was assured; just as she had hoped, she had succeeded in making her own impression on the film world. Alex, on the other hand, had again arrived at a professional impasse, and over the next year an unemployed Korda could do no more than stand idly by and watch the growing success of the other Corda's acting career.*

Finally, in early 1926, Lajos Biro came to Korda's rescue by writing an original film scenario for him, a starring vehicle for Maria: *Eine Dubarry von heute* [*A Modern Dubarry*—1927]. The film was made for Felsom during the summer of 1926 at the Ufa studios at Tempelhof and Neubabelsberg.

Biro had up-dated the Dubarry story, but the result was a complex and improbable script. The picture was obviously a showpiece for the talents and charms of Maria Corda and may have been made with the express design of capturing the attention of a Hollywood producer. Ironically, present-day interest in the film is confined not to the star, but to one of the dress extras, who soon after became one of Hollywood's greatest screen goddesses—Marlene Dietrich.

During the post-war period the American film industry was engaged in rendering financial support to the German cinema. In 1925 Adolph Zukor of Paramount and Marcus Loew of Metro-Goldwyn-Mayer jointly loaned Ufa $4,000,000, and as a result Ufa's distribution company was known for a time as 'Parufamet'. The Germans, however, were concerned about the influx of American films and the amount of money flowing out of Germany to America, and so they established a '*kontingent*', a quota system whereby a certain proportion of films screened in Germany would have to be made in Germany. (France and Britain were to follow suit.) To make the most out of this limitation, the American Fox Film Corporation, run by William Fox, organised a branch in Berlin—Deutsche-Fox—to make 'quota' pictures with Fox's German earnings which could no longer be remitted to the

---

* Maria spent the year in Rome and Vienna. She starred in two films, *L'uomo più allegro di Vienna* (The Gayest Man in Vienna—1925) directed by Amleto Palermi and *Gli ultimi giorni di Pompei* (The Last Days of Pompei—1925) which Palermi co-directed with Carmine Gallone and which also starred Victor Varconi. Late in 1925 she made a film for Pan-Film in Vienna; *Der Gardeoffizier* [*The Guardsman*—1926], directed by the German Robert Wiene, was, in fact, an adaptation of a Hungarian play which had been filmed in 1917 by Sándor Antalffy for Korda's Corvin.

United States. Korda's last German film was produced for this company.

*Madame wünscht keine Kinder* [*Madame Wants No Children*—1926] was taken from a French novel by Clément Vautel. Adolf Lantz and Bela Balazs, the Hungarian film theoretician, co-wrote the screen adaptation, and Maria Corda was again surrounded by an impressive group of actors and actresses. Filmed at Tempelhof during October and November 1926, the picture was another frothy French 'society' entertainment, probably much like *Der Tänzer meiner Frau*. Although released before *Dubarry*, *Madame wünscht* was the last Continental film which Korda was to make until his return from Hollywood in 1930.

Korda's knowledge of Hollywood and the powerful American film industry and its moguls had increased significantly since the days when he had ignored a letter from Adolph Zukor. Alex and Maria now realised that to reach the top in the film world meant to reach the top in Hollywood. Their (especially Maria's) hard work at self-promotion over the past five years finally paid off in the fall of 1926 when they were offered a contract by First National, the Hollywood production company, to come to work in Hollywood. Korda immediately took the contract to Heinrich Fraenkel, who describes the meeting in his book *Unsterblicher Film*:

In those days . . . I was German 'press chief' with First National, the big American firm which had engaged Korda. Since he couldn't speak English yet and knew little of America and Hollywood, he came to me with his lengthy contract, which he had not yet signed, and had me translate the most important points. Then he wanted to know whether one could live over there on $350 a week—I believe that was his beginning wage.

I said that he wouldn't starve on it, that after all his wife would also receive a (somewhat higher) salary and that the first rise would be due in six months; whereupon he elaborated his question as follows:

'Look,' he said, with that charming accent with which he always spoke German, English and French equally fluently and equally coloured with Hungarian. 'In Vienna I lived in the Imperial, ate at Sacher's and had my suits made at Knicze's. Here I live in the Eden, eat in the Bristol and go to Stavropoulos. Can I do that in Hollywood as well—with this contract?'

I said no, but added that the living and working conditions there were completely different and that this contract could only be seen as a springboard.

'All right then,' he said, 'I'll sign. If they don't let me do what I want over there, I'll simply come back.'[4]

In the first week of December 1926 Alex and Maria sailed from Europe aboard the *Olympic* on their way to New York and Hollywood.

1. Lotte H. Eisner, *The Haunted Screen*, London, Thames and Hudson, 1969, p. 140.
2. *Ibid*, p. 89.
3. *The Bioscope*, 24 February 1927, p. 71.
4. Heinrich Fraenkel, *Unsterblicher Film*, München, Kindler Verlag, 1956, pp. 138–9, translated for the author by Priscilla Murphy.

# CHAPTER FIVE

# The Best Forgotten Years—Hollywood

HOLLYWOOD, California had been the American film capital for less than ten years when the Kordas arrived in 1927. In that time the Hollywood system of film-making, the pattern of its companies and studios had become well established. However, there were already signs that the American film industry was burning itself out after a decade of feverish activity. In those years before sound, the Hollywood studios were engaged in a race to bolster audience interest in silent films by drafting stars and directors from Europe in the hope of spicing up the standard Hollywood product. As one journalist wrote in November 1926:

> Like schoolboys we listened at the feet of fabled foreigners while they told us how to run our own business. We harkened to the sacred pronunciamento of Bernard Shaw, who said with the Shavian sneer: 'No American director should be permitted to make a moving picture until he has served apprenticeship to some of the German or Scandinavian masters of this trade.' We took Shaw's advice and imported a flock of Germans and Scandinavians and Russians.[1]

This 'flock' included directors like Mauritz Stiller, E. A. Dupont, and Victor Sjöström and stars like Greta Garbo, Lars Hanson, Pola Negri, and Emil Jannings. They were all brought to the West Coast in the early twenties, and Alex and Maria were simply the latest in a long line of foreign imports.

The Kordas' exodus to Hollywood had, in fact, come too late, for the tide had turned rather quickly against these 'invited invaders'. The novelty of foreign talent had worn off, and both the industry and the public felt that many of their films had not lived up to expectations. For their part, some of the foreign artists found the Hollywood studio system too rigid and could not, or would not, adapt themselves to it. The Kordas were to be no exception. Although First National was more interested in the star 'Corda' than the director 'Korda', neither of them would be treated particularly well by Hollywood.

First National had been founded in 1917 by a group of twenty-five cinema exhibitors. Throughout the late teens and early twenties the company was in fierce competition with Adolph Zukor's Paramount, and this resulted in both companies becoming enormous vertical combines with interests in film exhibition, distribution, and production. Richard Rowland, vice-president and general manager of First National, had been one of the founders of Metro Pictures (later to be merged into Metro-Goldwyn-Mayer) and had engineered the 1921 production of *The Four Horsemen of the Apocalypse*, which brought instant fame to its star Rudolph Valentino. It was Rowland who offered the contract to Alex and Maria, and he and the studio obviously hoped to groom Maria into another Pola Negri and perhaps thought that Alex might do for First National what Ernst Lubitsch, one of the most successful imports, had done for Paramount.

On his arrival the thirty-three-year-old Korda was impressed by the Hollywood scene. 'Hollywood still kept,' he later admitted, 'a little of the old adventure and glamour—not much, but enough for us, the younger generation, to see traces of it, like the worn-off gilt on a piece of old silver.'[2] Of course, he also felt dislocated, as he hadn't felt in Vienna or Berlin. He knew neither the language nor the country's habits and tastes, but, more importantly, he knew almost nothing about the bureaucratic Hollywood routine. He was to make many mistakes. As he told a reporter in 1936: 'I was so glad to be in Hollywood, but I walk first on the left foots, and then never could I bring up the right foots!'[3]

His first months under contract were enough to dampen his initial enthusiasm. In an article in the *Sunday Chronicle*, H. W. Seaman describes the events leading up to Korda's first directorial assignment:

. . . from the first he found Hollywood a hard nut to crack. For months he reported daily at First National studios, said 'Yes' a few times, and waited for something to do.

One day he was called into a conference. 'You are Hungarian, aren't you?' he was asked. He said 'Yes.'

'Well, we are going to make a Hungarian picture—all about gipsies. There's a butler in it and we think he ought to wear a military uniform and click his heels and bow. Is that right?'

'Yes,' said Korda, and got the job of directing the picture. It was 'The Stolen Bride', starring Billie Dove. To add a touch of verisimilitude Korda had the butler kneel and kiss her feet.

This was considered very nearly a master touch. . . .[4]

*The Stolen Bride* (1927) was shot at the First National studio in Burbank during the summer of 1927 and was praised on its release for its elaborate sets and authentic costumes. The story dealt with a love quadrangle across 'class' barriers: a Countess in love with a peasant but betrothed to a Baron, who in turn is in love with a dancer. It was a theme that Hollywood was exploiting at the time, and Korda was to direct three more films along similar lines.

After the moderate success of this first film came the picture upon which most of Korda's limited Hollywood success rests, *The Private Life of Helen of Troy* (1927). Maria Corda had been signed to play Helen 'after much discussion and disagreement' among the First National executives, and the film was to be directed by George Fitzmaurice, a French director who had just finished *Son of the Sheik* (1926). Some time in mid-1927 Fitzmaurice was taken off the picture, and the assignment was given to Korda.

The film was fresh and witty and approached history from a new angle, an angle supplied by John Erskine's novel *The Private Life of Helen of Troy* and Robert Sherwood's play *The Road to Rome* upon which the script by Carey Wilson was based. In previous costume films, such as Korda's *Samson und Delila*, past historical events had usually been used as lessons for the present, but in *Helen of Troy*, history was shorn of its significance, and the characters were comically exposed as everyday people with everyday problems. The great drama of Paris's stealing of Menelaus's wife Helen and the Trojan War which was its consequence thus became the subject for a satirical sex comedy. Helen is no longer a tragic heroine, but a bored wife and coquette who welcomes the flattery and attentions of other men. Menelaus, usually portrayed as the mighty Greek whose pride and honour demanded both recovery of Helen and revenge upon the Trojans, is now shown as a weak, adoring husband who is normally willing to put up with his wife's escapades and who only reluctantly goes to war when things have gotten a bit out of hand.*

*Helen of Troy* gave Korda a chance to demonstrate his talent for handling actors in light comedy roles. Lewis Stone (Menelaus) and Maria Corda (Helen), in particular, are allowed to play their parts with enthusiasm, but without histrionics. Maria never looked more glamorous, for the role took advantage of her classical features. Like many late silent films, the picture suffers from the absence of sound. There is a profusion of dialogue titles, and Korda later lamented that the film had not been shot as a sound film, since the dialogue was all-important. Much of the film's success, in fact, depended on the language of the characters, for they 'spoke' in contemporary American idioms: 'The human knee used to be a joint; now it's an entertainment,' and 'Marriage is only exchanging the attentions of a dozen men for the inattention of one.' As we shall see, these lines are strikingly similar to the dialogue in most of Korda's later sound films.

The production values of the film were outstanding in the best Hollywood tradition. The lighting and camerawork gave the film a polished and dazzling visual quality, and the cameraman Lee Garmes certainly deserves all the credit for this, for as he said of Korda: 'He had no knowledge of lighting; he was interested only in the story and the acting.'[5] The costumes and sets were slightly futuristic, and this helped to divest the film from any concern with historical accuracy. One of the highlights of the film was the (thanks to *Ben-Hur*) obligatory chariot race. The editing was done by Harold Young, the Hollywood technician who, like Garmes, was to work often with Korda both in Hollywood and London.

*The Private Life of Helen of Troy* was premiered on 9 December 1927, roughly the first anniversary of Korda's arrival in Hollywood. It was

---

* The epilogue to the film provides a good example of the film's light and satirical approach. Helen asks a servant to fetch her some housework, for she has decided to become 'domestic'. Menelaus overhears this and is pleased that Helen has at last settled down. The Prince of Ithaca is then announced; he has heard of Helen's great beauty and wants to meet her. Menelaus permits the meeting, for he is confident that Helen has learned her rightful place. Helen enters all aglitter and openly flirts with the young man who is finally led to her chambers. Menelaus, momentarily crestfallen, recovers quickly, leaves his wife and the young man alone, and suggests to a palace guard that they go on a fishing trip. The Trojan War has changed nothing after all.

the last wholly satisfying film which Korda was to make in America, and it had a lasting influence on Korda's career. The film's satirical treatment of history and sex was something to which Alex was to return again and again.

However, Korda's enthusiasm for Hollywood had paled considerably. He was too cynical to take the system and his press clippings seriously, and yet too serious-minded to revel in the absurdity of the whole milieu. He felt an outsider even in the émigré community, and his primary concern was to amass a quick fortune and leave Hollywood as soon as possible.

Alex hadn't been in Hollywood long when an elaborate practical joke was played at his expense by a master of mischievousness, Ernst Lubitsch. It happened one Sunday morning when Lubitsch and some friends from the 'German' colony in Hollywood were taking a walk in Beverly Hills. The story is retold by Heinrich Fraenkel, one of the accomplices in the crime:

> . . . we came to Alexander Korda's house, found the door unlocked and went in. The house was completely deserted—perhaps the Kordas were also taking a walk—and suddenly Lubitsch had the idea to simulate a burglary. Quickly we took some ashtrays, books, glasses and whatever else was standing around, shoved everything under the couch, rolled the carpet up, made as much of a mess as we could in a great hurry—naturally we didn't want to be surprised by the owners, who were sure to be returning soon—and walked quickly back to Lubitsch's house.
>
> From there we had an American actress whose voice Korda didn't know call him up . . . [purporting to be from] the local editor's office of the Los Angeles Times. A burglary had just been reported, did it involve Mr Korda, the well-known film director?
>
> Korda confirmed this, and then upon questioning by the 'reporter' had to give a detailed summary of his career.
>
> 'What do you think of America?' was the first question prompted by Lubitsch in a whisper, and 'How do you like it in Hollywood?'
>
> On these subjects, too, Korda gave exhaustive (though perhaps not entirely truthful) information. Then he was asked what had been stolen in the burglary.
>
> 'Some particularly valuable books,' he said, now rather agitated,

'also a Persian rug and probably some of my wife's jewellery, she's just now counting the pieces. We haven't been able to establish yet exactly what is missing.'

Five minutes later Lubitsch had another American woman call Korda, and shortly thereafter another one; each one supposedly a reporter from one of the other two big Los Angeles daily newspapers. Each time he had to give an account of his whole life story and career—this he naturally wasn't loath to do—and each time he was asked how he liked it in Hollywood, what he thought of Hollywood, and whether he found American women prettier than European women—all typical American reporter questions; and each time he had to make a detailed statement about the stolen valuables.

This he did with much gusto and imagination, for by the third telephone call his wife's pearl necklace was amongst the stolen goods. Was this an especially valuable heirloom, the reporter now wanted to know. But before Korda could think of a suitable reply, Lubitsch came to the long-planned point, took the receiver uot of the American woman's hand and called out in good Berlin slang: 'Man, just have a peep under the sofa.' Then he hung up.[6]

After only two films it seems that Korda had already been typecast as a director of 'actresses' and 'foreign locales' by the studio executives. Of his last eight Hollywood films all but one were vehicles for a female star, and only one was set in its entirety in America. Korda wasn't a good enough director nor were his films successful enough to allow him any freedom of choice in his subject matter or in the casting. He was learning that to get along in Hollywood even a director had to become a convincing actor: '. . . all producers have to act through their eyes,' he once remarked. 'It takes a long time to learn that, but, when I had mastered it, I became the best "Yes-man" of the lot. That's why I got on so well there for a time. But I couldn't stick that course. I stuck it only as long as it served my purpose.'[7] More accustomed to European (and his own) production schedules, Alex disliked the standardised working hours in the studio, and he was amazed at the lack of good scriptwriters in the studio stable. He must therefore have been overjoyed in 1928 when he began work on a film written by his old friend Lajos Biro, now a successful Hollywood film-writer.

Their collaboration, *Yellow Lily* (1928), was no more than a carbon copy of Korda's first film, *The Stolen Bride*. Both films starred Billie

Dove, were set in Hungary, and dealt with love between members of two different classes. For variety, the roles were reversed, and Miss Dove played the commoner (Judith Peredy) pursued by the Archduke Alexander, played by Clive Brook. The film is technically unimpressive, although photographed by Lee Garmes and edited by Harold Young. The lighting is poor, and the only camera movement in the entire film is an awkward and out-of-place back-tracking shot at the very end. The film is partially redeemed by the acting of Clive Brook who is perfectly cast as the heartless Archduke, the suave seducer.

With his next two films, *Night Watch* (1928) and *Love and the Devil* (1929), Korda continued his career as a director of undistinguished programme pictures. Both films were concerned with married women who are discovered in a bedroom with a man other than their husband (the bedroom 'discovery' featured in several of Korda's Hollywood films). In each case someone is shot—either the discoverer or the man involved—and the disgraced women are in the end able to avert further calamity through self-sacrifice. The former film, another Billie Dove vehicle, presented difficult problems for the film-maker, since it was almost entirely set on a French battleship at the start of the First World War. Karl Struss, the famous Hollywood cameraman, later discussed the problems: 'On *Night Watch* . . . we shot an awful lot of it in a tiny eight by ten cabin on a battleship, with a full ceiling and pipes in perspective. It was one of the first times full ceilings were used.'[8] *Love and the Devil*, Korda's last silent picture, is important as the last film in which Korda was to direct Corda.

The Korda marriage had for some time suffered under the strain of two strong and ambitious artistic temperaments. In an interview in 1927 Maria made it clear that she accepted Alex's direction only in the studio, that she played the dominant role once they were off the studio floor. 'At home . . . I am the director,' she is quoted as saying. 'When it is dinner time, or time to go somewhere, then Mr Korda takes direction from me. He does it agreeably. We do not argue the matter, for he recognizes that in the home—I am the director.'[9] From all accounts, their home life was not as peaceful as Maria was willing to admit, and, according to one source, Maria had a childish, but effective way of making her point in an argument—she broke Alex's cigars in half. Even in Hollywood, they were separated for long periods of time while Maria starred in films in Europe. Maria had, in fact, been a party to England's attempt in the late twenties to attract Hollywood stars and had gone there in 1928 to make *Tesha* (1928), a melodrama directed by Victor Saville.

A technological innovation, the sound film, was to cause further tension in the Korda household. Once the 'talkie' madness had been accepted by the Hollywood studios as something more than a passing craze, Maria's career was almost over. Like so many foreign stars, Maria spoke with a thick accent, and studios were reluctant to entrust roles to men or women whose speeches might not be understood by the American public. The inevitable decline in her career meant a turnabout in the Korda–Corda relationship. Previously, Maria had been the more successful partner; it was her talent, after all, which had brought the couple to Hollywood. The realisation that her substantial ten-year career in films was at an end and that Alex's career was not similarly jeopardised must have caused her great frustration and must have precipitated the collapse of the marriage. In 1930 they were divorced.

During those last months Alex had turned once again to his family. Zoltan had stayed in Berlin trying to find work, but Alex managed to convince him to come to Hollywood where he was sure to find employment. (Alex also suggested that the California sunshine and dryness might cure Zoltan's tuberculosis.) In late 1929 or early 1930 Zoltan arrived in Hollywood, and Alex must surely have welcomed his brother's presence during his last traumatic year in America.

> How nice it would be if I could say that the moment I heard the first talking film my prophetic soul said enthusiastically: 'This is the future of the film industry, I shall never touch a silent film again.' Alas, it would not be true. As a craftsman I was interested in this new tool . . . but I disliked it very much indeed. It can be imagined, then, how I felt when I was told in Hollywood that my next picture would be a talking picture.
>
> . . . Anyway, whatever my artistic beliefs may have been, one has to eat and the weekly pay cheques certainly wouldn't have come if I had said to the powers who ruled the vast studios that I did not believe in this new gadget. Nor can I say that I really disbelieved in it, either. It is all a question of the angle from which you approach your craft.[10]

Korda was not alone in his shortsightedness about sound, the 'tool' which revolutionised the film industry. Many producers and directors had reservations about the new gadget and only reluctantly made the

Sándor Korda – Budapest 1916.

Antónia (Maria) Farkas – *c.* 1918 – a
starlet under contract to Corvin.

Korda's film journal, 'Mozihét' (Ciné-Weekly)

Cover – New Year's issue 1918.

Editorial page – 13 August 1916.

Eight years later, now Maria Corda, Alex's wife
and a European screen star.

Advertisement for Korda's film *Szent Péter
esernyöje* (Saint Peter's Umbrella)—(1917).

Action on a stage at Korda's studio – sketch 1917.

Valéria Berlányi, György Kürthy, and Aranka Laczkó in
*Fehér éjszakák* (White Nights) (1916). The first major
Hungarian production directed by Sándor Korda.

Korda in Austria: the spectacle – *Samson und
Delila* (1922).

Korda in Germany: the society drama –
*Eine Dubarry von heute* [*A Modern
Dubarry*] (1927).

transition to sound film-making. Korda's two previous films had, in fact, had 'sound' in them, but only sound effects and music. *The Squall* (1929) was his first 'talking' picture and, incidentally, was the last film Korda was ever to make with a Hungarian setting. Korda, rather selectively, remembers:

> I was working in the First National Studios in Burbank, and the company had just been taken over by the Warner Brothers, the initiators of the sound film, who started their ride to great fortune and fame with Al Jolson's *Singing Fool*. There was only one sound channel, and this was used during the day-time in Warner Brothers studio, and at night-time by First National Studios. I had to make my picture at night. It was a ghastly picture and I do not even remember what it was called. I only remember that it was the first talking picture with Loretta Young and Myrna Loy. Many years later I reminded Myrna Loy of this adventure and she said to me with a smile, 'That was a long time ago and I was then a child actress,' and I told her, most ungallantly, 'Yes, and I was a child director.'[11]

Korda's appraisal of *The Squall* was pretty accurate.

In the film Miss Loy plays Nubi, a 'Gypsy Charmer', who takes shelter, in the middle of a squall, in Farmer Lajos's house and promptly has the entire male population of the family madly in love with her. Her husband finally arrives and leads her away from the farm where serenity is restored. According to *Variety*'s reviewer the use of sound was extremely naïve:

> Like the opening and closing of some theatrical shows of yore, a gang of geese and some oxen indicate the beginning and ending of each day by being paraded out of the barnyard in the morning and returned in the evening. The first few times their passing is interesting, but after that the blare of sound quacks and scientific renditions of chicks clucking become irritating.[12]

Hollywood producers, quick to exploit the talkies, were in a panic to find enough new film subjects. Their solution exacerbated the fears of the proponents and opponents of sound, for they resorted to re-making old silent films with added dialogue and, often, songs. Korda's last films for First National, *Her Private Life* (1929) and *Lilies of the Field* (1930), were two such productions.

*Her Private Life* was a remake of *Déclassée* (1925) which had been directed by Robert Vignola and which, in turn, had been an adaptation of Zoë Akins's 1923 play of that title. Billie Dove starred this time as Lady Helen Haden, an Englishwoman whose love for a young American, Ned Thayer, played by Walter Pidgeon, leads to an ugly divorce for her and to her penniless flight to America. After numerous hardships, she accepts the proposal of a rich American who steps aside in the final reel so that Helen can marry Thayer. *Lilies of the Field*, filmed previously in 1924 by John Francis Dillon, starred Corinne Griffith (the star of the earlier version). She recreated her role of Mildred Harker, a woman who, like Helen Haden, has to suffer the consequences of an ugly divorce. Her 'descent' to the life of a Broadway showgirl (living only for 'jazz and cocktails') is sentimentally explored and is the occasion for some imaginative stage musical productions. Neither film was particularly successful, and Korda finally decided to break with First National.

In September 1928 Korda had signed a new, two-year contract with First National which stipulated that he would receive $1,750 a week in his first year and $2,250 in his second. There had also been a provision for an optional third year at $2,500 a week. This was a long way from the original $350 a week, but even though Alex was earning close to $100,000 a year, he had many expenses and never seemed to be able to save money. His plan was to save $100–250,000, to send himself back to Europe, and to set up production there. However, his house on North Rodeo Drive in the heart of Beverly Hills, his wife and the divorce settlement, dinner parties, and a brief trip to Europe in 1930 all played havoc with his great plans. Furthermore, Alex had invested some of his money in the American Stock Market, and that went in the Wall Street Crash of 1929. But, in spite of his financial losses, Korda had reason to be a little optimistic in early 1930.

Ned Marin, the producer of all but one of Korda's First National pictures, had left that studio to work with Fox Film company. Although he had some months left on his contract, Korda quickly settled with First National (or rather Warner Brothers, since they now owned First National) and followed Marin to Fox with a $100,000-a-year contract. W. B. Courtney colourfully describes Korda's first day on the Fox lot:

> It was one of those real-estate-prospectus California mornings which make you walk like a midshipman and feel sunbeamy and pious although you may have just stolen your aged father's nest-egg earnings as a professional convert in the Angelus Temple. No

morning, however, in California or elsewhere, can be glamorous or bright enough to match the good will of a young man who is newly come to Mecca; who has arrived at the capital of his ambitions, the principal city of his dreams, after years of labor in sparse outlying vineyards.

The hundred-thousand-dollar-a-year contract our hero had signed added its best of smugness to his mood, of course; that was a lot of pengoes in his own far land, and it made him feel consequential. He was, therefore, positively transfigured by friendliness to all the world as he strode for the first time as a salaried employee across the great Coyote lot. . . .

Anyhow, it was Monday. Our lad, hastening toward his virgin desk, saw the Big Shot coming across the yard. There were many reasons for the rather explosive 'Good Morning!' which greeted the Big Shot as he passed abreast of his latest hireling; the innate courtesy of the latter, his experience of such matters in the Old World, his buoyant spirits this day, and his belief that a wage larger than the Regent got back home bore fellowship with it. But he may as well have tipped his hat to a fire hydrant. The Big Shot's austere eyes took no more grip on him than a hot knife takes on butter; the Big Shot's face, dramatically set in a reflection of deep thoughts, was just about as friendly as a coral reef.

'Maybe he's hard of hearing,' thought our young man, as he walked on, a little dashed. Then he heard a bloodless feminine squeak. 'Oh, Poppy! Yoo-hoo! Good Morning, Poppy!' He turned, and saw a marcelled buttercup waving to the Big Shot from a dressing-room window half the yard away. Big Shot was agog with fraternal attentiveness: 'How are you today, darling?' he called.

The new man resumed his way, disquieted. 'Of course, it is possible he did not recognize me,' he figured. 'We had only seventy-one private conferences before I signed the contract.' Later that day he passed the Big Shot again; and greeted him quite as firmly as on the first occasion—but without result.[13]

The 'Big Shot' was Winfield Sheehan, head of the Fox Film Studio in Hollywood. Sheehan had built up Fox's picture-making prestige, but had refused to help William Fox, the company's founder, when his position was threatened by a group of financiers. Sheehan's lack of support facilitated the company's decision to oust William Fox in 1930.

From Winfield Sheehan and Sol Wurtzel, the production supervisor, Korda learned all about Hollywood's bag of dirty tricks.

Korda's first assignment at Fox was a better-than-average programme picture, *Women Everywhere* (1930). It was a musical adventure story about cabaret singers and French legionnaires in North Africa, and Korda was able to work with both Lajos Biro and Zoltan Korda, who constructed the script in collaboration with Harlan Thompson and George Grossmith, the English actor. Korda's first impression of Grossmith is recorded by H. W. Seaman:

> When Korda first saw him, a cultured Englishman of 60 or more, with a smile that revealed teeth like a piano keyboard, Korda did not know that that smile and those teeth were famous wherever Englishmen gathered.
>
> At the end of the first day's work in the studio, when Korda sat in the projection room and saw the result on the screen, he turned to Biro and said: 'That man! Never shall I be able to do anything with him.'
>
> He changed his mind later, but even before . . . he came to know Grossmith off the screen and away from the studio. . . . They used to meet in the studio restaurant.
>
> 'England ought to be making the best pictures in the world,' Korda would say.
>
> 'Well,' Grossmith would reply, displaying his teeth, and sucking air in at the corners of his mouth in the Grossmith way, 'Why can't we three—you and Biro and I—go to England and make them?'[14]

In two years' time this off-hand suggestion was to be put in operation.

*Women Everywhere* was released in June 1930, and at least one reviewer picked it out as 'one of those gems occasionally found in the herd of program pictures . . . way ahead of many of the talkers ballyhooed on Broadway'.[15] Sadly, the film did nothing to improve Korda's standing at the studio. He was offered a series of dreadful scripts which he managed at first to refuse without jeopardising his contract. He eventually had to accept *The Princess and the Plumber* (1930). In 1936 Korda bitterly recalled:

> It was a bad story. . . . I hated to make it. But I had to make it under my contract. I was mad at the whole business. But that's the way in America. They know everything about everything else out

there in Hollywood. The great big Panjandrums don't know how little they are, really.

There were lots of things that Hollywood could teach me, and there were lots of things I wanted to learn. They weren't the things that the great Panjandrums thought they were teaching me, but they didn't know that. It pays to say 'Yes' at times.[16]

When the film was almost finished, Korda took it along to the projection room to be screened for Sheehan and Wurtzel.

'Pretty good,' said Winfield Sheehan, 'but don't you think it wants a little—something?'

'Yes,' said one of the assembled Yes-men. 'What it needs is a little menace.'

'Menace! That's the stuff,' said Sheehan. 'Can you put some menace in it, Korda?'

Korda stood up and faced the throng. Bracing his shoulders and clearing his throat, he said in a loud voice: 'No!'[17]

It was not the expected response, and Korda was unprepared for the consequences.

The studio 'Panjandrums' move quickly in the face of such outright disobedience. Korda had, in fact, shot the scene which 'needed menace' three times, each time filming his own version or variations of it. None of these versions pleased the executives, and Korda's stubbornness led Sheehan to replace him. Although Korda retained screen credit, the film was actually completed by John Blystone, a more dependable Hollywood programme picture director. Furthermore, according to Heinrich Fraenkel, shortly after the projection room episode:

... [Korda] was called into the Head Office and told something like this—I can't vouch for the exact figures, but they must be fairly near the facts:

'Mr. Korda, your contract has another 30 weeks to run at $1,500 a week, that's $45,000. Here is a cheque for $25,000. Would you like to accept it and tear up the contract?'

Korda was angry and refused; whereupon he was politely told that, of course, he had the right to sit out his contract, but he'd have to go into the 'Dog House'. To be sure, they were polite enough to avoid this familiar Hollywood phrase. But the immediate practical consequence was that he had to exchange his beautiful bungalow—an airy office with an antechamber, its own little garden and bathroom—for the seediest and smallest of offices.

Naturally he was allowed to make the room a bit homier at his own expense. He could have a carpet laid, books and patience cards brought in and even a radio, all very necessary acquisitions—after all, he had nothing to do in his tatty doghouse 9 hours a day (with a one-hour lunchbreak) but sit out his contract. His first and most urgent reading was a close study of that lengthy contract, which contained—in return for the single right to a weekly cheque (which he now had to pick up himself, rather than having it delivered)—numerous rules with which one normally didn't have to concern oneself: above all, keeping punctual office hours, or not smoking in certain corridors of the administration building and the studio. Any infringement of such rules at that time would have meant a breach of contract and summary dismissal for Korda, in other words the loss of tens of thousands of dollars.

He held out the test of nerves a couple of weeks, then reported to the Head Office and declared that he was ready to cancel the contract. He promptly received his compensation cheque, but now it was only for $15,000. The couple of weeks playing stubborn had cost him a lot of money.[18]

Korda had allowed himself to be caught in the famous studio 'demotion' ploy, a typical practice used against dissident employees. As Korda found out, this was only a prelude to the more serious humiliations to come.

Korda was unemployed, but worse than that he was unemployable. Word had gone out from Fox, and Alex found that the other Hollywood studios wouldn't touch him, apart from Columbia whose boss, Harry Cohn, made a one-picture offer that was not accepted. In Hollywood, cut-throat competition and stealing of talent among studios were normal practices, but, at a moment's notice, the whole community could effectively close ranks against anyone brave enough to challenge the system. The black-listed individual became a leper, even to his friends: no one wanted the taint to rub off on them. Korda was demoralised. His only recourse was to get out of Hollywood while he still had some dignity left. 'It was one of the best moves I ever made in my life,' Korda later said, 'and it is a good rule to follow whenever you are in a hole. Wasn't the ego in me worth fighting for? I asked myself, and I concluded that, if it wasn't it wasn't really worth having.'[19]

By 1930 Alex Korda had served a long apprenticeship in the international film industry without gaining any substantial stature. Nevertheless, his four years in Hollywood were the most valuable in terms of his later career. He had seen at first-hand the technical professionalism of the studio craftsmen—the editors, cameramen, costume and set designers—but had been surprised by the lack, at least in his own experience, of good scriptwriting departments. He now recognised that an effective independent film production company could only operate with its own studio, that without this, producers and directors were totally at the mercy of the men who controlled the studio. Above all, Korda had been impressed by the power and international influence of the Hollywood film. If he were to survive in the international film industry, he would have to beat Hollywood at its own game. To conquer Hollywood from abroad, a producer needed to know what subjects, what types of films appealed to the American film-going public, and this Korda had learned. He had even found a specific film genre—the historical satire of *The Private Life of Helen of Troy*—which particularly suited his directorial talents and public tastes. Finally, Hollywood had forced Alex to shed his artist's naïvety: a successful career, he realised, depended as much on a shrewd business sense as it did on artistic talent and professional expertise. How well Korda had assimilated all these lessons, Hollywood and the film world were soon to discover.

Many say that Alex Korda would never have made it in Hollywood even if he had received better 'breaks'; the place, they suggest, was too primitive and crude for his more refined nature. More to the point, Hollywood was too big for Korda in those years. Continental film directors, many with more talent than Korda, over-ran the studios, and Korda was simply unable to distinguish himself above the 'flock'. In assessing Korda's accomplishments during his entire film-making career, someone once said that his greatest achievement was to make everyone forget that he had ever worked in Hollywood.

1. Alfred Dace, 'Invited Invaders', *Motion Picture Classic*, vol. XXIV no. 3, November 1926, p. 18.
2. Sir Alexander Korda, 'The First Talking Pictures', *loc cit*.
3. W. B. Courtney, 'New Worlds for Alexander', *Collier's*, 15 February 1936.
4. H. W. Seaman article for *Sunday Chronicle*, 7 March 1937.
5. Charles Higham, *Hollywood Cameramen*, London, Thames and Hudson, 1970, pp. 38–9.
6. Heinrich Fraenkel, *op cit*, pp. 170–1, translated for the author by Priscilla Murphy.
7. Philip Johnson, *loc cit*.
8. Charles Higham, *op cit*, p. 127.

9. Maria Corda in 'Should Husbands Direct Wives?', *Motion Picture Classic*, vol. XXV no. 3, May 1927, p. 70.
10. Sir Alexander Korda, 'The First Talking Pictures', *loc cit*.
11. *Ibid*.
12. *Variety*, 15 May 1929.
13. W. B. Courtney, *loc cit*.
14. H. W. Seaman, *loc cit*.
15. *Variety*, 25 June 1930.
16. Philip Johnson, *loc cit*.
17. H. W. Seaman, *loc cit*.
18. Heinrich Fraenkel, *op cit*, pp. 164–5, translated for the author by Priscilla Murphy.
19. Philip Johnson, *loc cit*.

# CHAPTER SIX

# Recovery in Paris

IN later years Korda liked to promote the story that he had left Hollywood with only twenty dollars in his pocket. Although the exact figure sometimes varies, the story was probably close to the truth. Korda had touched bottom in Hollywood, both in his career and his personal life, and he went back to Europe in 1930 to pull himself and his career together.

As his last 'home' in Europe, Berlin seemed the best place to begin this recovery. Korda had already made useful contacts in the German film industry, and old friends like Lajos Biro were then working in the German capital. Even before he arrived there, Alex had planned a possible course of action. He hoped that Ufa or one of the other major German companies might finance a programme of three or four films a year which would have a good chance of conquering the American market and for which Korda would arrange French and British financing and distribution. He wanted these to be inexpensive and quickly made films with enough box-office potential to provide Korda and his associates with a liveable income.* But Korda left Hollywood with no guarantee that his plan might be supported and with the nagging suspicion that the political climate in Germany might undermine his venture anyway.

* Korda even proposed a more economical way to make multi-language versions (usually shot simultaneously with the original): shooting, cutting, and previewing the German film first and only then copying it in French and English. This procedure, which would cut down on the amount of film shot for the subsequent versions, was exploited by Korda in Britain during the thirties.

Korda's reservations about returning to Germany were based on the significant changes which had occurred there during his absence. Hitler's National Socialist Party had come to prominence, and in September 1930 the party had, in fact, won a hundred and fifty seats in the Reichstag elections. It is possible that Korda witnessed the Nazi demonstrations in December against the screening of the American film *All Quiet on the Western Front* (1930), directed by Lewis Milestone, a film which looks at young German soldiers during the First World War and which suggests that the cause of the drive towards nationalist-motivated wars permeate the whole of society and is reinforced by the educational system. Ian Dalrymple, the English film writer, producer, and director who later worked with Korda in Britain, has remarked that 'the rising Nazi Party filled [Korda] with foreboding for the future of Ufa, and of civilised life'.[1] Korda made one half-hearted attempt to arrange a picture deal with the theatre director Max Reinhardt and the Hungarian film director Gabriel Pascal, but this collapsed, ostensibly because the financial terms were unacceptable to Korda. Alex left Berlin after only a few weeks.

In Berlin Korda and Biro had run into Steven Pallos, another Hungarian, who was working for a French film company. They spent several hours in a hotel lounge proposing plans for the 'ideal' film-making organisation. Korda put forward his case:

'What we want,' said Korda, 'is a studio town—huge studios surrounded by a model village in which the workers can live. It is no use thinking about making little pictures. We must have big ones that can be shown to the whole world.

'The thing can be done. I am just back from Hollywood and I have learned how not to do it. It cannot be done there.'

'Then where?'

'England,' said Korda.

There was silence for a moment; then Biro and Pallos both nodded. All Hungarians are Anglomaniacs. All who can afford English clothes wear them. English literature, English plays, even English jazz bands are the best; why not English films?

'Exactly what I asked George Grossmith,' said Korda.[2]

Gone were the ideas about quickly made and inexpensive films. His imagination rejuvenated, Korda now saw the future in terms of an immense studio complex capable of fostering large-scale productions.

But how was such a venture to be financed? Pallos came up with a possible solution:

> 'All right,' he said, 'we'll go to England. But we can't go there at once. We need some money. First let us go to Paris and make some. Already they are making talkies there in three or four languages. I've got to go back to Paris in the morning. Will you two come with me?'[3]

Alex Korda left for Paris with Pallos and Biro the next morning.

Korda and Biro were both immediately employed by Paramount Pictures' French subsidiary in Paris. France, like Germany and Britain, had established certain regulations to protect its national film industry from American domination. Since Paramount could not remit all its earnings in France to the United States, the company had a substantial quantity of 'frozen francs' which it used to produce films in France. At its studio in Joinville on the outskirts of Paris, Paramount ran an active production centre, where, among other things, versions of the company's American films were re-made simultaneously in different languages for the European market. Korda's first assignment at Joinville was to direct the German and French versions of Harry D'Arrast's *Laughter* (1930).*

Cinema audiences today are totally unfamiliar with the vast majority of Korda's films made prior to 1931, for the few prints still in existence have not been screened publicly for several decades. *Marius* (1931) is the first Korda film which has survived and which is still widely shown, on television, in cinemas, and in universities, as one of the 'classics' of the early sound film in France. It is the first 'great' film with which Korda was associated, although he has not been given much credit for the film's status or success.

This credit was to go to Marcel Pagnol, the French playwright who wrote the 'Marseilles Trilogy' of which *Marius* was the first part. *Marius* was written in 1928, but it was not performed until March 1929,

---

* The films were entitled *Die Manner um Lucie* (1931) and *Rive Gauche* (1931). It was standard practice for the versions to be filmed at the same time (the French cast stepping on to the studio floor to recreate the scene which the German cast had just finished playing). Although the principal actors were different for each version, the technicians, including in this case the Hollywood cameraman Harry Stradling and editor Harold Young, usually worked in the same capacity on each film.

after the success of Pagnol's previous play *Topaze*. With an outstanding cast headed by Raimu, the popular French music-hall comedian, the play was an immediate theatrical triumph. It was set in Marseilles and, with a mixture of romance, sentiment, comedy, and local colour, described the lives of a Marseilles café owner, César (Raimu), his restless son Marius (Pierre Fresnay), the young girl who loves Marius, Fanny (Orane Demazis), and the shop owner Panisse (Charpin) who wants to marry Fanny. Although the story revolved around these four, the play introduced several priceless character roles: the fat ferry-boat captain and notorious cuckold, Escartefigue (Paul Dulac), the dandyish and gullible 'outsider' from Lyon, M. Brun (Robert Vattier), the daft sailor, Piquoiseau (Mihalesco), and Fanny's portly mother, Honorine (Alida Rouffe). The characters all spoke in regional dialect, and the play was full of the flavour of the Midi.

Pagnol had resisted the offers of several film companies who wanted to adapt his plays, for he feared that they would not be scrupulously faithful to the stage versions. Robert T. Kane, head of Paramount's French studio, made the necessary assurances to Pagnol, and a contract for *Marius* was signed in mid-1931. When Kane told Pagnol that he had hired Alex Korda to direct the film and that more familiar French actors might be cast, Pagnol's fears multiplied. According to the French film historian Charles Ford, 'Korda took the bull by the horns and told Pagnol: "I didn't arrive in France yesterday. I've seen your play twice. I'll go again with you this evening. It's a pleasure watching such actors work. We will use them in the film." '⁴

The film was shot at Joinville between June and August 1931, under the watchful eye of Pagnol. Korda and Pagnol became good friends, and the collaboration went smoothly. It has been suggested that Korda's contribution to the film was minimal, that he merely directed a faithful translation of Pagnol's screenplay, but quite what this means is uncertain. Pagnol had clear notions about the actors and the direction, but he had no prior film-making experience. Did he dictate the camera movements? the length of shots (as he did in *Marius*'s sequel, *Fanny*— 1932)? the lighting of the scenes? Or did Korda make suggestions in these areas which were then offered for Pagnol's approval? To be sure, Korda would not have over-ridden Pagnol's objections, but to suggest that he added nothing to the film completely underestimates the film experience which Korda, not his collaborator, had.

For one thing, Alex Korda was responsible for the evocative Marseilles waterfront set. He had been unsatisfied with the first set constructed for this all-important Marseilles street where all the action takes place. He convinced his brother Vincent to come to Paris. Ian Dalrymple continues:

> It was in Paris that Vincent joined what he calls the circus, having been summoned by his brother from his happy life of high painting and low subsistence in the south. Alex took him on to a set which purported to be Marseilles and said: 'Vincent, you know Marseilles.' 'Yes, Alex,' replied Vincent. 'Tell me, Vincent: is this like Marseilles?' 'Not at all, Alex,' replied Vincent; and his career as a painter was over, at any rate for twenty-five years.[5]

Vincent designed the sets for *Marius*, and for every one of Alex's major films over the next two decades, becoming along the way one of the leading art directors in the British film industry. Edward Carrick, the British art director, has stated that Vincent was 'not wedded to the idea of film-making . . . and would have probably become a very great painter had he not been engulfed in his brother's work'.[6] But Alex wanted to keep the family together, and after 1931 the Korda brothers became an inseparable film-making team.

Released in Paris in October 1931, *Marius* was initially rewarded more in commercial returns than in critical acclaim. It was condemned as 'canned theatre' by those who had been inundated by a spate of filmed plays—the immediate source plundered to fill the demand for stories with dialogue—and who feared the demotion of cinema to the status of a theatrical recorder. It was, on the whole, an uninspired period in the cinema, and the critics' over-reaction to *Marius* was perhaps justified at the time. Nevertheless, the film weathered these criticisms and has gained a more tolerant following over the years. There is, it seems, always room for effective, visual translations of stage plays in the total scope of film-making, and *Marius* is one of these.

Although more 'stage-bound' than the other two films forming the trilogy—*Fanny* was filmed in 1932 by Marc Allégret, *César* in 1936 by Pagnol himself—*Marius* is generally accepted as the most successful of the three. It is certainly the best written, but it is also the best directed. Korda makes no awkward attempt to 'open up' the play, as Allégret and Pagnol were to do; but the preponderance of long takes and obvious 'entrances' and 'exits', although unavoidable, tends to keep the audience at a distance. To reduce this distance, to transform *Marius* into a 'filmic' experience, Korda and his cameraman employed three basic techniques: panning, angled shots, and dramatic lighting effects.

From the opening sequence we are aware of the roving camera 'eye' which pans across the Marseilles harbour, the quayside, and finally the street where César's bar is located. When Marius, whose desire to become a sailor has turned into an obsession, walks outside his father's bar and stares longingly at the ship docked in front of him, the camera slowly follows his gaze to the ship and back again in one long, smooth movement which binds Marius to the object of his fantasies. Later, as Marius leads the willing Fanny to his bed, the camera moves along the walls of his room (which looks like a ship's cabin), further illuminating the private world in which Marius alone lives. One of the most interesting camera movements is the slow pan from the balcony of Fanny's flat, past the stage wall which separates the outside from the inside of the flat, and into the kitchen. This is a parallel to the previous pan, and it ties Fanny to the 'kitchen' just as the former ties Marius to his 'cabin'. It is also the movement of a 'voyeur' and gives us a silent indication that what occurs indoors (pre-marital sex) is quite isolated from the world outside. Korda, whose earlier films betray if anything a lack of concern with camera movement, has here subtly employed movement as a means of discovering more about the characters and the relationship between their external and internal worlds than is given in the dialogue.

The most effective angled shot comes near the beginning when Marius, in a profile close-up, discusses the magic of the sea with the ferry-boat captain Escartefigue. The shot is taken from slightly above his head so that the bodies and feet of people passing in the busy street in front of the café are visible. There is also an effective aural transition as the steam whistle of the ferry is immediately cut to the kettle whistle of the bar's coffee-maker. Both effects emphasise the contrast Marius feels between the solitary life of the open sea and the busy, but restricted life he leads in Marseilles.

Fanny's flat, where the two lovers keep their rendezvous, is always shown in romantic half-light. During a highly dramatic moment, Fanny's bedroom appears in sombre shuttered light, and the flickering beam from the nearby lighthouse through a window is used to reinforce the ever-present call of the sea which eventually separates the two lovers. In *Marius* Korda has utilised lighting and the camera's point of view to provide the psychological mood that the stage play could not give, without in any way restricting his actors.

The acting is, after all, what makes the film so delightful to watch. Although it was the film debut of most of the cast, they adapted their stage performances into vibrant film performances without resorting to stage theatrics and without missing a beat in the speed of their delivery.* Raimu, who later starred in Julien Duvivier's *Carnet de bal* (1937) and Pagnol's *La Femme du boulanger* (1938), displayed in this his first film all the qualities which were to make him the leading French character actor of the thirties: '. . . the endearing humanity, the restrained power, the perfect timing, the inimitable sense of comedy . . . with the slow smile, the shrewd philosophical eyes, the accent thick as bouillabaisse'.[7] Charpin, as Panisse with his wide cummerbund and tight shoes, is the perfect companion-foil to Raimu's César, and the entire cast is well served by Pagnol's script and Korda's direction, both of which expose the 'simple virtues' as well as the 'amiable weaknesses' of the characters. Certain scenes remain unforgettable: Raimu's lesson in how to mix a drink and pour wine properly, Marius's 'slow burn' as he watches old Panisse lecherously courting the young Fanny, the notorious card game with Raimu clutching his chest and exclaiming '*Mon cœur!*' as a signal to his thick-headed partner Escartefigue, and the elaborate ruses used by father and son in order to sneak off to their respective rendezvous.

Korda's direction seems to slip only occasionally: the sudden, bulging eyes of Pierre Fresnay every time he hears the blast of a ship's horn is an extension of silent film exaggeration inconsistent with the rest of the acting,† and the model lighthouse which looms on screen as soon as the lovers climb into bed is a rather feeble symbolic device. Otherwise, the simple sexuality of the film was deftly handled, the abandoned Fanny's pregnancy being carefully intimated in only the last few feet of the film. Even so, the subject matter was daring enough for *Marius* to run into censorship problems. It was refused a certificate in England, and when it was finally released there in 1949, Alex Korda had already been a prominent member of the British film industry for fifteen years.

One night, Lajos Biro, who had been writing scripts for Paramount and had gone to England a few times to work for Gainsborough Films, was summoned to a conference at the Hotel Raphael where Korda was staying. Korda, Pallos, and a solicitor were there, as were the papers for the setting up of the film company which they had jointly discussed in

* It would be instructive to compare this version with the German one *Zum Goldenen Anker* (1931) which Korda directed at the same time, or with the Swedish and Italian versions directed by John W. Brunius and Mario Almirante respectively. The films must surely have suffered in translation.

† Fresnay was to give a more subtle performance, his best, as Captain Boieldieu in Jean Renoir's *La Grande Illusion* (1937).

Berlin. The company was to be called Pallas Films, after the Greek goddess. They bought the film rights to three 'hot' properties of the time— *Le Controlleur des Wagon-lits*, *Train 3-47*, and *The Girl from Maxim's*— but the trio's plans were temporarily cut short in the autumn of 1931.

A group of Paramount executives had been making the rounds of their foreign subsidiaries and had been displeased with the work emanating from their British branch. Korda was asked if he would accept a contract with Paramount British. This would provide Korda with his first taste of England and the British film industry, and at the same time he could earn some money to help establish his own company. Korda accepted and left Paris in November 1931. He was thirty-eight.

1. Ian Dalrymple, 'Alex', *The Journal of the British Film Academy*, Spring 1956, p. 5.
2. H. W. Seaman, *loc cit*.
3. *Ibid*.
4. Charles Ford, 'Marcel Pagnol', *Films in Review*, vol. XXI no. 4, April 1970, p. 200.
5. Ian Dalrymple, *loc cit*.
6. Edward Carrick, *Art and Design in the British Film*, London, Dennis Dobson, 1948, p. 13, p. 80.
7. *Daily Telegraph*, 26 September 1949.

PART TWO

*England and Recognition*

# CHAPTER SEVEN

# The Birth of London Films

SIX months after Alex Korda landed in England, in April 1932, the following pastiche appeared in a British film trade paper under the title 'The Director':

> I am Monarch of all I survey,
> My right there is none to dispute.
> Give me a good story, good pay,
> Good staff, then (maybe) I'll shoot.
>
> I'll take stars from all round the map.
> A Yank who can't act but who's skittish;
> A German, a Frenchman, a Jap . . .
> And produce you a picture that's British.[1]

No one could then have imagined how applicable this verse was to be to the British career of Alexander Korda, the Hungarian who would within eighteen months astound the international film world with a single film about an English king. Both the man and his film became the foundations of British hopes for waging a successful campaign against Hollywood's domination of world markets. If Korda had not come to England, the British cinema of the thirties might well have taken a different course. For the rest of his career Korda brought ambition, recognition, imagination, and glamour to an industry that needed his optimism and his showman's talent.

By 1931 the British film industry was already in a depressed state, and there were several reasons for this. It was widely felt that the

country's climate and the small size of its home market were not con-
ducive to large film-making enterprises. Britain's economic doldrums,
the conservatism of its big businessmen, and, with a few notable
exceptions, like Michael Balcon and Victor Saville, the scarcity of
British film producers with a flair for salesmanship did not help the
matter either. In France and Germany, painters, writers, and musicians
lent their support to the growth of the cinema. In England film was
looked on with much suspicion and even condescension. Hit by the
advent of sound and unable to afford multi-language versions, the
British film industry was bound in slavery to the American market by
a common language. British producers had attempted in the late
twenties to fight back by coaxing Hollywood or foreign actors to
London in order to achieve wider box-office appeal, but the experiment had failed. Hollywood remained the 'promised land', and anyone
who wanted to succeed in films bent over backwards to get an invitation to cross the Atlantic.

'Audacity' and 'imagination' were the two qualities which British
film people lacked and which Alex Korda had in seemingly inexhaust-
ible abundance. The country needed an industry leader with faith in the
potential of the native cinema and with bold ideas of how to inject
spirit and hope into the rest of the industry. The British welcomed men
like Alexander Korda whom they felt might accomplish this rejuvena-
tion.

This was a marked contrast to his reception in Hollywood. In an
article in February 1932 entitled 'Welcome Visitors', a journalist stood
up for the newcomers:

> We should welcome American and Continental directors as
> long as they justify themselves by helping to make better and more
> widely acceptable British pictures. Men like Alexander Korda,
> Paul Stein, Mervyn Le Roy, and Rowland V. Lee should not be
> regarded with jealousy and suspicion simply because they do not
> happen to be British-born. Their skill and experience are their
> passports. . . .[2]

England needed Korda, but Korda's need for a place to settle down and
construct a stable life and career was just as great. He was fed up with
his gypsy existence and needed a home where he could bring together
all his ideas and his experience in the undertaking of a grand enterprise.
It was the first time since Hungary that Korda's strong ambitions were

not at odds with the prevailing climate of an industry or country. The timing, for once, was just right.

Alex took a small flat in Duchess Street in the centre of London and immediately began work on the first film of his two-picture deal with Paramount British. Paramount's subsidiary in London, like other American film subsidiaries, was at that time producing films to comply with the Cinematograph Films Act of 1927, which, among other things, required film distributors to handle a certain percentage (starting at 7½ per cent in 1929) of 'British' films each year. This 'quota' was intended as a protection against the onslaught of the American film, as a means of promoting the exhibition and distribution of British films. The distributors' quota, however, made the situation worse. American companies quickly realised that by producing their own films in London—they were legally 'British' as long as they fulfilled certain requirements—and by specially commissioning films from British companies, they could regulate the costs of the films which they were being forced to promote and distribute. These films were hastily made, cheap productions which rightfully earned the name 'quota quickies'.* Most of Korda's earliest British films were 'quota' pictures for Paramount.

Paramount British was, however, willing to spend more money on its own quota films than on those commissioned from other British producers. For Korda's first picture, *Service for Ladies* (1932), the company brought the British actor Leslie Howard back from Hollywood, where he had already made a name for himself, and apparently paid him a salary of £500 a week. When told that the film's director was Alex Korda, Howard, whose real name was Stainer and whose parents were Hungarian, was supposed to have replied: 'Korda? I have heard of Maria Corda, the actress. Any relation?'

The film was a remake of an earlier Paramount film which Harry D'Arrast had directed in 1927 with Adolph Menjou in the title role. The story was taken from Ernest Vajda's novel *The Head Waiter* (the working title for Korda's version), and it told of the rags-to-riches rise of a head waiter who is mistaken for a prince. It was the same kind of light, superficial exploration of high society with which Korda had been associated in Germany and America. Besides Howard, the cast in-

---

* British film-makers were paid £1 a foot for these four- to six-reelers. They, of course, tried to make the films for less than the £4–6,000 fixed sum. This was a far cry from the £30,000 average cost of films produced by British film companies during this period.

cluded George Grossmith and Benita Hume, supported by Morton Selten, the seventy-two-year-old actor who became one of Korda's favourite character players. The film was edited by Harold Young who had worked on *Helen of Troy* in Hollywood and who was soon to take over the editing department of Korda's own company.*

Paramount officials and the British public were impressed by the 'polish' of *Service for Ladies*. 'A visiting executive from the mother-studio,' to quote Ian Dalrymple, 'was so startled by its *expertise* that, on learning its moderate cost, he shouted: "Say, it isn't your job over here to compete with us in Hollywood!" '4 Dalrymple continues with a tale which perhaps puts the film's merits in perspective:

> . . . a probably apocryphal story tells of a debate between Zolly and Alex some years later on the set at Denham. *Service for Ladies* had entered into the argument, which Zolly pooh-poohed as a 'lousy' film, Alex rather naturally maintaining its excellence. All work on the floor stopped while the brothers retired to the projection theatre and the film was winkled out of the vaults and run for them; whereupon, at the end, Alex pronounced with his small-boy grin: 'Zolly is right. It is lousy.'5

In late November 1931 Paramount announced that Alex Korda would direct a screen adaptation of Rudyard Kipling's *The Light That Failed*, but for some reason the project was abandoned.† Two months later Korda began work on his second contract picture, *Spring Cleaning*, from Frederick Lonsdale's play. The film's title was changed to *Women Who Play*, but Korda was not to direct the film.

> 'He was not happy with it,' H. W. Seaman writes, 'and could see only failure ahead.
>
> 'One night he was riding home from Elstree along the Barnet By-pass when his car, a Paramount car with a Paramount chauffeur, crashed. Korda escaped with injuries just serious enough to make it impossible for him to work for a few weeks. Paramount paid him damages and released him from his contract, and he was free.'6

---

* In 1931 Korda had sent for Young to take charge of the editing department at Joinville, and he then brought him to England. Harold Young's wife writes: 'Harold being Irish and Korda being Korda they did not always agree but always seemed to work things out as they had respect for each other.'3

† *The Light That Failed*, directed by William Wellman and starring Ronald Colman, was finally made by Paramount in 1939.

*Women Who Play* (1932) was directed by Arthur Rosson and apparently lived up to Korda's expectations. It was the first, but not the last time that Alex Korda would be saved by a car accident.

Free from contract commitments, Korda was ready to embark on his most important project since the founding of Corvin in 1917. Early in 1932 Korda summoned his two brothers to London, Vincent coming from Paris and Zolly from Hollywood. In February Korda gathered his entourage together and founded a company which was christened London Film Productions. (There had been a previous film production company with this name—London Film Company, set up in 1913—but it had ceased operation long before 1932.) The board of directors for London Films was comprised of the men who financed the company's incorporation: George Grossmith (Chairman), Lajos Biro (who shortly resigned, as business matters didn't interest him at all), Lord Lurgan, J. S. Cerf (who represented French Pathé interests), Captain A. S. N. Dixie, John Sutro (who looked after the investments of his father, Leopold Sutro, a city banker), and Alex Korda himself.

Where Korda got the money to pay for his share of the investment in London Films during its first year has been the subject of much speculation. Korda probably did not have a lot of money at the time, but he had directed three films in 1931 and must have put aside some of his salary for investment in the company which he, Biro, and Pallos had organised in Paris. However, in a letter to *The Sunday Times* in 1970, Alex's son Peter made the following statement:

> It was my mother's not insubstantial financial aid that enabled my father to transfer his film career to London in 1930.
>
> If my father became a leader of the British film industry (as has been claimed) then it can accurately be stated that without that financial assistance the British film industry would never have experienced, even briefly, the European, and respectable, influence that he was able to apply.[7]

Maria Corda apparently did come to London in early 1932, and she may well have given Korda financial backing for his company. Although others have assured me that this suggestion is preposterous, I have no reason, and no evidence, to discount Peter's explanation. One thing is clear: during its first year London Films just managed to stay solvent.

A five-room office in a mews off Grosvenor Street (No. 22) in Mayfair served as headquarters for the fledgling enterprise. It was a luxurious location for a young company, but Korda was always adamant that his people should work in the best surroundings. Economies were enforced in other areas. The office staff, for instance, was kept to a minimum: a typist, a publicity director (John Meyers), and a casting director and general production manager (George Grossmith, Jnr). The company functioned as a family business. Lajos Biro took charge of the script department, Vincent headed the art department, and Harold Young supervised the editing department. It was a shrewd move to have so many of the staff either related to Korda or in some way tied to the company, for when money was in short supply, as it often was, most of the 'creative' staff were willing to forego their salaries so that the office staff could be paid.

Finance for actual film production had been arranged through two sources. London Films obtained a contract from Paramount to make a series of quota films, and in February Korda had also gone to see Michael Balcon at Gaumont British. The two men had first met in Berlin when Alex was working with Josef Somlo and Herman Fellner, and Balcon now helped to arrange the (100 per cent) financing and distribution of Korda's first project, *Wedding Rehearsal* (1933), through Ideal Films, a part of the Gaumont British organisation. On the 5th of March 1932, the first promotional advertisements for London Films' up-coming productions appeared in the press. Three weeks later came the news that Big Ben had been chosen as the company's trademark. This was Korda's own idea; he knew that it was a prestigious symbol which would be easily recognised almost everywhere as representing a 'British' film. Korda always enjoyed being asked if there was any special significance in Big Ben striking a certain time at the beginning of his films. His answer was that that was when the sun had finally come out and the shot could be taken. In actual fact, the trademark went through at least one transformation: from Big Ben shown at night from a distance in the early films to the more familiar daytime shot of the actual tower seen from close range.

Once financing had been obtained, Korda's first priority was to expand his impressive production staff. Besides Lajos Biro, the script department now housed the talents of Arthur Wimperis, who had written titles for silent films (including Maria Corda's British film *Tesha*) and who was hired to write the dialogue (usually the 'jokes') for Korda's films, the novelist and playwright Anthony Gibbs, and the playwright Dorothy Greenhill. Vincent was joined in the art department by Oskar Werndorff, the German designer who had worked on

Korda's last two German films. Harold Young had Stephen Harrison to help him with the editing chores, and Bernard Browne, Phil Tannura, and Robert Martin were London Films' first cameramen. In almost every case the 'foreign' member of the staff had at least one English counterpart, and this was not accidental. Muir Mathieson, who was a twenty-year-old music student at the time, provides us with the reasoning behind this mixture:

> When Korda set up his London Film Productions here, he had a German music director, Herr Schroeder, who had been an opera coach or something in Cologne or one of the minor German opera houses. His [Schroeder's] brother-in-law had been in Hollywood with Korda, and he recommended getting hold of Schroeder when Korda came here to London.
>
> In order to get a work permit for the German, they had to make the excuse that he was training an Englishman, in this case a Scotsman. So my old friend Grunbaum from the Royal College sent me along to see this Schroeder and then Korda, and I became assistant music director at £4 10s. a week. . . .[8]

Schroeder didn't last long at London Films, but his 'assistant' became the most influential and prolific talent in British film music.

Korda also realised that his company needed a stable of contract players. In order to avoid paying exorbitant sums to borrow 'name' talents for all the roles, he decided to find new, less expensive 'faces' with whom he could surround the few 'names' he could afford. The call went out, hundreds of young aspirants were interviewed, and in April 1932 came the announcement of Korda's four new starlets: Wendy Barrie, Diana Napier, Joan Gardner, and Merle Oberon. Each one had been chosen to fit a particular stereotype—Joan and Wendy were Korda's idea of the typical English girl, Merle was the 'exotic', and Diana 'the high class beetch' (Korda's words). According to Diana Napier, they were offered a five-year contract at £20 a week. To provide romantic interest for the starlets Korda recruited several young actors, including Robert Donat, Emlyn Williams, John Loder, and Maurice Evans. The casts were almost always headed by more established players such as Roland Young, George Grossmith, Lady Tree, Leslie Banks, and Edmund Gwenn. This economic mélange of experienced and non-experienced players provided a two-fold benefit for Korda: audiences would be drawn to the films by the established names, and, by constantly promoting new actors and actresses, Korda would gradually create a demand for them as well. This was Korda's method of making a 'star'. It was an activity which he thoroughly enjoyed and one at which he was quite successful.

Although five of Korda's first six films were quota pictures, Korda approached them as he would any other production and probably spent more on them than was normal for the time. He needed to be proud of the films, for they were to be the foundations of his career. To ensure that the films were competently made, he hired well-known directors to make them. London Films' inaugural effort, *Wedding Rehearsal*, was not a quota production, and Alex saved the direction of this picture for himself.

At one time or another two 'Lords' have been credited with the idea behind *Wedding Rehearsal*—Lords Vansittart and Castlerosse. It sounds like the kind of story which the English upper classes might enjoy telling about themselves: the bachelor Marquis who makes matches for all the eligible girls his mother has proposed that he should marry until he, too, falls in love (with his mother's secretary). The dastardly complications of marrying within and without one's social class and the added confusion when twin daughters are involved (double roles again) offered Korda the type of material which he had handled several times before, and he again tried to approach it in a satirical, even sarcastic manner.

Unfortunately, the sarcasm and the satire have to yield fairly early to the overburdened plot machinations—how to get everybody married off in less than an hour. The beginning had prepared us for a slightly different film. Accompanied by loud music and voices chanting out numbers in thousands, the opening scene reveals the machinery of Fleet Street churning out newspapers with headlines about thousands being killed in an eruption of Mount Vesuvius and about the imminent danger of war. A man dressed in morning coat rushes into the city editor's office, a cry of 'stop the press' is heard, and a new headline, all about the 'Binley–Foster Wedding', is substituted. From there the film proceeds to a working class flat where the husband has come home to find his wife gone to stand in a crowd to watch the wedding and his daughter engrossed in the newspaper account. He rants about the needless waste of society weddings, but finally succumbs to his own curiosity and peers over his daughter's shoulder to read the account himself. From then on Korda's own fascination with the English aristocracy precludes anything but a lovable portrayal of the eccentric, idle rich whose only occupation seems to be matchmaking (seven couples are united by the end of the film).

The cast is equally divided between the 'older generation' (the experienced actors) and the 'younger generation' (Korda's new faces), the former almost making up for the awkwardness of the latter. Lady Tree, Roland Young, Morton Selten, and Kate Cutler seem most at ease; their lines are also the best. When Reggie, the bachelor Marquis (Roland Young), and his mother (Kate Cutler) go through the list of girls suitable for marriage, Reggie manages to find something distasteful about each one . . .

> Reggie: Such a long nose.
> Mother: That nose came down straight from the Normans.
> Reggie: But does it have to come down so far?

Lady Tree effortlessly steals every scene. As the quiet and naïve Lady Stokeshire, mother of the twins, she somehow gets away with her reply to Reggie's comment that she should be an optimist: 'I saw one last week and he said my eyes were all right.' When given the duty of telling her about-to-be-married daughters the facts of life, her discomfort is beautifully portrayed. Nervously and unconsciously tying her handkerchief around the arm of a chair, she broaches the touchy subject: 'In these days almost everything is made by machinery; this might have given you the wrong ideas.' Sadly, the rest of the actors, including George Grossmith who is more concerned with caricature than character, cannot maintain Lady Tree's standards.

Joan Gardner and Wendy Barrie just manage to pull off the Roxbury Twins by their spunkiness and the fact that they do look and act like twins. The juvenile leads, John Loder and Maurice Evans, are wooden and lifeless, and Merle Oberon and Diana Napier seem totally at a loss as to how to behave, let alone act, in their roles. Merle Oberon had only been given the role after a motor accident caused the removal of the first 'Miss Hutchinson', the beautiful girl behind the secretary's thick glasses, and she is sadly miscast. Diana Napier, who was soon to give up acting and marry Richard Tauber, the operatic singer and film star, reminisced about Korda's limitations as a director:

> But what Korda couldn't do, he couldn't make people act if they hadn't got it in them, so he glamorised them . . . He was more interested in the decor than the actor, I think, or the im-

pression it was making or the richness of it, or having real jewellery on you instead of artificial jewellery.[9]

Over the years Korda was to lose touch more and more with his actors as he pursued bigger and better visual effects and superficial polish.

In one of the final passages of dialogue in *Wedding Rehearsal*, a metaphorical analysis is applied to the subject of marriage in a discussion between Reggie and Major Harry Roxbury (Morton Selten):

Roxbury: What do you think about marriage?
Reggie: Have you ever bought a tie? You see one and you say 'I want it'. It's expensive, but you buy it and you put it on. It's just the shade you wanted. But then you take it home, and in daylight it's not what you wanted at all.
Roxbury: Somewhere there's a tie that suits you all the time. If you give it away and then see it on someone else, you realise that you really wanted it.

This exchange provides Reggie with a closing line as he comes to the realisation that he is in love with 'Hutchy': 'I believe you're the tie I gave to my butler.' These lines, and the ones quoted earlier, are clear indications of the direction which the dialogue in Korda's films was to take, a direction the signposts of which are a lack of subtlety and an excessive dependence on epigrammatic exchanges, rather childish humour, and unimaginative metaphors.

*Wedding Rehearsal* is, not surprisingly, good to look at. The decor of country estates and town mansions are impressively recreated, and the photography, though not inventive, is adequate. The ambitious attempt at an innovative mixture of image and sound during the opening montage of newspaper headlines and press machinery is rather crude, but it was an interesting experiment and does prefigure a similarly conceived, but successful scene at the beginning of Korda's *Things to Come* (1936).

The film made little impact on the British public when it was released in January 1933, and it was never released in America. In a cutting analysis of Korda's work written in 1937, Marcel Ermans, the French critic, suggested, 'If I were Korda, I would get up in the night, steal the negative, and quietly drop it in the Thames.'[10] On the other hand, many people remember the film with great fondness, perhaps for its attempt at sophistication and for the fine performance of Lady Tree. A piece of fluff like this, however, cannot survive uneven acting and dialogue, especially when coupled with an over-complicated plot, too facilely rendered.

Korda acted as 'producer' for the five quota pictures which London Films made for Paramount in 1933. He chose or approved the scripts, cast the players, decided which technicians and directors were to work on them, and, with one exception, left the directors alone to get on with the job. They were all contemporary stories, and although interiors were shot at British and Dominion's Elstree Studio where Paramount rented space, most of the films took advantage of extensive location shooting. Some reviewers applauded them for 'bringing Britain to the screen', but, like most quota films, they were brought to very few screens or were shown during such peak attendance hours as early morning, when the cleaning staff outnumbered the cinema-goers.

*Men of To-morrow* (1933), the first of the series, was directed by Leontine Sagan, the German theatre director whose entire film reputation rests on her frank and brutal study of life in a German girls' school, *Mädchen in Uniform*, which caused a critical stir on its release in 1931. Eager to leave Germany, she accepted Korda's invitation to make a film in England 'suited' to her special talent, a film about another group of students—undergraduates at Oxford. The story, an adaptation of Anthony Gibbs's play *Young Apollo*, was a perfect vehicle for four of Korda's fledgling stars: Merle Oberon, Robert Donat, Emlyn Williams, and Joan Gardner. It was the first film to recreate the Oxbridge university atmosphere, and Sagan's handling of the actors and the location shooting in Oxford was widely praised. Unfortunately, the final product failed to do justice to Sagan's treatment of the story's original, downbeat theme—the disillusionment of an undergraduate 'sent down' from Oxford for writing a diatribe about the university.

An article in the film journal *Close-Up* points to a possible cause: 'One suspects . . . that she was not given a free hand—one knows that the filming was attended by what are politely called "difficulties", and it would seem that the "toning down" of the hero and the featuring of young married bliss almost exactly reverses the director's own feelings in the matter.'[11] Zoltan Korda's co-direction of the film with Sagan may have been the source of these difficulties. Sagan's film-making experience was limited and it was not unreasonable to offer her more experienced advisers, but Zoltan was an unlikely choice. In addition, although Sagan did edit one cut of the film herself, extensive re-editing was done (by whom it is not clear) in order to shorten the film's length. Sagan complained that this re-editing ruined the rhythmic balance of the editing and shifted the emphasis of the story. This is the first of several instances where Korda was criticised for damaging the work of directors in his employ.*

*That Night in London* (1933) was a lightweight drama about a country bank clerk who steals from the bank in order to have one night on the town before he commits suicide. He (Robert Donat) meets a 'real' crook (Miles Mander) on his way to London, and the remainder of the film describes Mander's attempt to rob the clerk with the assistance of his sister (Pearl Argyle), who, in the end, saves the clerk's money and his job. The film was directed by Rowland V. Lee, the American director who had served his apprenticeship in Hollywood under Thomas Ince and had subsequently made *Alice Adams* (1926) and *The Mysterious Dr Fu Manchu* (1929). One still from the film, which shows Donat and Argyle dancing in what must be a night club, gives us some idea of the spartan production values in quota films, for the scene offers no detail and no atmosphere and is far inferior in these respects to, for example, the night club scenes in Korda's *Das unbekannte Morgen*, made ten years before, or the party sequence in *Eine Dubarry von heute* (1927).

*Strange Evidence* (1933) was a classic whodunnit story in which all the main characters gather in the family home to resolve a mysterious murder. Directed by another American, Robert Milton, the film's only noteworthy achievement was that Korda had coaxed Leslie Banks, the British actor who had forsaken Britain for Hollywood and had just made his first really successful film there (*The Hounds of Zaroff*—1932), back to England to star in the film.

The experienced American director Allan Dwan had no more success with his quota film, *Counsel's Opinion* (1933), than Rowland Lee had had with *That Night in London*. A review of Dwan's film in *The Observer* (7 May 1933) gives us a good indication of how these films were received:

* The British film director Thorold Dickinson, who did the English subtitles for *Mädchen* with Sagan, provides this interesting note (letter to the author 5 February 1974):
'We all knew she was a stage director and knew nothing about film and its techniques: Carl Froelich [the German film director] had done that for her. So when Korda booked her for Men of To-morrow, we knew what was going to and did happen. Even Korda could not save it. He would never have booked her if she had been British.'

London Film Productions is a firm that has always found it difficult to shake off the impression that it is making bright, sophisticated pictures for a college union, but there is perhaps more naïveté than usual about this comedy of a divorce counsel who imagines himself mixed up in his own case. The director is an American, Allan Dwan, who must either have come or gone away with odd ideas of British humour; he tries to inject a bit of professional De Mille gaiety into a Louis XV night at a London hotel, but otherwise leaves his team of stage humourists to get their laughs when and how they can. Binnie Barnes is easy to look at, but gives you nothing beyond her lines; Henry Kendall has an impossible young man to play, and does his job faithfully.

Korda must have believed in *Counsel's Opinion*, however, for he remade the film in Technicolor in 1938 under the title *The Divorce of Lady X*.

The last of the quota films, *Cash* (1933), was Zoltan's first solo directorial assignment for London Films. Edmund Gwenn starred as an embezzling bank clerk, and Wendy Barrie and Robert Donat played the romantic leads. The moral of the film seemed to be that a superficial display of hard cash was all that one needed to win financial support from the big investors in the City of London. (As we shall see, Korda soon accomplished this feat himself with even less effort.) Robert Donat's biographer, J. C. Trewin, describes a public screening of *Cash* which Donat attended: 'When *Cash* was put into a Sunday night programme at the Plaza [Paramount's "showcase" theatre], the audience guyed it from the moment the warning, "British Made Picture", filled the screen. "It insults your intelligence, doesn't it?" said Robert's neighbour. . . .'[12]

Korda's quota pictures may have done nothing to improve the standard of these formula-made features, but given the reason for their existence (a handy loophole in a law restricting the screen monopoly of American films) and the conditions under which they were made (the fixed delivery prices and even lower production costs), this would have been an impossible and worthless task anyway. Although it gave some film-makers, like Korda, a chance to direct pictures, quota film production didn't deserve to succeed, for it was an affront to both British film-makers and the British public and gave British films a bad reputation.

In its first year the small mews office of London Films had at least been active. The groundwork for the future had been laid, but Korda had built up an organisation far too competent and too grandiose to content itself with quota film production. In the autumn of 1933 Korda was to prove himself more than a small-time quota producer and director. He did this with just one film, *The Private Life of Henry VIII*.

1. John Harlow, 'Rhymes of the Studios', *Film Weekly*, 29 April 1932.
2. *Film Weekly*, 20 February 1932, p. 1.
3. Letter from Mrs Emily Young to the author, 24 August 1973.
4. Ian Dalrymple, *op cit*, p. 6.
5. *Ibid*.
6. H. W. Seaman, 'How Korda Finds His Stars', *The Sunday Chronicle*, 14 March 1937, p. 4.
7. P. V. de Korda, letter to the editor, *The Sunday Times*, 8 October 1970.
8. Interview with Muir Mathieson conducted by the author, 17 July 1973.
9. Interview with Diana Napier Tauber conducted by the author, 22 July 1973.
10. Marcel Ermans, '*Alexandre le Magnifique*', *World Film News*, 1937, vol. 2 no. 3, p. 6.
11. *Close-Up*, vol. 9 no. 4, December 1932, p. 296.
12. J. C. Trewin, *Robert Donat: a biography*, London, William Heinemann, 1968, p. 69.

# CHAPTER EIGHT

# The Private Life of Henry VIII

IT did not take long for Alex Korda and his group of polyglot Continentals to become the focus of attention in the British film world and especially in the British press. In the midst of an industry already characterised as glamourless and rather parochial, London Film Productions offered an exciting contrast, an alternative image of how films should be made and how the men who make them should look, talk, and behave. Journalists flocked to Grosvenor Street to find out more about the ambitions and ideas of this newcomer who seemed to be preparing himself for an extended stay. One journalist dubbed Korda's offices 'International House' and described with much fascination his first visit there in August 1933: 'I am credibly informed that eight languages are in current use among the personnel. From the German conversation between two members of the staff in an ante-room I passed in to be greeted in Hungarian-accented English by Korda, who sat speaking Italian into a telephone.'[1] Upon first meeting Korda a reporter was usually most impressed by his politeness, grace, and sheer physical 'presence', and descriptions of him bordered on the lyrical: '... a modern film executive, pacing the office floor as he talks, smoking, in endless succession, his continental cigars ... tall, spare, quiet, in his early forties, with glasses that hide the thought in the eyes behind, and something leonine in the head and gait'.[2]

Early press coverage, of necessity, was confined to the cosmopolitan nature of the London Films company and its chief, for up until August 1933 Korda's film-making record had made little impact on the

industry. Even the film which Korda directed in Paris in December
1932, *The Girl from Maxim's*, was not released until January 1934.
Korda had become restless in his role of 'producer', and as he
already owned the film rights to Georges Feydeau's play, he decided to
return to Paris to direct it, both in English and in French. He left
David Cunynghame in charge in London. (Cunynghame had first
met Korda in Paris where he had been Paramount's official overseer of
Korda's studio activities. He remained one of Alex's closest friends and
associates over the next twenty-five years, working on most of Korda's
films in the capacity of production manager.) Alex took with him to
Paris his brother Vincent (to design the sets) and most of the cast for
the English version, including Lady Tree, George Grossmith, Frances
Day, Leslie Henson, and Stanley Holloway.

The making of the film was beset with minor calamities which provide some amusing and useful insights into Korda's film-making
priorities. Production apparently came to a standstill one day when
Frances Day refused to wear the cotton undergarments designed for
her by Jean Oberle. In order to play her role as 'the girl from Maxim's'
she demanded silk under-garments which, as she put it, 'wouldn't
bunch'. Order was quickly restored as Alex, a bit exasperated, boomed
out: 'Make them silk! Then maybe we can make a feelm.'[3] The
production progressed a bit further, until Korda realised that the film
was way over budget. He decided that some economies must thereafter be observed, and he gathered the film crew together to announce
his new course of action. He had weighed everything very carefully,
he told them, and now knew where the axe would have to fall. His
solution? To fire the young lady who answered the telephones.
Reported in the French press, this story helped to launch the legends of
Korda's particular kind of extravagances.

Set in the 'Gay Nineties', *The Girl from Maxim's* was a lively musical
comedy which showed at least enough promise to interest Metro-
Goldwyn-Mayer in remaking it in Hollywood. Metro cabled Korda:
'REQUEST OPTION FOR REMAKE RIGHTS OF DAME
DE CHEZ MAXIM. WIRE FINANCIAL CONDITIONS.'
Alex quickly sent off his terms and awaited Metro's answer. It came the
next day and, to his amazement, simply stated, 'OUR LAST OFFER
£35,000.' Taken aback, Korda asked his secretary to bring a copy of
his cable to Metro. The telegram read: 'RELINQUISH RIGHTS
FOR £40,000. KORDA.' Sure enough, his secretary had made a
small, but convenient typographical error. Korda had, of course,

meant dollars, not pounds. He naturally accepted Metro's offer, making $175,000, not $40,000, on the final transaction.[4] Given the late release date of the film, we must assume this lucky deal occurred some time after the phenomenal success of Alex's *The Private Life of Henry VIII* (1933).

There are at least three stories in circulation about the genesis of *Henry VIII*, although they all begin from the same premise: that Alex was looking for a 'vehicle' for Charles Laughton and his wife, Elsa Lanchester. Miss Lanchester had met Korda while Laughton was in Hollywood making *Payment Deferred* (1932), and Korda suggested to her that they star in a film called *A Gust of Wind*. Nothing came of the project, but when Laughton returned to England, he often met with Korda to discuss different film ideas.

According to the first story, one day a London cabby singing the Harry Champion music-hall number, *I'm 'Enery the Eighth I Am*, gave Korda the inspiration to make a film about this well-remembered English king whose personal life presented such a natural film scenario. The second story is that during a meeting, a statue of Henry VIII in the room caused Laughton's agent to remark on the resemblance between Charles and the monarch. And the third story is that in another meeting in Paris, probably while Korda was directing *Girl from Maxim's*, the idea simply came up in a discussion between Alex and Laughton about possible film roles suited to the actor's talent. All the versions might, in fact, be true, all parts of a sequence of events. The first story was Korda's own favourite, and he seemed to delight in leading journalists to believe that he had known nothing about Henry VIII until he came to London.* Soon after Korda's return from Paris preliminary work was begun on the project.

Lajos Biro wrote the original treatment with the help of Philip Lindsay, the 'historical consultant'; yet we can be sure that both Korda and Arthur Wimperis had a hand in it even at this stage. In an article entitled 'Why Film Authors Are Not Stars', Arthur Wimperis humorously outlined the relative positions which these three men had during this and many subsequent collaborations.

> In my own case there are three of us in collaboration—first and foremost Alexander Korda (privately known as Alexander

* This was, of course, not the case; in 1920 Korda had made *The Prince and the Pauper* which was set in Henry's reign and in which he obtained a highly praised performance from Alfred Schreiber in the role of the king.

the Cruel, owing to the merciless manner in which he dismisses our pet ideas!), who has forgotten more about story construction than most people ever knew.

Then Lajos Biro, famous Hungarian playwright, novelist, and publicist, who is architect in chief; last and least, myself, who writes that brilliant dialogue, which you never hear because it gets cut out by A. the C., and contributes those witty scenes, which you never see for the same reason.[5]

The script in its first drafts only dealt with Henry and his fourth wife, Anne of Cleves (to be played by Elsa Lanchester), but as the script conferences progressed (seven complete scripts being written and thrown away in the meantime) one wife after another was added, until five out of Henry's six wives were included. Perhaps the Henry–Anne of Cleves story could not be padded out to feature-film length. Perhaps they simply got carried away with what was, after all, a thumping great idea. Perhaps Korda felt he had to use all his female contract players. For whatever reason, the broadening of the film's scope was the key to its commercial success. Since the title had worked once before and since the approach to history was basically the same, Korda christened the project *The Private Life of Henry VIII* and began the arduous task of finding finance for it.

The task was difficult, because 'period pieces' had long been out of fashion. Korda soon realised that he couldn't even give the thing away. As he himself admitted, 'The costume picture was the most disliked thing in the world. My colleagues said the public would not stand for it—they even told me it would be unwise to use King Henry's name in the title and wanted me to call the picture *The Golden Bed*.'[6] Korda tried Gaumont British, but after the meagre results of *Wedding Rehearsal*, neither Michael Balcon nor C. M. Woolf felt they could risk more money on Korda's new film. Other companies were sounded out, but the reaction was always the same: the project was condemned as box-office poison.

Finally, one of George Grossmith's friends, Richard Norton (later Lord Grantley) and his associate Murray Silverstone came to Korda's rescue. They both liked Korda's script and attempted to get support from United Artists, the American film company for which they both worked. Founded in 1919 by Mary Pickford, Douglas Fairbanks, Snr, Charlie Chaplin, and D. W. Griffith, United Artists was set up expressly to produce and distribute the films of the founders and of other selected independent producers. By 1933 the company was searching for new producers, new products, and after an initial negative response from the New York sales manager, Norton cabled Joseph Schenck, president of United Artists, and Samuel Goldwyn, an owner–member, and convinced them to give the Korda project some financial backing. Although the reported figures vary, UA came through with somewhere between twelve and twenty thousand pounds, enough to get the project off the ground.

There had been a slight 'catch', however, for the British producer Herbert Wilcox at that time had an exclusive contract with UA which prohibited the company from distributing other British films. Alex phoned Wilcox and persuaded him to exempt *Henry* from this ban. Probably as compensation, it was decided that the film would be shot at Wilcox's British and Dominion Studios, where production began in the late spring of 1933.\* From the start Korda had no idea whether he would ever get the money to finish the film, but he seemed to delight in such crisis-ridden film-making situations. Korda believed that films 'grew', and like an artist who refuses to finish a painting once the cartoon has been carefully drafted, so Korda lost interest in films that were progressing too smoothly.

Now, for the first time since leaving Hungary, Korda was faced with an inadequately financed project which required all his resourcefulness in the production stages. The cast and film crew had faith in Korda and what he was trying to do, and many of them agreed to share the risks with Korda, either going without or reducing their salaries and waiting until the film was released to receive proper compensation. Vincent Korda designed the sets which were constructed quickly and economically, so much so, in fact, that some of the actors were afraid that the sets would come tumbling down around them at any moment. The number of costumes was kept to a minimum, usually by having the players wear the same costumes throughout most of the film. It has been reported that some scenes cost as little as £10 or £12 to shoot, thus off-setting the costs of the more elaborate scenes, such as the banquet sequences. Georges Périnal, the famous French cinematographer who had worked with René Clair on *Le Million* (1931) and *A nous la liberté* (1931) and had shot Korda's *The Girl from Maxim's*, had been coaxed to London by Korda, and his exquisite cinematic

---

\* In 1937 Korda repaid his debt to Wilcox. He gave Wilcox £50,000 studio credit at Denham (Korda's studio) which allowed him to make *Victoria the Great* (1937).

'eye' not only disguised the flimsiness of the sets, but actually gave the whole film a lavish and glossy appearance.

The picture was completed in five weeks, thanks to the last minute financial support of another film 'patron' discovered by Korda—Ludovico Toeplitz de Grand Ry. Son of an Italian banker, the gargantuan, bearded Toeplitz (nicknamed, because of his appearance, 'Henry IX') gave Korda enough money to finish the film and became, for a short time, his business partner. After *Henry*, Toeplitz began interfering in Korda's plans, and the partnership was dissolved. As a financial settlement Toeplitz was offered ownership of either *The Girl from Maxim's* or *The Private Life of Henry VIII*. He must have regretted his judgement, for he chose the former film which at that time seemed to have more commercial potential.

One man who did see *Henry's* possibilities was Douglas Fairbanks, Snr, who as a United Artists founding member had the film screened at a special preview. Deeply impressed by the film's quality and international box-office potential, Fairbanks immediately offered Korda a long-term tie-up with the American company. Negotiations were completed by the middle of August 1933 and a new 'one million pound alliance' was announced to the trade press. London Films would produce six to eight feature films a year for United Artists at an average cost of £100,000, and there were ultimate plans for the building of a studio for Korda's company. The goals of the United Artists–London Films alliance were made clear right from the beginning: 'The aim of the new organisation will be . . . to bring back to England many great English artistes who have not heretofore produced in this country . . . [and] other artistes of world-wide importance, although not of British origin, will be invited to join and to produce their pictures here.'[7] Thus, United Artists, then suffering from a decline in picture output, was to have a fresh source of feature films marketable in America, and Alex was finally to have the proper backing for his film-making schemes. The first pillar of Korda's film empire had been put into place.

Knowing the necessity for a British film to do well in America if it was to earn a profit and infected with new confidence in the film's value, Korda decided to stage the film's grand premiere in America. On the 12th of October 1933, *The Private Life of Henry VIII* opened at Radio City Music Hall in New York and proceeded to break the box-office record for first day admissions by taking £7,500. In its first week the film earned back more than half its production cost, which had been close to £60,000.* Two weeks later, *Henry* reached the Leicester Square Theatre in London, and from comments in the press the next day it was clear that London Films' promotion of the picture as 'the film that will make screen history' was not an exaggerated pun. A colossal success, the film made £500,000 on its first world run and was still earning £10,000 a year twenty years later. It was the first British film to conquer the American market, and it inspired a tremendous film-making 'boom' in Britain. For these reasons *The Private Life of Henry VIII* has ever since been considered one of the most important films in the development of the British cinema.

*Henry*'s success had little to do with 'novelty', for the 'keyhole' approach to history was not new. In the immediate post-war period writers and film-makers had explored the ways in which history and historical figures could be 'humanised', and this trend led to films like Ernst Lubitsch's *Anna Boleyn* (1920) and Korda's own *Helen of Troy* (1927). In this respect *Henry* was a late-comer, a belated apotheosis of a genre which treats history lightly, satirically, and at times irreverently. Korda's use of an unfashionable approach was therefore a gamble, but there were several definite advantages to it. Henry VIII was an historical character about whom almost everyone knew something—if only the number of his wives—and the 'private life' treatment allowed Korda to deal with the most familiar episodes of Henry's personal life while excusing him from having to delve into the historically significant events of Henry's public life. The political and religious ramifications of Henry's reign were simply outside the scope of the film.

For Korda, the 'humanising' technique depended on setting up the audience's vicarious identification with the remote historical figures. In one of the first sequences the audience is encouraged to make this connection. As the crowd gathers to witness Anne Boleyn's execution, our attention is focused on an ordinary couple who have come (like the audience) to watch the big event:

> Wife: *Poor* Anne Boleyn! I do feel so sorry for her! *Would* you mind taking off your hat, Madam—we can't see the block . . .
> Is it true that the King marries Jane Seymour tomorrow?
> Husband: To-day, they say.

* £60,000 promptly became the 'magic' cost figure for films made by other British companies.

Wife: *To-day?*
Husband: Yes . . . What it is to be a King!
Wife: Meaning what?

The film must at the same time explode the distance between past and present by emphasising the basic 'humanness' which makes the characters accessible to the audience. Therefore, in another early scene, Katherine Howard discusses Henry's decision to execute Anne Boleyn with the other court ladies, and the following exchange take place:

Katherine: Well, if the King were not a king what would you call him?
First Lady: What would *you* call him?
Katherine: I'll tell you—
(*Henry enters room unseen.*)
Henry: No. Tell me . . . Well, what would you call me?
Katherine: I should call you—your Majesty—a *man*.
Henry: Why, so I am—and glad of it!

The rest of the film is an exploration of Henry's humanity during which Korda substitutes the stereotyped image of Henry as 'Bluebeard-King' for an equally stereotyped characterisation of a 'vulnerable man'.

Although Korda's Henry is tender and sentimental as well as blustery and vulgar, the emphasis is always on Henry as 'victim' of manipulating women. The two wives who don't comfortably fit into the image which Korda and company have constructed—Catherine of Aragon and Jane Seymour—are both disposed of as quickly as possible. Catherine of Aragon never appears, for as the film's very first title tells us: 'Henry VIII had six wives. Catherine of Aragon was the first; but her story is of no particular interest—she was a respectable woman. So Henry divorced her.' Jane, the simple girl whom Henry deeply loves, dies in childbirth after four brief appearances in the first third of the film. The great repercussions of Henry's marriage to and divorce from Anne Boleyn are not discussed at all; her fate has been sealed before the film opens. Henry does seem in control of his life up to Jane's death, but after that point the film settles into a series of 'feminine games' played at Henry's expense. The greater part of the film deals with Henry's courtships and marriages to Anne of Cleves and Katherine Howard, two women who are, in fact, in love with someone else. Anne of Cleves, in easily the best scene in the film, outmanoeuvres Henry both in cards and in the marriage game. Katherine Howard, who from the beginning has shown her talent for flattering Henry's ego, plays hard to get and wins the prize in the end, although she lives, or rather dies, to regret it. At the film's close Henry has become just another hen-pecked spouse whose wife, Katherine Parr, natters away at him about watching his diet and keeping warm.

For a film which is supposed to be a 'private life' exposé, the treatment of sex is quite naïve. There is some charm to this at first, but it wears off as the film reverts again and again to lengthy bedroom 'preparations' as a substitute for showing even a bit of what follows the preparations. Not once, but three times we are subjected to scenes of Henry's old nurse (Lady Tree) fumbling around Henry's bed, twice depositing a magic charm under the covers in order to ensure a male heir. Yet Henry himself is shown in bed only twice—once playing cards with Anne of Cleves, the other time when he has exhausted himself after trying to prove his masculinity in a wrestling match.

The bedroom naïvety comes off beautifully in the scene where Henry reluctantly enters the royal bedroom to face his fourth wife, the even more reluctant Anne of Cleves. Charles Laughton and Elsa Lanchester are perfectly cast and do wonders with the following dialogue:

(*Anne is in bed munching an apple; Henry enters.*)
Henry (*roaring*): Did they not give you enough to eat, Madam?
Anne: Don't shout at me—just because I'm your wife.
Henry: My wife? Not yet!
Anne: My mother told me—first he say the marriage is not good —then he cut off the head with an axe-chopper!
Henry: That is an exaggeration, Madam.
Anne: Then why you say that I am not your wife?
Henry: Why, Madam, a marriage ceremony does not make us one!
(*Anne shows her ring to Henry.*)
Henry: Oh, yes, yes, I know—but—we have to—
Anne: What?
Henry: Oh, well, all that stuff about children being found under gooseberry bushes—that's not true.
Anne: Oh, no—it was der shtork.
Henry: The stork!
Anne: Der shtork flies in der air mit der babes und down der chimney drops—
Henry: Er—no, Madam, that isn't true either. When a hen lays an egg, it's not entirely all her own doing.

Anne: You mean sometimes it was der cuckoo?
Henry: Yes—it was the cuckoo . . .

In *Henry VIII* 'food' is often used as a substitute or euphemism for sex. Twice after Henry has 'lost' a wife we are treated to a huge banquet scene where Henry morosely but voraciously gorges himself on food. Food is also verbally equated with sex or marriage throughout the film. Witness the following lines of dialogue from the two banquet scenes, spoken by the kitchen staff who are preparing Henry's elaborate dishes:

Pastry-cook: Ay, marriage is like pastry—one must be born to it!
Second cook: More like one of these French stews, you never know what you're getting until it's too late!

And:

Cook: They're not trying to make him marry *again*?
Carver: I'd like to see them, after that German business.
Woman: After all, you can't say he hasn't *tried*!
Wife: Tried too often, if you ask me, to say nothing of the side dishes—a little bit of this and a little bit of that! What a man wants is regular meals.
Cook: Yes, but not the same joint every night! A man loses his appetite after *four courses*.
Woman: How do you mean—'four courses'?
Cook: He got into the soup with Catherine of Aragon, cried stinking fish with Anne Boleyn, cooked Jane Seymour's goose, and gave Anne of Cleves the cold shoulder!
Wife: God save him! It's no wonder he suffers in the legs.

Although these metaphorical passages, reminiscent of the dialogue in *Wedding Rehearsal*, are primarily belaboured attempts at jokes, they reveal the pervasive sexual innocence of *Henry VIII*.

Korda was not unaware of the film's particular treatment of sex and, moreoever, considered it appropriate to the 'English' subject. Shortly after the film's premiere, he told one journalist:

Your French audience is ready for a great deal more frankness and breadth in the statement of a sex situation than the English. But that is no reason why British films with sex themes or incidents should not be enjoyed in France. If anything in the treatment strikes a Frenchman as being prim and proper or discreet to the point of absurdity, by his lights, he will still accept it because it is English—*if* the whole character of the film is English.[8]

This thoughtful explanation does not, of course, provide an answer to why almost all of Korda's films, regardless of setting, betray a sexually innocent streak. As a film-maker Korda *was* concerned with the 'flavour' or 'suggestion' of sex, and he wanted to satirise the games of sex, love, and marriage which people play. His approach, however, was coy rather than subtle or suggestive, and unlike directors like Ernst Lubitsch—whose subtle sexual innuendoes formed the basis of the 'Lubitsch Touch'—Korda relied on the sexual *immaturity* of the audience. Because he wanted to reach the widest possible audience, Korda played to the 'lowest common denominator' of that audience; but his under-estimation of the public's sophistication—which was re-inforced by Korda's own boyish innocence, a quality which he maintained despite all the outward display of worldly cynicism—only really succeeded in *Henry VIII*.

The talent for handling actors in comedy roles which Korda had already shown in *Marius* was again demonstrated in *Henry*. Charles Laughton, Elsa Lanchester, and Binnie Barnes (as Katherine Howard) play the three strongest characters around whom Korda has wisely centred the story. The other wives and lovers, although well cast, were mere 'icing' on the cake. Many critics have given Charles Laughton complete credit for the film's success. Marcel Ermans, for one, has noted that: 'Laughton is one of the principal comedians of our age, and the Shakespearian insolence of his interpretation saved Korda's film.'[9] John Grierson, the founder of the British documentary movement, preferred to see Laughton's portrayal as a triumph of the native vitality and vulgarity of the English music-hall tradition.[10] Laughton's puffed-up monarch was a sympathetic character, alternately vulgar, morose, forceful, and vulnerable; and for a man who had to immerse himself completely in whatever role he played, the performance was certainly a personal triumph which earned him an Academy Award for Best Actor of 1933. In a huge cast, only Elsa Lanchester and Binnie Barnes were able to match Laughton's seemingly effortless acting. The delightful bedroom encounter between Laughton and Lanchester was naturally heightened by the fact that the two were in fact married. Second only to this scene is the one in Katherine Howard's bedroom where Katherine, wanting a crown not just a bed partner, cleverly wards off the randy King's advances. It is significant that the film's two sub-plots revolve around the 'true love' affairs of Anne of Cleves and Peynell (John Loder), and Katherine Howard and Thomas Culpeper (Robert Donat). In both cases, the devotion and courage of Anne and Katherine in their love for other men merely emphasise the loveless grounds of their 'marriages' to Henry and, in the end, make Henry appear more shallow and foolish.

Both the dialogue and actual structure of the narrative were criticised by contemporary reviewers and critics. The script for *Henry* was the first film script to be published in book form in England (Methuen, 1934); yet it hardly deserved such an honour, for the dialogue lacked imagination and even the irony and satire were too facile and at times juvenile. The narrative was mechanically structured around anecdotes in Henry's life and was far too episodic and repetitive (e.g. the numerous bedroom, barber, and banquet scenes). The repetition of scenes was perhaps necessitated by the film's small budget, for it was only practical for the film-maker to make the fullest use of sets already constructed. Moreover, since the sets, for economy's sake, were designed to be viewed from only a few pre-arranged angles, there is little camera movement in the film. Georges Périnal's ingenious camerawork at least helps to make us less aware of the similarity of the sets and scenes, and his actual shots and close-ups were painstakingly composed.

As in *Marius*, clever, though not original, use was made of aural transitions. In the first example a close-up of the French executioner whistling as he awaits the arrival of Anne Boleyn is immediately followed by a shot of a palace hall where we hear the same tune being whistled by Henry as he makes his first swaggering entrance in the film. A few scenes later, the hammering sound of men building Anne's scaffold dissolves to the sound of Henry tapping his fingers against a window pane as he impatiently awaits the cannon shot which is to signal Anne's execution. In each instance Korda has directly linked Henry with the men who are to assist in Anne's death, the act being accredited to the man who commanded it.

Alex Korda always maintained that he could not understand why *Henry VIII* had been such a box-office success. Although public responsiveness to a certain film is difficult to analyse, the most reasonable explanation for *Henry*'s success must surely be that Korda had taken a titillating subject, cleaned it up, played it for laughs, and made it wholly acceptable to audiences everywhere. The glamour and pageantry, the pretty girls and Laughton's performance merely enhanced the subject's more basic appeal to curious, but inhibited people who wanted to see a 'sex romp' where the emphasis was on the 'romp', not the 'sex'. The few vocal critics of the film were quickly drowned out by the overwhelming public acclaim. The film caught the public's fancy, just as the BBC television dramatisation of *The Six Wives of Henry VIII* was to do forty years later.

For Korda it was a tremendous gamble which had paid off. Lajos Biro once admitted: 'Korda had put his shirt, coat, hat, and everything he had, on Henry. If it had failed, he would have been cleaned out.'[11] *The Private Life of Henry VIII* instead became the catalyst to the most fascinating period in Korda's life and career, for he was too ambitious to rest on his laurels. As he later said: 'Anyone can make a success in show business. The problem is how to survive your success, how to build on it.'[12] As a constant reminder of the ephemeral nature of show business success, Korda had a favourite photograph which he delighted in showing to journalists, one of whom described the ritualistic display in these words:

> I walked with him to a corner of his office. He picked up a small framed picture. 'Here is a souvenir I carry with me always,' he said.
>
> The picture showed a Paris street. In it is a peeling tattered poster announcing 'Charles Laughton in "The Private Life of Henr..."'
> The poster is tacked to the side of a French street lavatory.
> Korda smiled. 'There it is to remind me ... of what comes after glory.'[13]

1. Stephen Watts, *op cit*, p. 12.
2. C. A. Lejeune, 'Alexander Korda: A Sketch', *Sight and Sound*, vol. 4 no. 13, Spring 1935, p. 5.
3. *Picturegoer*, 17 December 1932.
4. *Rundschau*, 3 March 1967, translated for the author by Priscilla Murphy.
5. Arthur Wimperis, 'Why Film Authors Are Not Stars', *Picturegoer*, 24 March 1934.
6. From *The Golden Years of Alexander Korda*, Robert Vas's BBC-TV documentary, originally shown 27 December 1968.
7. *Kinematograph Weekly*, 24 August 1933.
8. Stephen Watts, *op cit*, p. 14.
9. Marcel Ermans, *op cit*, p. 7.
10. John Grierson, 'The Fate of British Films', pamphlet reprinted from *The Fortnightly*, July 1937, p. 9.
11. Phillp Johnson, *loc cit*.
12. David Lewin, *op cit*, Chapter Three, 28 January 1956.
13. *Ibid*.

# CHAPTER NINE

# The International Film

THE financial success of *The Private Life of Henry VIII* gave hope to the British film industry and marked Britain's final graduation into the international film world. It was like a graduation diploma for Korda as well, for he had demonstrated that he was more than a refugee from Hollywood with only enough talent to make quota pictures for an American subsidiary. There were those who preferred to hold their applause until Korda could prove himself to be more than a 'one-picture' man, but many others were anxious to cast him in the role of a possible saviour of the British film industry. Korda professed his reluctance to undertake such a role in 1935: 'The responsibility,' he wrote then, 'would be too great.'[1] Nevertheless, for three years, from the autumn of 1933 to early in 1937, Alex Korda was the most important single figure in the film industry in Britain, the man whose progress, whose successes and failures were the focus of everyone's attention. This period in his career has since been called the 'golden years of Alexander Korda'.

Korda believed that he had the solution to Britain's film-making doldrums, and *Henry VIII* had provided the necessary evidence to prove that his solution had merit. The most famous 'British' film of all time had been constructed, as many pointed out, by three Hungarians (two Kordas, one Biro), a Frenchman (Périnal), and an American (Harold Young). The inherently British subject had been viewed through 'foreign' eyes, and their vision had created an 'international' picture out of 'national' subject matter. The policy of 'Internationalism' became, in Korda's own words, 'the bulwark of London Films'.[2] He no longer questioned the validity of his assumptions, and his reasoning went like this. The goal of any national film industry must be to make its presence felt in the international film world. Any goal less ambitious is self-defeatist and doomed to failure because it limits the imagination and creativity of the artists working in the industry. To compete in the international market means to compete with Hollywood, and successful rivalry can only be achieved by winning over the huge American market itself. A film-maker must therefore make films which will appeal to international (especially American) audiences and must have some assurance that his work will be widely distributed abroad (especially in America).

What were the ingredients for an 'international' film? In an article on this subject Korda first made the point that

> ... the phrase 'international film' is a little ambiguous. I do not mean that a film must try to suit the psychology and manners of every country in which it is going to be shown. On the contrary, to be really international a film must first of all be truly and intensely national. It must be true to the matter in it.[3]

To Korda the concept of a 'well-defined nationality' depended entirely on a film's conforming to the audience's preconceived notions of the 'reality' which the film is expressing or describing. He used the American gangster film genre as an example.

> The American gangster films ... owe their appeal to their fidelity to events with which the world is familiar. They are essentially American in every detail. . . . If a gangster in an American film is depicted drawing a gun from his hip-pocket, nobody in Britain is likely to object on the grounds that it is not a common practice for Englishmen to carry guns.[4]

The international film was to be one which relied on stereotyped situations and characters peculiar to one country, but recognised immediately by audiences of other countries.

Korda quickly hastened to add that this policy did not mean that national films could only be made by 'native' film-makers.

> An outsider often makes the best job of a national film. He is not cumbered with excessively detailed knowledge and associations. He gets a fresh slant on things. For instance, I should hate to try to

make a Hungarian film, while I would love to make one about the Highlands that would be a really national Scottish film—and indeed I plan to do so. The best Hungarian film I have ever seen was made by the Belgian, Jacques Feyder.* I believe that Clair could make a better London picture than any of the English directors—a London film that would be international. I know there are people who think it odd that a Hungarian from Hollywood should direct an English historical film, but I can't see their argument.

The greatest folly is to set out to try to suit everybody. It is the sure road to insincerity and artificiality. The result will be a mongrel film which belongs to no country.[5]

Although he mentions a 'Scottish' film and a 'London' film in his remarks, Korda was not concerned with only making films with a well-defined *British* nationality, and a major criticism of Korda's international policy was that it resulted in British-made films without any British character. That it was not his intention to explore only British subjects is clear from Ian Dalrymple's assessment in his perceptive article 'Alex' in *The Journal of the British Film Academy*: 'From the start Alex never made "British" films: he made films in England for international exhibition among the best of American, French and German product.'[6]

Korda did, in fact, make some films that can be truly described as 'British'—his 'Empire' pictures, for example—but he was always aware that a film-maker could only go so far into a British subject before jeopardising the international marketability of the film. He elaborated this point in 1938:

> Our difficulty . . . is that you cannot convey a proper sense of the English spirit . . . unless you go down to the roots. Roots strike deep into history and may be very local things. In America, where roots are near the surface, they are not easily interested in what lies deep down in other countries, and unless we can interest America there may be no great market for our films. The most definite phases of life in this country, for screen purposes, are not local but national. We have no material that quite corresponds to 'Western' stories, for example, though we can occasionally turn

* Korda is referring to *L'Image*, which Feyder made for Vita-Film in Vienna in 1924–5.

out a film, such as 'Edge of the World'*, which is an epic of local life. I think that we are compelled, as far as world markets are concerned, to stick to stories based on broad issues of the national life, though I am not going to dogmatise about it. All that we can say, based on screen experience, is that stories that dig deep into national roots start with a handicap.[7]

Another criticism of 'Internationalism' as defined by Korda was that films designed to perpetuate or feed off existing stereotypes of thought and behaviour are seldom films which will further the development of the cinema. They would, instead, be films which would hinder its growth, for they add nothing new, they break no new ground. Yet, again, Korda's policy was intended to support a programme of quality entertainment pictures. If the programme was successful, so Korda's argument went, then there would be money enough for more audacious, artistic endeavours.

The problem of finding adequate American distribution for Korda's films was supposedly solved by his distribution link with the American United Artists company. Although UA was to provide backing for actual film-making, the company's ability to secure wide distribution in the American market was, however, severely hampered by the small size of its own American cinema circuit and the company's policy against 'block-booking'.

Most of the Hollywood production companies owned their own exhibition circuits, but UA's chain (a few first-run cinemas in key, large cities) was a very minor one compared to those of Paramount, Fox, Warner Brothers, or RKO. This meant that United Artists had to promote and sell its films to other independent exhibitors in order to obtain a wide showing, and this task was complicated by the UA constitution which required that the films must be sold individually, not as part of a package deal of several pictures. The anti-'block-booking' policy had little adverse effect on the American UA output, for the films of Mary Pickford, Douglas Fairbanks, Snr, and Charlie Chaplin could easily be sold under any terms because of the stars' audience-drawing powers. To sell British films with as much success was a different matter. American exhibitors shied away from them, complaining that 'accent' differences, less familiar stars and subject matters, and inferior production values made them unprofitable com-

* *The Edge of the World* (1937), a film about Scottish islanders, was written and directed by Michael Powell.

modities. UA, therefore, had problems promoting its British products, and, as writer Alan Wood admits, as a consequence 'most Korda films never reached the sophisticated city audiences; they were shown in little out-of-the-way small-time cinemas, to precisely those audiences who were likely to be puzzled by them'.[8] It took some time for Korda to realise the built-in weakness of his organisational connections with America.

The prosperity of London Films had its effect on Alex Korda's lifestyle. He moved from his suite in the Dorchester Hotel to a large mansion at 81 Avenue Road, a fashionable street of impressive residences winding north from Regent's Park. Korda's home was filled with modern paintings, several by his brother Vincent, and endless shelves of books. His son Peter lived with him, and the house was the centre for Korda's after-office work and leisure. He gave many formal and informal dinner parties, the guest list usually including his brothers, Lajos Biro, Arthur Wimperis (who was considered 'official court jester'), and at least one or two honoured personages, often foreign and just as often from some other profession—a well-known physician, writer, politician, or diplomat. Dinner conversations were never confined to 'shop-talk', although Korda was always eager to hear the film ideas of his friends from outside the film world. Often, after dinner, script conferences were convened which sometimes lasted all night. These were usually preceded by a few hands of bridge, a card game which Korda was supposed to have disliked, though he played it incessantly.

When alone, Alex often played Patience and read; his leisure reading was non-fiction, for, as he once admitted, 'I only read fiction professionally.'[9] An extremely hard worker, Korda, so it has been claimed, never slept more than a few hours each night, perhaps one reason for his ever-present 'tiredness'. Upon meeting Korda, people were surprised by the limp handshake and the tired eyes behind the horn-rimmed glasses. Korda referred frequently to how 'tired' he was, but one close associate felt that this was more an acquired 'mannerism' than an actual physical condition—Korda rather enjoying giving the impression of an over-worked executive. Unlike Vincent and Zoltan who were generally less sophisticated and certainly less concerned about 'appearances', Alex was always a conservative, impeccable dresser. At a premiere, in his office, on the studio floor, or on location, Korda was immaculately accoutred: a pipe or cigar in hand, a walking stick hanging on his arm, and his soft-brimmed hat pulled tightly down on his head. 'He is over six feet in height,' film critic and journal-ist C. A. Lejeune noted in 1936, 'but he doesn't give the impression of being a tall man. He wears his overcoats very long, winds himself in woollen scarves to cross the lot, crams his hat low on his head, and walks with his hands thrust deep into his pockets, hunched into his wrappings like a cocoon.'[10]

From photographs we can see that Korda's weight often fluctuated (being a connoisseur of fine food did not help), and in later years for reasons of health he was forced to limit his intake both of cigars and gourmet food, constraints which he found particularly annoying. Alex's first big meal of the day was at eleven o'clock, and he would schedule meetings during normal lunch-time hours. This led to the mistaken impression, held by many, that Korda worked straight through mid-day without pausing for a meal. To keep himself going through the day and night, Korda consumed great quantities of coffee—there was always a pot percolating near by—and apples, his favourite fruit. He was a man with a great deal of nervous energy for whom crises and arguments were needed stimuli. He was to precipitate his fair share of both over the next years.

The next films which Korda produced were attempts to repeat the success of *Henry VIII* by adapting the private life formula to other historical figures. He gave some thought to characters whose lives international audiences might be familiar with and then took a quick look around to see which artists he had under contract. The Viennese actress Elisabeth Bergner and her Hungarian film-maker husband, Paul Czinner, had come to England in 1933 and were contracted to London Films.* Flora Robson, the English stage actress, was under contract, and because of the United Artists tie-up Korda also had the Douglas Fairbanks, both Junior and Senior, at his disposal. In addition, there was Korda's own stable of up-and-coming starlets. Two projects finally emerged from the story conferences: *The Rise of Catherine the Great* (1934) and *The Private Life of Don Juan* (1934).

*Catherine the Great* was an adaptation of the Hungarian play *A carno* (*The Czarina*) which Lajos Biro and Melchior Lengyel had written in 1912. Biro had adapted it once before, for Ernst Lubitsch's silent film *Forbidden Paradise* (1924) with Pola Negri starring. For the Korda version Biro, Wimperis, and Marjorie Deans re-worked the story, taking

* One story has it that when Korda was desperately trying to find end money for *Henry*, he offered Bergner's contract to Paramount as part of the deal.

the usual liberties with historical facts. For example, in order to make Catherine's extra-marital indiscretions palatable to the mass public, the writers substituted the romantic excuse that these affairs were 'manufactured' by Catherine to win back the love of her husband, Czar Peter, by playing on his jealousy. Elisabeth Bergner was cast as this 'virtuous' Catherine, Douglas Fairbanks, Jnr, in a stroke of ingenious casting, portrayed Czar Peter, and Flora Robson played the over-amorous Empress Elizabeth, Peter's aunt. Korda utilised the same technical crew that had worked on *Henry*: Périnal at the camera, Vincent designing the sets, John Armstrong the costumes, and Harold Young working as editor. Kurt Schroeder, Korda's music director, had 'disappeared' after *Henry*—presumably after some controversy with Alex—and Muir Mathieson took on his job.

Bergner's husband was to direct the film, but shortly after filming began troubles arose between Czinner and Korda. Korda was not pleased with Czinner's handling of the actors other than Elisabeth Bergner and began intruding to direct some of the scenes himself. In Robert Vas's BBC documentary *The Golden Years of Alexander Korda*, Elisabeth Bergner remembered with understandable bitterness the rather tense situation: 'Well, he wasn't a very good director and suddenly after *Henry* he thought he was, and he could butt in and say it should be done this way or another way and forgot our contract which didn't allow him this. So we had fights. . . .'[11] It is difficult to determine exactly which scenes Korda personally directed, although there are some clues. In her biography of Flora Robson, Janet Dunbar states that Korda directed all Miss Robson's scenes, and she also gives us at least one technical reason why Robson's portrayal of the man-hungry Empress is too strident:

> Czinner, directing the film, understood Elisabeth Bergner and could deal with her particular temperament. Alexander Korda sometimes took a hand, and it was he who directed Flora. Her voice was too powerful for the microphone positions, which shot high in the air when she spoke; there were so many adjustments that in the end her voice came through sounding high and thin. Korda did not always allow for the fact that full-bodied acting came out as over-acting on the screen: he placed his cameras and microphones too near the set. What was needed was understatement, not strong projection. Flora was instinctively aware of this, but one did not argue with Korda. When she had some real

acting to do she could forget her difficulties, but in the artificial love scenes and, worst of all, in the sentimentalised death-bed fade-out which came later, she found it hard to relax.[12]

Diana Napier, who played Peter's mistress Countess Vorontzova, claimed that Korda directed her scenes as well: 'To be quite honest,' she told me, 'and I've got a very good memory, I just don't remember Paul Czinner on the set, not in my scenes anyway.'[13] Despite Korda's blunt interference in the film's direction, *The Rise of Catherine the Great* remains one of the most satisfying films produced by London Films.

One reason for this is that the narrative line allows for character development. The strengthening of Catherine's personality—the frightened German princess becoming a self-assured and competent ruler—is contrasted with the gradual mental disintegration of her husband. The parallel rise and decline of the two major characters has added drama, because we are made aware of the strong emotional feelings between them. The character of Catherine and, to a lesser extent, those of Peter and Elizabeth are analysed and 'humanised' in greater depth than had been possible in *Henry* where the emphasis was placed on comedy, not tragedy.

Another reason for the film's merit is that the pageantry is not conceived as window-dressing. From the opening shot in Peter's hunting lodge through the scenes of the grandiose Russian court, atmosphere and not just 'gloss' is created, and the intimacy of scenes is heightened rather than destroyed by the elaborate decor. The best example of this is the extravagant dining room scene where Peter unsuccessfully tries to humiliate Catherine by making her sit at the far end of the table over which he and his mistress are presiding. The tension is too much for the guests who ask to leave and are finally dismissed by Peter, who then joins his wife at the end of the table and taunts her with suggestions of how she will be treated 'in the nunnery'. Refusing to be intimidated by him, Catherine simply continues to eat her meal in silence. The camera lingers on what had become (in Peter's words) 'just an intimate little dinner', and this is the last scene in which the couple are shown together (Catherine has Peter arrested shortly thereafter).

Both Bergner and Fairbanks give extremely sensitive performances. Paul Czinner seemed to know intuitively how to capture the movements of his characters on film, and with the assistance of Georges Périnal he was able to compose frames of extraordinary cinematic beauty. The film, however, was only a moderate success in commercial terms (grossing about £350,000). That it was not as successful as *Henry* has been attributed to audience unfamiliarity with Russian history, although a more serious drawback was that the film was released in direct competition with an American film about Catherine, *The Scarlet Empress* (1934), directed by Josef von Sternberg and starring Marlene Dietrich. In his film, von Sternberg was concerned more with creating an epic romantic fantasy than with recreating Russian history, and this, plus the film's more provocative sexuality, gave it an inevitable edge over the Korda version in the American market. Nevertheless, *Catherine* was a worthy successor to *Henry VIII*; as a piece of cinema it is, in fact, far superior to its predecessor.

Korda's meddling during the production of *Catherine the Great* was the first warning of Korda's inability to restrain himself in the role of 'producer'. He wanted every film which came out under his banner to have the Korda 'stamp', but if he couldn't direct every film himself then this meant that he would have to supervise every production on the floor: watch the day's rushes, make or demand alterations or re-takes, and take over directing if the director was not willing to accept his 'suggestions'. Douglas Fairbanks, Jnr, once said that Korda wanted to be every man in the army; Korda preferred a naval analogy. He told C. A. Lejeune in May 1934:

> '... to go back to our symbol of the ship, a good ship's captain must know everything that his staff knows, from the chief engineer to the cabin boy. It is just the same with pictures. If all my cutters would be ill tomorrow I could cut the picture for them. I would do it slowly, and not quite so well as they would, but I should do it nevertheless. One has to be able to do a little bit of everything in order to direct a picture ... You've got to be able to steer the ship single-handed if needs be.'
>
> 'You put a terrible lot,' I said, 'on one man's shoulders.'
>
> 'You've got to in this business,' he replied. 'That is one reason why I choose pictures that will not take me away too far and too long. I should like to make a film of India ... but that not only costs a great deal of money, but would keep me away too long from a very young company.' [14]

There is, of course, nothing wrong with a director or producer knowing 'a little bit of everything' about film-making. Moreover, Korda was not alone in his attitude towards his company's productions, for famous producers like Samuel Goldwyn, David O. Selznick, and Irving

Thalberg, all of whom had less practical experience in film-making than Korda, often meddled in the work of the men whom they employed. None the less, many people have called Korda a 'prime interferer', a man unable to have confidence in the directors he had chosen to work for him, a man unable to delegate authority. He was sometimes justified in his interference; very frequently, he was not.

In 1934 Korda's pretensions took another turn. He began to see himself as a 'patron' of the arts and sciences much like the patrons of the Italian Renaissance. It appealed to him to be offered the opportunity to finance a documentary film at the request of Julian Huxley, the noted English biologist and writer. Huxley wanted to make a film about the habits of the gannets, the sea birds, and Korda accepted the project with the stipulation that the film should be titled *The Private Life of the Gannets*, in order to link it with *Henry VIII*. Osmond Borradaile and John Grierson photographed the film in the spring of 1934, and it was released as a 'curtain-raiser' to *Catherine the Great*. The film is both informative and visually beautiful and won the Academy Award for Best Short Subject (One-Reel) in 1937.

In a discussion of Korda's venture into documentary, Basil Wright, the British documentary film-maker whose own *Song of Ceylon* (1934) was made at the same time as the Gannet film, offered this interesting comparison between Korda and John Grierson, the film producer who was the moving force behind the British documentary film movement:

> ... they were both real patrons in the old sense of the word—like the Florentines and so on—and *when* Korda had the money he got Julian Huxley to do *The Private Life of the Gannets*, and he got the great Bauhaus man Moholy Nagy to do a film about lobsters— I can't remember *why*: what really happened was, presumably, that Moholy Nagy needed money, and Korda found the means of giving him some money. Just as with Grierson—if Lotte Reiniger was found in England short of cash, she got a job from Grierson at the Post Office [the GPO Film Unit]; and Len Lye's experiments with colour were all supported by Grierson. Just in the same way Korda did *The Private Life of the Gannets*. Moholy Nagy was Hungarian, of course. But at the same time it was a marvellous thing to do.[15]

A sidelight here is an interview which Korda had with Paul Rotha, the film historian and documentary film-maker. Korda told Rotha that the film he would most like to be remembered for was *The Private Life of the Gannets*. Basil Wright comments:

> I'll tell you why he said that. . . . Because he was saying it to Rotha, who was documentary, and he would play it that way, I think. If someone else had asked him, he would have said something else. He was a real chameleon-like character. He had tremendously swift reactions. Change your colour quickly if it concerns your reputation or if it concerns money to make a film.[16]

This chameleon-like trait was one of the keys to Korda's success in handling other people.

In January 1934, journalist Jympson Harman spent a few hours in the midst of a story conference held in Korda's Mayfair office. The picture under discussion was *Exit Don Juan*, the follow-up to *Catherine the Great*, which was finally retitled *The Private Life of Don Juan*. As was usual, the cast of characters present included Arthur Wimperis, Lajos Biro, and Alex, and Harman's account provides us with some idea of Korda's production routine and working habits.

> 'Alex, I did a couple of comedy scenes yesterday,' reports Mr. Wimperis. 'Splendid, my dear fellow; thanks very much,' Mr. Korda replies. 'And I have just found two lovely lines about marriage. They're from Samuel Johnson.'
> In response to my question, Mr. Korda says, 'Yes, I would certainly engage Dr. Johnson for talkie dialogue if I could.'
> 'It's an agony, concocting a film story,' says Mr. Korda. 'We have been three months on "Don Juan", and it is not ready yet. But it will be; it is going very nicely.
> 'Seventy-five per cent of the work in a film is done in the scenario stage. A film is made or ruined then. Even when you think you are ready and are actually shooting you are sure to find scenes that need re-writing.
> 'I always say, if we are going to make a film ninety minutes long, then we shall have ninety problems to solve before we start. Every minute is a problem.'[17]

At this point Alex left the room, and Harman asked Arthur Wimperis about how a story line was developed.

'One usually starts with a star. You seek a subject to suit that star's personality. Let us say he is Douglas Fairbanks. We want to give him something different. Don Juan is mentioned.

'Well, that wouldn't be bad. But how to make Don Juan new? How about dealing with Don Juan in middle life—just becoming a bit bored with keeping assignations, climbing ladders, and so forth? Yes, that's not a bad idea.

'We begin to turn it over—Mr. Korda, Lajos Biro . . . and myself. We sit around together all day perhaps. The hours go on and nothing happens. Dinner-time comes and Alex says "Let's have something to eat. Perhaps we'll get an idea." We have a dismal meal. Alex sighs and says "What about the Bridge?" Contract is always our stand-in when we are just fed up with the sight of each other's faces. Still the idea won't come . . .

'The other night at 1:30 Alex phoned for three taxicabs. We were giving it up. The cabs arrived. We strolled downstairs, weary and dejected. Suddenly one of us said, "What about having a scene like this . . .?"

'We turn upstairs again, and discuss the idea like demons. At two o'clock one of us exclaims, "Good heavens! those cabs are still outside!" "It does not matter," says Alex, "I will send them away." '18

Wimperis then mentioned to Mr Harman that he called Alex, Alexander the Cruel. When Korda returned to the room, Harman asked him about this appellation. 'He can say what he likes . . . We got beyond the ordinary rules of politeness at story conferences long ago. If an idea is poor we never say gently, "But don't you think, old fellow . . ." We say, "That's a rotten idea," and that's that.'19

Korda's way of tackling a script was fairly orthodox; at that time most film-makers tended to start with the stars and then find the right stories and characters to suit them. Korda recognised the box-office value of stars and felt he could depend on the flexibility of his screenwriters to develop a story around the chosen ones. Korda's emphasis on the importance of the script stage in the making of a film comes as no surprise. Yet, the script of *Don Juan* did not develop into a cohesive whole, betraying instead the piecemeal way in which Korda, Biro, and Wimperis had gone about creating the narrative and dialogue. The

English playwright Frederick Lonsdale was also brought in to work on the script, though the final script bears the traditional stamp of the Korda–Biro–Wimperis collaborations and Lonsdale must have had little influence.

In the story, a middle-aged Don Juan (Douglas Fairbanks, Snr) arrives back in Seville to discover that a youthful impostor has been courting the bored wives of Seville and that his own wife Donna Dolores (Benita Hume) is threatening to have Don Juan sent to jail. Told by his physician to curtail his balcony-climbing activities, Don Juan has a last fling with the beautiful dancer Antonita (Merle Oberon) and returns home to find that the impostor has been killed that same night by an irate husband. Seeing a chance for some peace and quiet, Don Juan refuses to reveal the truth, and after going to his 'own' funeral, he leaves Seville for a rest in the country under the alias of Captain Mariano. After six months and several unsuccessful romantic adventures (Don Juan realising the importance his name and legend had in his previously successful encounters), he returns to Seville to reclaim his identity as Don Juan. No one, of course, believes him. In desperation he interrupts the opening night of a play about 'his' life to proclaim his true identity. The incredulous audience turns to Donna Dolores for confirmation, but she calls him an impostor. A tamed Don Juan is finally reunited with his wife.

When Korda got down to translating this plot on to the screen, the weaknesses of the script became more apparent. In Korda's conception, to quote Ian Dalrymple, '. . . a film consists of some dozen truly-found and richly-played sequences, neatly chained by the necessary links'.[20] The description of the *Don Juan* script conferences—with Korda, Biro, and Wimperis searching for isolated scenes which might hopefully add up to the 'whole' of the film—certainly confirms this conception. Yet, if these isolated sequences are not chained together properly (they weren't in *Don Juan*), then the audience is left with a series of anecdotes or episodes which do not coalesce. Each episode in itself is carefully constructed, but Korda—either afraid that the audience has missed the plot or point or worried that the fragmented story needed something more to hold it together—has insisted on repeating scenes, actions, and even dialogue throughout the film. In *Don Juan* nothing happened once—it happened two or three times, and this way of composing a film led almost inevitably to a heavy and static cinematic structure which, according to one critic, was the greatest fault in Korda's productions.

Central Europeans, particularly Hungarians, have considerable dramatic gifts: they are imaginative and confident, they do not fear failure; in fact they fear only one thing, namely that the public may not understand the plot. As opposed to our young authors, who cannot or will not construct their work properly, they build a structure so solid, so heavy, so cumbrous, that it dwarfs everything and crushes the life out of the play. If by ill luck the story is dull or stupid, the spectator finds himself faced with a useless mechanism which functions to no purpose—unbearably explicit. He feels like jumping up and shouting: 'Please, please! I understand the plot, I understand the plot. Have a heart! I've had enough. How do you expect to move people to laughter or tears if you spend all your time telling them the plot?'[21]

Frenchman Marcel Ermans has made a valid point, for the belaboured working and reworking of the stories for Korda's films drained the vitality of the original conception right out of them. Even when Korda hired other scriptwriters, their work all seemed to go through the Korda–Biro–Wimperis machine. (These three men were fulfilling the 'dramaturge' role which Korda had envisaged back in 1917 in Hungary.) Korda obviously believed in and was loyal to his collaborators, but it is a pity that after the dismal failure of *Don Juan* Korda was still not able or willing to recognise that the fault was in the script itself.

The debunking of a legendary figure which had worked so well in *Henry* was taken to the extreme in *The Private Life of Don Juan*, and the hero became a pathetic, comical character who was more at the mercy of clever women than Henry had ever been. Korda tried without success to capitalise on similarities in the characters and lives of Henry VIII and Don Juan. One specific comparison which underlines the weakness of the later picture is provided by two similarly conceived scenes in both films: the attempted seduction of Katherine Howard (Binnie Barnes) by Henry and Don Juan's equally unsuccessful rendezvous with the kitchen maid, Rosita (also played by Binnie Barnes). In *Henry* the episode shows the king as a convincing seducer; if Thomas Culpeper (Robert Donat) had not interrupted the scene even the clever Katherine might well have succumbed to Henry's charm. In *Don Juan* the hero is a rather mechanical lover who can only reiterate the dreadful romantic patter which he had always used on his women, and Rosita is simply not impressed. In the end the audience can only view

Don Juan as a clownish, ineffectual man. Certainly this was part of Korda's intention, but audiences needed to believe that Don Juan had at one time had some sparkle, some flamboyance in order to appreciate the irony of what he became in later life. The image of Don Juan that Korda created was just not strong enough to sustain interest in the film.

Alex Korda was conscious, however, of how he had misused the talents of Douglas Fairbanks in this film. Fairbanks was unable to give any 'weight' to his performance, the main problem being his voice which was neither deep nor rich enough to carry off the characterisation of the Great Lover. His physical appearance somewhat made up for the weakness of his voice: every time he took up a sword or bounded over a balcony we could believe that this was the legendary Don Juan, but the moment he uttered a line the spell was broken. The actual dialogue did not help matters either. As in *Helen of Troy* and *Henry*, modern idioms of speech were used to point up the irony and satire of the approach, but lines such as the one belted out by one bored Seville wife to another ('Hey, Conchita, Don Juan's in town!') or Don Juan's cynical reply to a young lover ('All girls are different; all wives are alike') are pathetic in their cheapness. Korda seemed to have forgotten his own dictum about being 'true' to the matter of the film, for he has told an extremely romantic 'Spanish' story in distinctly unromantic mid-Atlantic dialogue.

The film is naturally stocked with a bevy of young starlets. Merle Oberon has little to do except look seductive, which she manages to accomplish with great style, plus a little bit of ham. Athene Seyler, playing the proprietress of the country inn, steals the film from both Fairbanks and the younger actresses in one brief scene. Binnie Barnes obviously enjoyed her earthy part as the country wench unimpressed with the 'style' of Captain Mariano. Credit again goes to Vincent Korda for the set designs, in particular the stunning recreation of the country inn with its central courtyard and numerous balconies, and to John Armstrong for the picturesque costumes.

The film was a commercial failure. Korda later waxed philosophical about the whole question of success and failure in film-making when he said: 'So in films one success is not enough. You need to have the courage to fail. People should not be afraid of failure. They should have the courage to nurse a success and then forget it and move on to something else. Never think of what's done—think of what's to do.'[22] Korda's refusal to promote the Hollywood maxim that a producer or director was only as good as his last film was perhaps one of his major contribu-

tions to the British cinema. Even before *Don Juan* was finished, Korda
had begun another picture which would allow the international public
to forget the failure of his Don Juan film.

*The Scarlet Pimpernel* (1934) was a project which Korda saw as another
opportunity to prove his theory about the international film. It was
based on the Hungarian writer Baroness Orczy's popular novel about
the daring deeds of English aristocrats during the French revolution,
and in selecting this work Korda was not only thinking about its
adaptability to the screen, but also counting on the 'pre-sold' audiences who would go to see the film because it was from an already
successful literary work (the novel had also been turned into a popular
play in 1905). Since Korda was consciously looking for a film subject
which would regain the American audiences who had flocked to see
*Henry VIII* and had since shied away, he chose to have the film 'made'
by a group of Americans who might visualise the film in such a way as
to appeal to the American public with which they were more familiar.
A promising young American director, Rowland V. Brown, who had
made his reputation with *Quick Millions* in 1931, was engaged to direct
the film. Robert Sherwood, the American dramatist who was later to
script such classics as *Rebecca* (1940) and *The Best Years of Our Lives*
(1945), joined Biro and Wimperis in writing the final scenario;* and,
instead of Frenchman Périnal, Harold Rosson, the Hollywood camera-

---

* Early on, the American playwright S. N. Behrman, who wrote the scripts for
*Queen Christina* (1933) and *Cavalcade* (1933), was employed for three weeks to do
a treatment of *The Scarlet Pimpernel*. He took the treatment to Korda's house for
a dinner-story conference:

'Dinner that night at Korda's,' Behrman remembers, 'was very pleasant;
there were Korda, his brother Vincent, the artist, Biro and myself. Vincent
was quite different from his older brother; he was small, dark and intense,
passionate for primitive African art and sculpture and his own work. "When
he's not painting," Korda said, "he's thinking about it. He is never away from
his easel. . . ."

'I read the treatment aloud after supper, explaining that I had allowed
myself to burst into dialogue when I felt like it. I read the scene I had written
for Leslie Howard. They liked it. For the rest, Korda pointed out that if I
were to follow the dramatised version of the book at all, several of the
scenes I had outlined at the end would be structurally impossible. But it
was all very relaxed, none of the life-and-death tension of the Hollywood
conferences.'23
Of Behrman's work all that remains in the film is the one Howard scene where
Sir Percy is giving instructions to his tailor about a new suit.

man, was also hired. Vincent again designed the sets, and the American editor William Hornbeck cut the film. Besides the cast and Arthur Wimperis, the only other British employees were Arthur Benjamin and Muir Mathieson (who were responsible for the music) and John Armstrong and Oliver Messel (who designed the costume). This 'British' costume picture was therefore an Anglo–American–Hungarian team effort.

There were the usual problems with the script; several versions were put to paper, the final one probably being rewritten as the film progressed slowly over the summer of 1934. Difficulties immediately arose between Brown and Korda over the former's conception of the film which did not coincide with the latter's. How much of the film was actually shot by Rowland Brown is not certain, although Mrs Harold Young remembers that he only worked on the film for a couple of days. The difference of opinion between Brown and Korda must have been of some magnitude, for Korda decided to replace him.* Korda directed the film for a time, but eventually turned the project over to Harold Young, his American editor, who had just directed two pictures in London for Warner Brothers. As with *Catherine the Great*, Korda kept close tabs on the rest of the film's development.

In the biography of Leslie Howard (who portrayed Sir Percy Blakeney, the 'Scarlet Pimpernel'), the author describes her father's impressions of Korda and his film-making habits:

> An Hungarian, dark and slightly sardonic, Korda had an arresting personality, and though some people considered him a skilful and slightly pretentious fraud, his supporters viewed him as a genius. Leslie never placed him entirely in one category or the other. Always scornful and sceptical about Korda's omniscience, frequently intrigued and impressed by his mind, Leslie found working with him a somewhat mixed pleasure.[24]

During *Pimpernel* the 'mixed pleasure' included Korda's 'most aesthetic approach to film-making': ' . . . if it were a beautiful day full of sunshine and the song of birds he would cancel work. He allowed nothing to interfere with the pleasures and comforts of life.'[25] Korda's habits on the sound stage or on location were notoriously leisurely— he hated to begin work early and would often disappear to conduct

---

* Brown's career took a sharp nosedive after this episode. Although he directed a few more films, he was never to fulfil the promise he had earlier shown.

business in his office after having prepared a scene for shooting—but he rarely cancelled work simply because it was a nice day. More than likely, this was a flamboyant gesture to cover the fact that the script had not yet been ironed out or that Korda had not yet settled the matter of who was to direct the film. There were almost always practical considerations behind Korda's more unorthodox and ostentatious gestures.

Unlike its three predecessors, *The Scarlet Pimpernel* owed no specific allegiance to history, and the main characters were depicted in the exaggerated and vivid way which is possible when dealing with fiction. As with *Catherine*, the plot is secondary to the character development; the adventurous exploits of the Pimpernel (except for his first escapade when, dressed as an old hag, he eludes the French officers with his cart-load of French aristocrats) were underplayed in order to emphasise the duality of the Pimpernel's life in England as Sir Percy Blakeney. The film really hangs on the tension between Blakeney and Chauvelin, the evil Frenchman out to discover the Pimpernel's true identity (played with obvious relish by Raymond Massey). It is a delight to watch the two characters, as in a chess game, trying to outmanoeuvre each other. Rumour had it that Korda had intended Charles Laughton to play the Pimpernel. Although he better matched Baroness Orczy's description of the character, Laughton would have perhaps been too clownish in the role. Whether discoursing on the latest fashion in cuffs or reciting his doggerel about himself ('They seek him here. They seek him there. Those Frenchies seek him everywhere. Is he in heaven? Is he in hell? That demmed elusive Pimpernel.'), Howard is the perfect fop. Merle Oberon played Lady Blakeney, and it was her largest role to date. As one critic remarked, she looked far too exotic (she was supposed to be French), and as an actress she was too weak to elicit any sympathy for her character.

The film begins to crumble about two-thirds through the narrative. The final encounter between Blakeney and Chauvelin is rushed, as if the film-makers had spent too much time setting up the story and were straining to tie up all the loose ends in a few minutes of screen time. A better concept of structure would have avoided this final confusion, but this was always Korda's weakness. The end was, as it seems, gratuitous. Korda had been looking for a suitable, stirring 'tag' ending and came up with the idea of having Sir Percy say to his wife as they stood on the deck of the ship returning them to England: 'Look, Marguerite, England!' Korda was supposed to have then added:

'They'll have to applaud after that.'[26] The film has been applauded as the best comedy ever to come out of London Films, and its success led Korda to make two sequels: *The Return of the Scarlet Pimpernel* (1938) directed by Hans Schwartz and starring Barry K. Barnes and *The Elusive Pimpernel* (1950) directed by Michael Powell and Emeric Pressburger, in which David Niven plays the lead.

In the first fourteen months of Alex Korda's 'golden years' he had released four films, two of which—*The Private Life of Henry VIII* and *The Scarlet Pimpernel*—were enormously popular both at home and in America and had, therefore, justified Korda's faith in 'Internationalism'. *The Rise of Catherine the Great* and *The Private Life of Don Juan* were failures, although the former film deserved much better treatment than it received. A fifty per cent average in film-making was not bad, and though four films in a year may sound a small quantity, it was probably what Alex would have considered the right amount for a company's yearly output. (In his last twenty-five years Korda made on average only four films a year.) For better or worse, the Korda 'stamp' had been imprinted on each of the films, for he had directly involved himself with their production. There were signs of a growing over-confidence in Korda's estimation of his own capabilities and of an inability to keep himself restrained in the producer's role, but these months had provided the British cinema with much hope and even more glamour.

1. *Film Daily*, 14 February 1935.
2. *Ibid.*
3. Stephen Watts, *op cit*, p. 13.
4. *Ibid*, p. 14.
5. *Ibid*, pp. 14–15.
6. Ian Dalrymple, *op cit*, p. 7.
7. G. A. Atkinson, 'That Amazing Mr Korda', *Answers*, 14 May 1938, p. 12.
8. Alan Wood, *Mr Rank*, London, Hodder and Stoughton, 1952, p. 63.
9. Paul Holt, 'A Cabby Decided His Future', *Daily Herald*, 9 May 1953.
10. C. A. Lejeune, 'The Private Lives of London Films', *Nash's Magazine*, September 1936, p. 80.
11. From Robert Vas's BBC documentary.
12. Janet Dunbar, *Flora Robson*, London, Harrap, 1960, pp. 160–61.
13. Interview with Diana Napier Tauber conducted by the author, 22 July 1973.
14. C. A. Lejeune, 'If I Had a Million—Alexander Korda', *Picturegoer*, 5 May 1934, p. 5.
15. Interview with Basil Wright conducted by the author, 17 July 1973.
16. *Ibid.*
17. Jympson Harman, ' "It's an Agony" says Mr Korda', 8 January 1934, no further information, Alexander Korda microfiche, BFI Information Department.
18. *Ibid.*
19. *Ibid.*

**Korda in Hollywood**

Alex Korda in his mid-thirties at the time of *Helen of Troy*.

His one Hollywood success – *The Private Life of Helen of Troy*
(1927) starring Maria Corda as Helen, Lewis Stone as
Menelaus.

The friendly card game: Paul Dulac (*lower right*), Robert Vattier (*hidden*), Raimu, and Charpin – *Marius* (1931).

*Marius* and *The Girl from Maxim's* were two of the films Korda directed in Paris.

Attentive listeners: Stanley Holloway, Gertrude
Musgrove, Leslie Henson, and Frances Day –
*The Girl from Maxim's* [*La Dame de Chez
Maxim*] (1934).

The most famous film in the history of the British
cinema – *The Private Life of Henry VIII* (1933).

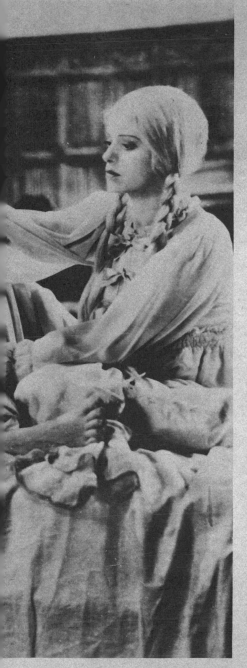

The bedroom scene: Charles Laughton (Henry) and Elsa Lanchester (Anne of Cleves).

Alex, on platform, directing scenes at Hampton Court.

Another 'Private Life': *The Rise of Catherine the Great* (1934) directed by Paul Czinner – Douglas Fairbanks, Jnr (Czar Peter), Flora Robson (Empress Elizabeth), and Elisabeth Bergner (Catherine).

The Last 'Private Life': *The Private Life of Don Juan* (1934)
directed by Korda, starring Douglas Fairbanks, Snr (*lower
right*).

Korda, a new partner-member in United Artists, amongst his associates: Douglas Fairbanks, Snr, Korda, Mary Pickford, Murray Silverstone (?) (*behind*), Charlie Chaplin, A. H. Giannini, and Samuel Goldwyn.

20. Ian Dalrymple, *op cit*, p. 7.
21. Marcel Ermans, *op cit*, p. 6.
22. David Lewin, *op cit*, Chapter Three, 28 January 1956.
23. S. N. Behrman, *People in a Diary: a memoir*, Boston, Little, Brown & Co., 1972, p. 204.
24. Leslie Ruth Howard, *A Quite Remarkable Father*, London, Longmans, 1959, p. 176.
25. *Ibid*, p. 198.
26. From Robert Vas's BBC documentary.

# CHAPTER TEN

# Financial Scheming

DESPITE the mixed box-office record of his previous three films, by 1935 Alex Korda was still riding high on the success of *Henry VIII*. He was one of the few British producers who, when asked what sort of pictures he would make if given ideal conditions, could honestly answer: 'If I could make any pictures that I wanted and no others? . . . *But I do!*' [1] His popularity as a film director had risen to such an extent that he was ranked first in a British poll conducted to ascertain the public's 'favourite directors'. Although pleased by this national acclaim, Korda was probably more delighted with the ripples of envy and concern that he was creating in Hollywood. One of the greatest personal triumphs of Korda's career came during his summer 1935 trip to Hollywood, where 'for the first time since his disgrace . . . there were genuflections by the greatest and hosannas from the highest . . . [and] the lesser rajahs could not get close enough to catch his eye'. [2]

The reason for the trip was that the film-maker who had made a backdoor exit from Hollywood five years earlier was now to be offered a full partnership in the United Artists company whose other partners now included Mary Pickford, Douglas Fairbanks, Snr, Samuel Goldwyn, and Charles Chaplin. The irony of the situation was not lost on Korda, who later remarked in an interview with David Lewin: 'They threw me out of Hollywood and I was broken-hearted. You are always broken-hearted when you leave Hollywood. Then I made "Henry VIII" in London and I went back and nothing was too good for me. I was a partner with the people at the top—the people who did not know me originally.'[3] Business negotiations among United Artists members were, however, notoriously difficult, for all the partners were extremely shrewd and protective of their own interests. Mary Pickford, 'America's Sweetheart', was even nicknamed 'The Iron Butterfly' by the others because of her tough business sense. Korda described a fairly typical meeting of the United Artists executives in these words:

> They were great days at United Artists—the only trouble was that the others were seldom talking to one another. Yet there was a by-law of the company which said that all decisions had to be unanimous. So whenever we met the lawyers came too. Goldwyn brought four lawyers . . . Mary Pickford three . . . Fairbanks three, and Chaplin two. I had one—I would talk to anyone.
>
> So we all sat inside the offices and the lawyers talked terms or deals in the garden.[4]

On the 5th of September the announcement of Korda's new 'owner-member' status with United Artists was released to the press. There is a uniform omission in the press notices of any reference to the price Korda had to pay to become a full partner, which leads us to believe that, as Paul Tabori intimates, Korda paid nothing. In actual fact, Korda made no immediate payments; the understanding was that he would pay for it in instalments over the next few years, which he did.

On the same day that the news of the Korda–UA deal hit the newspapers, Alex was honoured with a dinner by the directors' branch of the Academy of Motion Picture Arts and Sciences. As might be expected, the after-dinner speakers treated Korda's earlier Hollywood experience with discreet humour. According to a contemporary account,

> [Darryl Zanuck] sounded the keynote of the dinner when he facetiously told Korda he was complete proof that producers are unnecessary. 'You had producers, supervisors, and all possible assistance when you were here five years ago and ended up without a job. You went to England without any of them, and now come back five years later and get a testimonial dinner.'[5]

Korda was determined to accept the Hollywood 'about-face' gracefully and during his speech was quick to dispel any industry concern that he was out to take revenge on Hollywood by 'raiding' the Hollywood stables.

In France, Germany, and England, when a picture is finished the first thing they want to know is what Hollywood thinks of it. It is not the aim of England to raid Hollywood. You may read about the rivalry between British and American producers, but it is all idle talk. I assure you nobody in England thinks on terms of rivalry from any other point of view than now exists between Hollywood's own producers.[6]

The last sentence does, of course, leave the door wide open, and there were some in Hollywood who saw Korda's new power position as a threat. One studio executive sourly expressed this feeling to a magazine reporter:

Alexander Korda can stand on the corner of Hollywood Boulevard and Vine Street and wave a checkbook and all our actors and actresses, stars and featured players, and cameramen and technicians and writers and directors would desert our studios and pour around him from all over town and follow him just like the way the rats of Hamelin (he said Hamburg, so help me) ran after the Pied Piper. They're calling this fellow Alexander the Great—but he's Napoleon, too, if you ask me. He's just about the czar of the international film business today.[7]

This comment, coming as it probably did from one of the 'lesser rajahs' in Hollywood, was not necessarily indicative of the reactions of all the producers to Korda. It is hard to believe that the bigger moguls were overawed by or worried about the drawing power of a single foreigner. Nevertheless, the major Hollywood executives did think it wiser to embrace Korda—by planning co-production deals and talent exchanges or by offering Korda jobs in Hollywood—rather than to exclude him and thus, perhaps, precipitate an intense Anglo-American film rivalry.

Alex arrived back in Britain in late September with great plans for the future. He announced that during the next year twenty feature films would be made in London by his company and his United Artists associates, and the budget for these productions would be somewhere in the region of £2,000,000. The British public was told to expect Charles Chaplin, King Vidor, Frank Lloyd, and Edmund Goulding to be directing films on this side of the Atlantic in the near future. Korda also returned on the *Berengaria* with the man whose presence had helped consummate the U A deal, who was now a member of United Artists as well, and who had been for almost a year the 'angel' of London Films, Sir Connop Guthrie KBE. Guthrie was the man most responsible for bringing City finance, in the shape of the Prudential Assurance Company, to the aid of the British film industry, in the shape of Alex Korda and London Films.

By the middle of 1934 Alex had realised that he would need some kind of dependable film finance if London Films was to continue producing quality pictures. He could not rely on the profits from his own films, for financial returns, especially from overseas markets, took a long time to filter back to the producing company. He could not attack a whole production programme in the same way he had approached the finance for *Henry VIII*, since to make a series of films which could compete in world markets he needed vast resources, not just the haphazard investments of wealthy film enthusiasts like Ludovico Toeplitz. The men who controlled the City, that is to say the bankers and investors of London's large financial companies, looked like a promising group of potential film industry supporters, but these men were by nature and necessity most conservative, not the sort to take gambles in a field of production as risky as film-making. In addition, the majority of them had a fairly low opinion of the cinema. That one of the City's largest companies was persuaded to invest in the Korda enterprise was, therefore, quite remarkable.

We must quickly add that the Prudential was given a healthy push in the direction of film finance from an unlikely source. As Ian Dalrymple explains:

> The Prudential Assurance Company had so ably instilled into the little men and women of Britain the virtue and advantages of providence, that they were trapped in the toils of their own benevolence and burdened with the task of investing over a million pounds a week. Characteristically, their eyes turned overseas, but at this point we learn of an almost incredible intervention. . . . A Tory-dominated National Government brought pressure to bear on the Prudential to make a substantial contribution towards the expansion of British film production.[8]

So the eyes of the Prudential turned back towards home and the British film industry. Their search for a beneficiary to receive their somewhat forced largesse ended during the summer of 1934 when an Australian, Montagu Marks, suggested Alex Korda and London Films to them. Working as the liaison between Korda and the men from the Pru, Percy Crump and Sir Connop Guthrie, Marks was finally able to convince them that Korda needed the money and that with London Films' track record (i.e. the success of *Henry VIII*) they would not be throwing their money away. On Guthrie's approval, the Pru undertook the support of London Film Productions and in exchange obtained all the preferred shares in the company and a lien on all productions, present and future. Guthrie was immediately placed on the board of directors, and Marks was made General Manager. The deal promised Korda both backing for his films and capital for the future building of a film studio with colour facilities. The Pru's first cheque (for £250,000) was received with wild excitement in the Grosvenor Street offices; and for a start, London Films leased the Isleworth Studios, at £35,000 a year, and was able to announce by October a capital investment increase from £141,000 to £825,000.

With the Prudential and United Artists as the two pillars of his empire, Korda was able to undertake the kind of film-making enterprise about which he had been dreaming for many years. His appointment as Chairman of the London Films' board of directors in June 1935, upon the death of George Grossmith, further enabled him to take complete and sole control of the company's policies and future. During the past year there had apparently been minor intrigues perpetrated by some of the board members and aimed, we are told, at ousting Korda. Resignations and new appointments had taken care of this internal friction, and by 1935 Korda found himself in a powerful position with guaranteed financial security and with no one in the company to override his decisions. Yet he was now responsible to the men who were financing him; and, therefore, the next years bear witness to Korda's development not only as a big-time film producer and impresario, but also as a shrewd entrepreneur, a man forced to keep the ever-present Prudential watch-dogs at a safe distance and reasonably satisfied.

To intimate that Alex Korda personally invented the many practices that he took advantage of as a film executive would be to deny credit to all those ingenious film men who preceded him in the wheeling-and-dealing business of film production. He was neither the first nor the last to use them; neither was he the only British producer to capitalise on the vagaries of film production and promotion. He was, however, the first British film producer to refine these practices, to make them so much a part of his flamboyant style of film-making that to the casual observer they appeared to be mere eccentricities of the man's enthusiastic, artistic temperament. Korda's charm was powerful enough to get him over many hurdles in the coming years, but, as Douglas Fairbanks, Jnr, once remarked, 'You can't succeed over a long period with charm alone, and he had a very, very shrewd business sense'.[9] An examination of Alex Korda's entrepreneurial skills may undermine the image of him as a Bohemian film-maker, the 'dreamer with his head in the clouds', which the press, for one, loved to perpetuate. On the other hand, this image has for too long obscured a whole facet of Korda's character.

The practice which most frustrated the rest of the film industry was Korda's habit of buying up the screen rights to almost everything remotely adaptable to the film medium. Short stories, plays, novels, biographies, all forms of literature were included in Korda's buying sprees. Although this practice has usually been attributed to Korda's overambitious vision, it was, in actual fact, a fairly standard, self-protective policy which most film producers with money behind them followed. If you buy up a property as soon as it comes on the market rather than wait to obtain the film rights until after you are ready to go ahead with the production, then you will invariably pay less for the rights. Moreover, whether or not Korda actually planned to film these acquired works was immaterial, since eventually someone else might want to film it, and they would have to come to Korda to buy the rights at a higher price. The reselling of film rights represented a major source of additional revenue for many film companies. The only way the policy could back-fire was if Korda's original instincts about the property's screen potential were faulty. It is almost impossible to assess the success–failure rate of Korda's instincts in this, for, as we shall see, those screen rights which Korda did resell at fabulous prices made news, whereas those which he may have sat on for years have been forgotten.

Another indication of Korda's shrewdness with respect to film rights was provided by one of his ventures into theatrical production in 1934. London Films announced plans to rent a West End theatre and to produce stage plays under the supervision of a Hungarian stage producer Professor Eugene Robert. We have been led to believe that this was purely a beneficent gesture on Korda's part—lending support to a needy compatriot—but we must also take into account the official reason given to the press: 'If the play has a successful run we shall make a film of it. The reason for renting a theatre is to avoid paying heavy film rights to the author of a play which has had a successful run.'[10] (The one and only play attempted by Professor Robert and London Films, a private life of Napoleon and Josephine, was a complete failure.) To Korda's credit some of the items which he bought *were* gestures of pure generosity shown towards authors and friends who happened to need cash. For example, although he paid Winston Churchill £10,000 for his *Marlborough*, Korda did not make any concrete plans to film it.

For every film that Korda made in Britain, there were at least one or two other projects which were announced but never made. The trade journals are full of announcements from London Films of some glorious new production schedule with films listed by the dozens and budgets of six or seven figures frequently mentioned. In the appendix, included with Korda's filmography, is a list of close to one hundred of these projects which never came to the screen. This may only scratch the surface, for publicising projects was one of Alex Korda's strong points, expressing as did his talent as a film showman. His background as a journalist had taught him the art of film promotion, how to whet the public's appetite. Then, too, Korda was a dreamer, 'an idealist more interested in the plan itself than the execution of it'.[11] Looking at the list of projects, we can see that his dreams were quite often ingenious and imaginative, but occasionally far-fetched or unrealisable. At times the practice simply got out of hand. One magazine editor described it as 'dangling carrots in front of the public nose, only to snatch them away again when he discovers that he cannot deliver the goods', and went on to suggest that Korda should be more careful in the future.

> He has got into the habit of allowing his publicity organisation to use his dreams as propaganda for his genius. He should stop that. Too many schemes that don't come off convey an impression, not of genius, but of waste and indecision.
>
> Let Mr. Korda dream in private, not in public. And let him permit his dreams to be known only when he is reasonably sure of being able to put them into practice.[12]

There were, then, drawbacks to Korda's announcing projects publicly, for it could easily destroy rather than build confidence in his company and in himself. And building confidence in London Films and Alex Korda was the primary reason behind the practice, which served a calculated purpose in Korda's relationship with the Prudential.

In Jeffrey Dell's novel about the British film industry in the thirties,

*Nobody Ordered Wolves*, the hero, Phillip Hardcastle, is a screenwriter employed by Napoleon Bott's Paradox Pictures Corporation. After several months, the young man has finally discovered that each film produced by the company seemed to go through exactly the same stages. His elaboration of Bott's method of making films both reminds us of Korda's production routine, and provides us with a clue perhaps to Korda's own well-timed programme announcements.

> Every picture made or contemplated by the company passed through a recognised routine which was as follows: When a subject was first chosen, one or more highly paid playwrights or novelists would be invited to make a treatment. Their treatment would be handed to Mr Bott and pronounced useless. Other playwrights or novelists, still more highly paid, would then be engaged and their work be duly condemned. By this time the date when the picture was scheduled to go on the floor would long since have passed. Reports of the postponement of the picture would appear in the Press, and there would be considerable panic among the office staff. Rumours of impending bankruptcy would spread like wildfire through the studios. Mr Bott would make a statement to the Press announcing a staggering programme for the coming year. He would then call a story conference and, after inviting and disposing of other people's opinions, dictate a story outline which was invariably a great improvement on all earlier efforts. The picture would then go on the floor; but, after shooting for some weeks, Mr Bott would decide that the story was no good. A further story conference would be summoned and Mr Bott would re-write the entire story, enthusiastically encouraged by such of the authors as were still assigned to the picture. No suggestion made by any writer was, so far as Phillip ascertained, ever accepted by Mr Bott after the first few weeks of his employment; the only persons whose ideas were sometimes embodied in the story being visiting celebrities from other walks of life. Thinking over what Mr Bott had accomplished that morning, Phillip marvelled anew at his inventive facility. The fact that no picture had ever yet been completed made it no less creditable.[13]

There were more Korda programme announcements in 1935 than in any other year of the thirties. (1937, the year of the industry-wide crisis, ranks second.) But, between December 1934 and December 1935, London Films had produced only one film, *Sanders of the River*, and the men at Prudential Assurance were probably beginning to doubt the wisdom of their investment. To counteract the rumours that London Films was grinding to a halt and to keep the Prudential executives from descending too often upon him with embarrassing questions, Korda apparently decided to use some simple reverse psychology. A producer who is planning a whole series of films costing millions of pounds could hardly be said to be on his 'last leg', and it followed that the Pru's investment, which had not produced many results so far, was being used to set up these new projects. Programme announcements were, in other words, a useful ploy. They kept the public in a constant state of expectation, they kept one's rivals and critics slightly off-balance, and they kept the company's creditors quiet.

Although we have already encountered some examples of Korda's press statements, it is perhaps fitting to quote Jeffrey Dell's version of a typical Bott announcement, for in style and imagination it certainly captures the flavour of those bulletins which London Films released during the thirties.

... those recurrent rumours of impending disaster for the company had revived ominously during the last few days. Everyone was saying that Bott was finished and that he couldn't get another penny from the city.

But as Phillip drove into town, his eye was caught by a news-placard which said:

### 'SENSATIONAL FILM DEAL'

He drew into the kerb, bought a paper and found Mr Bott beaming at him from the front page. He read that Paradox Films had just signed up seven of the principal Hollywood writers for what was described as 'the most ambitious programme ever announced by a British Film Company.' It went on to say that, during the ensuing twelve months, Mr Bott proposed to make seventeen first feature pictures at a cost of something over a million pounds and quoted him as saying that he was satisfied that British pictures had not hitherto been giving nearly enough consideration to the writers' side of the business. This state of affairs he intended to revolutionise by employing in his scenario department not only the best scenarists Hollywood could provide but also great names in other spheres of literature, men of the calibre of Mr George Bernard Shaw, Mr Somerset Maugham, Mr J. B. Priestley and Mr H. G. Wells.

After a momentary qualm over the phrase 'of the calibre of,' Phillip went home greatly comforted, as doubtless did many of the company's creditors.[14]

It will soon become clear that Korda's appeasement of the City men depended on several other practices as well, all of which were much less manifest to the public and the film industry.

In late 1939 a British film director was being given a guided tour around the vacant Denham Studios, home of London Films between 1936 and 1939, when he espied rows of film cans lined up on the shelves of the studio vaults. His guide was Richard Norton, who had been one of Korda's associates since *Henry VIII*, and the director asked Norton what were in all the film cans. They were mostly, Norton replied, reels of films which Korda had 'shelved' for one reason or another. Reading through the labels on the cans, the two men started to envisage a film which might utilise some of this never-released material. The film opens with the London Films trademark, Big Ben, chiming forth in close-up, and as the camera tracks backwards an enormous foot becomes visible, then a leg, then the whole man, who is in actual fact sitting astride a model of the Houses of Parliament. So begins 'The Denham Studio Mystery', a thriller which takes place on the sound stages of Denham where a film (any film from Korda's shelves) is being made against a backdrop of murder and intrigue, a fanciful product of two men's creative imaginations, sparked by an afternoon stroll through the cluttered vaults of London Films.

The vaults at Denham were full because during the thirties Alex made or acquired numerous films which he could not or would not release. Some were foreign-language films which Korda had bought and imported for the express purpose of filming an English version. This was a most expeditious and inexpensive way to make films, for the English film-maker could both use the original film as a model and, if need be, keep large portions of the original footage (e.g. location and background footage, crowd and large-scale action scenes) in the adapted version. Yet only four English-language remakes were ever completed by London Films—*Moscow Nights* (1935), *Forget-Me-Not* (1936), *Prison Without Bars* (1938), and *The Rebel Son* (1939)—and the rest of the originals just sat on the shelves. Some of the films in the vaults were actually Korda productions which were either finished or in various stages of completion. Almost all the films on Korda's shelves represented 'white elephants', pictures which would very probably never make a profit if they were finished and released; but this did not mean that they were totally without value.

Here Alex Korda was employing a fundamental principle of film-making economics. As Jeffrey Dell's hero Phillip has it explained to him:

> 'It's one of the basic secrets of successful film promotion! ... If those pictures were released they'd be colossal flops. They wouldn't be worth fourpence. But you see, all the time they stay on the shelf they go in the balance-sheet as assets. They're stuffed with what is called production-value ... and their present value is what they cost us to make. .... Quite a useful sum to carry forward each year.' [15]

There are two particularly fascinating cases of this 'shelving' technique as it relates specifically to Alex Korda. One involves *The First and the Last*, a film scripted by Graham Greene, directed by Basil Dean, and starring Laurence Olivier and Vivien Leigh. The film was shot over the summer of 1937, and as it was not very good, its box-office potential was considered to be nil. It stayed in the vaults from 1937 until 1939 when it was bought (having been re-titled *Twenty-One Days*) by Columbia Pictures, presumably on the hope that the success its two young stars had gained in the meantime would be enough to sell the picture. The film was a failure on its release in 1940; but for two years Alex had been able to claim the film as an asset, and in the end it was Columbia who bore the financial failure of the film.

The other picture, *Conquest of the Air*, was a feature about the history of aviation which combined documentary footage with numerous dramatic reconstructions. Planned as early as 1934, the project was constantly being shelved, picked up again, and reshelved. Over a two- or three-year period at least five directors worked on the film, and most of the staff and players of London Films had a hand in the production. There is some controversy over when the film was actually released; some of the material was assembled and previewed in 1938, although it wasn't until late in 1939 that Charles Frend, an editor and director, compiled all the material into the film which was finally released in 1940. Before 1938, however, Frank Wells, H. G. Wells's son and a Korda employee, had gone to Alex's office to ask him if he could be allowed to 'get this film finally knitted up and finished'.

'No, Frank,' replied Korda, 'a film when it is not finished is an asset, but when it is completed it is a liability.'[16]

The one aspect of being a big film producer which Korda enjoyed above all others was his ability to be a 'star-maker'. To Korda, 'a real star is a name which will induce people to stand in a cinema queue on a rainy night',[17] and during his lifetime he discovered or helped develop a number of 'real stars' such as Laurence Olivier, Vivien Leigh, Robert Donat, and Merle Oberon. His attitude towards his stars was primarily paternal. Even during a rather trying period in his working association with Robert Donat—the actor who most owed his stardom to Korda— Alex's chastising letter to Donat's financial adviser displays a wealth of emotion and paternal disappointment.

> I defy you or anybody to show me an example where a producer dealt more honourably with an actor than I have dealt with Donat throughout his career . . . I am a very patient man and my personal liking of Donat and his wife made me overlook a lot of things. His indecision, his fear of committing himself, I regarded as an out-come of his too suddenly successful career. But looking at it all from a distance, I simply feel that I am no less necessary to Donat's future and no less useful to any actor's career than any actor in the world can be to me . . . I was hurt, and I want you to know it.[18]

Korda believed that stars should not expect to be mollycoddled or over-indulged, especially given the salaries they received. To make films with an international appeal a producer had to rely on the drawing power of star names, and Alex was willing to pay well for the stars that he borrowed—for *Knight Without Armour* Marlene Dietrich received £50,000. But it was cheaper for Korda to build up his own stars, and this is what he preferred to do.

Unlike fan magazine writers and public relations men, Korda did not even pretend to believe in the concept of 'overnight' stardom. In Korda's view, a star was made over a period of time, in a series of films, through a gradual process of familiarising the public with a new face and creating an audience demand. When he put a potential star under contract, he had a clear idea of the type of image which he felt would best exploit that artiste's looks, voice, and dramatic or comedic capabilities. He believed that a producer let down both the audience and the star if he gave the star roles which deviated too much from that image, as happened, Korda would suggest, when Clark Gable was allowed to play in *Parnell*. This probably accounts for Korda's attempt to discourage Vivien Leigh from playing Scarlett O'Hara in *Gone with the Wind*. His attitude, incredibly short-sighted though it was, was based on his conviction that the O'Hara role was too out-of-keeping with the Leigh image—the impetuous, but sweet English 'rose'—which Korda himself had been trying to promote.

By creating and doggedly adhering to a particular star image, Alex frustrated many of his contracted artistes who considered their acting range to be far more flexible. In this, Alex's actors seemed to fare better than his actresses, as was the case in the film industry in general. It was even more frustrating, however, for those performers who were kept off the screen for months or years while Alex searched for the 'right' role for them. For ten months at the peak of his career—just after *Mutiny on the Bounty* (1935)—Charles Laughton sat idle; for the first year of her contract, Vivien Leigh was not once used by Korda; and after *Catherine the Great* in 1934, Flora Robson did not make another film until *Fire Over England*, three years later. Whether they worked or not, they, of course, were paid their salaries, and most of them were allowed, especially if their contract so stipulated, to do work on the stage. But by being too careful Korda also lost the element of 'exposure' which was vital to star-making, for an audience too long deprived of seeing a new star will tend to lose interest altogether. Korda simply didn't make enough films to keep all his stars employed and in front of the public. One solution to this was for Korda to loan out his stars to other producers. By doing this, Korda was able to keep his stars working and his company's coffers full.

Lord Uxbridge, one of Napoleon Bott's associates in *Nobody Ordered Wolves*, explained the economic principles behind star-building, as practised by most film executives, in this way:

> 'It's elementary!... Unless you put an artiste under a long-term contract someone pinches her directly she begins to show a glimmer of acting ability. What you do is to build her up gradually opposite half a dozen different leading men, then you can loan her out at five times what you're paying her. That's the average company's principal source of revenue...'[19]

Although several actors and actresses were built up by Korda in this manner, the best single example of Korda's star-making talent is provided by the story of the rise of Merle Oberon, dance hostess and film extra who became an international film star and, eventually, Lady Korda.

Estelle Thompson was born in Tasmania either in 1911 (according to most reference books) or in 1917 (according to Miss Oberon's latest claim) and came to London, via India, in the late twenties. As Queenie Thompson she became a dance hostess at the Café de Paris in 1928, and she began working in British films as a dress extra in 1930. Despite an appearance in Korda's *Service for Ladies*, it was not until she was making her sixth film, Harry Lachman's *Aren't We All* (1932), that Alex Korda, then preparing his second quota picture at the same studio, really discovered her. From all accounts the 'discovery' took place in the studio commissary where, so Paul Tabori tells us, Maria Corda (then visiting her ex-spouse) pointed her out to Alex. She was asked to make a screen test for Korda and afterwards was signed to a £20-a-week contract as the resident 'exotic' in the London Films stable of starlets.

There was some initial disagreement over her name, for Alex had wanted to change it to Stella Merle. Miss Thompson stormed into Korda's office, told him that the new name made her 'ill', and emerged as Merle O'Brien, later to be altered to Merle Oberon. The 'Oberon' came, as the publicity department was quick to point out, from *A Midsummer Night's Dream*; Korda obviously felt that its foreignness suited the image that he planned to create for her. Although she had been tested for the lead in *Wedding Rehearsal*, Alex now considered her too 'vampish' for the part and assigned her instead to *Men of To-morrow* in which she was to play the temptress Ysobel D'Aunay. But, as Merle herself explains, she did get into the cast of the earlier *Wedding Rehearsal*, though totally by accident.

Although Korda had signed me as an exotic type, my first movie role was that of a mousey English secretary. The picture was 'Wedding Rehearsal' and Ann Todd, who was well established by then, was to play the feminine lead. On the very morning that the picture started, Ann was injured in a motor accident and I was rushed into her role. There was some doubt that I could play it with my almond-shaped eyes and olive complexion, but I carried it off so well that Korda nearly removed me from the cast of 'Young Apollo' [*Men of To-morrow*] in which I was to play a collegiate vamp.

'You can't do this to me,' I protested. 'It's lack of imagination, that's what it is. I do one thing well and you think I can't do the kind of thing you signed me for.'

'Will you test again?' Korda asked.

'Certainly,' I said.

I won the role all over again and escaped being typed in the perpetual role of the drab girl.[20]

She does not, in fact, 'carry off' the part in *Wedding Rehearsal* very well, and Alex never again tried to 'deglamorise' her in this way, wisely deciding to emphasise instead her exotic features in roles which did not demand too much of her admittedly limited acting ability.

Although her role in *Henry VIII* as Anne Boleyn had involved only two pages of script, it launched her career. By her beauty and a few 'poignant' gestures she managed to capture audience sympathy for the frail and tragic Queen in a few minutes of screen time. After *Henry*, offers started coming in from Hollywood, and as Korda had forgotten to renew her contract, she was technically free to accept one of them (one company was willing to pay her $30,000 for a single picture). She went to see Korda to tell him of her plans.

> 'My agent accompanied me to Korda's office,' Merle recalls. 'The moment Korda said he wanted to see me alone, I knew I was a dead duck. I was so soft. I was terribly grateful, I sat across from him while he put on a grey face and said, "If my own brother had done this to me, I couldn't feel any worse." The upshot of it was I signed with him for another seven years for no raise in salary.'[21]

Merle had fallen prey to the Korda charm and cunning, as would many other stars, film-makers, and City financiers over the years.

Aware now of Hollywood's, and perhaps his own, growing interest in the future of Merle Oberon, Korda began an earnest campaign to promote her as a film star. She moved out of the ranks of the Korda starlet stable to become one of London Films' leading ladies. She was first cast opposite Douglas Fairbanks, Snr, in *Don Juan*, and then played opposite Leslie Howard in *The Scarlet Pimpernel*. During the slow-down at London Films which followed *Pimpernel*, Merle was 'loaned out' to other film producers, first in England and finally in Hollywood. She co-starred with Charles Boyer in *The Battle* (1934), a British film directed by Nicholas Farkas, who had worked as Korda's cameraman in Vienna and Berlin, and she appeared in Bernard Vorhaus's musical

*Broken Melody* (1934). Alex then arranged, for a tidy sum, a loan to Samuel Goldwyn which led to a two-year stay in Hollywood. She starred in Sidney Franklin's *The Dark Angel* (1936) with Fredric March and in William Wyler's *These Three* (1936) with Joel McCrea and Miriam Hopkins. She was even promised the lead in David O. Selznick's production of *The Garden of Allah*, and when the part went instead to Marlene Dietrich, received a settlement of £18,000 for a picture which she didn't make. When she returned to London Films in 1937, she was a film star of some magnitude. In four years Alex had manufactured a glamorous international star of his own and had also created a Galatea with whom he was inevitably to fall in love.

Negotiating partnerships, finding financiers, buying subjects, announcing projects, shelving products, and making stars—these were important functions of the film executive's role as it was envisaged by Alex Korda. The deals and practices all played their part in the building of Korda's empire, and without some of them, especially the arrangements with the Prudential and United Artists, the enterprise would have folded from lack of sufficient financing.

As company business and administration began to involve more and more of Alex's time and energies, he was gradually taken further away from the studio floor. He undoubtedly resented the mutual exclusiveness of the roles of film executive and film producer—since he singlehandedly tried to maintain both positions for as long as he possibly could—but by 1935 he had made his choice. Thereafter, the pace of Korda's life had to accelerate, for to keep up with the Hollywood men who were now either associates, rivals, or both, he had to stay constantly one jump ahead of them. Korda was aware of this when in 1935 he paraphrased the Queen's advice to Alice in *Alice in Wonderland* as he felt it applied to film executives: 'We must run always fast if we want to stay in the same place, and run twice as fast to go more places.'[22]

1. C. A. Lejeune, *loc cit*, (Korda's emphasis).
2. W. B. Courtney, *loc cit*.
3. David Lewin, *op cit*, Chapter Two, 27 January 1936.
4. *Ibid.*
5. 'Industry Leaders Pay Honor to Korda', 5 September 1935, unmarked press cutting, Alexander Korda microfiche, BFI Information Dept.
6. *Ibid.*
7. W. B. Courtney, *loc cit*.
8. Ian Dalrymple, *op cit*, p. 9.
9. From Robert Vas's BBC documentary.

10. *Kinematograph Weekly*, 26 July 1934.
11. C. A. Lejeune, *op cit*, p. 4.
12. Herbert Thompson, 'Korda the Dreamer', *Film Weekly*, 20 June 1936, p. 3.
13. Jeffrey Dell, *op cit*, pp. 101–2.
14. *Ibid*, pp. 107–8.
15. *Ibid*, p. 140.
16. Frank Wells in an interview conducted by Robert Vas, for Vas's BBC documentary, but not used.
17. David Lewin, *op cit*, Chapter One, 26 January 1956.
18. J. C. Trewin, *op cit*, p. 87.
19. Jeffrey Dell, *op cit*, pp. 121–2.
20. Merle Oberon, 'How I Broke Into The Movies', *Los Angeles Daily News*, 19 May 1953.
21. *Ibid*.
22. *New York Times*, 16 August 1935.

# CHAPTER ELEVEN

# A Showman at his Best

PLEASED by the prestige and climate of prosperity which London
Films pictures had brought to the British cinema, and welcoming the
expansion in film production which was thereby created, film journalists were at first loath to examine the artistic merits of Korda's first
films. There were critics like Graham Greene who regularly roasted the
extravagant Korda productions; but on the whole the popular film
press, either 'snowed' by Korda and his publicity machine or afraid to
explode public confidence in this possible film saviour, avoided any
critical analysis of the actual products. In 1935 one courageous journalist, Freda Bruce Lockhart, attempted to 'look a little deeper' at the
previous Korda films and concluded that the 'private life' series and
even *The Scarlet Pimpernel* were lacking in almost everything but
superficial gloss. As she wrote in an article entitled 'Is He Really
Alexander the Great?':

> They have been polished, sophisticated, tasteful, pictorially
> beautiful, lavish in settings and costumes, and played with dis-
> tinction—all qualities still rare enough in British films to be
> valuable. *But they are not qualities which can compensate for the
> absence of any element of vitality in a picture. The primary essential of
> any first-rate film is sincerity of intention, continuous concentration upon
> the theme, either on the telling of the story, on the expounding of an idea,
> or on the drawing of characters, and this Korda has never achieved.*
> Although it may seem sacrilege to call the films . . . *dull,* in

none of . . . [them] has he shown any genuine feeling, any vital unity of thought, or even the conviction necessary to tell a story well. Always the essential core of the picture is neglected in favour of extravagant embroidery.[1]

Although she questioned whether these early efforts were significant contributions to the cinema 'in a creative sense', she foresaw a more substantial artistic future for London Films with the recently announced 'signing' of directors like René Clair, Anthony Asquith, and Robert Flaherty. She applauded Korda for the 'wisest step' in his career: 'At the crucial point, where a smaller man would have used his fame to put across his own mediocre goods, he has been able to take the long view and to recognize that his own genius is as a producer, a patron, an impresario, and not as a director.'[2]

It is a blunt, perceptive article which gives Korda much credit for his organisational abilities, his professional perfectionism, and his international outlook. The article did, however, upset Korda, for in one of his few forays into journalistic rebuttal Korda answered it the next week.

The two things which Korda seemed to resent most in the article were the writer's questioning whether he had made a creative contribution to the British cinema and her suggestion that he should stick to producing, not directing films. In response to the first issue Korda proclaimed that everything he had done in setting up London Films and in gathering together talented people from all over the world was a creative contribution to the native industry. Although there is truth to this claim, Korda seems to have missed, or avoided, the real point, which is that if the noblest intentions result in mediocre films, then the value of the contribution is much diminished. His answer to the second point is most informative, as it represents one of the first public announcements of his intention to move away from film directing in order to concentrate his energies on film producing.

> If I feel that my career lies generally in production rather than in direction, that is my own affair; and if I occasionally find a picture that I want to direct myself, that is my privilege and I shall indulge it . . . I want to *stay behind* pictures, well behind them, doing what I have to, bringing in the best brains I can find for the service of the industry.
>
> And if my next five pictures explode, as the last writer put it, 'the public faith in Korda as a "great director"', so much the

better for me and the public. That was always one of journalism's sillier ideas.[3]

His next five pictures—culminating in the two most ambitious projects of his career, *Things to Come* and *Rembrandt*—increased, rather than diminished the public's faith in Alex Korda as director and producer.

On the other hand, they did explode credibility in Korda's stated desire to stay 'well behind' pictures.

*Sanders of the River* (1935) was the first Korda film to explore what the writer and historian Jeffrey Richards calls the 'Cinema of Empire'.[4] That a Hungarian film producer should rediscover the British Empire as it was envisaged by Kipling, A. E. W. Mason, and Edgar Wallace, and put it on to the screen is not as strange as it first sounds. Korda was, after all, a confirmed Anglophile who saw the Empire builders as the embodiment of all the most noble traits in the English character and spirit. In his films about the Empire he wanted to sing the praises of, as the opening titles of *Sanders* express it, those 'handful of white men whose everyday work is an unsung saga of courage and efficiency', 'the Civil Servants—keepers of the King's Peace'. During a time of mounting Fascism, Korda saw this patriotic expression, this exaltation of efficient law and order meted out not by fear or tyranny but by love and understanding, as a perhaps necessary counterbalance.

Not to be overlooked, these stories about the Empire were great, action-packed adventure yarns, infinitely cinematic and especially suited—thanks to their reliance on stock characters and stock situations —to international distribution. They also exploited yet another untouched audience market, the Empire itself. In January 1935, three months before the release of *Sanders of the River*, Korda discussed with a reporter his plans to capture the Empire market.

> Korda pointed out to me that his company earns more money in America, per film, than any other British concern . . . But, at the same time, his complete receipts from Australia are considerably less than the profit he has already made on the run of the Pimpernel picture at the Leicester Square Theatre.
> . . . Korda, having become horizon-conscious, is going out for Empire markets in a big way. He intends to make pictures with specific appeal to different parts of the Empire.[5]

Thus, Korda had several reasons for using the Empire as a source for film projects, reasons which were based both on personal politics and on concrete business aspirations.

Alex also had, in his brother Zoltan, a director who thrived on making these kinds of pictures, but for different reasons. Zoltan, who had not modified his earlier left-wing political leanings as Alex had, was less concerned with fostering the Empire spirit than with exploring the 'native' existence. His son David says: 'My father loved Africa; he loved the black man; and he loved adventure stories.'[6] Zoltan and Alex had enormous rows over almost all the Empire pictures, mainly because of their different conceptions of what the films should express. One of their more notorious arguments centred on whether in thanking a native a white man would shake his hand. Korda thought not; Zoltan insisted that he would and eventually won on this point. The 'handshake' between white man and black not only became the most moving, though too self-consciously 'poignant' scene in *Sanders* but also provided the final dénouement in Zoltan's later South African film, *Cry, the Beloved Country* (1952). But, as can be seen by the rest of *Sanders* and by most of the Empire films as a whole, Alex more often won on the fundamental issue of basic interpretation.

Although the working title of the film was *Kongo Raid*, *Sanders of the River* was from the beginning ostensibly based on the Edgar Wallace novel. Zoltan and two film units left England for Africa two weeks after the opening of *Henry VIII*, in late August 1933. Zoltan headed the unit which started filming location material in Lagos, and a game hunter, Herr Grosse, took the second unit from Dar es Salaam into the interior. There were innumerable mix-ups during the location shooting, for communications between the two units and between them and the head office in London were difficult to maintain. At one point each unit was apparently filming to entirely different orders, from two entirely different scripts. In addition to this location footage—which provided the back projections for the film—aerial shots of African wild life were taken by the famous German pilot, Ernst Udet.

Zoltan returned to London with enough material to make a dozen ethnographic films—hours and hours of film and sound track of native music and native dances—but the problem was how to make a feature film out of all this documentary material. Alex, Lajos Biro, and Jeffrey Dell began a series of lengthy script conferences during which the film started to take shape. To film the actual plot line it was necessary to re-create the African settings in the English countryside, and to popu-late the African villages Negroes were imported from as far away as

Cardiff and put in camps close to the studio. The American actor and singer Paul Robeson was persuaded to star as Bosambo, presumably after seeing the native footage which Zoltan had shot. He was less pleased when he encountered the actual script which emphasised the paternalistic, patronising attitudes which he found distasteful. Nina Mae McKinney, the American actress who had given such a powerful performance in King Vidor's *Hallelujah* (1929), was totally wasted in her role as Bosambo's wife, and Leslie Banks as Sanders played with classic restraint the role of 'District Commissioner'.

Even at the level of narrative *Sanders* is confusing and inadequate, the back projection is poor, and as usual in Korda's films, the final product reveals the mixed and confused intentions of director and producer. As Miss Bruce Lockhart points out in her article: 'The interest is so continually side-tracked into an unrestrained display of native dancing and scenery, or irrelevant photographic virtuosity that the thread of the story is irretrievably lost, and we are left with the impression that the story was only a peg on which to hang a remarkable collection of news-reels of African life.'[7] As pure entertainment, the film succeeded commercially because of, not in spite of, this constant dependence on native dances (there are five in the film) and 'native' songs (e.g. the 'Canoe Song' and 'Battle Song' sung so stirringly by Paul Robeson). The 'Canoe Song', in fact, became a popular hit.* Over the years the film has understandably drawn criticism from the left and from the African community. Even though jingoism and imperialism are concepts which have long been in disrepute, films like *Sanders* always retain an historical interest as documents of the ethos of an earlier time.

In 1933 Korda had mentioned an interest in making an 'international' film about Scotland and had suggested that Frenchman René Clair would be ideal for directing a film about London which would be truly 'international'. Two years later the ideas were combined when René Clair made *The Ghost Goes West* (1935) for London Films. Korda's scriptwriters had for some time unsuccessfully tried to adapt

---

* In 1942 British film-maker Thorold Dickinson, while stranded in Stanleyville during location-scouting for his *Men of Two Worlds*, was stunned to hear the natives canoeing down the river singing this theme song from *Sanders*. Mischa Spoliansky, who wrote the music for *Sanders* to Arthur Wimperis's lyrics, told the author that the phrases in the song were actually lifted from the original native music tapes which Zoltan had brought back. The natives that Dickinson heard were singing the original.

Eric Keown's *Punch* story 'Sir Tristam Goes West' into a star vehicle for Charles Laughton. In the autumn of 1934 Clair, who by this time had shown an especial skill for the sound film (*Sous les toits de Paris*—1930, and *Le Million*—1931), arrived in London with his latest film *Le Dernier Milliardaire* (1934), a satire on Fascism and dictators which had been soundly rejected by French audiences. Upset by the film's reception in France, Clair was more than happy to sign the three-picture contract which Korda offered him the day after the film's London premiere. The first projects he discussed with Korda came to nothing, and he was eventually saddled with the already unfruitful 'Scottish' project.

During the spring of 1935 René Clair and American Robert Sherwood rewrote the script for this 'Scottish' comedy which takes a large satirical swipe at American philistinism and materialism. By playfully stressing stereotypical elements of the Scottish and American characters —loyalty of clansmen, rivalry between clans, and financial niggardliness on the one hand; financial extravagance, love of competition and modern gadgetry, and manic striving for 'culture', borrowed or otherwise, on the other—Clair and Sherwood created a scenario which fulfilled Korda's prerequisites for a successful international film. The story revolves around Murdoch Glourie (Robert Donat), the Glourie ghost, an unhappy eighteenth-century spirit who has been condemned to haunt Glourie Castle until he avenges a rival clan's insult, and Donald Glourie (also played by Robert Donat), the current destitute inhabitor of the castle who is forced to sell his castle to an American 'Food King', Joe Martin (Eugene Pallette). The castle and ghost are transported to the United States where, among the palm trees of Florida, the castle is faithfully reconstructed. There the ghost finally takes his revenge on a MacLaggan descendant and is released from his earth-bound existence. Romantic interest is provided by the 'Food King's' daughter, Peggy (Jean Parker), who falls in love with Donald, even though she has mistakenly assumed that the romantic Murdoch and his shy descendant are one and the same. Despite Clair's initial quandry as to how to render the ghost on film and differences of opinion between Korda and Clair as to the proposed star (Laurence Olivier was Clair's choice), shooting finally began on the film in mid-1935.

When Alex returned in late September 1935 from his Hollywood trip, he apparently took a look at Clair's rushes. He wasn't happy with the transition scenes aboard ship—when the castle is being taken from Scotland to New York—and so he threw out some of Clair's footage, remaking certain scenes himself and 'pushing around' parts of Clair's other material. Clair was understandably distressed by Korda's interference and at one time considered taking his name off the film. In the end, though the film is scarcely one of Clair's best, the result was better than might be expected given the behind-the-scenes troubles, and partly justifies French film historian George Sadoul's comment that Clair avoided becoming a victim to Korda and his '(deluxe) sausage-making factory'.[8]

The film shows a delicacy of touch which is missing in all other Korda films. What is most enjoyable is the cool, almost off-hand acting style of the leading players. As in other Clair films, the principal characters maintain an aloofness and nonchalance to the calamitous situations in which they find themselves. This underplaying, throughout Donat's dual role and especially when the Martin family has to confront the actual existence of the ghost, accentuates the lightness and comedy of the story. The Clair 'touch' is also evident in the prolonged scene between Donald Glourie and his many creditors. Their determination in staying around until they get their money, their chasing Donald and Peggy through the castle, and their willingness to provide still more supplies (and even to act as butlers) for a dinner which may clinch the sale to the Americans invoke situations and images easily reminiscent of similar episodes in Clair's Le Million. Thanks to both Clair's directing and Sherwood's dialogue, the Martins escape becoming caricatures, mere objects for satire. Their lines (e.g. Peggy Martin's throw-away one-liner as she is being given the guided tour of the castle: 'You don't know what it means to us to see something that's not new'; and Mrs Martin's unprompted dinnertime admission: 'Ever since I had my nervous breakdown, I've been psychic') lack the assertive nature of Korda's usual film dialogue, based as they are on real 'character' rather than on the theatrical, Shavian concept of characterisation so prevalent in the thirties.

Even after the clashes on The Ghost Goes West, Clair continued to work for Korda, and although their working relationship was often strained, it apparently didn't seem to affect their personal friendship. This was characteristic of almost all of Korda's associations. Alex took a dispassionate attitude towards studio and legal battles and believed that there was no contradiction in treating with open friendliness someone whom you were taking through the law courts or with whom you were constantly at odds on the studio floor. On the whole he simply refused to make a 'drama' out of a business or work disagreement, and although his outbursts of temper were thunderous, they were also short-lived. He seldom criticised members of the film industry, probably because he realised that the film world was capricious and that yesterday's 'enemy' might well be today's 'friend'. Those who took Korda too seriously were exasperated by his unflappable nature. Yet those who had most reason to dislike Korda found it difficult to 'hate' him. As one person who fits into this latter category said, in correcting Kenneth More's statement that 'He was a giant, and I loved him': 'No, he was a bastard, but we still loved him.'

The Clair-Korda liaison was finally brought to an end when the project which he and R. C. Sherriff had been working on—a film based on the English song, *A Bicycle Built for Two*—was summarily scrapped. There had been precedents which demonstrated Korda's difficulties in handling film directors with individualist talents, and the pattern was now firmly set. R. C. Sherriff wrote:

> He would bring in famous directors like René Clair, give them their heads, then find himself at odds with them because he felt the urge to stamp his own personality on their work. Maybe he was right. He wanted every picture to have the Korda stamp, but the only way to do that was to make them himself from start to finish . . .[9]

Ian Dalrymple, in his article on Korda, mentions the problems with *The Ghost Goes West* and then adds:

> . . . from this time there were to be increasing signs of his inability to delegate or accept the ideas of others, of the sort of producer he was becoming. Alex was a brilliant bringer-out of artistes, but, with one or two exceptions, not of directors: and it has to be said that he would employ men of artistry, imagination and individual gifts, in the full appreciation of their worth, only to cloud their originality and break their morale. But it has also to be said that he was frequently justified in his interference by the result at the international box-office.[10]

It is interesting that both Sherriff and Dalrymple put the same codicil on their criticisms of Korda—that his policy was (perhaps or frequently) proved right in the long run. With *The Ghost Goes West* this was certainly the case for, although we will never know what the total film as Clair envisaged it would have been like, the final Clair-Korda result was immensely successful at home and overseas.

The Glourie Castle had been constructed on some property northwest of London where, in the distance, an enormous studio complex was being built to house Korda and his company—Denham Studios. The planning stages for this enterprise take us back to the summer of 1934 when Montagu Marks convinced the Prudential that instead of paying out rent for studio space it would be more profitable over a long period of time for London Films to have its own studio and thus fixed assets. The Pru agreed to back the plan, and in September, Jack Okey, an art director who designed some of the Hollywood studios, was brought to London to confer on possible sites and to design the actual studio. After seeing and temporarily deciding on a site in Elstree, Marks and Okey were shown another estate, north of Denham Village, called The Fishery. They quickly realised the property's potential, for with its 165 acres of meadows and forests and the River Colne, which wound through the property, it provided the perfect setting for almost any film location. Marks immediately bought a thirty-day option on the estate for £100,000, even though Korda, then in Spain, had counselled him against making any commitments until his return. After Korda had seen the grounds and had become excited that they should clinch the deal with all haste, Marks finally presented the *fait accompli* to a much relieved and appreciative Korda. Within a few months exteriors for films then in production were being shot at Denham, and the actual construction of the studio, which would take the better part of a year, commenced in June 1935.

The original designs for Denham were ambitious, without being unreasonably extravagant. An early sketch for the studio shows a large, sterile administration building, but Korda, who always believed that work should be conducted in gracious surroundings, decided instead to refurbish the 'Old House' of the estate. This building served as head-quarters for the studio executives and for several studio departments, such as casting and brother Vincent's art department. The stables were turned into editing rooms, and the gardener's cottage, chosen by Muir Mathieson for its distance from Alex's office, became the music department. But the eyes of the Prudential, or perhaps those of the contractors, grew larger and larger, envisaging a studio whose vast proportions far exceeded the needs of Korda's one company. Perhaps carried away himself with the expanded plans, Korda did not demand the modifications which might have kept Denham at a manageable size. The construction of this 'enlarged' version of Denham progressed with no hitches until shortly before the official studio opening when, in the early morning hours, one of the stages burned down. Although the cause of the fire was never clearly ascertained, the Prudential, as Denham's insurer, ended up paying £45,000 for damage done to property belonging to the film company in which it was also the chief investor.

When finished, Denham was truly a film 'city', the 'studio town' which had only been a distant vision in Alex's mind five years before. There were seven sound stages (not the three that Korda had planned), fifteen 'star' dressing rooms, a studio restaurant (French chef included), projection theatres, and property, make-up, and hairdressing centres. Denham also had its own water supply, electric power plant, zoo, infirmary, and workshops. In addition, nearby were the Denham Laboratories, the end product of Korda's long negotiations with Herbert T. Kalmus, the American pioneer in colour cinematography and film processing, to bring the Technicolor process to England. Alex had for some time been enthusiastically promoting and getting his friends to invest in different colour processes and had even predicted, rather prematurely, that all films would be in colour by 1938. Now, thanks to the financial backing of S. G. Warburg of the Continental banking family, he had the first Technicolor laboratories in England and was himself part owner of Technicolor's incorporated company. From his magnificent all-white office with flowers, statues, and paintings in abundance, 'a chip shot from his nearest secretary and a half-mashie from the door', Alexander Korda ran the most up-to-date, best equipped film studio in Europe, and he populated this international film centre with some of the finest technicians and talents in the film world.

The jokes about the predominance of American and Continental employees at Denham are by now legendary. The British flags which flew over Denham were said to represent the number of British film men (in different accounts varying from one to five) employed at the studio, and one of Korda's British workers was once reported to have put up a sign on his door that read, 'British Consulate'. The greatest one-liner ever to become attached to Korda also emerged at this time: 'It's not enough to be Hungarian, you must have talent too.' But many of Korda's critics were quick to respond that for a while it did seem as if it were enough to be Hungarian, or at any rate foreign. Alex did feel more at ease surrounded by foreigners—he found the English a bit too cold and straight-laced—and he felt a loyalty to émigré Continentals, some fleeing from the Nazi regime, who were in a tight spot with regard to employment and finances, for he had travelled that road himself. Nevertheless, one has to sympathise with the fairly widespread feeling among many in the British industry that their film business was being invaded by aliens. In a review (not of a Korda film) for *The Spectator*, Graham Greene spoke out quite bluntly on this subject:

> England, of course, has always been the home of the exiled; but one may at least express a wish that *émigrés* would set up trades in which their ignorance of our language and culture was less of a handicap: it would not grieve me to see Mr Alexander Korda seated before a cottage loom in an Eastern county, following an older and a better tradition. The Quota Act has played into foreign hands, and as far as I know, there is nothing to prevent an English film unit being completely staffed by technicians of foreign blood. We have saved the English film industry from American competition only to surrender it to a far more alien control.[11]

To give Korda his due, an employee's nationality was not usually a prime determining factor in Korda's hiring practices. He wanted the 'best' people to work in his studio, and where the 'best' people came from was immaterial. Relying on already established talents was, of course, the easy way out; all Korda needed was enough charm to persuade them to come and enough money to pay their price, and Korda had both. But he could afford neither the time to 'discover' new talents nor the risks involved in using unknown or untested people on expensive productions, and was concerned only with immediately filling up his studio with productions which would have a certain guaranteed 'quality' and thus, hopefully, a guaranteed international box-office potential. His thinking that the 'best' people will automatically produce 'quality' films was the kind of showman's assumption which must have sounded good to the financial backers who were paying for the scores of contracts; yet even the finest technicians are only as good as the film material which they are given to work with. A brilliant lighting cameraman, set designer, or editor can improve the quality of a bad film, but his craft cannot be expected to compensate for a weak story or indifferent acting or direction. By laying so much stress on the hiring of famous technicians, Alex put himself out on a limb, for he was now burdened with the responsibility of keeping them all busy and of utilising them in projects that were worthy of their talents.

Although many British technicians did, in fact, get their start at

Denham Studios, their departments were largely run by Americans or Continentals. Editors like Charles Crichton and Henry Cornelius, both of whom later became established British directors, began as assistants to Hollywood men like Harold Young and William Hornbeck, and several cameramen, including Osmond Borradaile, Robert Krasker, and Wilkie Cooper, served their apprenticeships under Georges Périnal—who shot seventeen films for Korda—or under talented Americans, such as James Wong Howe, Harold Rosson, Charles Rosher, and Harry Stradling, who were less regularly employed at Denham. American special effects expert Ned Mann was responsible for training a number of British technicians, as were Guy and Pat Pearce, the Hollywood make-up artists whom Korda brought to his studio. Many young art directors were likewise trained by Vincent Korda, although the best assignments often went to other Continentals, for instance Andre Andrejew or Lazare Meerson. Only three British men—costumer John Armstrong, conductor Muir Mathieson, and sound recording director A. W. Watkins—were actually in charge of their respective departments. Even though Mathieson's music department did have its European contingent as represented by Mischa Spoliansky and Miklos Rozsa, the regular participation of British composers, among them Arthur Bliss, John Greenwood, Arthur Benjamin, Geoffrey Toye, and Richard Addinsell, made it the most 'British' of Denham's many units.

To assemble this impressive list of film talent, one which was envied by film producers around the world, no expense had been spared and no half-measures had been taken. The list was as large and enterprising as were Korda's ambitions for Denham.

Alex Korda ruled Denham like a benevolent autocrat. All authority rested on his shoulders and every problem, no matter how small, went straight to his office. It was Korda alone who smoothed ruffled feathers, who provided encouragement when it was needed, who decided if the star or the costumer was right in their disputed choice of an appropriate dress, who kept people apart if necessary or brought them together, who issued polite but firm reprimands, and who in general kept the vast human and non-human machinery of the studio moving along with some semblance of order and efficiency. If a director didn't appear for work, the resolution came in Korda's office.

'One day at Denham,' writes David Lewin, 'a Continental director did not turn up on the set.

'By telephone from his hotel the director explained his absence: "It is my day for not being well," he said.

'The matter was reported to Korda. He called the director immediately: "My dear fellow," he said, "I hear you are not well today. But I look in my diary and I find next Thursday is your day for not being well . . ."

'The director reported for work within an hour.'[12]

The demands on Korda as chief studio executive were, in fact, so enormous that it is surprising that in the first few months at Denham Korda returned to the studio floor to 'indulge' his 'privilege' by directing a picture that he really wanted to direct—*Rembrandt* (1936).

*Rembrandt* was the first film to be shot in its entirety at Denham, but several films had been planned or made during the shift from Worton Hall Studios, Isleworth to Denham which should be discussed first. Anthony Asquith had been signed to a contract with Korda in 1934, presumably on the basis of his film-directing experience—he had already directed eight films—but possibly more because he was the son of Lord Oxford and Asquith, a former Prime Minister. (Korda was an admitted 'snob' in such matters and also employed at about this time Oliver Baldwin and Winston and Randolph Churchill.) Asquith's first film was to have been *Twenty-Five Years of the Reign of King George V*, a series of dramatic reconstructions of events written by Winston Churchill for the King's Silver Jubilee in 1936. The project was abandoned early in 1935,* and Asquith was subsequently assigned to *Moscow Nights* (1935).

*Moscow Nights* was one of the Korda films which derived from existing French films, in this case Alexis Granowsky's *Les Nuits de Moscou* (1934). Asquith and Eric Siepmann worked on the script which was most likely taken from both the French film itself and the original novel by Pierre Benoît. The French film and stage actor Harry Baur, who had starred in the original, came to London to re-create his role as Brioukow; and the romantic leads were played by two new Korda contract players, Laurence Olivier and Penelope Dudley Ward. The cast also included four of Korda's (and Britain's) most dependable character actors: Morton Selten, Athene Seyler, Hay Petrie, and Morland Graham. The acting was the only distinguished thing in this cliché-ridden, melodramatic spy story, the direction of which was

* See page 255.

condemned by Graham Greene as 'puerile'. Alex, with his incredible talent for cutting his losses, managed to sell the film in a 'package deal' to another company, C. M. Woolf's General Film Distributors.*

A documentary (*Wharves and Strays*—1935), a short film (*Miss Bracegirdle Does Her Duty*—1936), and an animated cartoon (*The Fox Hunt*—1936) were all made under Korda's auspices during this interim period. Alex always professed an interest in making short subjects, documentary or fiction, but his plans continually fell apart after the first experiment. Encouraged by the reception accorded the Huxley documentary, Korda financed a twenty-minute cinematographic study of the docksides of London, which was directed and photographed by Bernard Browne, one of Alex's assistant cameramen. Browne was also involved in the 'Miss Bracegirdle' short which he and Hollywood cameraman Lee Garmes shot and Garmes directed. Elsa Lanchester, who was then 'between films' in her contract with Korda, was offered the role of Millicent Bracegirdle, 'more to keep me quiet than anything', as she put it. 'Although the character that I played was good,' writes Miss Lanchester, 'the film as a whole did not come to life and was not up to standard. . . .'13 Impressed by the work of Walt Disney, Alex had also embarked on another ambitious plan. He hired two animators, Hector Hoppin and Anthony Gross, to organise an animation department at Isleworth. The enterprise yielded only one eight-minute Technicolor cartoon, *The Fox Hunt*, before the project was abandoned. Whether Alex's interest or his finances waned after the first cartoon was made is not clear. This spurt of short-film production activity came to an end in 1936 when Alex was forced to concentrate all his energy, ambition, and imagination on larger projects, the largest of which was *Things to Come* (1936).

It is a leviathan amongst films. It makes Armageddon look like a street row. It shows science flourishing the keys of Hell and Death, and creating from the ruins of Everytown crazy labyrinthine cities radiant with artificial light, teeming with crowds of art-starved people craving for old excitements and former thrills. A stupendous spectacle, an overwhelming Dorean, Jules Vernesque, elaborated 'Metropolis', staggering to eye, mind and spirit, the like of which has never been seen and never will be seen again . . .

* This perhaps explains why Max Schach, the most universally disliked producer ever to work in British films, and his Capitol Films appear on the film's credits, for Schach was then closely tied to the GFD company.

as a scathing commentary on the martyrdom of man and the vanity of human wishes, there will never again be a film of greater significance than this.[14]

This description of *Things to Come* did not emanate, as one might suspect, from the publicity department of London Films, but was rather one film reviewer's impressions of the 'colossal' film which resulted from a collaboration between the writer H. G. Wells and the film showman Alex Korda. Wells's *The Shape of Things to Come* had been published in 1933, and in it Wells discussed relevant contemporary issues and envisaged the world of the future. Korda read the book, and the 'Jules Verne streak' in his imagination was fired by the cinematic possibilities of the material. Wells was extremely receptive to the idea of creating an entertainment film from his philosophical book; and after several amiable meetings with Korda in 1934, an agreement was reached, presumably signed on a postcard, whereby Wells would be commissioned to write the film scenario.

It was an audacious move on Korda's part, for although he respected Wells's genius, he had no guarantee that Wells would be able to write for the cinema. Trying to make his story cinematically viable was, in fact, Wells's major problem, as he himself later admitted.

> Alexander Korda offered to make a film which was, as far as humanly possible, exactly as I dictated.
>
> The task of putting my imaginative story into screen form was, however, far more difficult than I had imagined, and took much longer than I thought it would.
>
> It is only now that I realise how little I knew about the cinema when I wrote the scenario. Many of the sequences which slipped quite easily from my pen were extremely difficult to screen, and some were quite impossible. But that did not matter.
>
> The film has emerged spiritually correct, despite the fact that it now embodies many alterations suggested by Alexander Korda, William Cameron Menzies, and a score of other people.[15]

In the end Wells wrote three complete film treatments. The first was apparently unfilmable, and the second was scrapped for the same reason, although the characters and basic plot of the second script became the framework for the third and final scenario. Korda, Biro, and Cameron Menzies—the Hollywood art director whom Korda had hired especially to direct the film—tactfully coaxed Wells into thinking in more practical cinematic terms, but it was probably with some misgivings that they finally accepted the third version and began preparatory work on the actual filming.

As finally approved, the film describes three 'future' periods of civilisation as symbolised by the metropolis 'Everytown'. In each period we witness the struggle between the progressive and anti-progressive elements in the society: the scientists on the one hand, the reactionary bullies on the other. There is also the symbolic character of the hesitant 'Passworthy' who must learn, like the audience, that war is futile and that the progress of science must not be feared. On Christmas Eve 1940, the world is plunged into a thirty-year war which leaves Everytown decimated. The people have fallen prey to a black plague, the 'Wandering Sickness', which has finally run its course by 1970. Civilisation has been replaced by a group of tribal communities run by petty 'Chiefs' who still war with each other for possession of the few resources left on earth. Into this chaos comes John Cabal, member of a 'brotherhood' of scientists who have survived the worldwide upheaval and who now intend to save the world through science and reason. 'Wings Over the World', as the movement is called, succeeds in conquering the now medieval Everytown, and the city is gradually rebuilt into a scientific Utopia. By 2036 the scientist-leaders are preparing to send the first couple to the moon, but the artists of the community are enraged by this 'inhuman' march of progress. They organise a mass revolt to attempt to stop the moon shot. As their attempt fails and the space 'bullet' races towards the moon, Oswald Cabal, John Cabal's descendant, ponders with Raymond Passworthy the choice left to mankind.

> Passworthy: Oh God, is there never to be any age of happiness? Is there never to be any rest?
> Cabal: Rest enough for the individual man. Too much and too soon, and we call it death. But for Man, no rest and no ending. He must go on—conquest beyond conquest. First this little planet and its winds and ways, and then all the laws of mind and matter that restrain him. Then the planets about him, and at last, out across immensity to the stars. And when he has conquered all the deeps of space and all the mysteries of time, still he will be beginning.
> Passworthy: But we're such little creatures. Oh, Humanity's so fragile, so weak. Little, little animals.

Cabal: Little animals. If we're no more than animals, we must snatch each little scrap of happiness and live and suffer and pass, mattering no more than all the other animals do or have done. Is it this, or that? All the universe or nothingness? Which shall it be, Passworthy? Which shall it be?

The first two phases of the story posed the fewest problems to the production team. The 1940 scenes were simply treated as contemporary sequences with modern-day London serving as the model for this Everytown of massive office buildings, cinemas, and department stores. The bombing of the city and the symbolic battle scenes were more or less convincingly achieved by the use of miniatures, photographic superimpositions, and back projection work. The 1940 set, in ruin, was the basis for the 1970 'devastation' setting, in which there were some nice touches such as the horse-drawn automobile and the costumes which were thrown-together remnants of such clothing, uniforms, and material which would have survived the wartime holocaust. With the rebuilding of Everytown the special effects men took over completely. The excavation and factory machinery which appeared so mammoth on the screen were all miniatures, although they were built in larger scale than was usual with miniature work (the later space gun was apparently twice the height of a man).

Alex had hired the Hungarian artist Laszlo Moholy-Nagy to design the sets for the last 2036 vision of Everytown, but this may only have been intended as one of Korda's generous gestures, for these designs were never used.* Instead, Vincent Korda, with the help of Menzies and Wells, undertook the challenge of cinematically visualising the Wellsian world of the distant future. First in models and finally in actual sets and miniatures, Vincent created this future city of uncluttered rooms, functional furniture, tubular glass elevators, monorails, immense apartment blocks, helicopters, gigantic television screens, and spaceships. The pouter-pigeon, mini-skirted, and unisex costumes of the future world were designed by John Armstrong and René Hubert according to Wells's own suggestions. These later scenes heavily depended on several special photographic techniques to achieve the required effects: to enable the director to show actors and huge sets in the same composition, lower storeys of buildings were constructed in full scale, upper storeys in miniature, and the two images were united by the 'split screen' method. Less effective was Ned Mann's use of

*Anthony Gross also started, but abandoned an animated sequence for the film.

puppets moved along conveyor belts in miniature sets to simulate the crowds rushing towards the space gun. Although using these special effects did keep down the film's cost and although several of Wells's scenes were omitted as the production progressed, the film still ended in costing—at close to £300,000 ($1·5 million)—more than any other Korda project at the time.

It was not only in visual terms, however, that *Things to Come* was an ambitious project. From the very beginning Wells was interested in having the film's musical score play an integral role in the overall conception. Wells and the composer Arthur Bliss had lengthy discussions about the music, including one famous disagreement over the music which was to accompany the factory machinery section of the film (Wells argued that the machines of the future would be silent). The experiment of interweaving music and visuals is only really successful in the opening scene, where the visual montage of Christmastime shopping and newsplacards spelling out the threat of war is accompanied and dramatically heightened by the musical blending of traditional Christmas carols and an ominous, thundering melody which intensifies as the visual images become more emphatic. Other musical passages, in particular the 'March of the Children', are less effectively integrated with the film and are more appreciated when heard on their own, in concert or on record. *Things to Come* was, in fact, the first film to have its musical soundtrack recorded commercially.

For all its production values, *Things to Come* could not avoid the pitfalls which lay in wait for films conceived along these epic lines. In a film which is in itself a trilogy, the film-maker is somewhat forced to manufacture a dramatic climax for each episode, and ideally the last climax should be the most powerful. The main weakness of *Things to Come* is that the climax of the first episode—the war—is the dramatic high point of the entire film. These first sequences, culminating in the vignette of the wounded enemy aviator (John Clements) giving up his gas mask to a young girl whose town he has just bombed with poison gas, describe with great emotion and some authenticity a cataclysmic event which the manufactured dramas of the other two episodes cannot match. The conquering of the 'Chief' by 'Wings Over the World' in the second part is both too inevitable and too comic to be emotionally powerful, and the drama fabricated for the last episode depends on assumptions too dubious to be very convincing.

In this last part Wells's vision seems to have become timebound to the past and present, for the Wellsian dichotomy between artist ('Theotocopulos', Sir Cedric Hardwicke) and scientist ('Oswald Cabal', Raymond Massey) which forms the basis for the last climax at the space gun would surely be an anachronism in the world of 2036. As Alistair Cooke pointed out in his review, the visual beauty of this future world destroys the foundation upon which the Wellsian debate is constructed.

> When it comes to considering what sort of rooms we shall be living in in forty years . . . your guess is as good as mine. But it could hardly be as good as Vincent Korda's. By a few imaginative strokes on his drawing board he has made the piece a lovely thing to look at. At the same time, with the same stroke, he has been guilty of a rousing act of insubordination. For his drawing board and his models, come to life in the film, dispose of an argument that wastes a lot of words and all of Sir Cedric Hardwicke's part. It is the gayest mockery of the whole piece that Mr Korda's sets relegate Mr Wells's dialectic to the last and not the next century. According to Mr Wells, in another hundred years, after the intervening holocaust, the relation of artist and scientist will still be at the stage it has now got to in our country in the sixth form of schools; it's that charming superstition which the nineteenth century still leaves us groping through—the idea of a scientist as a man brewing smells and destruction in a test-tube, and the artist as a long-haired youth with the first claim on beauty.
>
> . . . Mr Korda's settings visibly demonstrate, that the artist as beauty specialist will be a vulgar survival . . .[16]

To make the film satisfying as entertainment the film-makers felt they needed the tense drama which the race for the space gun is supposed to provide, but one regrets Wells's having facilely put up the 'artist' as the antagonist. Raymond Passworthy would have perhaps been a better, more 'human' foil for Oswald Cabal, although, as portrayed, he would never have been able to 'command' the masses as Theotocopulos does. We must, moreover, regret the rhetoric used in the confrontation between 'art' and 'science', for it is naïve and unpersuasive, sounding more like a debate between two Victorian actors playing two Victorian schoolmasters. In the closing moments of the film, Wells sabotages his own message: the scientist Cabal never publicly responds to his critics; and the space shot goes ahead not because Cabal has at the last minute 'reasoned' with the malcontents, but simply because he has reached the space gun first. A science which so disregards the honest questioning of people *should* perhaps be feared. Wells may have intended this as the final irony; why else would he have created in the symbolic figures of John and Oswald Cabal such cold, smug, and unsympathetic men.

William Cameron Menzies's experience as an art director was invaluable in his actual directing of the film's dominating visual aspects. He was less adept in his handling of the actors, for it seems that he simply left each actor to create his own role as he saw fit. In keeping with Wells's dictate that the characters in the story were not intended to be individuals, but 'symbols', most of the actors solved the problem of how to portray a 'symbolic' role by over-acting. There is little or no subtlety in any of the performances, nor is there much, if any, humour. Ralph Richardson plays the swaggering 'Chief' in a style reminiscent of W. C. Fields and Charles Laughton and is the one source of light relief in an otherwise dry and heavy film. Edward Chapman (as Pippa and Raymond Passworthy) and the ladies in the film, especially Margaretta Scott, tend to be less wooden than the rest of the cast; and it is a pity that the second half of Miss Scott's dual role (as Rowena Black—Cabal's ex-wife—in the 2036 episode) was cut out of the film, for it might have added some warmth to the later scenes and presented us with a more human picture of Oswald Cabal. Raymond Massey and Cedric Hardwicke suffer the most at the hands of the Wellsian symbolism; they are given no chance to be more than theatrical representations of calm, intellectual scientist and violent, emotional artist.

Alex Korda and H. G. Wells had both closely watched over the production of the film and were proud of it when it was completed. They hoped that the film's universal themes and characters would appeal to international audiences, although before the film's release the two men declared publicly totally different intentions behind the making of the film. Wells stated that 'this picture is not intended as an indictment of civilisation so much as an evening's entertainment',[17] whereas two weeks earlier Korda had given another impression to one reporter:

> Alex is an implacable idealist, with the orthodox hates of ignorance, dirt, greed, injustice and war. He hopes that his picture, The Shape of Things to Come [sic], soon to be released, will be a document for peace. But he is unsure: what's the use of trying to turn people against war by telling or showing them its horrors? 'Human imagination is feeble,' he says, 'whereas human courage is unbelievable.'[18]

In its attempt to wed 'entertainment' and 'message' the film ultimately fails to do justice to either. The film did, however, find an audience;

most people were attracted to the film by the promise of stunning visual effects and because of curiosity about the 1940 war prophecy. The critics were almost evenly divided between those who loved the film and those who hated it, those who applauded it for being the first film to make an audience 'think' and those who condemned the film's own thinking, believing, as one critic put it, that 'no convincing good will come of fooling around with the next world until you have some understanding of the complexities of this one'. Ralph Richardson's performance so (understandably) upset Mussolini that he apparently had the film banned in Italy.

*Things to Come* did not make a profit, and some have attributed this lack of real financial success to the complacent, isolationist attitude of a time when people did not want to be made aware of the pessimistic, frightening forecasts for the immediate future which the film offered. In its sheer scale and visual achievements, the film provides us with a measure of Alex Korda's ambitions as a film showman. In its pretensions to be more than entertainment, it was in a sense Korda's attempt to answer those critics who proclaimed the shallowness of intention in his films. It was typical of Korda that he would go to an opposite extreme, and take on one hundred years of civilisation, to make his point.

*Rembrandt* was the first Korda production to go on the floor at Denham Studios, and it was probably the last film which Alex Korda expected he would direct. For both these reasons the project was a very special one for him. Korda's love for and appreciation of great literature was only surpassed by his admiration and passion for masterpieces of the visual arts. Over the years he acquired a personal collection of paintings, watercolours, drawings, and bronzes by artists like Van Gogh, Cézanne, Utrillo, Maillol, Degas, Gauguin, Renoir, Bonnard, and Soutine, an impressive collection of which he was immensely proud and the merits of which he would spend hours late at night discussing with friends and fellow connoisseurs. There had been passing references to famous painters in two previous Korda films (Holbein in *Henry VIII* and Romney in *The Scarlet Pimpernel*), but with *Rembrandt* Korda had the chance to pay a lasting tribute to one uncompromising artist in particular and to the 'artist' in general.

In the two years since *The Private Life of Henry VIII* Korda had failed to find a suitable next role for Charles Laughton. Laughton was announced for the leads in *The Scarlet Pimpernel*, *The Ghost Goes West*, and *Things to Come*, but the parts eventually went to other Korda players. For almost a year Korda and Laughton worked on an adaptation of Edmond Rostand's *Cyrano de Bergerac*; but one week they disagreed on the script, the next week they argued about casting, and the following week they could not agree on the appropriate false nose. The project was finally cancelled,\* to be replaced by the idea of making a biographical film about Rembrandt. Early in 1936 Alex was in Paris for Laughton's appearance at the Comédie Française, and after the performance they went to Amsterdam for a little reconnaissance. Back in London Korda decided to hire the German playwright Carl Zuckmayer, author of *The Captain of Köpenick* (1928), to write the scenario for the Rembrandt film. Typically, Korda then got Lajos Biro, Arthur Wimperis, and June Head to work on the script in order to translate Zuckmayer's German sentimentality into a more acceptable English idiom.

Korda and Laughton were concerned with exploring the man behind the paintings—the supreme egoist, impassioned craftsman, and peasant philosopher who refused to let financial adversity, his too early success, and society's artistic short-sightedness hinder the development of his talent. Since these qualities of Rembrandt's character were more apparent in his later years, it was decided that the story should commence at the turning point in Rembrandt's career, in 1642 when he had just finished his commissioned painting of the Civic Guard, 'The Night Watch', when his beloved wife Saskia died, and when he began to lose the favour and patronage of the Dutch bourgeoisie. The rest of the film is a series of vignettes describing his last years: his depression over the death of Saskia, his disinterested attitude towards his increasing poverty and eventual bankruptcy, his unsuccessful attempt to return to the peasant life of his family, his constant search for new sources of artistic inspiration, his love affair with the servant girl Hendrickje Stoffels, his distress over her fatal illness, and his last, solitary year.

Weeks and months of exhaustive research went into the preparation of the film. Almost everyone on the staff spent some time in Holland, poring over paintings, engravings, books, any source which would afford information on details of seventeenth-century Dutch architecture, furnishings, and costuming. It was a sudden time-shift for men like

---

\* Korda, however, held on to the film rights. Over ten years later, unaware of Korda's prior claim, the American producer and director Stanley Kramer announced his intention to make *Cyrano* with Jose Ferrer. Korda threatened to sue. The dispute was solved by Kramer buying the rights from Korda, who made a handsome profit.

Périnal, Vincent Korda, and John Armstrong, all of whom had just finished work on the twenty-first-century episode of *Things to Come*. Never had the flexibility and adaptability of Vincent Korda's talent as an art director been better demonstrated than in his extraordinarily detailed designs, in the space of a year, for projects as different as these two films. In an appreciation of Vincent's contribution to British cinema, Edward Carrick wrote:

> Vincent Korda has always been in the enviable position of being able to build lavishly, but his ideas have also been on a scale worthy of lavish treatment. In his approach to the designs of a set he searches in all directions for clues that will reveal to him the secrets of his own imagination. He appreciates the composite form of the film and makes use of every contribution of worth that is forthcoming in his art department.
>
> His set designs often vary in style and execution; when I once asked him what his favourite medium was he replied: 'anything that's around at the time.' To him the finish of the drawing matters little in comparison with the set. The set is the finished work.[19]

Although Vincent's sets for *Rembrandt* were too pristine, too 'unlived-in' to be wholly satisfying, they gave the film an at least outward appearance of authenticity. Georges Périnal, by capturing the particular 'north light' which illuminated Rembrandt's studio and his paintings, created pictorial compositions which seem—in gesture, lighting, and physical arrangement—to be examples of Rembrandt's own paintings come to life on celluloid. The careful concern with appropriate costuming helped to accentuate the differences between characters and classes: the dandified burghers and their starchy ladies, the simple peasants, the cavaliers, and the ever bohemian Rembrandt. Even the music, composed by Geoffrey Toye, was actually based in part on traditional Dutch folk melodies. Charles Laughton, who believed that the only way to 'act' a role was to 'become' the character, outdid everyone in the amount of research which he conducted in order to imitate the outward appearance and thus hopefully to capture the inward vibrations of the painter's character.

Looking at *Rembrandt* as a whole, what Korda and Laughton have achieved is the humanisation of a great artist. Although the film may be similar in structure to Korda's 'private life' films, the satire that was so much a part of these previous films has no place in this serious study of a complex man. The biographical facts of Rembrandt's life are more or less adhered to, and Korda for once refuses to reduce his analysis of the protagonist to a facile stereotype. Laughton apparently believed that Korda should have gone further in showing the more unattractive side of Rembrandt's character, but what Korda has shown, he has shown lovingly, but without fear of being critical. Laughton's Rembrandt has a child-like exuberance for life and a reverence for love: 'When one woman gives herself to you, you possess all women. . . . Call her by one name only. I call her Saskia.' When love and success desert him, he becomes morose and bitter: 'What is success? A soldier can reckon his success in victories, a merchant in money. My world is insubstantial.' He derives strength from his religious faith, from his work, and from the people around him who provide his artistic models and who create around him a protective cocoon. He is at times bliss-fully unaware of the sacrifices being made by others for him, and yet those who sacrifice for him do so out of love for him and belief in his talent. In the 'last year', Laughton's Rembrandt explains his philosophy in words taken straight from Ecclesiastes:

> All is vanity and vexation of spirit. In much wisdom is much grief, and he that increaseth knowledge, increaseth sorrow: wherefore I perceive that there is nothing better than that a man shall rejoice in his own works—for that is his portion.

The successful humanising of Rembrandt is made possible by three stellar acting performances. Whereas in other Korda films there is a tendency towards caricature, here, despite some occasional 'mugging', we can believe in the actors as the people they are representing. We need only compare the performances by Laughton and Lanchester here with their roles in *Henry VIII* to understand the subtlety which they as actors and Korda as director achieved in this film. Gertrude Lawrence, in a more frenetic role as Rembrandt's housekeeper, provides the perfect contrast to the gentle spirit of Hendrickje Stoffels. Unfortunately, so much attention was focused on the main characters that the large supporting cast, with the exception of Edward Chapman and Roger Livesey, appear to be no more than pasteboard film extras.

Although narrative construction is a major weakness in Korda's work, *Rembrandt* is more persuasive at this level. There is a jumpiness or fragmentation of the plot, difficult to avoid in a biographical film, which might have been ameliorated by better transitions (the recourse to dissolves is not satisfactory). Certainly it lacks a conventional dramatic structure, for *Rembrandt* is a series of 'tableaux' often without dramatic links between them. On the other hand, there is scarcely a superfluous scene in the whole film; each one is thematically linked to the overall portrait of the artist which Korda is trying to express. *Rembrandt* has been criticised, as was *Things to Come*, for 'shooting its climax too early'. One critic observed: 'This picture certainly could have been much better if it had been three-fourths rise and one-fourth fall. We should have had the climb of Rembrandt to fame, with hints of the independence which were [sic] eventually to be his undoing; then the blow-up; then a rapid tobogganing to poverty and oblivion.'[20] Korda did not, however, want to make a classic tragedy. He was concerned with how Rembrandt coped with his fall from success, not how he got there in the first place. It is arguable that a fuller explanation of his rise might have set the stage a bit better, but to suggest that Korda should have relegated all his explorations into Rembrandt's character in his declining years to one-fourth of the film is to ask him to have directed a different picture and to have misunderstood the subject of the film.

The repetition to which one becomes accustomed in Korda-directed films is evident in *Rembrandt*, but with one exception it is a strength, not a weakness in the story. The dialogue between Rembrandt and Hendrickje when she first sits for him is repeated just before her death: the dialogue is simple, and the repetition is an element of the romance. Even the repetitive events in Rembrandt's life—the deaths of Saskia and Hendrickje—are handled cleverly. Rembrandt's love for Saskia is expressed via his own words (she is never seen in the film) and mainly from two scenes which occur after her death: when Rembrandt paints her portrait from memory and when he writes her name in the dust on the table in her empty room. In Hendrickje's case, the growing love between the two is shown, and her quiet death and the impact her death must have had on Rembrandt is left to the imagination. By treating the deaths in these different ways, Korda has spared the audience from having to experience the same emotions twice.

The film's major flaw is the over-reverent attitude it takes to its subject. Rembrandt's religiosity is described in three different scenes during which Laughton recites from the Bible. These scenes are self-conscious and too obviously 'recitations' by a great actor. In his review of the film Graham Greene pointed out the pomposity of one of these recitations:

When Rembrandt reads the Bible at his father's table, you would think, from their expressions of amazement and rapture, that these pious peasants had never heard the Bible read before. Their faces are like warnings to us that these are solemn words beautifully uttered and that though they may have nothing to do with the story, we, too, ought to be, nay, must be, moved.[21]

(Biblical quotations, like epigrams and coy metaphors, are no substitute for good dialogue, a fact which Korda never assimilated.) The 'reverent' approach is also manifest in the slow pace of the film, which, like the recitations, tends to give scenes an overly explicit 'poignancy'.

As a director, Alex Korda often gives the impression that he avoids close-ups because they waste film time which could be better spent displaying the fabulous sets that he has had created. In *Rembrandt*, although the sets are key to the film, so are the close-ups: the faces of Rembrandt, Hendrickje, burghers, beggars, and cavaliers. It is interesting that Korda had planned on using shots of Rembrandt's paintings throughout the film but was dissuaded because he felt that these, especially the self-portraits, might destroy audience identification of Laughton with Rembrandt. Instead, Korda and Périnal probed the faces which inspired the artist's paintings. Besides the bitter comments about art and about the artist as 'beggar' to his patrons, Laughton's Rembrandt does not discuss his craft either. Nevertheless, Korda's philosophy is clear: the artist's life and his art are one.

When Korda made *Rembrandt*, he discarded his formula for successful international film-making. Gone were the easily identifiable stereotypes and stereotypical situations, and gone, too, was any chance of the film becoming a commercial success. Its lack of conventional narrative structure and its 'high brow' subject further weakened its box-office potential. When Alex was warned of this, he was reported to have replied: 'I know—but it's very beautiful.'[22] It was beautiful, and it was a critical success. After a triumphant premiere in Holland, the audiences, as expected, stayed away from the film. The box-office failure of *Rembrandt* depressed Korda, for he probably felt that although he wasn't a distinguished director, his work on *Rembrandt* had shown him at his very best and at his most courageous. *Rembrandt* was certainly Korda's finest directorial achievement, and as such it was a fitting close to Alex's 'golden years'.

1. Freda Bruce Lockhart, 'Is He Really Alexander the Great?', *Film Pictorial*, 26 October 1935, (Miss Lockhart's emphasis).
2. *Ibid.*

3. Alexander Korda, 'Korda Hits Back', *Film Pictorial*, 2 November 1935, p. 12, (Korda's emphasis).
4. Cf. Jeffrey Richards, *Visions of Yesterday*, London, Routledge, 1973.
5. Anon., 'He Hopes to Win Empire for British Talkies', 28 January 1935, unmarked press cutting, Alexander Korda microfiche, BFI Information Dept.
6. Interview with David Korda conducted by the author, 20 September 1973.
7. Freda Bruce Lockhart, *loc cit*.
8. Georges Sadoul, *Dictionnaire des Films*, Paris, Editions du Seuil, 1967, p. 86, my translation.
9. R. C. Sherriff, *No Leading Lady*, London, Gollancz, 1968, pp. 294–5.
10. Ian Dalrymple, *op cit*, p. 9.
11. Graham Greene, *The Spectator*, 5 June 1936.
12. David Lewin, *op cit*, Chapter Five, 31 January 1956.
13. Elsa Lanchester, *Charles Laughton and I*, London, Faber and Faber, 1938, p. 187.
14. Sydney W. Carroll, *Sunday Times*, 23 February 1936.
15. J. Danvers Williams, ' "I Wrote This Film for Your Enjoyment" says H. G. Wells', *Film Weekly*, 29 February 1936, p. 8.
16. Alistair Cooke, *Garbo and the Night Watchmen*, London, Secker and Warburg, 1971, pp. 128–9.
17. J. Danvers Williams, *op cit*, p. 7.
18. W. B. Courtney, *loc cit*.
19. Edward Carrick, *op cit*, pp. 80–1.
20. Don Herold in Alistair Cooke's *Garbo and the Night Watchmen*, p. 71.
21. Graham Greene, *The Spectator*, 20 November 1936.
22. Paul Tabori, *op cit*, p. 165.

# CHAPTER TWELVE

# *Crisis—1937*

IN 1936 it looked as if nothing could spoil the continuing success story of Alex Korda and London Films. There was a trade boom in all sectors of the film industry, and everywhere men from the City were searching for new 'Alex Kordas' in whom they could invest some of their money. It was appropriate that the man so responsible for this growth and prosperity throughout the British film world became a naturalised British citizen during this year. Alex's gypsy existence, his years as an 'outsider' came to an end one day on the set of *Rembrandt* when a huge party was given to celebrate the notification of his official naturalisation. Korda's assistant at the time, Eileen Corbett, described it:

> His naturalisation papers came through while we were filming *Rembrandt* . . . Charles Laughton proposed a toast to Alex and then when we'd all drunk to his health as a new British citizen we called upon him for a speech; and he stood up behind the trolley—the props had rigged up a Union Jack up from the gantry above and they let this Union Jack down behind Alex—and he stood up there with his glass in his hand and he said: 'I have only one thing to say —to hell with the bloody foreigner.'[1]

Korda was at his best when he had a country, or a national film industry, to fight for and when there was some crisis situation to overcome. He now officially had the country; he was soon to have the crisis as well.

The British 'way of life' which Korda embraced so wholeheartedly was the way of life of the rich, the aristocratic, or the influential. 'All Hungarians love the English,' Korda once said, adding, 'it is their snobbism and I am a snob.'[2] His unabashed social ambitions were not difficult to achieve, for unlike the stereotyped image of the vulgar and culturally ignorant film producer, he was a man of immense charm, social grace, and culture. He was not, however, above quite openly using his position to further his establishment in the upper echelons of society. Offering contracts or employment to titled or famous people was a part of Alex's policy noticed and usually accepted by those who worked for him, as A. W. Watkins, London Films' director of sound recording, later revealed:

> We used to have all the local debs as crowd artists. It wouldn't be allowed today because they have got to be members of the Union, but in those days it wasn't quite the same. I felt at that time that here was a person who wanted, in a very nice way, to climb the social ladder . . . which, of course, he did.[3]

Although Korda gravitated towards people of influence or social standing and took advantage of their dilettante's interest in film-making, he was not an effusive social gadabout, the typical cocktail party 'mixer'. He was easily bored with people who, in his terms, had nothing interesting to say. When I questioned people who knew Korda primarily in a social context, they all tended to draw the same picture of Alex as they remembered him in social situations. Upon entering a room filled with people, Alex would survey the gathering, pick out the most interesting man in the room, and spend the rest of the evening deep in conversation with the selected person. Those he preferred to talk to were usually not film-makers—rather politicians, writers, or financiers—just as his own conversation, more often than not, was on any subject other than films and film-making.

In conversation with Alex the first thing everyone noticed was his accent and his particular way of speaking English. R. C. Sherriff once analysed Alex's speech in these words:

> Like most Hungarians, he had a gift for speaking English more effectively and attractively than the English did themselves. He spoke it softly and immaculately, feeling his way carefully through an unfamiliar tongue as if he felt privileged to speak it and was at pains not to distort or abuse it. It was as if he were learning to play

a delicate musical instrument, finding notes and rhythms that English people never troubled about.

He was shrewd enough to know the value of his attractive accent. I once asked him how he managed to get so much money out of the hard-headed, tight-fisted financiers in the city when our own native film producers couldn't raise a penny out of them. He waved the question aside with a modest little smile, and said, 'It is easy. You ask for it in broken English.' [4]

For several years during the thirties many believed there was more than a grain of truth in Alex's facetious response.

Most people who came in contact with Korda were amazed at the breadth of his knowledge and interests and found it quite striking that a film producer should be so widely read and so well informed. During any conversation and with equal ease Alex could recite a verse of poetry, discuss the aesthetic merits of a particular artist or art work, emphasise a point with a Latin quote, or assess the current world political developments. He was a witty raconteur, and although seldom given to bursts of laughter, he had an ironic, dry sense of humour. The British film-maker Roy Boulting admitted that Alex was 'one of the two greatest conversationalists I've ever known', the 'other' being Winston Churchill; [5] and Kenneth (now Lord) Clark recently remarked, in dismissing the idea that working in film and television was somehow inferior to working in the traditional art world, that 'in any case how many people in the art-world are as intelligent as Alexander Korda?' [6] Yet, in all fairness, there were others who discerned a lack of depth in Korda's conversations. One person even assured me that Korda prepared himself in advance for a social gathering by reading up on some subject or another and then poured forth with this recently acquired information throughout the evening. He was widely cultured, but he also knew what subjects would appeal to certain people and often, as we have already seen, said those things which he thought you wanted to hear. This chameleon-like aspect of Korda's nature does make it almost impossible to judge the depth or sincerity of Korda's comments, actions, or intentions.

The different roles which Alex Korda played, the various sides to his personality, confound attempts to place him in a well-defined category. Artist and businessman, film director, producer and studio executive, showman and impresario, father figure both in his professional and personal life: he played all these roles and could change from one to another with the blink of an eye. Each image demanded certain elements of his personality to dominate, however briefly, other parts of his nature. At times he was tactful, generous, and understanding, at other moments stubborn, calculating, and authoritarian. In explaining the nature of his relationship with Alex, Ralph Richardson has said:

> His manner to me was mostly one of ironic weariness. He gave me the impression that I slightly bored him—very likely I did—but at the same time he drew one towards him . . .
>
> Though not so very much older than I am, I regarded him in a way as a father, and to me he was as generous as a prince.
>
> But Alex could be maddening too, and one could be tremendously exasperated by him. These moments came, I think, from the fact that he had a great number of sides to his nature—like an enormous crystal revolving on its orbit—and one never knew which facet might present itself. After struggling with a problem, one would be stunned to find the edge confronting one would be completely at variance with one's own ideas based on previous discussion. Instead of a helpful reflection of one's thoughts, one found only a refraction, a swift darting away from understanding. Agreement would vanish and one would be left feeling only the hardness of a glass wall and a consequent frustration of mind that set it splintering into a thousand fragments of rage. One would be left feeling like that for a while and then would realise that Alex had cast another aspect, more enlightened and more original and helpful to one's problem. Alex always understood. In all my moments with him I always sifted some gold.[7]

Alex's unpredictability was further compounded by his impulsiveness.

> . . . when he erupted, the explosion was violent, and all within reach of it felt its blast. In these moods he was imperious, capricious, and could dominate anybody. The truth was perhaps that he was always inclined to act on impulse rather than after reflection, a tendency which led to his greatest triumphs as well as his more grandiose disasters. After all, impulse goes hand in hand with enthusiasm, and Alex above all was a great enthusiast.[8]

Expanding on film-maker Sidney Gilliat's above analysis of Korda, we can conclude that it was precisely because of Korda's multi-faceted personality that he was able to succeed for so long in so many different roles. The complexity of Alex Korda's nature set him apart from other film producers, made it difficult for the industry to sympathise with his problems,* and certainly caused conflicts within Korda himself; but a man of lesser complexity, with fewer inner resources to draw on, would not have possessed Korda's prodigious imagination and ambition and would never have taken the risks which Korda did.

The one facet to Korda's personality which was both the most obvious to other people and the most useful to Korda himself was his magnetic charm. To quote again from Ralph Richardson's reminiscences:

> What might be called the secret of Alexander Korda could be discovered in the first five minutes of meeting him. . . . There were as many layers and stratas and veins in his nature as in any man's, possibly more, but the one bright golden vein, this secret, by its very nature, lay near to the surface, so it might be seen at once. This rare and indefinable possession was, in my opinion, chiefly responsible for his greatness. It was his gift of charm—and a strength of personality that could well be described as hypnotic. Hypnotists, they say, are unable to make their subjects do anything against their inner will. Alexander Korda was continually making people do things against their will but seldom against their interest.[10]

Korda's charm was indeed his secret weapon. Actors, actresses, film directors and producers, and financiers all came under his spell and found themselves helpless to refuse Alex anything, whether it was roles they didn't want to play, films they didn't want to make, or money they didn't want to part with. His quiet, persuasive charm was coupled with an instinctive knowledge of how to turn aside a threatening encounter, how to claim a victory without even fighting the battle. He achieved this by refusing to accept the defensive position in any encounter, by striking a pre-emptive blow which set his opponent permanently off-balance.

* As C. A. Lejeune wrote in 1936:
Korda has probably given more headaches to more people than any man in the industry; he is tiresome, unaccountable, outspoken and cold-blooded in his judgments, and he suffers fools, not only not gladly, but not at all. Except for his intimates, who are quite simply devoted to a man whom most of the world has never seen, there are few people who mention him with tolerance. He is not spoken of, for instance, with the affection, rather gentle, always sympathetic, that is reserved for Mickey Balcon of Gaumont British. Somebody, somewhere, all the time, is being sorry for Mickey Balcon. Nobody, so far as I know, is ever sorry for Alex Korda.[9]

In handling the less tense situations with people who posed little threat to him, Korda would utilise one of his more common ploys. He would greet them immediately with an allusion to his own 'tiredness' or to the big financial troubles which were weighing on his mind. This usually elicited a sympathetic response and totally disarmed the visitor, who, of course, did not want to add his or her problems to Korda's already burdensome list. In more delicate encounters, especially with angry employees, Korda had to be more ingenious in his manoeuvres. An actress's rage could usually be turned aside by a well-timed compliment. As Margaret Leighton once recalled:

> I'd decide to storm in and see him—have it out with him and put up my own ideas . . . But there he would be in his office smiling, happy to see me. 'Ah, but what a charming dress, my dear Margaret,' he would say. 'A delightful French creation.'
>
> And then I'd say it was nothing—just an old something I had altered the night before. And before I knew what was happening we would chat happily about clothes and all my set speeches of protest would be forgotten and I'd be outside his office again.[11]

With others the compliment might be slightly more backhanded. During Korda's post-war years at Shepperton Studios, he had several directors working for him, more or less as independent film-makers. According to producer Ivan Foxwell,[12] one day Leslie Arliss—one of these directors—met Foxwell in the outer room of Korda's office. He was hopping mad about some disagreement with Alex and was solemnly practising a soliloquy to be used in his argument. Primed for the battle, Arliss stepped into the inner sanctum to Alex's welcoming words: 'Leslie, they say you are a very bad director, but I don't believe what they say.' Non-plussed, deflated, Arliss abandoned the set speech, as had Miss Leighton and as had many others.

As one-time 'Fleet Street liaison' for London Films, the writer Moore Raymond had the opportunity to observe and to experience personally the exasperating, but effective Korda charm.

> The first thing I discovered was that everybody went into Korda's office at the double—and came quietly out looking slightly dazed.
>
> I've gone into his office urgently wanting a decision about something he'd kept postponing.
>
> I've walked resolutely down the long and beautiful carpet, past

the valuable paintings and the library of books in five languages—
absolutely determined to get the man to make up his mind.

He would get up from his desk, put his arms around my
shoulders, and murmur: 'Moore, I theenk . . .'

The next thing I knew I was standing outside his office, watching
the tall mahogany doors with crystal-glass handles being closed in
my face, with Alex saying, softly through the crack: 'Moore, you
coom and see me tomorrow.' He'd hypnotised me all the way
down that carpet from the desk to the door.[13]

Although employees were most often exposed to the Korda hypnosis,
they were not the only ones on whom it was used. Financial backers
were equally at risk. 'To put it rather viciously,' comments Basil
Wright, 'with Korda it is the blind man who *gave* him the penny from
the tray—Korda didn't have to steal it. And the blind man felt happy
and privileged that he'd done so.'[14] It would be foolhardy to insinuate
that the men from the City who financed Alex Korda were like 'blind'
men—they were far from it—although in the beginning they too were
about as helpless and obliging when put face to face with the Korda
charm. Throughout the collapse of the British film industry in the late
thirties, Korda managed, albeit with more and more difficulty, to keep
thousands of pounds coming in from the City. In the end not even
Korda's charm could stop his film-making empire from crumbling.

Even before the industry-wide crisis occurred, there were signs of
strain in the Korda empire, which now centred around the activities
at Denham. Alex himself had been apprehensive about the future of
Denham Studios from the very beginning. Lew Thornburn, long one
of Korda's associates, later described a sad moment just prior to the
official opening of the studio to Ian Dalrymple, who retells it in his
article on Alex.

Alex, on a late tour of inspection with him one Saturday afternoon,
and having trudged the whole forbidding length of the notorious
corridor, sank wearily down on some synthetic stonework, and
looked drearily into the future. 'I have made a terrible mistake,' he
said.

As Dalrymple goes on to explain:

The mistake was not the building of a studio at Denham as a home
for London Films, of a size which he might himself keep occupied,

and for which he might reasonably assume responsibility; but his folly in allowing himself to accept the contractor's grandiose conception, with the enormous load it would lay on him, and the confusion of his own plans by the need to foster alien projects.[15]

As a producer Alex Korda could not expect to make more than three or four films a year, and the seven Denham stages could not operate year round on that small number of films. Consequently, Alex was forced to rely on renting studio space to other companies and on negotiating production contracts with independent film-makers and with other studios. Although these films were made at Korda's studio and often employed many of his own band of technicians and staff, they were not strictly speaking Korda films, for Alex had little or nothing to do with the conception or execution of most of them. (The Korda link with some of them—e.g. Victor Sjöström's *Under the Red Robe* (1936)— was so tenuous that the films have quite rightly been excluded from most Korda filmographies.) They did at least allow the studio to function at close to full capacity, but at a great cost to Korda's own energies which were of necessity diverted from his own projects to the increasingly difficult job of keeping the monster Denham fed.

To understand the crisis and slump which hit the British film industry in 1937 we must first have some idea of the specific nature of the trade boom which preceded it and the part which Korda played in it. From 1933 to 1936 expansion had occurred in all sections of the film business, in exhibition, distribution, and production, but it was in the production sphere that the boom was most noticeable. Between 1925 and 1932 the number of new production companies registered in Great Britain had averaged about thirty-seven new units each year.[16] In 1934 this figure more than doubled; and, in 1935 alone, one hundred and eight new film-making concerns were formed. In the decade between 1928 and 1938 studio stages had almost quadrupled in number, while actual studio space had increased more than sevenfold. Of even more importance was the fact that the total value of British films in production had gone from £500,000 in 1928 to £7,000,000 in 1937. This growth, though rapid, was considered by all to be a positive, healthy trend. Unfortunately, the assumptions on which the growth was based and the actual financing behind it were not as sound nor as prudent as they appeared to be.

The assumptions and financing peculiar to the thirties expansion derive directly from Alex Korda and the example which he provided for the rest of the industry. The international success of *The Private Life of Henry VIII* and the financial investment of the City in film production, which began with the alliance between the Prudential and London Films, can be accredited with beginning the British production fever. Inspired by the world markets conquered by *Henry VIII*, British and émigré film producers started making extensive plans for film companies and film productions based on the Korda 'mould' and found that City firms—also impressed with the monetary returns on Korda's film—were now more than willing to make heavy commitments to the film industry.

There were three particular aspects of this film expansion which set it apart from more normal and stable forms of industry growth. First, this increase in film investment was purely speculative, 'based almost entirely on *expectation* without any concrete results to justify that optimism'.[17] Since the older British production companies had not been showing significant profits, this new optimism was based on the mistaken premiss that the success of *Henry VIII* signalled a reversal in the previously unreceptive attitude of overseas markets to British films, the results of which, it was reasoned, had not yet had enough time to filter back to the industry. Rather than seeing *Henry* as an isolated case, a freak occurrence, film-makers and financiers instead judged it as the forerunner of a new era in which British films could expect to reach international markets.

Second, the financing of these companies was effected by tremendous increases in short-term loans, rather than on increases in actual working capital (which happens in normal boom circumstances and which allows the companies to liquidate their previous loans as opposed to incurring more and larger loan obligations). As of October 1936 sixteen of the new production firms (including London Film Productions) had a combined working capital of £835,000, while their debentures, mortgages and short-term loans amounted to a staggering £4,197,000. Taking all spheres of the film industry together, the first ten months of 1936 witnessed the increase of loans and mortgages to a total figure of over twelve and a half million pounds. The situation was made even more precarious by the fact that these financial investments had been undertaken by a relatively small number of City firms who were thus given great control and power over the industry's future. Without fully realising it, most film producers were almost totally at the mercy of a few City men who, at the first sign of crisis, could call in loans, thereby undermining the whole industry structure.

Third and last, the most misguided feature of this boom time was the peculiar nature of the film producers who received the benefits of the heavy City investment. In his history of the British film industry *Where We Came In*, C. A. Oakley observed that 'the profits made by *The Private Life of Henry VIII* were already becoming legendary, and people unacquainted with the industry supposed that [Korda's] flair for making successful films was someway linked with his mid-European background'.[18] So, the investors looked around for other émigré film producers; and their search was seemingly rewarded, for there were in Britain at that time numerous refugee film-makers or film promoters. As British producer Michael Balcon later recalled:

> There were many people who came to this country . . . Hungarians like Korda, Germans understandably getting away from the Nazi regime, Italians and others, often somewhat flamboyant figures who had meteoric careers in film production, most of them pale imitations of Alex Korda; Latin charm and *gemutlichkeit* are no permanent substitute for professional experience and training.[19]

It was a disastrous policy for the City to finance, on such a grand scale, men who were as yet unproven in Britain, who in some cases lacked any film-making expertise, and who often had nothing to recommend themselves other than their foreign accent. And as Alex himself said at the time: 'If an investor chooses to entrust his money to his tailor for the building of a ship, he deserves all he gets.'[20]

Facts and figures about the trade expansion and especially about the nature of the financing behind it were not fully disclosed until January 1937. A few months before, the Film Council, a research team organised to study certain aspects of cinema, had undertaken an examination of the structure and financing of the American film industry and had followed that up with a similar investigation into the British industry. The researchers, as John Grierson explains, 'wanted to look behind the gossip, rumours, hunches and half-truths of Wardour Street and create for ourselves a more satisfactory body of information'.[21] By making this information public, the Council hoped to effect a re-evaluation and re-thinking of the precarious financial structure of the industry. Instead, the publication of a summarised account of their findings in *World Film News* in January 1937 immediately precipitated a crisis situation. City companies ordered extra copies of the *World Film News* issue and were stunned to find out exactly how much they and their

City colleagues were expending on the industry in speculative loans. The result was fairly predictable: certain loans were called in and receivers appointed for the most insolvent companies, Twickenham Studios failed in January, other studios announced possible closures, and even London Films immediately announced pay cuts (although they were restored by the end of the year). The City's disengagement with the film business carried on for the next two years, causing a crisis which shook the foundations of the industry. Alex Korda, the man who however indirectly had helped the industry reach this crisis state, was one of the most vocal critics of the continual 'crisis talk'. He could afford to be, for he and his company had managed to weather the crisis quite well.

At the time of the crisis Korda and London Films were being financed in the main by two City firms, the Prudential and C. T. Bowring and Company, although the Pru took first place among the company's shareholders and creditors. In the fiscal year 1934–5 London Films had shown a loss of almost £30,000, although by May 1936 this loss had swelled to over £330,000. Unsettled by the financial losses and by Korda's apparent extravagances, the City men descended on Korda more and more regularly, demanding explanations for expenditures and firmly suggesting future economy. Korda would employ all his charm in circumventing their demands or suggestions; he would at times be most conciliatory, castigating himself unmercifully for his extravagance until the City men were themselves discomforted and glad to give him another cheque. On other occasions he would play a different game, coldly offering them the choice between taking his latest film, half-finished as it was, or helping him complete it. And he was always having to justify the amount of money which was being paid out for contracts.

To an outsider it appears that Alex Korda tried to put everyone in the British film world under contract to London Films. As an employee once remarked, it was no longer an honour to be signed to a Korda contract because absolutely everyone was offered one. Alex could never understand why anyone would refuse a contract, and he always countered a negative response in the same characteristic way. The actor (now Sir) John Clements described one contract encounter he had with Korda: 'He said to me, "John, come and sit down. Now we have offered you a contract, yes?" I said yes. "And you have said no." I said yes. He said, "What have we offered you—don't tell me—double it." That was typical of Korda.'[22] When the writer R. C. Sherriff was contemplating a contract with Korda for writing a script of A. E. W. Mason's *The Four Feathers*, he discussed the financial arrangements with his agent whose assessment of Korda's philosophy in the matter was most perceptive.

'So don't aim too high,' I told my agent. 'Don't ask for anything that might put him off.' But my agent knew more about these things than I did. 'Korda wouldn't offer you an important story if he didn't consider you were worth it,' he said. 'He doesn't think like these other producers. If you asked for peanuts, he'd value you in peanuts . . .'[23]

Alex did derive his estimation of a person's worth from that person's own estimation of himself, and he did tend to lose respect for those who accepted or asked for less than their talent could easily command, just as he lost interest in projects which people tried to sell to him on their 'economical' merits.*

While it could be said that the City men didn't understand that films take a long time to earn their money back and consequently panicked too often, too soon, it was also true that Alex was especially lavish in spending their money. Almost everything he ever did was 'big' in scope and thus in expense, and he almost always talked in six or seven digit figures. When the newspapers criticised the amount of money being lost in British film-making, Korda was quick to retort that an industry which makes money in millions of pounds when it is successful must expect, when it loses money, to lose it in millions as well. His attitude towards money has often been illustrated by the story of the five-pound note which he gave to his nephew Michael, saying, 'It's a gift. Don't spend it, waste it.'

Before and even after the film crisis in 1937 there was a lot of waste at Denham: talent wasted by being kept inactive and finally being used in inferior productions, money wasted on superficial production values, and time wasted in inefficient production methods. John Clements, who worked at Denham during this time, later admitted that he had not been 'terribly impressed' by the Korda extravagance.

---

* Mischa Spoliansky told me of an episode when he and Alex were discussing plans for making a film musical (a genre which Korda kept fairly clear of). Spoliansky outlined one of his ideas, and Alex seemed genuinely interested. As a parting remark Spoliansky off-handedly mentioned to Korda that the picture wouldn't cost very much to make. To this day Spoliansky is sure that this comment was the kiss of death for that particular project.

I found the waste of time, the waste of money, an irritant. It seemed to me to be all wrong to carry on in this way where money simply didn't count and nor did time, where virtually every prop you touched was something priceless out of the British Museum—the waste of time, the hours of talk, talk, talk, talk, loads and loads and loads of food from Fortnum and Mason . . . all going bad under the lights and I felt a bit contemptuous about all the ballyhoo of films and all the waste of money and energy on something which seemed to me to be pretty second-rate stuff.[24]

Even Korda's notion of 'economy' was incredibly frivolous; as David Lewin noted in a chapter of his *Daily Express* articles on Korda: 'Once he decreed that to save money his household should buy coffee by the pound—instead of three or four pounds at a time. But he sent his chauffeur-driven Rolls to Soho to pick up every pound.'[25] A studio-wide announcement of a forthcoming 'big economy drive' was quite likely followed by a memo from Korda stating that henceforth the windows would not be cleaned and a coarser grade of toilet paper would be used. By his reluctance to tackle the real source of the extravagance —the films themselves—Alex was stubbornly standing up for his conviction that 'big' films were the only ones worth making that big-time film-making on a par with Hollywood was the only alternative for the British cinema.

By the time of the crisis London Films had been able to show a profit over the previous eight-month period of £35,839. This timely recovery, coupled with Alex's own assurances with respect to future economising, forestalled the Prudential from abandoning London Films. Although making inexpensive, programme features was anathema to Korda, he was forced, by the size of Denham and the condition of the industry, to start thinking more along these lines. This meant the creation of a 'new Korda', as Alex himself revealed in an anti-crisis statement in late January 1937:

There has been panic, yes. But I am not afraid of it . . . I have learned several lessons. I have been forced to fix my mind on the finance of these films to the exclusion of all considerations. There have been times when it was all figures, when I felt more like an accountant than a film producer. My policy will still be to go all out for the big successes and I shall get them. It is true I shall be bearing this question of cost always in mind. That will be a new

Korda. I hope the old Alexander Korda will not be killed in the process.[26]

Although this pronouncement was surely a conciliatory remark aimed at silencing his critics and creditors, there are tones of resentment and bitterness in his comments here and elsewhere which lead us to believe that he viewed the crisis with personal indignation, as if the industry was purposely setting out to undermine all his work and achievements. Nowhere does he accept responsibility for the crisis, and he seems quite able to dissociate himself from the mistakes made by others. But then, how much blame should we put on Korda anyway?

I asked several people I talked to this question of how much Korda was responsible for the basically unsound boom period and its subsequent crisis. Even those who admired Korda greatly were willing to admit that Korda's particular model for making films and the way he had them financed both made and destroyed the British film industry. He gave the British cinema its first taste of international success and then undermined it all by trying to pull himself and the industry up too quickly. A more gradual rise might have been more financially sound and might not have frightened the City away from film investments in the future. Yet, thirty-six years after the crisis, Basil Wright offered this analysis:

> . . . in the great South Sea Bubble, the explosion of finance for films, after *Henry VIII*, I think it's only fair to say that the one person who left the nation enriched by it was Korda. But if you think of the other people, like Max Schach and everybody, who came in and in fact merely manipulated finance in grandiose plans for making films, some of which came off and some of which didn't, but never built a studio, never added anything to the sum of things for the industry—I think Korda comes out of the thing very well. You can't blame him entirely for this extraordinary, extravagant South Sea Bubble boom. . . . He had got the princely quality of the Renaissance; he made lots of mistakes—but he left us with a lot of bricks and mortar and some laboratories, *and* some good films, don't forget that.[27]*

---

* Certain City men were far less charitable towards Korda, as this entry (23 August 1938) from Sir Robert Bruce Lockhart's diary reveals:
Last night Bayliss-Smith, who is a leading chartered accountant and represents the creditors in some of the big cinema financial messes in this country, says the cinema industry here has cost the banks and insurance companies about

For a contemporary analysis of Korda's achievements and failings, we need only turn to *World Film News*, the magazine which had first exposed the industry's financial structure. A few months after that issue appeared, an article called '*Alexandre le Magnifique*' was published. In it was printed a translation of Marcel Ermans's critique of Korda in *Cinémagazine*, which had chastised Korda for his inability to recognise new talent and to delegate his authority and which concluded with these words:

> Well, it remains that Alexander Korda is an amiable gentleman who gives a livelihood to quite a number of worthy people. From the moral point of view he has a right to our esteem, and in the present state of society he represents a beneficent force. My natural indulgence causes me (not being myself a shareholder in London Films) to congratulate him in making money circulate. I have no regrets that this clever businessman has not been attracted to some industry other than cinema—automobiles, for instance, cement, or even preserves. No, I will not even reproach him with being an incomplete artist and a creator without resource. Nor do I find it a fault that he will only work in a brilliant and expensive atmosphere. I am sorry because he is simply an ambitious man, like any other ambitious man, and because his ambition is so naïve. Ah, if Korda had been a *farceur*, everything would be different, and how welcome he would have been these days when there are so few amusing picturesque and 'different' people.
>
> Let us be content to thank Alexander Korda for having built near London in the middle of an immense park the most expensively equipped studio in Europe. In our time, as we all know, the spiritual is obscured by the intellectual, and the intellectual by the technical. One should not be surprised to see palaces thrown up to shelter gigantic machines placed at the service of shallow ideas and making ephemeral and artificial productions. But one day perhaps some genius will arise to make use of the marvellous instrument which lies at Denham.

£4,000,000. Most of this lost by Jews—like Korda and Max Schacht [sic]. Latter already lost a packet for German Government before Hitler. Has now done same here. In Bayliss-Smith's opinion, and he would not say so lightly, Korda is a much worse man than Schacht. Schacht is just a slick Jew who sees financial moves ahead of the other fellow. Korda is a crook and, according to Bayliss-Smith, an evil man.[28]

On that day a brilliant director, a poet, a creator, a lion like Stroheim, or a magician like Murnau, will reign upon one or more of the floors at Denham, and we shall wink at each other and say, 'Old Korda knew what he was doing after all.'[29]

The editors of *World Film News* countered Ermans's amusing diatribe with their own assessment which was 'kinder to Korda and nearer the fact'. Their defence of Korda represents one of the best statements of what the British cinema owed to the work and ambitions of Alexander Korda.

Korda has been ambitious and his ambition has at least been the means of giving scale for the first time to British production. He has made it think of big things and has pointed, like Cortez, to the horizon. The results have been sometimes disappointing and more often than not his films have been more expensive than they should have been. All this because Korda has not succeeded in making organisation keep in step with that ambition. He has, in truth, not known how to surround himself. It is a colossal weakness in a man otherwise brilliant which may well prove his undoing: all the more so in a business, like film, where so many factors are involved in production and so many important responsibilities must be delegated. Korda has had the overmastering desire to create a great film tradition round himself and to do it quickly, but the very quality of his ambition may be too individualistic to be content with that position of *first among equals* in a group of great abilities which is the key to efficient film production. Not otherwise does ambition in the corporate creative process which is the cinema 'fall upon the other'.

But this need not blind anyone to the fact that Korda's quality has been of historic importance in the development of the British cinema . . . He is still, today, the only fighting figure in the British cinema independent enough and tough enough in the cause of the British film to match swords with the American bosses . . . One may not like the British films he stands for, and many wise critics do not. One may doubt the economics of his films and wonder at the economics of his studios, and many sensible observers do. One may sigh that his dreams and his schemes should so often be doomed to scrambles and tangled and second-rate execution, and embarrass themselves in their final cost. One may doubt, and many do, that he is the best leader for the British cinema; for he is on the one hand not a native, nor is he a born leader who knows how to keep strong people with him. But he is the only imaginative figure one sees in a bunch of dim-wits and the only courageous figure in a bunch of lily-livers. And that will do for now.[30]

1. From Robert Vas's BBC documentary.
2. Paul Holt, 'A Cabby Decided His Future', Daily Herald, 9 May 1953.
3. From Robert Vas's BBC documentary.
4. R. C. Sherriff, op cit, pp. 287–8.
5. Interview with John and Roy Boulting conducted by the author, 23 August 1973.
6. John Russell, 'A Guiding Star of Our Civilisation', The Sunday Times, 8 July 1973, p. 35.
7. Sidney Gilliat and others, 'Sir Alexander Korda', Sight and Sound, vol. 25 no. 4, Spring 1956, p. 215.
8. Ibid.
9. C. A. Lejeune, 'The Private Lives of London Films', Nash's Magazine, September 1936, p. 80.
10. Ibid.
11. David Lewin, op cit, Chapter One, 26 January 1956.
12. Interview with Ivan Foxwell conducted by the author, 23 July 1973.
13. Moore Raymond, 'Korda's Secret', Sunday Dispatch, 29 January 1956.
14. Interview with Basil Wright conducted by the author, 17 July 1973.
15. Ian Dalrymple, op cit, p. 9.
16. All statistics from Klingender and Legg, Money Behind the Screen, London, Lawrence and Wishart, 1937, or The British Film Industry, PEP Report, London, 1952.
17. Klingender and Legg, op cit, p. 54.
18. C. A. Oakley, Where We Came In, London, Allen and Unwin, 1964, p. 135.
19. Michael Balcon, op cit, p. 94.
20. Paul Tabori, op cit, p. 178.
21. John Grierson, Preface to Klingender and Legg, op cit.
22. From Robert Vas's BBC documentary.
23. R. C. Sherriff, op cit, p. 289.
24. From Robert Vas's BBC documentary.
25. David Lewin, op cit, Chapter Two, 27 January 1956.
26. Paul Tabori, op cit, p. 180.
27. Interview with Basil Wright conducted by the author, 17 July 1973.
28. The Diaries of Sir Robert Bruce Lockhart, London, Macmillan, 1973, p. 392.
29. Marcel Ermans, op cit, p. 7.
30. Ibid.

PART THREE

*Eclipses and Come-backs*

Zoltan Korda in 1941; a
director who thrived on exotic
adventure films.

Sabu and Kala Nag in
*Elephant Boy* (1937)
directed by Robert
Flaherty and Zoltan Korda.

Leslie Banks carrying the big stick as Sanders in Zoltan
Korda's *Sanders of the River* (1935).

Vincent Korda, the art director whose contribution to Korda's films is best exemplified in *Things to Come* and *Rembrandt*.

**The collaboration of Alexander Korda and H. G. Wells:**
*Things to Come* (1936) – directed by **William Cameron Menzies**

The First Part: Christmas 1940 in Everytown.

The Second Part: The victory of 'Wings Over the World'
(Raymond Massey) over the tribal 'chief' (Ralph Richardson)
– Everytown June 1970.

The Third Part: Everytown 2036.

Charles Laughton in *Rembrandt* (1936).

Korda and Friends

Denham Studio gathering – *c.* 1936 – including *front row:* Conrad Veidt,
Victor Saville, Anne Harding, Marie Tempest, Edward G. Robinson,
Googie Withers; *back row:* Flora Robson, Korda, Elsa Lanchester,
Douglas Fairbanks, Jnr, Marlene Dietrich, Richard Tauber, Diana Napier,
Elisabeth Bergner, Alan Hale (*behind*), and Murray Silverstone.

Korda, (?), Prime Minister Neville Chamberlain, and Victor
Saville at Denham in 1936.

Alex, Mrs Muir
Mathieson, and René
Clair in St Tropez in
1936.

# CHAPTER THIRTEEN

# A New Alexander Korda?

1937 was a pivotal year in Alex Korda's career. Prior to that year, he had been primarily a film director and producer, megaphone in one hand, cigar in the other, calling out directions in several languages on the studio stages of Europe and America. He had often undertaken more than one job at a time, but active film-making remained his chief concern. Korda had expressed a desire to disengage himself from production as early as 1935, yet it was only after 1937 that he became almost exclusively an executive producer, a film impresario, and a business manipulator. Between the outbreak of industry crisis in January 1937 and the outbreak of war in September 1939, Korda carried on in a supervisory capacity at Denham, but he directed no films during this period and was obviously happy to let his own directorial achievements rest on the merits of *Rembrandt*. He no longer felt the need or desire to 'prove himself' as a creative artist and was, in fact, to direct only three more films in the last two decades of his life.

The circumstances of the time did partially dictate this change of roles, but Korda was not antipathetic to leaving the studio floor to sit behind the administrator's desk. His stated fear about the possible 'killing' of the 'old Alexander Korda' had referred not to the demise of Korda as director, as personal artist, but rather to the possible loss of ambitious vision which the 'old' Korda had stood for and which the new economical times might make obsolete. Alex had what some people who knew him have called a 'power mania'. Although this assessment gives us a too stereotyped picture of Korda as a man possessed with an insatiable hunger for power, it is clear that Alex wanted to be *the* leader of the British film industry. If this meant vacating the director's chair, then it was a sacrifice which he was willing to make. Many felt, and still feel, that this sacrifice was a betrayal of the 'true' Korda—his creative self—but it can also be viewed as the final emergence, in a man of many parts, of that part which really was the quintessential Alex Korda.

By examining the films which were made for and by London Films during the pre-war period, we can note some of Korda's strengths and weaknesses as he began to fulfil his new role. Some of the films provide concrete proof that Korda's showmanship was unimpaired by the increasingly tense and financially tight film industry condition; some of them prove that as an executive producer Alex could promote distinguished, modest-budgeted films, as well as some rather undistinguished programme pictures. A look at Korda's frustrated and frustrating business deals over this period makes it apparent that as an entrepreneur his ambition was great, though his ability to realise his ambition was often less impressive, and that as a possible leader of the industry he had much to understand and much to learn.

Alex had always been extremely sympathetic to the plight of filmmakers and artists who, for one reason or another, found themselves stranded in London. As the European political situation became more threatening, more and more émigrés came to Britain, and the number of Germans and Hungarians employed at Denham steadily increased. Several of these men signed on with Korda shortly after reaching British shores; others gravitated towards Denham after first working for other British producers. As an executive producer Korda still operated under the theory that 'outsiders' make the best 'national' films, and he therefore put these men to work on projects which were frequently quite 'British' in nature and subject matter. To enhance the international quality and potential of these films, Korda then threw in a sprinkling of British and American technicians, directors, and stars. By this mixture Korda probably hoped to minimise, for commercial and even perhaps for political reasons, the 'Germanic flavour' which might otherwise have permeated the films.*

* Two films which fall into this category, *Men Are Not Gods* (1936) and *Forget-Me-Not* (1936), were actually completed before the film crisis. Both were 'women's pictures' in that they dealt with tangled marital and extra-marital relationships from the 'female' angle. Their plots harked back to the stories so

The most characteristic films of this group were produced by the German film producer Erich Pommer, previously a major figure in the development of the German cinema, who had signed a contract with Korda in November 1935. Pommer's Pendennis Production Company made two films at Denham in 1936–7: *Fire Over England* (1937) and *Farewell Again* (1937).

Ever since *Henry VIII*, Korda had wanted to make a film about Queen Elizabeth I, for as the other 'best-known' English monarch she represented the most likely and appropriate subject for a follow-up to *Henry*. Alex had already picked out his star, Flora Robson, but she and the public had to wait four years while Korda had several scripts written about the Virgin Queen. He finally bought the film rights to A. E. W. Mason's novel *Fire Over England*, and Clemence Dane, the British writer, was set to work adapting the novel for the screen. Korda then hired William K. Howard, one of Hollywood's most promising film directors (e.g. *The Power and the Glory*—1933) to direct the film, and Howard brought with him from Hollywood the cameraman who had shot almost all his American films, James Wong Howe, now con-

---

prevalent in the twenties, several of which Korda had directed, almost all of which had centred on the temptation of adultery. Will secretary Ann succeed in preventing actor Edmond from killing his actress-wife Barbara during a performance of *Othello*, an act of desperation attempted in order to clear the way for a union of the two lovers?—*Men Are Not Gods*. Will stenographer Helen resist the charms of a former sweetheart and remain faithful to her devoted opera singer husband? —*Forget-Me-Not*.

The former film was directed by Walter Reisch, a Viennese film-writer and director who had worked as Korda's assistant when Alex was in Vienna in the early twenties. *Men Are Not Gods* had the advantage of an excellent cast, with Miriam Hopkins coming from Hollywood to play 'Ann' opposite Gertrude Lawrence's 'Barbara' and Sebastian Shaw's 'Edmond', and an 'ace' Hollywood cameraman, Charles Rosher, who had won an Oscar for his work on F. W. Murnau's *Sunrise* (1927). As contemporary reviewers observed, the 'commonplace emotionalism' of the melodramatic dénouement greatly undermined the light comedy approach which Reisch had intended from the beginning, but the production values and the acting distinguished the picture from other films of its type. *Forget-Me-Not* was Korda's second English adaptation of an existing foreign film, although this time the original was a German film of the same title. It was directed by brother Zoltan and photographed by Hans Schneeberger, and the Germanic script was rewritten by two Englishmen, Hugh Gray and Arthur Wimperis. The film was planned as a vehicle for Italian singer Beniamino Gigli, whom Korda had hired in November 1935 to the accompaniment of much publicity. According to the critics, Gigli's singing was the only redeeming feature of an otherwise forgettable film.

sidered one of the masters of Hollywood cinematography. To design the sets for the film Korda obtained the talented Russian-born art director Lazare Meerson, whose work had added so immeasurably to the French films of René Clair, Jacques Feyder, and Marcel L'Herbier. Once this truly international team was gathered together, Korda left the actual execution of the film to Pommer.

The Armada confrontation and the rulers and courts of Spain and England provide the historical background for this fictional story about a headstrong young Englishman (Michael Ingolby, played by Laurence Olivier) who saves Elizabeth and England from a group of English traitors in the paid service of Philip of Spain. It seems ironic that in such a patriotic film the court of Philip would turn out to be far more interesting, in sets, action, and acting, than the Elizabethan court. Flora Robson is both plausible and sympathetic as Elizabeth★ and is particularly good in her more intimate scenes with Leicester (Leslie Banks), Burleigh (Morton Selten), and her fictional lady-in-waiting, and loved one of young Michael, Cynthia (Vivien Leigh). But the scenes in the English court are strangely lifeless compared to the swashbuckling and tense scenes set in Spain and Portugal. Raymond Massey in his portrayal of Philip II steals the picture, as do Tamara Desni (as Elena) and Robert Newton (as her husband Don Pedro) who present a far more believable and interesting couple than Olivier and Leigh, who give rather manic performances. That the central lovers are such a tedious pair and that Elizabeth in her constant interruptions of their scenes together appears to be more a nosey, over-protective nanny than a powerful ruler are serious weaknesses in conception. The film is constructed out of too many short, choppy scenes that seem to lead nowhere; a script which combined some of these shorter sequences might have made for a more cohesive whole. Yet, in its favour, there is much action in *Fire Over England* and some stirring Armada scenes, including some of the best model ship sequences in all of cinema. Richard Addinsell's music adds to the rousing spirit of the film and deserves to be numbered with the finest scores written for British films. Of all the films during this period made for Korda by others, *Fire Over England* is the most like an Alexander Korda production and owes much of its success to the Korda 'panache'.

Many of the people who had worked on the first Pendennis film were reunited for Pommer's second film at Denham, *Farewell Again*, which was retitled *Troopship* for its American release. Flora Robson and

★ She played the role again in Michael Curtiz's *The Sea Hawk* (1940).

Leslie Banks again starred, this time in a true story about a British troopship returning from a long tour of duty only to find it is immediately being ordered back to active service. Another American, Tim Whelan, directed the film, which though less epic in scope was even more 'British' than *Fire Over England*. Although an admirable little production, the film did not share the success of its predecessor.

Three other films of smaller scope and smaller budget were produced by Continentals for Korda before the war: *The Return of the Scarlet Pimpernel* (1937), *Paradise for Two* (1938), and *The Challenge* (1938). The first of these, as its title implies, was a sequel to Korda's earlier Pimpernel film. In his autobiography *Nice Work*, Adrian Brunel tells us a little about the making of this film and offers some fascinating insights into Korda's method of delegating authority.

> Apparently there was no story, but just the title, and so Alexander Korda engaged me to write the story and script with Arthur Wimperis . . . Further, we had the guidance of Korda's scenario-editor, Lajos Biro, who was most sympathetic to my idea for evolving a story of Robespierre and the Terror during the French Revolution which would remind audiences of Hitler and the Nazis.
> . . .
> I found the subject and conditions at Denham were encouraging—there was an air about the place in those days, which was obviously derived from Korda's personality—and in this atmosphere I think I did some useful work. . . .
> These happy and comparatively carefree days could not last forever, and when the production date neared I fell a victim to Alex's fatal fascination. He said he wanted to 'promote' me. He was too busy to supervise the picture on the floor and so asked if I would be his deputy, for which position we devised the 'credit' of associate-producer. (We already had an excellent producer, mainly on the business end, in the person of Arnold Pressburger, who became my friend and ally in the difficult job I had in tactfully trying to guide the most inelastic director it has been my lot to encounter. I guess Alex sensed what I was in for. I don't blame him at all. He was right to delegate the work, for since he is a highly skilled director, he is tempted to step in and undertake too much when his appointed director is apparently falling down on the job.) However, we survived the production, though it seemed in-

terminable, and Arnold Pressburger managed to get the film completed for about two-thirds of what Alex had estimated. In spite of some appalling bits, I insist that it was a very good film, and much of its effectiveness was due to Lazare Meerson, that genius amongst art-directors, as well as to the photography of 'Mutz' Green.[1]

Arnold Pressburger's association with Korda had begun in Hungary, and Pressburger had even produced one of Alex's Viennese films, *Herren der Meere*, in 1922. The 'inelastic' director was German Hans Schwartz, and I have been assured by many Pimpernel fanatics that Adrian Brunel's estimation of the film, which starred Barry K. Barnes, Sophie Stewart, Margaretta Scott, and James Mason, is quite just.*

These were some of the more or less 'alien' projects which Alex was having to foster at Denham in his capacity as studio executive. The émigré producers were able to work with greater autonomy than would have been granted prior to the economic crunch and the building of Denham, for Alex could not personally supervise all the films then coming out of his studio. By accepting the fact that he could no longer 'captain' every Denham production and attempting instead to work through 'liaison' men assigned to the productions, Alex had taken an important step forward. Nevertheless, the autonomy which these film-makers enjoyed would not have been possible if Korda hadn't viewed with basic disinterest most of the projects which were undertaken. Every 'prestige' production of this period *was* carefully

---

* Both *Paradise for Two* and *The Challenge* were produced by German émigré Gunther Stapenhorst and were part of the Denham economy drive of 1937. They were hardly the types of films which Alex would have sanctioned in his better days, but it was relatively easy to 'bring them in' for the sum (around £80,000) which Alex had proposed as the top limit for his 'non-prestige' productions. Although Alex had previously spurned the idea of personally supporting an 'inexpensive' musical production, he now allowed Stapenhorst and director Thornton Freeland to make *Paradise for Two*, in America *The Gaiety Girls*. British comedian Jack Hulbert and American actress Patricia Ellis were featured in this musical which was co-written by Robert Stevenson, who, twenty-five years later, directed the famous musical *Mary Poppins* (1964). *The Challenge* was a 'mountain-climbing' film, a German version of which was apparently made at the same time. Luis Trenker, a former mountain climber who made his film reputation entirely on German 'Mountain' pictures, starred in and co-directed this film about the conquest of the Matterhorn. Joan Gardner (who was by now Mrs Zoltan Korda) provided the 'romantic interest' in the thin story which was merely an excuse for some extraordinary Alpine photography (by Georges Périnal and Trenker's own cameraman Albert Benitz).

supervised by Alex, for if a project genuinely appealed to him, wild horses couldn't drag him off the set.

*The Man Who Could Work Miracles* (1937), for those not familiar with the film or the H. G. Wells short story from which it was taken, tells the tale of an unprepossessing Englishman, George Fotheringay (Roland Young), who is endowed by the 'Giver of Power' with the ability to work miracles so that the heavenly observers can find out 'what's in the human heart'. At first purely amused by his new magician's powers, George soon feels the burden of moral responsibility weighing heavily upon him and seeks out advice as to how he should use his 'gift' to the benefit of mankind. Utterly frustrated by the selfishness or short-sightedness inherent in the suggestions he receives, George finally decides to take matters into his own hands. In a grandiose palace he assembles all the world's greatest minds, past and present, and gives them all until morning to come up with a blueprint for a harmonious and peaceful society. When more time is asked for, the brash miracle worker responds by commanding the earth to stand still. In the cataclysm which immediately results, George gives up his powers, and the world returns to normal. We are left with the conclusion, as stated by one of the celestial giants (played by a barely recognisable George Sanders): 'Once an ape, always an ape.'

Made directly after *Things to Come*, the film was supposed to ride along on the publicity and success accorded the previous Wells–Korda extravaganza. Since Wells's presence throughout the former film's production had demanded constant patience, conciliation, and accommodation from the film-makers, this time Korda kept Wells away from the film as much as possible. (Korda apparently solicited Frank Wells's assistance in these manoeuvres.) Although Wells receives screen credit for the script, Lajos Biro was, in fact, the responsible party, which may have been an additional reason for keeping Wells at a distance.

A lover of fairy tales and visual tricks, Korda obviously wanted the fantasy elements of the story stressed, and the only sad thing was that he didn't get rid of all traces of the Wellsian 'message' which weigh the film down. The escapist and romantic qualities of the story—George being like a genie capable of granting an infinite number of wishes but unable to make the woman he loves love him—are destroyed by the 'serious' sociological debates which pepper the film. The picture therefore falls between two stools, and to compensate for the obligatory message, Korda, director Lothar Mendes, and the special effects team have offered us a whole repertoire of visual tricks. The tricks are, alas, less inventive than those which Georges Méliès devised thirty years before with cruder technical resources and less expense. The humour is not as biting as we might have expected or hoped for and lapses on occasion into pure vaudeville (e.g. Ralph Richardson's over-made-up role as the crotchety Colonel Winstanley). The absence of Arthur Wimperis from the script conferences may account for the heavy-handed and vulgar treatment of humour here, for in the past he had been the one who guided Hungarians Biro and Korda through the 'subtleties' of English humour.

The film had a mixed critical reception and was less commercially successful in Britain than in America on its general release in February 1937. If the film-makers' ambivalent intentions could have been sorted out and a more subtle approach applied, much could have been done with this film. Instead, this was one of the few cases where Korda *should* have spent more time on the preparation of a film.

Time in preparation was one thing which *Elephant Boy* had in abundance. Though not released until April 1937, the project originated in discussions between the documentary film-maker Robert Flaherty and Korda in early 1935. Korda had first met Flaherty in Hollywood at the end of the twenties and considered him one of the masters of cinema. In 1933 Alex mentioned Flaherty's first film *Nanook of the North* (1922) as one of two classic examples (the other was James Cruze's *The Covered Wagon*—1923) of the 'international' film. Flaherty's past experiences with film producers, the majority of whom had hired him for his documentary talents only to mould the resulting footage to suit their own needs, read a little like Red Riding Hood being betrayed by the come-on of the nasty old wolf. By 1935 Flaherty was in great need of money, and since in Britain the words 'profit' and 'money' were then inextricably linked with the name Korda, he decided to go to Korda with his idea for making a film about 'a boy and an elephant'. Korda was most receptive to Flaherty's ideas and to the thought of adding Flaherty's prestigious name to the London Films banner. Each man secretly believed that he was going to derive the greater benefit from their association. Arthur Calder-Marshall relates their initial parting in his biography of Flaherty entitled *The Innocent Eye*:

> But when the great Irish–American charmer was leaving the great Hungarian charmer, the latter gripped his right hand firmly

and patted his elbow with his left hand. 'We're both artists, Bob,' he said. 'We understand each other. Leave the contract side of our friendship in my hands.'

Flaherty agreed without a murmur to a contract which gave Korda overriding supervisory powers.[2]

Even before the contract was signed, Korda had won the first round. It was Korda who had first suggested Kipling's Indian story *Toomai of the Elephants* as a possible framework for the film. He told Flaherty that he would buy the film rights to the names of the characters and the title, and the story itself if Flaherty cared to use it. Korda was aware that Flaherty's approach to documentary film-making involved much exploratory shooting on location without any concern for following a story line. Consequently, he attempted to forearm Flaherty with some kind of basic plot, and something resembling a plot eventually evolved from Flaherty's conferences with Lajos Biro. After receiving official permission for the location work in India from His Highness the Maharajah of Mysore, Flaherty and his wife Frances left for India in February 1935 with Korda's cameraman Osmond Borradaile and production manager 'liaison' David Cunynghame, and with a promise from Korda that they would be financed for one year's worth of filming there. It was a gesture worthy of Korda's 'patron of the arts' self-image; it was also a commercial gamble.

The monsoon season plagued the production throughout the summer of 1935. By September Frances Flaherty was able to write that the casting (in particular the finding of a stable boy, Sabu, to star in the film) and the opening sequences had been completed. But Korda was already beginning to panic. As he later admitted: 'For months I heard absolutely nothing. Of course, I heard from the business manager . . . and money had to be sent to India, but still we had optimism, but . . . you know, when you spend money for eight, nine months and no film comes back, you start to get worried.'[3] Some time in the fall, Korda exercised his supervisorial rights and sent Hollywood director Monta Bell out to India to assist Flaherty. Instead of helping to speed up production as Korda had intended, Bell's intrusion led to a further waste of time and money. The unit's cameraman, Osmond Borradaile, filled in the details of this fiasco:

Borradaile . . . says that Bell told Korda about a book just published in New York, called *Siamese White*, about a ghost elephant. Korda liked this idea and sent Bell out to incorporate the ghost in the script. 'If it had not been such a tragic mistake, the whole affair would have been comic. Monta Bell didn't like the jungle and wanted to return to the bright lights as soon as possible. But he didn't get away before Flaherty received and read a copy of *Siamese White*, which turned out to be a story of a man named White, who lived in Siam—a bit embarrassing because an elephant had actually been white-washed to play the ghost. All the footage shot on this blunder—and a good chunk it was—went into the ash-can.'[4]

By the spring of 1936 the script was again going through daily revisions, and Alex had further hedged his bet by sending brother Zoltan to India to join Bell and Flaherty. At one point three units were independently shooting footage to entirely different stories. Korda finally called a halt to this veritable three-ring circus in June 1936.

Over fifty-five hours of film had been shot in India, all background material to a still non-existent story. This was a customary state of affairs on a Flaherty picture, for it was in the editing stages that he and a good editor would give a film its story and shape.[5] Yet Alex was by now looking for the quickest way to turn his investment into a conventional, commercially profitable feature film. Once back in England, Flaherty had almost no control over the last stages of production on *Elephant Boy*, as the film was finally entitled. British writer John Collier was brought in to construct a simple story which could be filmed at Denham and then interwoven with the Flaherty location material. Zoltan Korda directed these story sequences in six weeks, and William Hornbeck and Charles Crichton shaped over 300,000 feet of material into a film of just over 7,000 feet, half of which was pure Flaherty, half of which was pure Korda.

In spite of the erratic course which the production had followed, *Elephant Boy* was far more successful than anyone connected with it could possibly have imagined. It turned out to be a solid entertainment film (Korda's contribution) centred around a romantically observed and touching relationship between a boy, Sabu/Toomai, and his elephant Kala Nag (Flaherty's legacy). The fictional plot did take great licence with Flaherty's documentary facts, such as when Kala Nag's 'musth' is explained in the story as the elephant 'mourning' for his master's death; but its main virtue was its simplicity, a trait it shared with Flaherty's other works. Only Sabu's unnecessary prologue and the dreadful 'model elephant' and 'rubber feet' special effects of the Elephant Dance sequences do a direct disservice to the integrity of the Flaherty footage.

Many critics and historians dismiss the film, seeing in it only an example of how the innocent artist can be betrayed by the shrewd businessman. This question makes Flaherty more naïve and Korda far cleverer than either man really was in this instance and leads to the unfair conclusion that *Elephant Boy* is not worth our attention or discussion. After all, for one year Flaherty was able to film in India at Korda's expense, and some of his footage became the core of a popular commercial film. We may regret that *Elephant Boy* is not 100 per cent Flaherty, but in the final analysis 50 per cent of Flaherty is better than 100 per cent of many other directors. As a compromise between two very different concepts of film-making, this film does represent a fascinating case, especially fascinating since unlike so many other similar compromises the end result was *not* a disaster. Much credit for the film's profitable career must, of course, be given to Sabu, who came to England for the filming of the story sequences, whose performance endeared him to audiences around the world, and who stayed on to become one of Korda's star attractions of the late thirties.

The ironic epilogue to the two-year saga of *Elephant Boy* came later in 1937 when the film received the 'best direction' award at the Venice Film Festival. Against heavy odds, Korda's gamble on a 'prestige' Flaherty picture had in the end paid off, both at the box office and in at least some more critical circles. The actual method of production, or rather the lack thereof, does, however, reinforce some of our criticisms of Korda as a producer, in particular his impulsiveness, and even naïvety, with regard to the *Siamese White* episode and his tendency to wait until the last minute before coming in to salvage a production which, in his terms, had already gotten out of hand.

Walter Hudd, who played the rather bland 'Petersen, Elephant hunter' in the Flaherty–Korda film also had the dubious honour of being for many years the front-running choice for the lead in Korda's planned-but-never-made screen biography of Lawrence of Arabia. Korda had acquired the film rights to Lawrence's abridged autobiography *Revolt in the Desert* in late 1934 or early 1935, but he was wary of making the film without Lawrence's permission. In May 1935 Korda received an unexpected visit from Lawrence, who sanctioned the project but requested that it should not be made until after his death. Korda was surprised at Lawrence's stipulation; he was probably more stunned when Lawrence was killed in a motorcycling accident a week later. Although technically free to start the film, Korda did not begin serious preparations until 1937.

Miles Malleson had written the script for the film which, like the book, was to be called *Revolt in the Desert*, and Brian Desmond Hurst, the British director, was assigned to the picture. Exactly who was to play Lawrence by this time is not clear, for several people were constantly being announced and re-announced for the role. John Clements remembers:

> Alex sent for me to make a test . . . for Lawrence of Arabia, and I said that the part of Lawrence of Arabia is already cast with somebody else, who had been advertised for years to play the part . . . and had in fact appeared in Spotlight [the industry casting directory] for two years dressed as Lawrence of Arabia.
>
> He said, 'Don't be silly. Come and make a test.' . . . so I went . . . and I got the part. He said, 'You must be ready to go to Arabia in six weeks.' . . . I said, 'Yes, fine, I'd love to do [it],' and nothing happened—I heard nothing for six weeks, eight weeks, nine weeks, ten weeks, and then suddenly somebody showed me a newspaper which said—headline: LESLIE HOWARD TO PLAY LAWRENCE OF ARABIA. Three days later Clifford Evans was to play Lawrence . . . then Robert Donat . . . then I think I was to play Lawrence of Arabia and then I think Laurence Olivier and nothing more was said and that was the end of that.[6]

The project had actually progressed to the point where Brian Desmond Hurst was set to go to Jerusalem to scout locations. As Mr Desmond Hurst related it to me, he was sitting in the sea plane as it prepared to take off when he espied a launch coming up alongside the plane. The message was simple and direct; he was requested to return immediately to the studio. Once there Korda told him that the Governor of Palestine wouldn't countenance any large gathering of Arabs. Since the unit would have to depend on the native population as extras in many of the scenes, the film would have to be put off.

Not long after this Korda sold the film rights to another production company, probably because he needed the cash. Yet he bought the rights back in 1938 and briefly resurrected the project. It was in the Sudanese desert during the location filming on *The Four Feathers* that John Clements again heard about the film.

One day I was sitting in my tent in the Sudan taking off all the make-up I had in *The Four Feathers* . . . in a sort of hip bath when Zoltan Korda . . . who directed . . . *The Four Feathers* came into my tent. He didn't say anything; he just took a telegram out of his pocket and he handed it to me and it said words to the effect, 'After you finish shooting in the Sudan you and the cameraman and various members of the unit and Clements will stay behind to shoot exteriors for your next film *Lawrence of Arabia.*' I said nothing. I handed the cable back to Zolly. He said nothing, put it into his pocket. We never mentioned it again. We returned to England with the unit, and it was never mentioned again. And then I said . . . to Alex one day, 'Why, what's the matter with *Lawrence of Arabia*? Why haven't you made *Lawrence of Arabia*?' He said 'How can I make a film of *Lawrence of Arabia*? We are friendly with the Turks.' [7]

So, in the end, the need for British diplomacy got the better of Korda and the Lawrence project, and we are left guessing as to how the film might have turned out. It would hardly have been as outstanding as David Lean's *Lawrence of Arabia* (1961), which, after much casting indecision—Alec Guinness and Laurence Harvey being among those first announced as 'Lawrence'—finally starred Peter O'Toole in the role that had been promised to so many other British actors over the years.

In early 1937 one project overshadowed the *Revolt in the Desert* preparations and, for that matter, every other production on the stages at Denham. This picture was *I, Claudius*. For a film which was never completed, more has been written about it, more rumours and legends have arisen from it than from any other film with which Korda was associated during this period. Practically everyone involved with the production has expounded at great length on what went wrong with the film, though naturally the renditions vary. From these reminiscences we can piece together the progression of events and isolate the various conflicts of personalities, and in this endeavour we are greatly aided by Bill Duncalf's excellent BBC documentary about the making of the film, appropriately entitled *The Epic That Never Was*.

*I, Claudius* and *Claudius the God* were two companion historical novels written by British poet and Classics scholar Robert Graves and published in the mid-thirties. They dealt with the Roman Empire and in particular with the unexpected rise to power and eventual deification of one Caesar, Tiberius Claudius, the stammering, limping Roman historian, grandson of Mark Antony, grand-nephew of Augustus Caesar, and uncle of Caligula. Just as he had seen the 'epic' possibilities in Wells's *The Shape of Things to Come*, so Korda also saw the cinematic potential of Claudius's story. He immediately telegrammed Robert Graves.

> '. . . one day I got this cable from Korda that he wanted to buy the rights,' Graves later recalled. 'So I thought, fine. Korda was a remarkably good chap. He was cynical, but he was real. His only failing, if I might call it so, was making himself a centre of expatriate Hungarians and, really, filling up the studios with Hungarians who were not altogether qualified for the jobs which he gave them, especially in the English department.'[8]

Graves's criticism of Korda's Continental writing staff was based on his reaction when first shown the initial scenario for the Claudius film.

> I was eventually shown a bit of the . . . a bit of some sort of script in which a character comes in, I think it was Caligula comes in and says 'My armies are revolting,' which . . . seems rather odd use of English. There was a lot that was revolting in the script besides. I don't know who wrote it. Somebody, a character called Biro was somehow concerned, another Hungarian. And . . . I was allowed, even given money, to write the script, which I did, but, of course, that was filed somewhere.[9]

Graves was right, for Korda regulars Lajos Biro and Arthur Wimperis were both responsible for the early drafts of the script. In addition, Carl Zuckmayer had stayed on after *Rembrandt* to lend a hand with the writing of *I, Claudius*, and American scriptwriter Lester Cohen also assisted with the script as the production date approached. As was by now usual with Korda productions, there were many last minute revisions in the shooting script, and it was probably not fully realised by the time the film went on the floor.

Alex had envisaged the film as another vehicle for the talents of Charles Laughton; but, perhaps even more important, he saw, in the role of Messalina, a wanton young dancer and Claudius's third wife, a part designed to further Merle Oberon's career. At least that's how Miss Oberon saw it herself:

I was Alex's only star at the time, under contract to him I mean, and I had done nothing much—I was very young—but it had all been very successful. . . . I think Alex wanted to nearly make me 'the' big star, so he bought *I, Claudius* and cast Charles Laughton as Claudius, and Messalina for me. When Alex decided that he would get von Sternberg to direct me—'cause von Sternberg was a woman's director—he just wanted to give me everything he could to make me shine.[10]

This was undoubtedly in the back of Korda's mind when he hired Josef von Sternberg to direct the picture; yet there was more behind his decision than the hope that von Sternberg, the mentor of Marlene Dietrich, would be able to make Merle 'shine'.

Josef von Sternberg was in London recovering from surgery when Alex approached him with the *I, Claudius* project. Von Sternberg was under the impression that Korda had intended to direct the picture himself, and in reply to his question on this matter Korda related, to quote von Sternberg, the 'gruesome details of the difficulties he had endured in directing Laughton, interlarding his recital with effusive flattery of my ability to direct the devil himself'.[11] After *Rembrandt* Alex had apparently had his fill of Laughton's 'character immersion' method of acting (he was once reported to have said that Laughton needed a midwife, not a director), but we can still question why Alex chose von Sternberg to do the job for him. The answer perhaps comes from another version of the story which writer Doug McClelland has uncovered:

> A quarter of a century before von Sternberg's book appeared, *Hollywood* magazine writer Charles Samuel covered the matter with a wider lens. Laughton, it seemed, had agreed to do *I, Claudius* with his friend, the great art director William Cameron Menzies, directing. But Korda then ran into a financial snag and couldn't pay Marlene Dietrich the last $100,000 due on her $350,000 salary for *Knight Without Armour*, which she had just done for Korda. Dietrich said that if he would hire her discoverer, von Sternberg, to direct *I, Claudius* she would forget about the last payment. Korda agreed. Laughton was furious.[12]

Since this episode would have coincided time-wise with the industry crisis, we can well believe that Korda's finances were such that he couldn't pay the remainder of Miss Dietrich's salary. Von Sternberg must have been aware of the behind-the-scenes negotiation; that he would be loath to mention it in his autobiography, *Fun in a Chinese Laundry* (Macmillan, 1965), which is considered by most to be an overly self-congratulatory work anyway, is not surprising. Regardless of the way in which he was hired, von Sternberg was a director infinitely well suited to this kind of undertaking. He had a strong visual sense and had already proven his ability to explore decadent or foreign atmospheres in films like *The Blue Angel* (1930) and *Morocco* (1930). He also shared Korda's enthusiasm for the Claudius story and planned 'not only to bring to life an old empire and to depict the arrogance and decay of its civilization but to hold it up as a mirror to our own tottering values and to investigate the diseased roots of excessive ambition'.[13] He instinctively knew that *I, Claudius* was going to be a 'memorable' film and would later express deep regret that the picture had been abandoned, that, as he put it, 'actors had truncated my film'.[14]

The picture did prove to be 'memorable', but in a very different sense than von Sternberg and Korda intended. Budgeted at £120,000, *I, Claudius* went into production on the 15th of February 1937. Vincent Korda had designed the immense sets, and although there was a technical adviser employed to oversee the film's accuracy to historical detail, nothing was allowed to get in the way of von Sternberg's personal vision of the opulence and decadence of the Roman Empire. John Armstrong, a distinguished British painter in his own right and costume designer on *Claudius*, bore witness to this.

> One morning [von Sternberg] asked me, 'Have you any vestal virgins?' I said, 'Yes.' He said, 'How many?' I said, 'Six,' which was the authentic number. He said, 'How are they dressed?' I got him my drawing which I took from a statue in Naples. They were all well-covered with clothing with a kind of tiara on their head. 'Allure' was not allowed; in fact, they were buried alive if they broke their vow of chastity. He looked at the drawing and said, 'This won't do for me. I want sixty, and I want them naked.' He defined naked—bra and pants under a veil—and he said, 'I want them on the set tomorrow morning!'
>
> There was no arguing. I went off to London to hold a parade of extras to choose the girls, while the wardrobe set out to cut sixty circles of five-foot radius out of scenic gauze. Next morning the vestal virgins duly appeared on the set, diaphanous, holding tapers, and arranged up a magnificent flight of steps in the temple scene.

It looked lovely, but it had nothing to do with the Roman religion.[15]

And so the production went, with von Sternberg himself, clothed in
laced-up boots, riding breeches and occasional turban, looking no less
incongruous on the set than the sixty diaphanously clad virgins.

The cast now included, besides Laughton and Oberon, Flora Robson
as Claudius's octogenarian grandmother Livia, John Clements as
Messalina's lover Valenz, Emlyn Williams as the mad Caligula, and
Robert Newton as Cassius, a Roman guard and Caligula's murderer.
The actual shooting was begun in haste, and von Sternberg attempted
to rectify the situation with an intensive, day-long production and
rehearsal meeting. From the footage that remains of the film—much of
which is included in the television documentary—we can see that von
Sternberg's gruelling session had been fruitful. With little preparation
the actors managed to find the 'keys' to their particular characters: the
raspy voice and palsy of Livia, the sissy nuances in Caligula's gestures
and demeanour. Everyone seemed firmly 'in character', everyone, that
is, except Charles Laughton.

Laughton had, of course, taken a long time settling into the characters of Henry VIII and Rembrandt; but playing a stammering cripple,
a wise man pretending to be the fool that the Romans considered him
to be, was an even more demanding assignment. By the time the
cameras started rolling, he still hadn't worked out how he was going to
act Claudius, and everyone on the set was aware of the actor's distress.
Von Sternberg, who had little sympathy for Laughton's 'growing
pains', later wrote:

> There was a rumour that the capers indulged in by Claudius were
> part of a deliberate plan to wreck Alexander Korda, but I cannot
> give credence to this, as this was too perfect a performance. . . .
> Beginning with the first limp, he dragged a different foot each
> time, alternating according to his mood, and sometimes attempted
> to drag them both. . . . Promptly at nine he would enter a stage
> which had been prepared for the day's work, look everything
> over, and then declare that he would not be able to play his part
> there, as he had prepared himself to interpret a sequence for which
> no stage as yet had been made ready. This required an about-face
> on the part of everyone, and this soon became routine.[16]

Despite the inconvenience it caused to all concerned, von Sternberg was forced to devise ways to circumvent Laughton. Different sets were constructed on every available stage at Denham so that if Laughton was unable to play one scene, there was always another one ready to which the crew and players could move. During the shooting of a scene Laughton would occasionally disregard his directions and wander into un-lit areas of the set, out of range of the cameras, where he felt there were better vibrations. In concert with the talented Georges Périnal, von Sternberg so arranged the lighting of each set that 'every possible retreat' Laughton could find would be adequately illuminated. And at times no one but the crew knew when a scene was actually being recorded, for the knowledge that the cameras were filming tended to drive away the characterisation which Laughton had finally achieved during the rehearsals.

Finally one day Laughton found the inspiration for his Claudius; he discovered that Claudius was, in fact, King Edward VIII, who had abdicated just two months before the production commenced. Each morning a recording of Edward's abdication speech could be heard emanating from Laughton's caravan, and for a short while Laughton played Claudius in imitation of the former King. A distressed Korda, however, put an end to Laughton's unpolitic impersonation, and, according to one observer, the actor thereafter began imitating Groucho Marx instead. This does make it sound as if Laughton were out to sabotage the film, whereas his reactions were more probably just the result of his utter frustration with not coming to terms with Claudius and with not receiving from von Sternberg the encouragement which he required. We can witness in the existing footage Laughton gradually slipping out of character: the losing of the stammer and the voice inflections and the disintegration of his concentration. Von Sternberg was right: Laughton's acting difficulties were too painfully genuine to have been part of some childish conspiracy. But then we must also agree with Emlyn Williams's assessment which suggests that von Sternberg deserves some blame for not supporting Laughton, for only offering the actor 'frost', when what he needed was 'sun'. As a last resort von Sternberg appealed to Korda to try directing Laughton, but by this time even Alex was incapable of solving the actor's dilemma.

The demise of *I, Claudius* came suddenly. On Tuesday, the 16th of March, a month and a day after the filming had begun, Merle Oberon was involved in a car crash on her way to a fitting. She was thrown through the windscreen and suffered facial cuts and, it was later discovered in hospital, a concussion. She would be unable to work for several weeks, and, therefore, a few hours after the accident Korda suspended the production indefinitely. Everyone waited around for a time, wondering whether the film was to continue or not. In the end Korda decided to shelve the project, and Lloyds liquidated the £40,000 which had already been spent.

There has been much speculation as to why it was necessary to abandon *I, Claudius* outright. One of the more popular, and undoubtedly spurious theories was that government pressure had been brought to bear on Korda because the stammering Claudius might be construed as a reflection on the speech impediment of the new King, George VI. It seems absurd to go to such lengths to construct a plausible explanation. After all, the production was progressing very slowly, and Merle's absence would mean further delays in the shooting schedule and possible problems with the time limitations on certain contracts. Why couldn't Merle have been replaced? Looking at the scenes that have survived, we must admit that Merle was not giving a stellar performance as Messalina; yet replacing her would mean having to reshoot scenes with Laughton which had been tough enough to shoot the first time around. Emlyn Williams, who was giving a far better performance and who had probably shot more scenes than Merle, speculated: 'If the film had been going absolutely wonderfully and was going to be the greatest success in the world for everybody concerned with it at that moment, and I had been in that taxi [sic] and gone through the windscreen, even though I had shot all this stuff, I know that they would have replaced me.'[17] But the film wasn't going well, and Korda considered Merle irreplaceable. Alex once declared that 'the only thing worse than a producer falling in love with his leading lady is a producer falling in love with his leading man', and it must be added that by this time Korda was deeply in love with Miss Oberon and would have been extremely reluctant to continue with another actress in the role that he had so especially planned for her. Taking into account Korda's sentiments and the production's past history, it appears that abandoning the film was the most reasonable solution to a difficult problem.

Merle's accident was thought by many to have been a 'godsend',* yet today, as we watch what remains of *I, Claudius* in *The Epic That Never Was*, we share with von Sternberg and some of the actors their regret that events had worked so much against the realisation of the

* So much so that another rumour circulated to the effect that Korda had been the 'chauffeur' of Merle's car and had 'engineered' the accident.

film. When Laughton is at his best, for example in the scene in the Roman Senate when he is explaining the conditions upon which he would consent to become emperor, he brilliantly brings Claudius to life. It would have been, almost without question, his finest screen performance. And for us to be deprived of Emlyn Williams's Caligula is indeed a great shame. To my mind, it is not an overstatement to say that if the film had been completed it would have stood at the top of the list of Korda's cinematic achievements. Abandoned as it was, it instead symbolises that unattainable side of Korda's ambition, an ambition which was never quite able to realise itself.

During a most crucial time in his career Alex Korda had allowed himself to become embroiled in productions which had taken up far more time, energy, and money than should have been the case. *Elephant Boy* did, at least, survive its extraordinary production problems, but two of these projects were destined never to reach the cinema screens at all. As we shall presently see, it was not only in the sphere of production that Korda's ambitious plans were running into difficulties.

1. Adrian Brunel, *Nice Work*, London, Forbes Robertson, 1949, pp. 180–1.
2. Arthur Calder-Marshall, *The Innocent Eye*, London, W. H. Allen, 1963, p. 176.
3. *Ibid*, p. 178.
4. *Ibid*, pp. 180–1.
5. Cf. Editor Helen van Dongen's notes on Flaherty's *Louisiana Story* in Karel Reisz and Gavin Millar, *The Technique of Film Editing*, London, Focal Press, 1968, pp. 135–55.
6. Sir John Clements in an interview with Robert Vas, conducted for Vas's documentary, but not used.
7. *Ibid*.
8. From Bill Duncalf's BBC TV documentary *The Epic That Never Was*, originally shown 24 December 1965.
9. *Ibid*.
10. *Ibid*.
11. Josef von Sternberg, *Fun in a Chinese Laundry*, New York, Macmillan, 1965, p. 172.
12. Doug McClelland, *The Unkindest Cuts*, New Jersey, A. S. Barnes, 1972, pp. 110–11.
13. Josef von Sternberg, *loc cit*.
14. From Bill Duncalf's BBC documentary.
15. *Ibid*.
16. Josef von Sternberg, *op cit*, pp. 183–4.
17. From Bill Duncalf's BBC documentary.

CHAPTER FOURTEEN

# 'The Usual Denham Mouse'

FOR over twenty years Alex Korda was one of the most steadfast defenders of the British cinema. No matter how dire the circumstances appeared to be and despite the personal doubts which he may have felt, Korda refused to promote the alarmist forecasts announced by those he considered 'the worst enemies of British pictures . . . the depression-mongers'. Throughout the film crisis of 1937 he maintained the attitude that the British film industry should not view its problems in isolation, but should rather find encouragement in the healthy state of film industries in other countries, especially in America. Upon his return from Hollywood in June 1937 he remarked:

> I left England with depression over the film industry and found Hollywood on the top of a wave. Never has there been such aggressive spending, salaries have never been bigger; a million dollars is a moderate price for a film and they are getting their money back. In 1930–31 six of the major film companies in Hollywood were in the hands of receivers. Now only one is, and we get criticised because we spend £150,000 on a film.
>
> We have got to stand on our feet, and now it is certain that our productions will be sold in all parts of the world. Every picture will have American distribution.[1]

Although based on an unrealistic economic comparison between two countries whose film markets and industries were of completely different proportions, this type of pep-talk was a much needed antidote

199

to the contagious pessimism which was deflating the British industry. Korda correctly diagnosed that the industry's primary ailment was inadequate world distribution of British films, and his 'certainty' about better world marketing in the future derived from negotiations which had taken place during this Hollywood trip.

Alex had been unhappy for some time with the results of his association with United Artists. He felt that his own films were not promoted enough by United Artists in America and was probably exasperated by the lack of authoritative leadership within the organisation.* For several months stories had circulated about different United Artists members attempting to buy out the other members; according to *Variety*, 'there were rumours that [Korda] wanted to withdraw from his UA affiliation but was reminded his contract as a member owner had eight years to run and that he would be held to it.'[2] In Hollywood, in June, Korda started the ball rolling on an ambitious scheme which would have made Korda one of the most powerful film producers on the international scene. The scheme was simple, but staggering in its implications and its financial requirements. In partnership with the American independent film producer Sam Goldwyn, Korda planned to take over control of United Artists.

Like Korda, Goldwyn was a member owner of United Artists, and together they controlled 40 per cent of the company. The remaining 60 per cent was still held by three of the four founding members—Douglas Fairbanks, Snr, Mary Pickford, and Charles Chaplin. When Korda first approached Goldwyn with the take-over plan, Goldwyn

---

* With regard to the British home market, United Artists had helped secure more dependable exhibition of Korda's films by its acquisition, in 1936, of a 50 per cent interest in Oscar Deutsch's Odeon cinema circuit (for a reported price of £50). Deutsch, whose rapidly expanding circuit was by 1937 the third major exhibiting chain in Britain after Gaumont British and Associated British Picture Corporation, was eager to obtain first-class films for his two hundred and fifty cinema houses, and London Films and UA's other affiliates produced just this type of picture. Although all the UA producers would benefit from having a substantial foothold in a British circuit on which they could rely to give their films a fair showing, Korda obviously stood to gain the most by this direct link with British exhibition. Although Deutsch needed the UA tie more than UA itself did (as the sale price indicates), it is significant that it was United Artists who approached Deutsch, not the other way around. We can, therefore, surmise that Korda and perhaps Murray Silverstone, UA's head executive in Britain, played an important role in encouraging this Deutsch-UA connection which was so advantageous to London Films. In mid-1937 Korda became a member of the board of Odeon Cinema Holdings Ltd, the private company which controlled the whole Odeon organisation.

was apparently not interested. Korda then sounded out David O. Selznick, the independent producer, and the Hollywood director Frank Capra. They were both enthusiastic, but this deal also broke down, for reasons which Frank Capra later explained:

> ... Korda, David O. Selznick, and I formed a partnership to buy United Artists. We had visions of making millions by distributing our own films and those of other independent producers. The deal was all set. But Korda's irresistible charm ran into Selznick's immovable ego on the question of which one should be the new president of United Artists. I sat in the bleachers, while Korda made long impassioned speeches favoring Korda, and Selznick wrote equally impassioned, but longer, letters in favor of Selznick. ... As the oratory waxed, the deal waned—then died for lack of a president.[3]

In June Alex met again with Sam Goldwyn, and a deal was finally worked out to acquire the interests of the other three partners for £400,000 ($2,000,000) each. An undisclosed, but substantial amount of money was paid for the six-month options which Korda and Goldwyn were given. They now had six months to find the £1,200,000 needed to complete the transaction. Alex sailed triumphantly back to Britain and told the press for the first time about his 'practically completed' take-over bid.

Midway through the six-month period of grace the selling members were offered the option of taking their £400,000 in cash or in cash and stock in the company. Chaplin opted for the cash, whereas Fairbanks and Pickford decided to take £250,000 in cash and the remainder in company stock. This, of course, eased the financial burden on Korda and Goldwyn, for they would now only have to come up with £900,000 in cash. It was generally understood that two London financial companies had promised at least part of the money. The Prudential, which had already financed London Films to the tune of £2,000,000 (the figure widely reported at the time), was to provide some of the capital, and the Warburg banking concern, which had investments in Denham Laboratories, was probably the other City source. According to Paul Tabori, Oscar Deutsch headed 'a British group' (Odeon Cinema Holdings?) which was likewise involved in the financial pool. In America two firms had early on shown interest in the take-over, Lehmann Brothers and Kuhn, Loeb, and Company, but whether they actually promised any capital or not is unclear. There were even rumours that Metro-Goldwyn-Mayer's British subsidiary was either helping finance the deal or planning themselves to take over both Denham and London Films. These stories were emphatically denied by Korda in a statement to the press in October. In that same month Alex returned to Hollywood with two-thirds of the needed sum (i.e. £600,000) arranged.

No confirmation of the deal was immediately forthcoming, for now that the money was almost assured, the lawyers on either side wanted to examine closely the terms of the agreement and the various legal problems presented by the transfer of interests. During his stay on the West Coast, Alex kept in touch daily with London, often staying up until four in the morning to place his calls to Denham and listening to the dialogue rushes of films in production there played for him over the phone. Korda and Goldwyn had until the 23rd of December to smooth out the remaining legal difficulties. Two weeks before their option was to run out, however, the plan was abruptly scrapped.

The explanation which Korda prepared for the British public was, out of necessity, a bit vague. In January 1938 he announced that 'owing to the change in world conditions' over the past six months, the United Artists takeover no longer looked like a 'good investment'. 'It would have cost too much to borrow the money,' he admitted to the press.4 Korda had underestimated the enormity of the task of raising so much money during a precarious time in British film financing in general. We don't even know where, if anywhere, Korda had found the last £300,000, but we do know that those already financially committed to the deal were beginning to get cold feet. The London financiers were deeply perturbed by the legal troubles which the transaction was encountering, and, as one journalist revealed, 'It was feared that when the cash payments had been made there would be a shortage of ready money to finance production.'5 The financial difficulties alone were enough to undermine the deal, but there were two other issues equally as disturbing.

Alex was the only United Artists member owner burdened with the overhead of a large studio complex. In order to operate Denham at a profit Alex knew that he could not depend solely on a few 'prestige' productions. He had therefore requested that under the new agreements he should be allowed to produce films for distributors other than United Artists. This would give him the freedom to accept advantageous package production deals with other distribution companies (who might have better exhibition connections than UA), and he would still provide United Artists with several big productions each year. Fairbanks, Pickford, and Chaplin were divided in their opinions as to whether the company should be taken over by a producer who did not produce for United Artists exclusively. Since the company was already in a state of decline, they probably rightly feared that this provision would lead to a further emasculation of the company's position. From all reports it was 'The Iron Butterfly', Miss Pickford, who in the end vetoed this provision and thus made Korda's decision to drop the option more unavoidable.

The third contributing factor was hinted at only once in a newspaper column. The one-line reference stated: 'Government control of the United Artists film industry raised scores of legal snags, which lawyers failed to smooth out.'[6] Even though Sam Goldwyn and Alex Korda were to share the control of United Artists, the money for the take-over came primarily from British sources. Concerned with the politics and economics involved in this arrangement—which would inevitably increase the outflow of dollars to Britain—the United States government apparently opposed the deal by constructing as many legal impasses as possible.

After a midnight conference of the London backers and a quick exchange of telegrams with Hollywood, the project was officially abandoned on the 9th of December. The composition of the company executive and Korda's own status remained unchanged, but Alex did at least receive one small reward: the renegotiation of the existing UA policy with respect to British independent film producers. The new terms promised them distribution of their films at a cheaper cost and a fairer share of the profits. Notwithstanding this concession, Alex's attempt to break down the barriers to British film exploitation in America left him right back where he started.

Glowing reports of his adventure had filled the trade and daily papers for months; and while some viewed the abandonment of the project as a 'stroke of good luck'—'Master Korda . . . is really much better off if he is left to brood about camera angles in the projection rooms at Denham'[7]—others looked at it as another example of Korda's inability to realise his promises. Korda launched a pre-emptive attack on his critics in an article entitled 'What's *Right* with British Films':

I returned from Hollywood and New York the other day with a certain amount of enthusiasm for my job as a film producer, eager to get on with my new programme of pictures. In Hollywood I learnt once again what it means to move about in a place where success is more talked about than failure, where another man's triumph is welcomed by all his colleagues and competitors, where even when things are really bad they have a way of kidding themselves that all is swell.

And on my return I find the whole of the British film business wallowing, I am almost inclined to say, in an orgy of self-pity and depression, just because the infant business has been suffering a few growing pains.

Taking a long view of the situation I am in no mood for unhappiness about the future of British pictures. I know the business, have had my failures as well as my successes, and I am satisfied that British films have made very good progress during the past four or five years of building up a new industry against the most formidable opposition that any new business has ever had to face.[8]

Korda's talent for turning the tables on his critics, for shifting blame on to others, and for evoking confidence and resilience when the opposites were expected, was a quality of special value for a producer whose impulsiveness led so often to public disappointments.

Although much effort had gone into two abandoned film projects and an unsuccessful business transaction, Korda still managed to produce some notable films during this period, the most impressive of which was *Knight Without Armour* (1937). Consciously conceived in terms of the 'international' film, *Knight Without Armour* was, and is, the most satisfying of all the Korda films made to this formula. It had all the prerequisites: a romantic drama set during the Russian Revolution taken from the British writer James Hilton's novel, adapted by the famous Hollywood writer Frances Marion, and scripted by the Biro–Wimperis team; direction by Jacques Feyder, the Belgian responsible for such screen classics as *Thérèse Raquin* (1928) and *La Kermesse héroïque* (1936); set designs by the French art director Lazare Meerson; music composed by Miklos Rozsa; and cinematography by Hollywood cameraman Harry Stradling. Added to this was a stellar cast headed by Robert Donat and Marlene Dietrich. Korda had brought similar teams together before, but the resulting films were never as good as they should have been. How did *Knight* escape a similar fate?

The answer was Korda's choice of director, for Jacques Feyder was one of the cinema's most adaptable and gifted artists, a film-maker who excelled at recreating on film the atmosphere of a distant or unfamiliar historical period. Korda had acknowledged previously Feyder's international talent in his praise of *L'Image* ('the best Hungarian film I have ever seen'), and it was during the making of *L'Image* in Vienna in 1924 that Alex had first met Feyder. Korda obviously considered it a major coup to have convinced Feyder to work at Denham, but it is interesting to note that during the production Feyder himself struck a blow for the 'national' British film in a tirade against the sort of film that he was directing and Korda was continually promoting. It concluded: 'In short, English films about England made by English people. That is the ideal. No more foreign styles, no more foreign technicians, no more foreign film-craftsmen, no more foreign film directors . . . That means me. . . .'[9]

Both Korda and Feyder were directors preoccupied with cinematic detail, but whereas Korda's obsession went only as far as the superficial details of set and costume, Feyder's concern went much deeper into the subject's total atmosphere, into both character appearance and behaviour, and into mood re-creation. It was the money Korda spent on unnecessary details which later prompted John Clements to remark:

> I think Alex was a man who wanted the best and was not content with anything but the best. The fact that it wasn't necessary to have the best—that a background tapestry didn't have to come from the British Museum because it was out of focus anyway— would never enter Alex's mind; it had to be the best. In the same way in the theatre the nearest approach to him . . . was C. B. Cochran,* and there never has been anybody to compare with those two; and they both had really the same approach. Money was no object; it never entered their minds.[10]

Alex could not keep a tight rein on the budget of *Knight Without Armour*, and in the end the film cost close to £350,000, which excludes, we must suppose, the remainder of the salary which Alex was unable to pay Miss Dietrich. As had happened before, its prohibitive cost deprived the film of any chance to earn a profit. In critical terms, the film was far more successful.

* Sir Charles Blake Cochran (1872–1951) was a theatrical manager who promoted lavish, large-scale productions in the West End theatres and around whose life and work a recent stage musical, *Cockie*, was mounted.

The film should, of course, be judged a critical success more in relation to Korda's film-producing record than to Feyder's. It was received more warmly by English critics and audiences than by the Continental film-going establishment who compared it unfavourably with Feyder's earlier films. The picture was one of the lesser works of a talented film-maker—as both *The Ghost Goes West* and *Elephant Boy* had been—but it did represent one of the most consistently engrossing and entertaining films which came out of Denham, perhaps the only one that unquestionably rivalled the Hollywood product. It had in its favour an exciting and irresistible plot. Rather than face deportation for having translated some supposedly seditious Russian books, British translator Ainsley Fothergill (Robert Donat) accepts an offer to join the British Secret Service operating in Russia. Disguised as a Russian revolutionary, he is caught by the Czarist authorities, and sent to a Siberian camp from which he is liberated upon the Revolution. As a 'People's Commissar' he is entrusted with taking Countess Vladinoff (Marlene Dietrich) to Petrograd. Instead, he helps her escape (several times) from her enemies, and together they flee in disguise across Russia amidst the turmoil of the post-Revolutionary period. There is, naturally, a suitably climactic and happy ending (not to be found in the original novel).

Despite a slow opening, the script is tight, and the dialogue avoids the banalities we have come to expect from Messieurs Biro and Wimperis. Robert Donat plays with extraordinary subtlety a role steeped in ambivalence, frustration, and determination. In a large sense he makes up for Miss Dietrich's somnambulistic performance. Feyder's major achievement is to capture the total confusion of the time—the struggle of the Red and White Armies, villages conquered, lost, and reconquered by the two opposing factions, masses of refugees fleeing down dirt roads and stopping crowded trains on which they hope to ride to safety—without overwhelming the intimate central relationship which develops between the escaping couple. He accomplishes this in part by a careful balance between the film's quiet moments and its violent scenes. For example, the couple's pause in a deserted railway station where they begin to unwind by quoting poetry to each other turns suddenly to violence as the two are forced to protect themselves from two officers who have discovered them. There is, too, the pair's idyllic respite in the forest. While necessary for the development of the romance, this sequence also provides welcome audience relief from the emotional tension created by their constant flight. Finally, the dramatic scene as the two bluff their way through an identity check is followed by a fairly peaceful train ride shared with the officer (John Clements at his scene-stealing best) who has knowingly abetted their escape. This episode then closes with the officer's suicide, a desperate action staged to allow the couple to continue their flight to freedom. The critic Graham Greene, normally scathing in his reviews of Korda's films, highly praised Feyder's film, and his comments explain how the director technically achieved his successful blend of story and background:

> No Denham stamp has obliterated [Feyder's] private signature— the very rare use of long shots—long shots used like close-ups to punch an effect home, not as by most directors to get through the duller parts of a narrative. To me the most aesthetically satisfying of all cinematic shots is—in rough script terms—the medium close shot, and this is the distance at which Feyder remains consistently from his characters: close enough for intimacy and far enough for art.[11]

All in all Alex had much reason to be proud of the picture and of the degree of independence which he had at last been able to give a film-maker of such individualistic talent. *Knight Without Armour* remains a prime example of the type of picture which Korda wanted to promote in Britain; yet its financial failure must surely have caused even Korda to doubt the economic viability of his 'international' policy. In the ensuing years Alex did modify his production programme, but by that late date neither minor nor major economies could save the situation.

Although not released until September 1937, *Knight* was actually a hold-over from Denham's extravagant, pre-crisis days. The films shot after January 1937 were on the whole much less expensive, though not necessarily less ambitious, than their predecessors. Four of the more interesting of these films were produced by Victor Saville, the independent producer who had joined London Films in March 1936 and who had already established his reputation as one of the two (the other was Alfred Hitchcock) most polished and professional of Britain's film directors. He had worked for many years at Gaumont British and had demonstrated his Hollywood-like expertise with musicals like *The Good Companions* (1932), *Evergreen* (1934), *First a Girl* (1935), and *It's Love Again* (1936), all starring the vivacious British actress, singer, and dancer, Jessie Matthews. Saville enjoyed a rather unique position at

Denham as the only British producer working on his own in the midst of a foreign enclave. He had little difficulty in asserting his independence in the otherwise Korda-dominated environment of the studio and in two years produced four quite substantial, moderately budgeted films: *Dark Journey* (1937), *Storm in a Teacup* (1937), *Action for Slander* (1937), and *South Riding* (1938).

Saville personally directed two of these pictures, the first and the last. *Storm in a Teacup* was co-directed by Saville and Ian Dalrymple, who also collaborated on the scripts for three of the films, and the American director Tim Whelan was responsible for *Action for Slander*. Most of the technicians and players came from the London Films staff and stable, but *Dark Journey* was the only film of the group which bore the 'Denham stamp', a term here meant in the same derogatory sense that Graham Greene had implied in the above-quoted review. Lajos Biro and Arthur Wimperis had tailor-made this improbable and naïve tale of French and German espionage and counter-espionage for Conrad Veidt, the intelligent German actor who had just signed a contract with Korda and for whom Alex had difficulty in finding suitable and acceptable roles. (He was typecast here, as in the later *The Spy in Black* (1939), as the German spy for whom duty always, or almost always, comes first.) Luckily Victor Saville was able to follow this film with three strictly of his own choosing.

These three films represented the 'English films about England made by English people' of which Feyder had spoken. They were all critically praised for 'digging down' into just those 'British roots' which Korda had always avoided as box-office poison. Writing about the provincial romantic comedy *Storm in a Teacup*, which starred Vivien Leigh and Rex Harrison, Basil Wright was prepared to call it 'the first British comedy from an English studio . . . a film which is, perhaps for the first time, genuinely British'.[12] The second film dealt with the hypocrisies in the British concept of 'honour', an honour preached about but not practised by English officers and aristocrats. Its slim, downbeat story—the ostracism of a British officer and gentleman who is persuaded to refrain from defending himself from an accusation of card cheating, of which he is innocent—succeeds because of the convincing milieu and the fine acting of Clive Brook and a host of solid British character actors. *South Riding* was, however, the most ambitious of the lot, for the problems of English rural education and housing and the corruption of local government were subjects seldom treated, even lightly, in fiction films. The picture is thoroughly entertaining, which, under the circumstances, is a major accomplishment. The casting was superb, and the underplayed acting, a trait of all three films, gave the film a naturalness which Korda himself never really achieved. In fact, the simplicity and lack of pretension of Saville's Denham films show up the majority of Korda's own films for what they often are—vulgar and overblown attempts to make up for an emptiness of plot or idea or a shallowness of human characterisation by an emphasis on superficial production values. One is tempted to discuss these excellent films in more detail, but their very un-Korda-like nature and the minimal role which Korda played in their creation make them more appropriately the subject of another work, a long overdue re-appraisal of the career of Victor Saville.

We need only compare these films with contemporary Korda products to understand Alex's occasional lack of discrimination in his choice of film subjects. Two works in particular, *The Divorce of Lady X* (1938) and *Over the Moon* (1940), are relevant to this discussion, for why Korda picked these two projects over others certainly more worthy remains somewhat a mystery. Both were vehicles for Merle Oberon, but even that seems an inadequate excuse.

*Counsel's Opinion* had been an unimpressive quota quickie directed by Allan Dwan for Korda five years earlier. A better cast, a new title, Technicolor photography, and an appreciably larger budget (£99,000) did nothing to improve the material when it was remade as *The Divorce of Lady X*. A general rule of film production states that film remakes are never as successful as the original from which they are taken. This has, of course, never stopped film companies from making them anyway. Even so, most remakes are produced because the first film was itself a success and because the film-makers hope to capture the older, 'pre-sold' audience as well as the younger generation not familiar with the original. To plan a remake of an unsuccessful and inferior quota film appears an almost lunatic proposition. But Korda was apparently convinced that the subject warranted another version.

He assigned Tim Whelan to direct the picture and Ian Dalrymple to write the script (with Biro and Wimperis), probably in the hope that they would bring some life to the material as they had for Saville's *Action for Slander*, which vaguely dealt with the same British milieu. Adapted from a play, the film centres around a farcical situation: a young divorce lawyer finds himself prosecuting a case in which he himself is the supposed co-respondent. Merle Oberon was able to show off her talent for comedy, and Laurence Olivier, Binnie Barnes (who had played Miss Oberon's role in the earlier version), and Ralph Richardson support her admirably. None the less, we still come away wondering why it was all necessary.

*Over the Moon* suffered from an inconsequential plot: romanticising young woman inherits £18,000,000, squanders much of her money fulfilling her youthful fantasies, but is saved from this meaningless existence by the doctor who loves her. Similarly frivolous stories have been turned into films, but there appears to have been little justification for Korda's having planned this as a Technicolor extravaganza. (It must be remembered that a colour film was an expensive undertaking at the time.) The film was shot over the winter of 1937–8, but its release was delayed until February 1940. Korda obviously realised that he had a stinker on his hands and accordingly buried it in the Denham vaults where for two years it remained a financial asset. *Over the Moon* was co-directed by William K. Howard, the once 'promising' American director who had first come to London for *Fire Over England*. Howard also directed a modest but effective crime picture, *The Squeaker*, for Korda in 1937, but neither this film nor *Over the Moon* gave him much chance to demonstrate or to develop his talent. His long-time associate, cameraman James Wong Howe, later pointed out that Howard's career was being ruined by alcoholism. Utter frustration with his London Films contract, with the inferior films he was being assigned to, probably did nothing to alleviate his problems.

Although London Films had doubled its production output in 1937, the emphasis on quantity rather than quality had put enormous strains on Korda's resources as a producer. The Victor Saville connection had been an admirable solution to the need for an increased output, but other films, those produced by Korda or by Continental producers, represented, more than anything else, a grand waste of talent on second-rate projects. It was beginning to look as if, under the pressure of making 'bread-and-butter' features, the 'old Alexander Korda' would succumb after all. During Alex's last year as production chief of Denham Studios, the old Korda flair surfaced only twice more, in *The Drum* (1938) and *The Four Feathers* (1939).

The Korda stamp was imprinted on these two pictures principally because all three Kordas worked on them: Alex producing, Zoltan directing, and Vincent designing the sets. The three did not collaborate all that frequently, but when they did it was almost a foregone conclusion that a film about the British Empire would be the result.

*Sanders of the River* had emerged from their combined efforts in 1935, and the trio had, for better or worse, contributed to Robert Flaherty's vision of India two years later. The reasons why they chose Empire pictures have already been discussed—Alex's jingoism and his desire to open up a new film market, Zoltan's love of exotic adventure stories and of native populations. Like many ex-colonial officials, Alex never really gave up the British Empire nor his romantic and patriotic notion of the 'British' way of handling a situation.*

Whenever the brothers did work together professionally, they brought with them to the studio their healthy, if at times hypertensive, familial relationships. No one could call the Kordas a family of brooders. When things went wrong, when the inevitable disagreements appeared, volatile outbursts and enthusiastic reconciliations were sure to result. All three spoke English idiosyncratically, and their language was well peppered with appropriate or inappropriate expletives. (It was Zoltan, so the story goes, who angrily replied to a critic: 'You think I know fuck nothing about pictures! I tell you I know fuck all!') Most of their arguments, unfortunately for us, were conducted in Hungarian, so that those who witnessed them had no idea what all the fuss was about. Zoltan's son David remembers how, when he was growing up in California, he used to hear his father vociferously arguing in rapid-fire Hungarian with Alex, who was at the time six thousand miles away on the other end of the telephone. Although the content of these encounters we can only guess at, the form of their clashes does not have to be left to our imagination.

'I remember one day being in [Alex's office],' John Clements later reminisced, 'and we were talking about something or other when suddenly his two brothers, Zoltan and Vincent, came in screaming at each other and at Alex in Hungarian. Well, Alex took up the scream in Hungarian and Zolly started picking things up off the table and throwing them on the floor, and I really thought they were going to kill each other. I was sitting there in

---

* In the fifties Zoltan wanted to make a film from Pierre Boulle's novel *The Bridge on the River Kwai;* and although Alex did buy the rights, he refused in the end to allow Zolly to direct this picture. The idea of British prisoners of war actually aiding their enemies, regardless of the reasons, struck Alex as being definitely 'anti-British'. Alex then sold the rights to Sam Spiegel, retaining 10 per cent interest in the film which Spiegel was going to make with David Lean. Alex needed ready cash at one point and sold off his percentage for 'something like £10,000', thus proving that even Alex wasn't always the best businessman.

the middle of it, not knowing what they were talking about and suddenly, as suddenly as it started, it stopped and everybody embraced everybody, including me, and we all had a nice cup of tea and that was the end of that. . . .'[13]

The Kordas threw themselves whole-heartedly into their disagreements and their peace-making and obviously enjoyed themselves immensely in the process. This was the energetic, often maddening atmosphere in which the Empire films were created.

*The Drum* and *The Four Feathers* have more in common with each other than the Korda family collaboration. Both were action-packed stories taken from works by A. E. W. Mason, and they were photographed, in glorious Technicolor, by the well-established team of Georges Périnal, Osmond Borradaile (who did most of the exterior shooting), and Robert Krasker. Lajos Biro and Arthur Wimperis had a hand in both scripts, and in the capacities of editor and production assistant were two men, Henry Cornelius and André de Toth, who would later become film directors in their own right. Though very similar in their production teams, and thus in the resulting visual polish, the films are quite different and cannot really be considered companion pieces.

*The Drum* is an Eastern 'Western' of intrigue and ambush set in the then present-day North-West Frontier of India. The 'baddie' is the usurper Prince Ghul (Raymond Massey) who plans to secure his own rise to power and an all-out war with the British by the audacious act of massacring Captain Carruthers (Roger Livesey) and his regiment during their 'friendly' visit to the Prince's capital of Tokot. The situation is saved by the rightful ruler of Tokot, the 'goodie' on white charger, Prince Azim (Sabu). The film says much less about the Empire and Empire-building than the other Cinema of Empire pictures, for the action elements and spectacular visual effects dominate the picture leaving little room for polemics of any sort. The need for self-sacrifice among British 'keepers of the peace' provides the film's only message.

Having learned his lesson with *Elephant Boy*, Korda did not send the film company out to India for location shooting this time. Instead the exteriors were shot in the hills outside Harlech in Wales. This was an economical and convincing substitution which won the praise of many in the industry who were glad to see Korda using the resources closer to home. Solid performances by Roger Livesey and Valerie Hobson and the touching relationship which develops between Prince Azim and the young British drummer boy (Desmond Tester) helped to make the film a success. Sabu's world-wide popularity (after *The Drum* Sabu received, according to Korda, one hundred letters a day from his fans) and some of the best colour photography to date must, however, receive most of the credit for the film's profitable record. There is no doubt that Zoltan Korda had a gift for spectacle, a talent for getting audiences totally wrapped up in action sequences. Better dialogue would surely have enlivened the interior scenes where Zoltan was less assured as a director.

Although there was even more action in *The Four Feathers*, there was also more substance to the script, which was written by R. C. Sherriff. A. E. W. Mason's novel had been filmed at least three times before (in 1915, 1921, and 1929), and it was remade by Zoltan Korda and Terence Young in 1955. But the 1939 Korda version is without doubt the most famous of the group. Given the plot, it is no surprise that film-makers were so often attracted to the subject.

Young Harry Faversham (John Clements) comes from a family of military officers and heroes. Believing that he has no obligation to carry on the family tradition in a military career which he honestly feels himself unsuited to, Harry resigns his commission, whereupon he receives from three of his former comrades three white feathers, the symbols of cowardice. The fourth feather of the title is figuratively given to him by his fiancée Ethne (June Duprez) who also disapproves of Harry's decision. After his regiment leaves for the Sudan to fight the 'Fuzzie-Wuzzies' and 'Dervishes' alongside Kitchener, Harry realises his resignation had derived from cowardice, not from principles, and disguised as a Singali native he goes to Africa to earn the right to return the three feathers by saving the lives of his three fellow officers. By ingenious means Harry achieves his aim and proves his bravery beyond question. Back in England he reclaims both Ethne and his rightful place in the Faversham family.

Never in a Korda film had colour photography and location shooting been used to such good effect. Most of the exteriors were filmed in the Sudan (with a cast of thousands, or so it seemed), and the most stunning images were created there: scores of natives pulling small sailing ships along the Nile, the battle and final massacre of Captain Durrance's (Ralph Richardson) patrol, the journey through the desert with Harry leading the now-blind Durrance to safety through the parched landscape with ominous vultures hovering overhead, the natives amassing their forces, the soldiers drilling, the final victory at Omdurman. For authenticity and visual splendour these scenes have seldom been surpassed, and it is small wonder that location footage from *The Four Feathers* can be found in films made twenty years later, including *Zarak* (1956), *Master of the World* (1961), and *East of Sudan* (1964), as well as Zoltan's own remake *Storm Over the Nile* (1955).

Military officers were enlisted to advise on all details which would give a credible atmosphere to the picture. The 'soldiers' were taught to drill the same way soldiers would have in the late 1800s—the years in which the film is set—but the advisers' suggestions were not limited to the action sequences. Alex wanted accuracy, though not at the cost of the spectacle itself.

> '. . . there was a sequence,' John Clements remembers, 'where Aubrey Smith . . . gives a ball to the soldiers of his regiment . . . in his private house. And, of course, the military advisers were called in to have every detail of dress exactly correct. Ralph Richardson and I went to one of the most expensive Savile Row tailors in England for our uniforms. . . . Finally, the scene was called and we went down on to the set, and Alex Korda came on to the set and stopped dead, and said, "What is this?" We said, "This is the ball sequence." He said, "But what is this blue uniform?" And the military colonel, or whatever he was, said, "But that's correct. This is in a private house, not in the mess." "But this is Technicolor!!" he said, and the whole thing was changed and we were all dressed in red uniforms.'[14]

The country homes of the retired generals Faversham (Allan Jeayes) and Burroughs (C. Aubrey Smith) and Harry's London flat, with the rooftops of a London shrouded in smoke and fog visible outside the windows—these interiors provided a period flavour and atmosphere within which the actors were not just part of the decor. Moreover, the camera movement and visual technique, from the opening sequence onwards, were much more dynamic and imaginative than had been the case with other Korda spectacles.

The film is particularly engaging for the humour and satire which Sherriff was able to inject into the story: retired officers recounting in great detail and with much relish the horrific, but heroic deaths of former comrades, or General Burroughs's unsolicited and not quite truthful recreation of a Crimean battle with available apples, nuts, and a pineapple (the General himself) to represent the troops who were only separated by a 'thin red line' of wine. The acting performances and the script do justice to each other, making *The Four Feathers* along with

*Knight Without Armour* the two finest achievements of Korda's last years at Denham.

Irving Asher was an American producer who had earned a reputation as 'King of the Quota Quickies' at Warner Brothers' British studios at Teddington. He was just the man to whom Alex could delegate the more tiresome and uninteresting job of producing inexpensive Denham pictures, and on the 30th of May 1938 Asher joined the production staff at the studio. His first task was to produce the second of two English adaptations of foreign films, the formula which Korda always resorted to when he needed cheap films fast. As it turned out, neither film was as cheap or as quickly made as Korda would have liked, and the production histories of both films are quite amazing.

The first of these was *The Rebel Son* (1939). The story behind its making is quite complicated, but Adrian Brunel, who directed part of the picture, unravelled some of the mystery in his autobiography *Nice Work*. Apparently Alex had arranged a co-production deal with the French-based producer–director Alexis Granowsky for a film about Tarass Boulba at about the same time (1935) that *Moscow Nights*, another Granowsky–Korda co-production, was being made. The Boulba film was shot in Paris and Hungary in both English and French with Harry Baur, Roger Livesey, Anthony Bushell, and Joan Gardner in the leading roles. The writer Jeffrey Dell was sent along with the unit, ostensibly as dialogue director, but primarily as Korda's 'liaison'.

According to Adrian Brunel the resulting material was 'a boisterous cowboy horse-opera in a vague period setting' and was considered so bad by all involved that both versions were shelved before they were actually completed. On his own initiative, however, Granowsky resurrected the film, shot more footage, and with some success released the French version as *Tarass Boulba* in 1936. Impressed by Granowsky's salvage measures, Korda tried to do the same thing with the footage which was lying in his vaults. Brunel was given the task of re-writing the story, and he then 're-shot about two-thirds of the film in twelve days for £12,000'.[15] Although Brunel admitted that there was 'some satisfaction in trying to rescue a costly, wasted effort', this kind of satisfaction could not be shared by the public nor by the critics, who panned the film and chastised Korda for having wasted even more money on an unworthy project.

*Prison Without Bars* (1938) was Irving Asher's first Denham assignment. It derived from the 1933 French film *Prison sans barreaux* directed by Léonide Moguy which Alex had imported and promptly shelved. According to the British director Brian Desmond Hurst, the Continental producers Arnold Pressburger and Josef Somlo began the English adaptation of this film about a girl's reformatory with a director whom everyone now discreetly refuses to name. Unhappy with the director's conception of the film, the producers asked Desmond Hurst to look at the rushes with the hope that he would take over the project. As Desmond Hurst told me, these first rushes did make the women's prison 'look more like a finishing school than a reformatory'.[16] The director ran the original French version twice and then embarked on his own salvage operation. (It may have been at this point that Asher became associated with the production; Josef Somlo is not mentioned in the film credits.) Desmond Hurst was pressed to complete the film in all haste by everyone except Alex, who characteristically told him to 'take two extra weeks; just make a good film'. Like *The Rebel Son*, the film was criticised by the English reviewers who were probably tired of Alex's foreign adaptations. Nevertheless, *Prison Without Bars* had some success in America where it was assisted by the large coverage it received in *Look* magazine as the first of their traditional 'Movie of the Week' selections.

During his bid for co-ownership of United Artists in 1937, Alex had fought his partners for the right to produce films for other companies. Now, a year later, he signed his first 'outside' contract with another American company, Columbia Pictures. Irving Asher became directly responsible for these productions, the first of which was Q *Planes* (1939). The film was based on a news item which Alex had spotted as likely material for a screen story. Korda was usually quite wary of original film screenplays; they brought with them no prior publicity, no pre-sold audience, as did adaptations of popular plays or novels. But he could appreciate a well-conceived and constructed script, no matter the source, and Ian Dalrymple provided just that for the competent Q *Planes* picture which Tim Whelan directed. The other Columbia features, *The Spy in Black* (1939) and *Twenty-One Days* (1940), came from more traditional sources and were scripted by two men who were to make a mark in British films, Emeric Pressburger and Graham Greene. By introducing the Hungarian writer Pressburger to the British director Michael Powell for *The Spy*, Korda also helped to forge a film-making partnership which provided Britain with some of its best and most creative films over the next two decades.

'Alex Korda used to say that I was the greatest technician he ever knew in his film career,' Michael Powell has remarked. 'He was no technician, but he appreciated technical ability in others, and he gave me a job when nobody else would and when he didn't even know where his next million was coming from.' [17] In 1937 Powell was on the verge of abandoning the British film world for Hollywood, where his individualistic talent might be better appreciated; but his agent, Chris Mann, sent Korda a copy of Powell's latest film, *The Edge of the World* (1937), and, convinced of Powell's ability, Alex offered him a one-year contract. After some months of inactivity it was decided that Powell should direct *Burmese Silver*, a film written by Alex's close friend, the diplomat and statesman Sir Robert Vansittart. The director travelled to Burma for location reconnaissance, but upon his return he found that the project had been cancelled, presumably because of the unsettled international political situation. Powell was immediately assigned to the Asher–Columbia picture, *The Spy in Black*.

Asher and writer Roland Pertwee had already begun work on the film, an adaptation of J. Storer Clouston's novel about German spies and Scapa Flow during the First World War. Over-riding Asher's objections, Alex allowed Powell to visit the Orkney Islands in order to shoot some background footage. Asher was displeased with the footage; Alex and Powell were displeased with the script. The stalemate was resolved by the appearance of Emeric Pressburger.* Alex had given him a copy of the novel on the chance that he could come up with a better script, one which would, in particular, create a starring role for Conrad Veidt, whom Alex still had under contract. To the delight of Korda and Powell, Pressburger's script was extremely inventive, 'a real piece of conjuring' in which both the characters and the plotline were completely re-fashioned. In a recent discussion of the script Michael Powell offered this insight into the Hungarian mind, which, though prompted by his close association with Pressburger, could easily be applied to Alex Korda:

> The script was typically Emeric. Well you know it's the way the Hungarians see the world. They always see the world inside out. All their jokes are reverse jokes. They deal in paradoxes, that's why Chesterton is to them a revered writer. The man who is able to write, you know, brilliantly paradox after paradox—which Chesterton can do. It's very much in the Hungarian line of thought. [18]

* Pressburger was a story writer at the German Ufa company between 1930 and 1933. After Hitler's rise he went to Paris, and then to England in 1935.

The shooting script was written as the film progressed, and the result was an effective and atmospheric spy thriller. The film's box-office success, both in Britain and in America (where it was retitled *U-Boat 29*), owed much to the timeliness of its release in the opening months of the Second World War.

Towards the end of 1938 production at Denham was being maintained more by outside renters, especially MGM-British, than by London Films. Korda needed another film to fulfil his obligation to Columbia, but there wasn't a film completed or in preparation which would be appropriate. Alex arrived at an ingenious solution: to unload on Columbia one of the 'assets' lying in his vaults.

Part of the story behind *Twenty-One Days* has already been told. To recapitulate: Graham Greene had adapted John Galsworthy's story *The First and the Last*, and Basil Dean, the British stage and film director, had directed it at Denham in 1937 with Vivien Leigh, Laurence Olivier, and Leslie Banks. As Dean later admitted, Korda's main intention in producing the film was to give Vivien Leigh a 'star'-building role. The two 'lovers' of the film, Leigh and Olivier, had just fallen in love themselves, and no one, it seems, took the film very seriously. According to Graham Greene, who rather bravely reviewed the film himself, that was the only way one could approach the project.

> 'Galsworthy's story,' Greene wrote in *The Spectator*, 'was peculiarly unsuited for film adaptation, as its whole point lay in a double suicide (forbidden by the censor), a burned confession, and an innocent man's conviction for murder (forbidden by the great public). For the rather dubious merits of the original the adaptors have substituted incredible coincidences and banal situations. Slow, wordy, unbearably sentimental, the picture reels awkwardly towards the only suicide the censorship allowed—and that, I find with some astonishment, has been cut out. I wish I could tell the extraordinary story that lies behind this shelved and resurrected picture, a story involving a theme-song, and a bottle of whiskey, and camels in Wales. . . . Meanwhile, let one guilty man, at any rate, stand in the dock, swearing never, never to do it again. . . .'[19]

Korda had interfered constantly during the film's production. He rearranged shooting schedules at the last moment so that Leigh and Olivier could go to Denmark for a week to play in *Hamlet* together. He added a sequence, which he personally directed, in order to 'inject a more Continental atmosphere', and he changed the title to *Twenty-*

*One Days* from its original working title of *The First and the Last*. Basil Dean was never to see either the rough-cut or the finished product. In 1939 the film was finally sold to Columbia who held on to it for another year, hoping perhaps that audiences might be drawn to see it by the success its two stars had since achieved as Heathcliff in *Wuthering Heights* (1939) and Scarlett O'Hara in *Gone With the Wind* (1939).

When film people reminisce about the days of Korda's reign at Denham Studios we get the feeling that it symbolised for many of them a modern-day Camelot. An idealistic and optimistic climate had prevailed over the studio; those who worked there believed that they were part of a film-making élite producing outstanding pictures which would prove to everyone that Hollywood wasn't the only film capital of the world. Foreign stars, directors, cameramen, editors, designers, and composers had been attracted to Denham, and much home-grown talent had been discovered and nurtured there as well. Despite the enormous pool of talent at Denham, all too often the results were, to use Graham Greene's favourite epithet, 'the usual Denham mouse'. Yet several memorable films had been produced, and both the atmosphere and the films had been created or presided over by one ambitious and flamboyant man, Alexander Korda.

In viewing the history of the British film industry, what is particularly striking about the deep impression left on it by Korda's Denham is that the studio only operated for two and a half years under Alex's guidance. Whatever influence it had was created in that short span of time. By 1938 the Prudential, which had been gradually decreasing its commitment to Korda for over a year, could no longer support London Films. Korda had tried to trim the costs of his production programme, but the company's liabilities now amounted to over one million pounds. Korda's less expensive films had not been money-winners; neither, on the whole, were his costlier spectacles. Alex's commitment to Technicolor productions had pushed up the cost of films, and his own discrimination as to which films should be produced in colour was not always sound. The salesman supreme, Korda was no longer able to sell the Pru on promises and planned projects. They simply weren't sufficient collateral any more.

Late in 1938 the final blow fell. The Prudential decided that Denham Studios, as London Films' primary asset, should be taken out of Korda's hands. An arrangement was made by Korda's old associate Richard Norton which resulted in the amalgamation of Denham Studios and

Pinewood Studios (the near-by complex established in 1936 by J. Arthur Rank, the 'flour millionaire' about whom more will be said later). Although Korda had been involved in the negotiations, it is hardly likely he was in much of a position to affect the decisions one way or another. By the first of the year the deal was completed.

Alex considered the loss of Denham his greatest professional failure. A. W. Watkins relates this story:

> When Korda lost Denham, this was, of course, his greatest defeat. It had been his greatest production and also his greatest flop. I happened to go over to his office in the Old House, and he was sitting there a very dejected person, and he said to me, 'Look at what's happened. All I have left are a few shares which are practically worthless and some old films which are equally worthless,' and to me that was a very sad occasion indeed. I have never known a person of his great intellect so utterly downcast.[20]

Alex had tried to do too much, and he had tried to do it alone. Early in 1939 he was asked why he had attempted a task which was 'beyond the physical and mental strength of any man'. He replied:

> It was a task which had to be undertaken. When London Film Productions was born, British pictures were handicapped by the lack of well-equipped studios. If we were to challenge Hollywood, we had to have perfect technical equipment and a staff which could carry out the work efficiently.
>
> I took over the responsibility of carrying out that programme, and I think it has been achieved. Denham can rank with any studio in Hollywood, and it is manned by a fine staff.[21]

But now this well-equipped and staffed studio would have to operate without Korda controlling every move from his office in the Old House. The loss of Denham was a tremendous personal defeat, and Alex would have been even more despondent if he had known then that as a functioning studio Denham was not to survive past 1952. The studio had fed off the Korda charm and magic, and when Korda left, in a sense, he took the studio with him.

Twice in his life Alex Korda had been deprived of film studios which he had painstakingly constructed and for which he had great and ambitious plans. Now, in early 1939, he again had to call upon his inner reserves of optimism and self-confidence in order to continue his film-making career. The public was hardly aware of how 'downcast' Korda was by the loss of Denham, for he retrieved the situation quickly and gracefully. With his 'few worthless shares and equally worthless films', Korda carried on into another, and in many ways even more glamorous phase of his career.

1. Press cutting dated 14 June 1937, Alexander Korda microfiche, BFI Information Department.
2. *Variety*, June 1937, Alexander Korda microfiche, BFI Information Department.
3. Frank Capra, *The Name Above the Title: an autobiography*, New York, Macmillan, 1971, p. 215.
4. Alexander Korda, 'What's *Right* with British Films', *The Evening News*, 25 January 1938.
5. Press cutting dated 10 December 1937, Alexander Korda microfiche, BFI Information Department.
6. *Ibid.*
7. Press cutting dated 12 December 1937, Alexander Korda microfiche, BFI Information Department.
8. Alexander Korda, 'What's *Right* with British Films', *loc cit*.
9. Interview with Jacques Feyder, *World Film News*, March 1937.
10. Sir John Clements in an interview with Robert Vas, conducted for Vas's documentary, but not used.
11. Graham Greene, *Night and Day*, 30 September 1937.
12. Basil Wright, *The Spectator*, 18 June 1937.
13. Sir John Clements in an interview with Robert Vas, conducted for Vas's documentary, but not used.
14. *Ibid.*
15. Adrian Brunel, *op cit*, p. 182.
16. Interview with Brian Desmond Hurst conducted by the author, 8 August 1973.
17. From a speech given by Michael Powell at the Cinema City Exhibition at The Roundhouse, London, 30 September 1970.
18. Kevin Gough-Yates, *loc cit*.
19. Graham Greene, *The Spectator*, 12 January 1940.
20. From Robert Vas's BBC documentary.
21. R. Ewart Williams, 'Korda Begins a New Career', press cutting, Alexander Korda microfiche, BFI Information Department.

CHAPTER FIFTEEN

# The Old Korda Flair

THE ousting of Alex Korda as executive in charge of Denham Studios led to a wave of speculation in the industry and the press as to Korda's future plans. Eager journalists and wire services issued fantastic reports regarding the 'Alex Korda Mystery': Korda to make films in Hollywood, Korda to abandon the British film industry, Korda to give up film-making altogether. Most of these stories were promptly and categorically denied by the London Films head office. Towards the end of 1938 Alex clarified his position in an interview conducted at Denham:

> The rumours usually are that I'm a millionaire and am retiring from film production on my profits or that I'm broke and therefore have to leave it. Neither is true.
>
> What has happened is that I have given up the administration of Denham Studios. In future I shall be responsible only for the production of films and I shan't have to direct the routine affairs of the studios themselves.
>
> . . . I am glad that I can go back to production. I can go back, too, under better conditions. When you are saddled with the responsibilities of a studio, sometimes plans have to be made which are a handicap to the interests of a picture. To prevent studio space and technicians from standing idle, for example, a film may have to go into production a week or so before it is ready. Probably the result is that it lacks the little touches which make the difference between a good and an average film.

That will not be necessary in the future. I shall be able to make all my preparations *before* the picture goes on to the studio floor. I shall be able to wait until I get the right actor for a certain role.[1]

He went on to confirm that he would be producing four colour pictures, including the almost completed *Four Feathers*, over the next year at Denham, where he was now a tenant producer rather than the landlord. Alex's professed commitment to the British cinema temporarily scotched some of the wilder stories in circulation, but after Korda's quick trip to Hollywood in January 1939 rumours of his intended departure from Britain resurfaced. These rumours, partially based on Korda's own announcement that at least 'part' of his future production programme would be filmed in Hollywood, popped up again and again over the next twelve months.

In his face-saving assessment of the situation Alex had overstated the problems in running Denham which in practice he had never allowed to become real handicaps, but he was right to assure the public of the improvements in Korda productions which the re-organisation of Denham made possible. The changes at the studio, after all, meant little to a public only concerned with the final product. The London Films stable of players and artists remained intact, and the studio's facilities were still at Alex's disposal. The quality of his future films, therefore, would not be adversely affected by the changeover in the administrative hierarchy. Korda's statement does reveal his sense of relief at giving up the executive's burdens. 'He was always striving after something,' Muir Mathieson told me. 'The impression you got all the time was that he was striving always not to be second-rate.'[2] Denham, as much a Moloch and a battleground as a film-making Disneyland, had forced Alex at times to produce second-rate films. Now he would not have to accept any project that was not first-class. Confronted with a deep feeling of personal failure over the loss of Denham, Korda must have found some consolation in this recovery of production freedom.

The 'old Alexander Korda', the flamboyant artist, had survived the traumas of the film crisis of the late thirties; it was rather the 'new' Korda, the streamlined businessman, who had succumbed. At first even Korda's financial position did not seem too critical. He remained in his capacity as chairman and managing director of London Films, and he still had a controlling interest in Denham Laboratories and his United Artists partnership, both valuable commodities. In addition, Korda formed a new company, Alexander Korda Productions, in March 1939.

With a share and loan capital of £530,000, this company became specifically responsible for the films which Alex planned to produce at Denham. In that same month Korda started work on the first of these big productions, *The Thief of Bagdad* (1940).

The classic version of *The Thief* had been made with Douglas Fairbanks, Snr, in 1924, but Alex had no intention of using the earlier silent film as a model for his production. The script, written by Miles Malleson and Lajos Biro, was to be developed along entirely new lines in order to exploit several things: the popularity of Korda's two major stars, Conrad Veidt and Sabu; the technical expertise of Denham's special effects department; and, above all, the lavishness of Georges Périnal's colour cinematography and Vincent Korda's colour art direction. The film was conceived as a tremendous spectacle, an epic fairy tale with an international appeal, and its budget was as spectacular as its scope. Korda once explained to a journalist his attitude towards million dollar productions with a quotation from one of Madame de Sevigné's famous letters: 'I'm sorry I haven't time to write a short letter.' 'You see,' Korda elaborated, 'I can't afford to make a cheap picture.'³

Alex chose the German Ludwig Berger to direct this extravaganza. Berger had worked as a theatre director, for Max Reinhardt among others, before coming to films and, like Korda, had directed films both on the Continent and in Hollywood. Alex selected Berger presumably on the basis of his previous experiences with fantasy—e.g. *Der verlorene Schuh* [*Cinderella*—1923]—and with large-scale musicals—e.g. *The Vagabond King* (1930) and the colour film *Trois Valses* [*Three Waltzes*—1938]—but just how familiar Alex actually was with Berger's work, with the nature of his talent, is open to question. It was not unusual for Korda to hire someone for a specific job without taking into full account that person's prior work, the suitability of the person to the task *as Korda saw it*. From the outset Korda and Berger were at loggerheads over the conception of *The Thief of Bagdad*.

Berger, it seems, was primarily concerned with the actors. According to John Justin who played Prince Ahmad in the film, Berger was especially gifted in directing 'intimate' scenes between actors with a minimum of extraneous background detail. Michael Powell, whom Alex in desperation had asked to look at Berger's tests for the film, later remarked: '. . . I saw the tests that he had made, and they were wonderful. He had done all the tests with the actors, with Sabu, and he had done absolute wonders with the movement of the tests, movement of people. I could see that he was a man who could handle actors marvellously.'⁴ It mattered little to Berger if by focusing on the players in a scene he disregarded or sacrificed a grandiose scenic background. Alex, on the other hand, was a film-maker who tended to keep his camera at a distance from his actors in order not to waste the decor surrounding them. Korda wanted *The Thief* to be a spectacle and could not apparently abide the idea of his enormous and colourful sets taking a backseat to the actors.

Apprehensive about the fundamental differences between Berger's approach and his own, Alex was not prepared to give Berger a free hand to direct the picture along pre-planned lines. 'Berger wanted to get it all absolutely set,' Michael Powell recently explained. 'Alex wanted the whole thing to grow in the way that Alex usually made his big pictures. He wanted other people to do all the work, and he'd come in and criticise it.'⁵ If the film were carefully planned in advance, it would be more difficult for Korda to exercise this kind of last-minute, last-word control.

Korda's belief in films that 'grow' derived from a more serious problem which may have been one of his major weaknesses as a film producer. Once a scene was filmed, once Alex saw the rushes, he could usually grasp what was right or wrong with the sequence, but he had difficulty in visualising a scene—from the printed page, sketch, or model—before it was shot. If we accept this idea of a deficiency in Korda's visual imagination, then we can better understand certain quirks in his production methods, such as his lack of concern about whether scripts were finished before shooting began and the huge number of retakes which accompanied almost every Korda production. Since Alex's critical faculties operated best during the final stages of filming, everyone connected with the film had to remain flexible, ready to re-build, re-write, or re-shoot at a moment's notice, throughout and often beyond the production schedule. It was a lot to demand of film crews, players, and directors, and some, like Dr Berger, were unwilling to play the game according to Alex's rules.

Berger would not accept the conditions under which Korda wanted him to work, but neither would he relinquish his contract and bow out gracefully. Faced with a film director as stubborn as he was himself, Korda resorted to subversive tactics. He sought out and hired two other directors to shoot certain large chunks of the film. Michael Powell was chosen for his ability to handle the big spectacle and special effects sequences and was immediately sent to Cornwall to start the film. Tim Whelan was hired to shoot the 'action' scenes, the 'chases' and so forth, while Berger, for the time being, was allowed to film the 'love' scenes between Korda's two young stars, John Justin and June Duprez. With the film in this state Alex announced that he would return to film directing with *Manon Lescaut*, a project for Merle Oberon. Nothing came of these plans, and later in May Alex absented himself from Denham for a holiday in the south of France. He spent his holiday in the company of the actress who most owed her film career to Korda's star-building talents, and at Antibes on the 3rd of June 1939 Alex Korda and Merle Oberon were married.

Alex was forty-five at the time of his marriage to Merle. In the past year he had lost the 'boyish' quality to his appearance, for his hair had turned grey and rich living coupled with a total disinterest in physical exercise of any kind had finally resulted in the thickening of Alex's usually slim features. Age, however, added to rather than detracted from Korda's overall presence. Physically he became more distinguished and consequently more impressive. Mary Morris, one of the starlets working on *The Thief of Bagdad*, remembers Korda in these terms: '. . . sometimes one would see Korda suddenly. He would appear from nowhere—very elegant, very beautiful, in his way, magnificent grey clothes he used to wear. He was a grey man, grey face, grey hair, silver like a great god. To me he was a sort of godlike figure —a Zeus.'[6] Yet there is something disquieting about this description and, indeed, about other intimate portraits drawn by those more closely associated with Korda. In all of these there is a hint of an emotional emptiness, a loneliness or sadness underneath the surface.

The consensus of opinion is that Alex was not basically a 'happy' man, but the reasons for this have perhaps too facilely been ascribed to the inner conflict between the artist and the businessman. Certainly this conflict deeply affected Korda, but it is only the most outward sign of a more fundamental problem which was, in my opinion, the source of his unhappiness.

To find this source we must look at Alex's personal life, even though any such examination is hindered from the start by the singular lack of information or insights forthcoming from those who knew Korda best. Most, if not all, of Korda's papers were destroyed after his death, so there are no diaries or letters available which might shed some light on the matter. Korda declined to comment publicly on his private life, and the few published statements made by others are couched in fan magazine clichés almost useless to the researcher. Miss Oberon's comments, for instance, although extremely kind and full of the respect which she obviously felt for Korda, are, with few exceptions, unenlightening. Any picture that we construct must then be based on an analysis of the only known quantity we have to go on: the facts of the emotional environment in which he lived.

The stable home environment which Korda had enjoyed as a child was permanently disrupted by the death of Alex's father in 1906. Although the loss affected the whole family, it forced on Alex a role which few children are equipped or prepared to undertake.

> 'Korda told me,' recalls Ralph Richardson, 'that he became a father rather earlier in life than is usual—that is between the age of twelve and thirteen—because his father died. And then he and his brothers were left quite destitute, and he had to look after the other children and see that they went to school with their clean collars and clean behind their ears . . . he was the father of the family.'[7]

This sudden inheritance of the father's role apparently had several repercussions. It obliged Alex to accept an image of himself as a 'father figure', the financial provider and family disciplinarian upon whom everyone else is dependent. This role-playing resulted in the rapid development of certain aspects of his inner self—his determination to succeed, his self-reliance, his leadership qualities—while frustrating the normal development of other aspects. In particular, emotional flexibility—the freedom to express his own needs and to experiment with different types of relationships—was surely discouraged by Alex's having to take on this one-dimensional emotional role. (We can even posit the theory that Korda found in the cinema an acceptable outlet for the childhood romanticism and fantasy life that was at least partially inhibited by the sobriety of his family position.) Nevertheless, the important factor is that Alex was successful in his role as surrogate father. If the role had offered fewer positive rewards, it might never have become Alex's primary way of relating to other people.

His relationship with Maria Corda had its genesis in the paternal association of an established film-maker with the young actress whose career is guided by the producer–mentor, and this pattern was, of course, repeated in his courtship of Merle Oberon. But the dominant personality of his first wife plus the fact that her career overshadowed his after they left Hungary created a new emotional environment, a reversal of roles, with which Alex could not apparently come to terms. When the marriage dissolved, Alex once again put all his emotional energy into his relationship with his brothers who were quickly summoned to his side. Between 1932 and 1939, Vincent and Zoltan, their families, and Alex's own son Peter were the focal points of Korda's personal life. He derived much pleasure from his status as head of the family, and an episode remembered by his nephew David provides us with a warm picture of Alex during a visit with Zoltan and his family after the war:

> It was always a treat when he came to Los Angeles. He was a very generous man, and always great fun. He was entertaining, even for a child. I remember one night when he came over all dressed up to go to some great dinner party. I was being put to bed. I had a friend over, and we were both in our pyjamas. Alex immediately said, 'Oh, no, they are going to come with us.' So they bundled us into the back seat of the car, still in our pyjamas, and drove us downtown with them. We, of course, didn't stay, but Alex gave us each a silver dollar for each year of our age.[8]

The carefully delimited world that Alex constructed around his emotional self may have protected him from certain conflicts, but it did not necessarily guarantee his happiness, for this private world carried its own frictions and frustrations. The one relationship which should have come naturally to Korda and which should have been a source of great satisfaction to him was his relationship with his son. It seems, however, that Alex was never able to establish a strong rapport with his son, and his failure to do so must have contributed to his feeling of emotional impotence.

For most of his life Alex lived in a male-dominated environment with respect to both his family (the three brothers all had sons) and his inner circle of friends. Korda's closest friendships were frequently with older men like Lajos Biro, Arthur Wimperis, and Winston Churchill. These were men to whom Alex did not have to relate paternally (quite the opposite), men with whom he could be open, vulnerable, himself.*

---

* Of Korda's many close associates it was Lajos Biro who played the most pivotal role in Alex's career and life. C. A. Lejeune wrote in 1936:
> It is almost impossible to over-estimate the importance of Biro's friendship in the story of Alexander Korda. Few people, seeing the leonine, stocky old man with the slow English speech who rules over the fortunes of London Films' scenario department to-day, can realise how essential his presence is to the well-being of the chief who nominally 'employs' him. In all his

As had been the case with his own brothers, Alex liked to introduce his friends into his professional world, to give them jobs at London Films, and to encourage them to experiment with film-making. He was not beneath using his position to cultivate friendships; even so, he needed to feel, and usually did feel, that these friends sought him out for himself, not for the rewards he could bestow.

With most people and perhaps especially with women, Alex was suspicious of their motives for desiring his friendship or love. He probably wondered which Korda they expected him to play—the generous father? the eccentric artist? the shrewd businessman?—or worried that they might demand a role which wasn't in his repertoire. During their marriage Merle Oberon admitted that she thought Alex felt that he had never been loved for himself. That he may have felt this way is revealing enough, without us having to ascertain whether or not his fear was well grounded. It does shed light on the complexity of Korda's dilemma, for how could he expect to be loved for himself when his 'self' was hidden under façades which few were allowed to penetrate. Given his imprinted self-image and his emotional disappointments, it was much easier for Korda to live in semi-isolation, as he did for half of his adult life, than for him to experiment with other styles of life. Yet given his strong determination to make a success of both his public and private lives, it was impossible for him not to make an attempt to broaden the bases of his emotional relationships. Alex's marriage to Merle was one such attempt.

On the surface their marriage symbolised the ideal movieland

---

career, in success and disappointment, in Vienna, in Berlin, in Hollywood, in Paris, in London, Biro has never failed him; he has paved the way for Alex's coming, and covered the way for Alex's retreat.

There are two people in the world whom Alex almost fanatically protects from misunderstanding, and who, nevertheless, have been consistently misunderstood and underestimated in the story of London Films. The one is his brother, Zoltan, the other is Lajos Biro, who came into the picture while Zoltan was still an undersized and rather indolent schoolboy. Biro's common sense and slow authority are the bulwarks behind which Alex's talents have been able to grow and flourish. I have been in Biro's room at Isleworth when Alex came bursting in, escaped from a business conference. He sank into a chair, running his hands wildly through his hair. 'Biro, these people will drive me crazy. That fool so-and-so . . .' and so on to the end of the story. [Then] Biro, playing with his pen at the desk, began very slowly, 'Well, Alex, the way I see it . . .' and five minutes later Korda was back at his conference in full charge of the situation again.[9]

romance, the kind of glamorised 'girl-marries-boss' love story which provides perfect copy for fan magazines and gossip columnists. But the marriage was by no means a romantic inevitability, and to those who considered Alex not to be 'the marrying kind', it came somewhat as a surprise. Their courtship had, after all, been a long one, frequently interrupted by Merle's trips to Hollywood, and (according to Louella Parsons) Merle had even been engaged to Joseph Schenck, then president of United Artists, for a short time in 1936. From the start Merle was much in awe of Korda's culture and his power: 'hero-worship' was the word which she often used to describe her first attitude towards him. We have no reason to doubt that she grew to love him, for the infiltration of the Kordas' tightly knit, male-oriented family was a task which required real strength and devotion. If Merle became quite possessive of Alex, as some claim, she was probably motivated by the need to reinforce the bonds of their relationship. For his part Alex was, of course, extremely proud of the stunning film star he had helped to create. She represented his greatest success as a star-maker, and it was understandable that he should fall in love with her.

That they did not marry until Merle's career was well established (she had just completed *Wuthering Heights*), that they waited until she was less dependent on Alex as a producer and career manager, was proof to the world, and perhaps to themselves, that there were no ulterior motives behind their marriage other than the love they felt for each other. Alex may also have hoped that a more equal professional status would allow their relationship to develop beyond the mentor-prodigy (father–child) level on which it first operated. Professional and economic independence did not, however, produce the state of emotional interdependence which Alex was seeking, and the hoped-for change in the nature of their emotional interaction did not, it seems, occur. 'I remember saying to him once how much I loved him,' Merle revealed a few years ago, 'and he said "Yes, oh yes, just as you would love a father." ' 'But,' Merle concluded, 'I think he resented that.'[10] In spite of this, Alex and Merle did find happiness together for a time. They, of course, had no way of knowing that their rationally constructed marriage was soon to be disrupted by the chaos of the Second World War and the demands of their separate careers.

When Alex returned to Denham mid-summer, he once more became embroiled in the production of *The Thief of Bagdad*. He saw the rushes of scenes shot during his absence and outrightly condemned and scrapped certain footage, Ludwig Berger's foremost, at a loss of several thousand pounds. The whole studio re-geared itself for extensive re-takes and more directorial confusion. Vincent rebuilt and repainted sets to Alex's new specifications ('build it four times as big and paint it all crimson'), while Miles Malleson and Lajos Biro began producing daily re-writes of the script. Korda's lax production methods suited this last-minute, changeable manner of making films, and the situation on *The Thief* was by all accounts identical to that described by John Clements in referring to earlier Korda films:

> . . . you would be called on the set at nine o'clock in the morning. Well, when you got to know about the Korda methods, you turned up vaguely . . . at half-past nine or thereabouts, and you went into the restaurant and you had your bacon and eggs and coffee and a red-faced assistant director would say, 'You're wanted on the set immediately' and you'd say, 'Don't be silly. Go away.' And then you'd make your way to the make-up room and you'd sit down and have a nice cup of coffee with the make-up man and get made up and go to your dressing room and get dressed and sort of wander on to the set about eleven, knowing perfectly well that nothing would happen before twelve.[11]

The actors and film crew could at least reconcile themselves to these standard Korda practices. It was another thing for them to adjust to the special manoeuvres which Alex was resorting to in order to get Dr Berger off the picture.

Even though the film had been all but taken out of his hands already, Berger could not be persuaded to break his contract voluntarily. So, to everyone's consternation and amazement Korda adopted a tactic which exacerbated the crisis by making Berger's position intolerable. In one of the most aggressive and flagrantly rude manoeuvres of his career, Alex decided to co-direct all of Berger's scenes. The resulting fiasco, witnessed by John Justin among others, consisted of Berger and Korda arriving on the set each day, Berger instructing the staff and actors on the sequence to be filmed, and then Korda, often literally pushing Berger aside, giving his own orders to the assembly. The cast and crew, totally confused as to whose directions to follow, usually played the scene by ear and hoped for the best. Berger tolerated this humiliating treatment for some time, but he finally became demoralised and left the film. Ironically, he was to keep top directorial billing on *The Thief*, although little of his individual contribution could have possibly survived past the final cut.

Towards the end of the summer, as Britain prepared herself for the confrontation with Hitler which now seemed inevitable, production on *The Thief of Bagdad* was stepped up in the hope of completing the film before hostilities broke out. On the second of September, the day after the Nazis marched into Poland, Alex called together several members of his staff to tell them that London Films was going into the 'propaganda' business. Michael Powell, one of those contacted, recalls the events of that crucial weekend:

> One day Alex said: 'Mickey . . . I have arranged with the Government that you are going to work on *The Lion Has Wings*.'
> 'What's that, Alex?'
> 'Oh, it is a film we are going to make to show that we are going to win the war.'
> That was Saturday, and on Sunday we were all working—they were working to try and finish *Thief of Bagdad*, which was quite impossible of course—[and] there was an air-raid alarm and Chamberlain's speech. We all listened to it in a coal bunker at Denham, and then went back to work. And the next day I was in the air on *The Lion Has Wings*.[12]

The film's objective was to demonstrate to the British people the strength of the Royal Air Force, to reassure them that Britain's aerial defences were highly organised and able to cope with Germany's formidable Luftwaffe. It seems likely, though it has yet to be confirmed, that the impetus for making the film came from informal discussions between Alex and some of his political friends, perhaps Churchill and Vansittart.

Since the film's conception predated the actual declaration of war and since it went into production before official film propaganda channels and committees, such as the Ministry of Information Films Division, were organised, *The Lion Has Wings* holds a unique position in British film history. In a recent speech written for a conference on 'Film Propaganda and the Historian', Ian Dalrymple, who was in charge of the film, emphasised the unique features of Korda's essay into film propaganda:

> Apart from the then GPO Film Unit's spontaneous act in going out into the streets to photograph what was going on in those

FIRST DAYS,* the initiative in Britain for the use of the medium for war purposes came from private enterprise, in the person of Alexander Korda.

. . . Whether it was Alex's own idea or he had been unofficially urged to make it, I don't know: what I do know is that he had no financial help from Government: that, as his normal finance was tied up in major product awaiting exhibition, to complete the film he had to pawn his last Life Insurance Policy: that those working on it received token fees, and it was released to Exhibitors on minimal terms: finally, that apart from technical guidance, the content was spontaneous—nothing in it had been imposed by the Central Authorities.[13]

A remarkable co-operative effort, the film provided proof that under certain circumstances the Korda team could work efficiently and economically. The token fees paid to the crew and the performers— which, according to varying reports, ranged from £5 each for the actors to £50 for each director—helped to keep the production cost down to a modest £30,000. Shooting of scenes supplementary to the acquired documentary footage took less than two weeks, and the completed film was released by the first week of November, only two months after its inception. This speed was made possible by a well-planned division of labour and by the immediate support given to the project by other film organisations, like the GPO Film Unit.

'Those among us geared to undertake the film promptly set to work,' Ian Dalrymple explains, 'though with little conviction that we would complete it before the Germans blew us to bits. Michael Powell dealt with Fighter Command, Brian Desmond Hurst with Bomber; the GPO Film Unit supplied material from factories overnight; Alex himself inserted one or two staged scenes with Merle Oberon and Ralph Richardson, and our excellent American film-editor, William Hornbeck, and I compiled a rude opening sequence denigrating Nazism . . . after five or six weeks, we projected the show copy of a feature-length film to the inaugural chiefs of the Ministry of Information, to their stupefaction as to how the film had happened.'[14]

How the public would respond to *The Lion Has Wings* was another,

---

* *The First Days* (1939) was a twenty-three minute short made by four documentary film-makers: Alberto Cavalcanti, Humphrey Jennings, Harry Watt, and Pat Jackson.

far more vital question, one which we can deal with thanks to an interview survey conducted six weeks after the film's release by Mass-Observation, an organisation set up to analyse British public opinion.

Since Korda's chief aim was to reach the widest possible audience in the shortest possible time, he must have been gratified with the results of these man-in-the-street interviews, for by mid-December an exceptionally high percentage of the random sample (55 per cent) had actually seen the film. This large turn-out can be attributed both to the way in which Korda facilitated exhibition by distributing on 'minimal terms' without the traditional 'bars' or restrictions and to the 'sense of duty' which propelled the public to the cinemas. As Mass-Observation pointed out, the method of advertising the film, 'which sometimes took the form of aeroplane displays, but more often of civic receptions or formal parades of soldiers or air force men at the opening',[15] encouraged this feeling of public obligation to see the film. The public's reaction to *The Lion Has Wings* was revealed in some interesting statistics: although 71 per cent claimed to have 'liked' the film, only '44% found something positive to praise, while 43% criticised the lack of story and 27% criticised the propaganda element'.[16] These figures bear witness to the problems faced by Korda and company and indeed by most film-makers engaged in propaganda work: how to propagandise without losing audience interest and without assaulting or insulting the intelligence of the public. Neither 100 per cent documentary nor 100 per cent fictional construction or reconstruction, but rather an odd mixture of the two, *The Lion Has Wings* demonstrates what can happen when a film-maker tries to cover all bases.

The section of the film which generated the most enthusiastic response was that 'rude opening sequence' devised by Ian Dalrymple and William Hornbeck. In a montage of documentary footage, they intelligently and humorously paralleled scenes of British and German life during the thirties. Although a country at peace and another preparing for war offered an obvious contrast, Dalrymple and Hornbeck used three clever types of visual and aural juxtapositions to heighten the dramatic effect. Most of the sequence relies on the juxtaposition of image with image: for instance, shots of British sports activities are intercut with shots of Nazi military parades. At times certain images are linked with unexpected sound effects for purposes of satirical comment, such as the sequence where the Nuremberg Rally is accompanied by a herd of baaing sheep. Especially effective was the linking of two different image and sound scenes, as when shots of Hitler making impassioned speeches are followed with shots of British street hawkers hustling crowds with frenetic exhortations. The verbal commentary, spoken by E. V. H. Emmett in the English version and Lowell Thomas in the American, is kept to a minimum; the carefully manipulated images are left to speak for themselves.

Unfortunately, the main section of the film dealing with the opening hostilities of the war and the preparedness of the RAF lacks the subtlety and authenticity of the opening sequence. This was at least partially un-avoidable. In order to reconstruct history so recently past and preview events which were still in the future, the film-makers were obliged to use whatever material was available and invent the rest themselves. By combining bits of old propaganda film, old fiction film, newsreels and documentary footage with fabricated battle scenes, special effects and a fictional sub-plot, they could maintain a respectable chronology of events and give the film some shape. But the inadequacy of this mixture and the inconsistencies in the footage undermined audience credibility (at least in Britain) and thereby weakened the film's message.

The Kiel Canal Raid and the long sequence showing the British warding off a German air attack were especially criticised on these grounds. Even though the audience is informed that the Kiel Raid shown in the film is a reconstruction, the admission is hardly necessary. Graham Greene wrote at the time: 'The Germans, I believe, have re-marked that the Kiel battle was fought in the Denham film studios (rather tamely fought, it may be noted), and we become aware of some point in the jest as we watch imaginary battles . . . in which all the deaths are German and all the heroics English.' [17] The mismatching of aircraft types in these battle scenes elicited the following sarcastic com-ment from the magazine *The Aeroplane* in an article entitled 'The Unicorn Has Tailplanes': 'It is one of the most essential features of any air picture that the characters should take off in one sort of aeroplane, fly in another sort, and alight in a third entirely different sort. . . .' [18]

The film-makers' biggest single misjudgement was the use of footage from *The Gap* (1937), a recruiting picture which had been made to demonstrate the weakness of Britain's aerial defences. They rearranged the material in an attempt to disguise the original message and expected that they could rely on the public's short memory. However, one critic (Greene) and one in twenty of those interviewed had remembered the scenes and were put off by their use in a film 'preaching invincibility'. Most viewers were of course not affected by these discrepancies, but they did react with bewilderment to the sudden appearance of Flora

Robson as Queen Elizabeth I in scenes culled from Korda's *Fire Over England* (1937). Considering the confusion it caused, the attempted analogy between the Spanish Armada victory and eventual victory over the Nazis made no positive contribution to the film.

Given more time Korda might have had the entire film designed around a fictional narrative, as were later 'propaganda' films like Thorold Dickinson's *The Next of Kin* (1942). As it was, he anticipated those who might object to a feature film without a 'story' or known actors by injecting some 'love interest' into the film. This sub-plot with Ralph Richardson as a Wing Commander, Merle Oberon as his wife, and June Duprez as a pilot's sweetheart was, however, awkward, unconvincing, and politically naïve. In particular, much adverse comment was justifiably levelled against the final scene where Merle tells her husband that England is fighting for 'Truth, Beauty, and Fair Play, and . . . Kindliness'. 'As a statement of war aims,' opined Graham Greene, 'this leaves the world beyond Roedean still expectant.'[19] The addition of star names did not apparently increase audience attendance, as Korda may have hoped. Instead, this 'Kordage and Merlery', as *Documentary News Letter* called it, worked against the film: those who came to the film expecting a documentary were embarrassed; those who came expecting a fictional film were disappointed.

Because of its many shortcomings, *The Lion Has Wings* was only moderately successful as a propaganda film. Although praised by a majority of British critics, the film was not wholeheartedly supported by the British people for whom it had been made. It had, after all, painted an overly optimistic picture of the situation in 1939 (17 per cent of the interviewed public stated that they couldn't believe the film), and there was a feeling that the film shouldn't be exhibited overseas until this optimism had more basis in fact. Yet, as is often the case, the film did have a more enthusiastic reception outside the country, especially in America where more unfamiliar audiences did not share the critical objections of their British counterparts. By December 1940, twelve months after its initial release there, *The Lion* had secured a thousand bookings in the United States and was still doing good business. Reaction in Germany was not as contradictory as it may have seemed at the time. The Germans evidently threatened to 'bomb Denham out of existence' for having fostered the project; yet a story widely circulated told of a captured print of the film being shown in Berlin as a comedy.

For the way it had been produced more than the actual effect it had,

*The Lion Has Wings* was one of Alex Korda's most enterprising and courageous ventures. The film had provided Korda with a chance to prove his patriotism, a patriotism which had already manifested itself in his commercial films. It is quite likely that the public criticisms of his first propaganda effort taught Alex an important lesson, for, excepting a short he sponsored in 1943, the only other propaganda film which he made had its message disguised within a conventional narrative structure. As important as this lesson, was the breathing space the film allowed Korda. The outbreak of war had forced Korda to re-appraise his future plans, and *The Lion* had offered him a much-needed two months' respite, time enough for him to make some difficult decisions.

1. R. Ewart Williams, *loc cit*.
2. Interview with Muir Mathieson conducted by the author, 17 July 1973.
3. *Los Angeles Daily News*, 7 November 1941.
4. From Michael Powell's John Player Lecture at the National Film Theatre, London, 10 January 1971.
5. *Ibid*.
6. From Robert Vas's BBC documentary.
7. *Ibid*.
8. Interview with David Korda conducted by the author, 20 September 1973.
9. C. A. Lejeune, 'The Private Lives of London Films', *Nash's Magazine*, September 1936, p. 82.
10. From Robert Vas's BBC documentary.
11. Sir John Clements in an interview with Robert Vas, conducted for Vas's documentary, but not used.
12. From Michael Powell's John Player Lecture.
13. Ian Dalrymple, speech for 'Film Propaganda and the Historian' conference at the Imperial War Museum, London, held 9–11 July 1973.
14. *Ibid*.
15. *Documentary News Letter*, February 1940, p. 5.
16. *Ibid*.
17. Graham Greene, *The Spectator*, 3 November 1939.
18. *Documentary News Letter*, February 1940, p. 5.
19. Grahame Greene, *The Spectator*, 3 November 1939.

CHAPTER SIXTEEN

# *For Services Rendered*

'I HAVE been through so many revolutions and wars,' Korda told reporter Jympson Harman during the Munich Crisis, 'that I think another war will kill me.'[1] On the contrary, the Second World War rejuvenated Korda as it did many other film-makers whose spirits had been dampened by the economic doldrums of the late thirties. There had been some fear in the early days of the war that the Government might close cinemas and halt film production. But Government officials soon recognised the value of film as a booster of public morale, a provider of vital entertainment and information, even though they saw the need for a more rationalised industry, one which could effectively operate within the limits of wartime economies and shortages. To nationalise British film production seemed the best course of action, and so throughout the war the film industry was under the central control of the Ministry of Information who vetted all film project proposals and apportioned available film stock.

There was, and indeed had to be, a strong feeling of commitment among those film-makers who continued to work in Britain despite the hazardous conditions and the increasing shortages in resources, human and otherwise, and it was during this period that Korda found what he later called 'the greatest exhilaration of my life—the sharing of danger'. 'I began to feel, during those terrible days, that I "belonged",' Korda went on to say. 'Becoming a British citizen and taking a British passport was not, to me, half so important as the feeling that I belonged, the thought that I had put down roots here.'[2]

How then did it happen that Korda's activities during the war led some to condemn him as a deserter of that very nation to which he felt so committed? His actions certainly left him open to such an accusation, especially since the nature of some of his wartime work denied him the chance to reply to his critics with a full explanation. The controversy stems from the fact that for three years, from June 1940 to May 1943, Korda lived and worked in the relative calm of Hollywood. Why he went there and what he accomplished must therefore be closely examined.

In December 1939 Alex went to Canada and the United States to promote *The Lion Has Wings* and perhaps to see Merle who was already in Los Angeles under contract to Warner Brothers. Two weeks after his return Korda was forced to defend himself against a report in *Kinematograph Weekly*—confirming its 'forecast' of November 1939— that he was to leave England for Hollywood, there to produce and direct for Warner Brothers.* In an open letter to the rival *Today's Cinema*, Alex attempted to 'nail these lies publicly'. He denied that he had a contract with Warners [the confusion was surely caused by Merle's association with that company] and further stated that he had 'no intention of leaving England *permanently* to become a producer in Hollywood'.[3] He elaborated:

> ... I have very important business in America. My films cost a great deal of money. They have to bring back a great deal of money. My chief market, besides our own, is the United States, where my films play in about eleven thousand theatres. This business—and it is an important business these days as it brings foreign currency to England—took me to America about twelve times during the last five years. Each time I returned, I was amused to hear the usual Wardour Street rumours to the effect that I was supposed never to be coming back to England. I never bothered about these rumours coming from people who *talk*, who talk films

---

* The trade press had been more critical of Korda ever since the 1937 crisis, in many instances for good reason. The wartime press hysteria, directed against *all* Britons working in Hollywood not just Korda, reflected the industry's own insecurities, its constant expectation of defections to Hollywood of men and women of questionable loyalty. Korda, only a 'naturalised' Briton and thus a likely suspect from the start, fell victim to the press's zealous pursuit of scoops of this sort.

instead of making them, and who mind everybody's business except their own. But when a responsible paper . . .

. . . At some time or other, I may or may not make some films in America. But never more than a part of my programme. My organization, my Company and myself will remain a part of the British Film Industry. . . .[4]

He did confirm that Zoltan, who had just set up his own production company, Legeran Films, was going to America for reasons of his health.* He sarcastically denied, however, the suggestion that he was in financial difficulties and announced that his new film project *The Hunting of the U Boats* was to commence as soon as he received Admiralty permission. One month later Alex was back in Hollywood.

Although loath to admit it, Korda was in financial difficulty. He had exhausted his British sources, and the February–May trip was devoted to a search for American finance. He took a copy of *The Four Feathers* with him to use as 'collateral', and on it he secured two large bank loans in April. The Security National Bank of Los Angeles and the Bankers Trust Company of New York undertook to loan Korda $3,600,000: $3,200,000 of which was to be used to produce four pictures in America, the remaining $400,000 for two British projects. As these arrangements meant that a 'majority', not a 'part', of Korda's programme was to be made outside Britain, the announcement of the terms added more weight to the allegations against him. In all fairness, though, the bankers were the ones in the position to dictate the terms, and Hollywood-based production naturally provided more of a guarantee on their heavy investment.

During this trip Alex also laid the groundwork for the transfer of production on *The Thief of Bagdad* to America. The film had been 'near completion' for five months, but the war had made it impossible for Korda to send the crew out to Egypt and Arabia for final location shooting. Having invested far too much in the project to shelve it away in his vaults, Korda decided to transport key technicians and those members of the cast whose services were still needed to the Grand Canyon in Arizona, where these scenes were to be shot. He supervised this transfer during a brief trip to London in May 1940, and six weeks later everything was prepared for the final episode in the film's already chequered production history.

* Zoltan had tuberculosis. He spent the summer of 1939 in a Swiss sanatorium and went to Arizona and California in January 1940, where it was hoped the desert air might cure him.

Alex had other 'important business' in America, for he planned to re-issue several of his earlier films throughout the country in order to earn currency for the dollar-starved British Treasury. But these were all reasons for Korda's *going* to Hollywood. Was it necessary for him to *stay* there? After all, he could have organised the re-issue from his London headquarters, and with Zoltan and William Cameron Menzies in charge of *The Thief*'s American production schedule Alex did not need to be there himself. Even if Korda did feel a commitment to over-see this production, why did he stay after the film was released in December 1940?

The answer presumably was that Alex intended to produce covert propaganda films in Hollywood to win support for the British cause. Couldn't he have made these pictures in England? Conditions were certainly difficult there, but he did have enough finance for two projects. These would have to be smaller films, not the big Korda epics, but they could have served the same purpose, as *The Lion Has Wings*, for example, had done. When Jympson Harman pleaded with Korda 'to stay and make bread-and-butter British films', Alex replied: 'I cannot make that kind of film. A man can do so much, but he must have some enjoyment from it, if it is to be any good.'[5]

It was lame excuses like this one which encouraged Korda's critics to view his leave-taking as opportunism. They believed that Alex was simply afraid for his safety and later pointed to the dates of his most prolonged stay in Hollywood—June 1940 at the low point of the war to January 1942 after American entry—as support for their contention that Korda stayed away until the British position was more secure. Korda did have reason to fear for his safety as he was on the Gestapo Arrest List,* but as this list was released *after* Korda's departure, it could

* This list, officially entitled *Sonderfahndungsliste G.B.*, was put out by the Gestapo no earlier than July 1940.[6] It contained the names of those British people whom the Gestapo planned to interrogate once Britain was invaded. (The information had been collected by German agents between 1937 and 1940.) Each entry concluded with a series of code letters representing the particular department of the *Reichssicherheitshauptamt* (Nazi Central Security Agency) which would undertake that person's interrogation, i.e. the area in which the person was a potential threat. Korda's entry on page 109 reads:

> 119. Korda, Alexander, 16.9.96 [sic] Turkeve, Ungarn, Direkter (d) Korda Film-Productions Ltd., London N.W.1, Avenue Road, St. John's Wood, RSHA II D 5.

The 'II D 5' signified 'Investigation of the Opposition', 'External problems', 'the English "Imperium"' and referred presumably to Korda's film work in or not have influenced his decision. Unable to defend himself fully and motivated by a strong conviction in the importance of his 'mission', Korda left England knowing that he had singled himself out from the rest of the industry and that he would thereby incur the enmity and resentment of those who stayed behind.

For a short time early in 1940 Korda had toyed with the idea of working in Canada instead of the United States, but he had concluded that Canadian technical facilities were lacking for large scale production. Hollywood, of course, presented no such problem, and with headquarters on Las Palmas Avenue in the heart of the film capital and rented studio space nearby, Korda could quickly finish the long-delayed *Thief of Bagdad*. By the end of August Zoltan had completed the Grand Canyon scenes with Sabu and John Justin, and the few remaining pick-up shots had been filmed at General Service Studio in Hollywood, probably under the supervision of William Cameron Menzies. Twenty months after the project had commenced in England, during the first week of October 1940, *The Thief* was finally previewed for the press.

In plot, theme, and characterisation, this particular tale from the Arabian Nights collection has all the necessary ingredients for an action-filled fantasy film. The evil Grand Vizier Jaffar's attempts to usurp Prince Ahmad's kingdom and sweetheart develop into a classic competition between the powers of white and black magic. Both hero and villain possess their own bag of magical tricks. Jaffar's powers include the ability to 'blind' the Prince and turn his faithful comrade, the Thief, into a dog; a flying horse and a 'human' shiva are the kinds of 'toys' he uses to charm and eventually kill the heroine's Sultan father. The heroes, who possess no magical talents of their own, accidentally stumble upon their magical assistants: the bottled-up djinni; the All-Seeing Eye, which the Thief steals after a nasty encounter with its guardian, an outsize spider; and the flying carpet and magic bow and arrow, the instruments of their final victory over Jaffar. With such

---

regarding the Empire. The only other film producer on the list was Isidore Ostrer, whose code letters ('II B 2') designated 'the Jews', 'Ideological opposition'. It is significant that Korda was not considered under this category, but rather under one which related to the possible political ramifications of the films which he had produced. Others on this lengthy list included Noël Coward, Virginia Woolf, Winston Churchill, J. B. Priestley, and Aldous Huxley, and it comes as no surprise that Korda felt proud to be included in such illustrious company.

The transformation of Estelle 'Queenie' Thompson into
Merle Oberon. One of Korda's 'new faces' in 1932.

In 1938, the year before she became the second Mrs Korda.

At the Denham commissary in 1937: John Armstrong, (?), Alex, Merle, (?), and Josef von Sternberg.

Rex Ingram (Djinni) with an earful of Sabu in Korda's
fantasy epic *The Thief of Bagdad* (1940).

Vivien Leigh and Laurence Olivier as Emma Hamilton and Lord Nelson in Korda's wartime Hollywood film *That Hamilton Woman* (1941).

(*above*) Deborah Kerr and Robert Donat in the reunion scene in
*Perfect Strangers* (1945); the one production of MGM–
British–London Films.

(*below*) *An Ideal Husband* (1947), the last film directed by Alexander
Korda – Constance Collier (Lady Markby), Diana Wynyard (Lady
Chiltern), and Paulette Goddard (Mrs Cheveley).

Alex, a few months before his death, at a party with his
third wife Alexa and Salvador Dali.

Sir Alexander Korda in his office at 144/146
Piccadilly (*c.* 1947).

potential, it is sad that, like so many of Korda's epics, *The Thief of Bagdad* was only a spectacular, colourful balloon with nothing but hot air inside.

The critic for *Variety* was the first to prick the balloon, exposing the flatulence of what otherwise appeared to be a fantastic vehicle.

> 'Bagdad' may enjoy success in a few key spots as a roadshow attraction. It can also develop into a smacko grosser and holdover attraction in the regular houses. Both will generate in direct proportion to audience acceptance of the fantastic Arabian Nights fable presented as background for the more important colorful mounting.
>
> . . . audience interest is focused on the production and technical displays of the picture, and the unimpressive story and stagey acting of the cast fail to measure up to the general production qualities.
>
> Picture is not only over-length in itself, but contains numerous scenes that run too long. In many instances, the camera is held on a scene long after the action has moved on, and in other spots, scenes that have nothing more than pictorial beauty are cut in.
>
> . . . On both the acting and directing sides, picture is obviously deficient.[7]

Korda had managed with great deliberateness to dwarf the film's story, theme, and bold characters by an over-emphasis on the exotic setting and a concern for spectacle for spectacle's sake. Where a small set and clever editing would have sufficed, Korda chose to build one of the largest market place sets in cinema history, and the elephant which lumbers through the scene is not merely decorated, but painted pink. If Korda had given as much attention to the actors as he gave to the sets, the film might have indeed been a classic.

Referring to another film-maker, Alex once told David Lean: 'He's a bloody fool. He thinks he only has to direct the actors.'[8] Wise as this comment may be, Korda himself transgressed by making the actors secondary to everything else. In *The Thief*, only Conrad Veidt (as Jaffar) and Rex Ingram (as the djinni) escape the fate of the rest of the cast, who look like puppets being manipulated around a lavish stage. John Justin and June Duprez, as the two lovers caught in Jaffar's intrigues, are too inexperienced to stand out against the technical fireworks around them, something which Vivien Leigh and Jon Hall, the originally announced stars, might have accomplished. Although Sabu gives a sympathetic and lively performance as the Thief, neither he nor anyone else in the cast can hold audience attention the way Douglas Fairbanks, Snr, was able to do in the 1924 version of the film. The actors were not only inadequately directed—and by too many different men—but they were also hampered by a basically humourless script, one which by its seriousness drained the fantasy of much of its potential.

The film fails as much in execution as it does in conception. Static camera placements and a plodding editing style, which precludes any imagination in the scene transitions, are bound to undermine the exotic atmosphere so dependent on action, movement, and fluid or dynamic cutting techniques. It is not coincidental that all the best scenes, especially the opening harbour sequence with its sweeping and rhythmic camera movements and the scene of Sabu's discovery of the djinni on a deserted beach, are directed by Michael Powell, the only one of the five directors whose visual imagination was allowed free rein. The film is at least held together by the uniform high quality of the Technicolor photography and the set designs, and here Georges Périnal and Vincent Korda deserve all the credit (and received it in the form of Academy Awards for Color Art Direction and Color Cinematography). *The Thief* also won an Oscar for Special Effects, but many of the effects are below standard—witness the bad matching of the flying horse sequence and the at times unconvincing use of models.

Despite all these reservations, the film does contain some memorable characters and scenes: the menacing omnipresence of Veidt's heavily cloaked, piercing-eyed Jaffar, Rex Ingram's playful and mischievous djinni dressed only in loin-cloth and pony-tail, and Sabu's quest for the All-Seeing Eye in a Tibetan temple. If *The Thief*'s critical flaws did not deny it a respectable box-office career, this was because it appealed to the less discriminating, but commercially vital family entertainment market for which it was designed. And, of course, Korda's self-indulgence, extravagance and, above all, his appalling behaviour towards Ludwig Berger and others were forgotten as the receipts rolled in. When one of the actors suggested to Alex that they never again make a film in such a chaotic, often unprofessional way, Korda sloughed the advice off. Like most of the big-time film producers, Korda believed a film's success was justification enough for the means that had been employed.

Anyway, by the time *The Thief of Bagdad* was previewed, Korda's only concern was his new project, a propaganda film which led to censorship problems with the American guardians of taste and morals, to a subpoena from the United States Senate, and, some say, to a knighthood. The film was *That Hamilton Woman* (1941).

Korda's decision to make a pro-British propaganda film in America placed him in an awkward and vulnerable position. The British Government could demonstrate its support of Korda's plans by facilitating the transport to America of people Korda needed with him, but it could not openly sanction his propaganda activities in a neutral country. Political allies like Churchill and Vansittart certainly approved of Korda's 'mission' and may even have instigated it, as some suggest, but Korda was mindful not to betray whatever support he may have been given. Thus he was alone responsible for finding a suitable film project to arouse pro-British sentiments and for concealing the film's message with enough cinematic embroidery so as not to alarm American isolationists.

Korda knew precisely what kind of film would fulfil these requirements, and even before he left England he had considered several historical subjects from which obvious parallels might be extracted. On his trip from New York to Hollywood in June 1940 he found the right one while reading a book on naval history by Admiral Alfred Mahan. The Napoleonic Wars was to be the setting, Lord Nelson and the British campaign against Napoleon was to be the parallel, and Nelson's love affair with Emma Hamilton the embroidery. Once decided, Korda lost no time in setting up the project. He immediately contacted R. C. Sherriff in England and persuaded him to come to America to co-write the script with Walter Reisch. After some initial hesitation Laurence Olivier and Vivien Leigh, then in New York with their production of *Romeo and Juliet*, accepted Korda's offer to star in the film.

Encouraged by the need to keep costs down and to get the film exhibited as soon as possible, Korda, for the first time in ten years, produced a film cheaply and directed it quickly. On one stage of the General Service Studio Vincent Korda constructed a large set of the Hamilton's villa in Naples (where much of the action occurs) within which numerous set-ups could be filmed without additional structural changes. Naval battle sequences were kept to a minimum, and models were used for those scenes, like the Battle of Trafalgar, which were essential to the story. The film began shooting during the first week of October 1940 and was finished six weeks later. In the rush to get the film completed, it was the scriptwriters who suffered most. R. C. Sherriff later wrote:

> ... only the first sequences were down in dialogue when they began to shoot the picture.
>
> From then on it was a desperate race to keep up with them. It was like writing a serial story with only a week between your pen and the next instalment to be published. We would slog along all day on scenes that would be wanted before the week was over, and I would take them back to my hotel and work most of the night smoothing out the dialogue. . . . There wasn't time for the leisurely script conferences I'd been used to. We'd sit round in the lunch-break eating sandwiches and drinking coffee, and talk about the scenes that Reisch and I had just brought in. . . . Sometimes the stuff we wrote didn't measure up to what Alex Korda and the others wanted. Then Reisch and I would have to go away and spend the afternoon rewriting it.[9]

Despite the hectic pace, an enthusiastic, collaborative spirit animated the whole production team, almost all of whom felt a strong commitment to the film's patriotic intentions. However, the making of a Korda film was usually accompanied by some crisis, and the Hollywood censor provided the requisite trauma during the last weeks of production on *That Hamilton Woman*.

Hollywood had for years operated under a self-regulatory pre-censorship system whereby the designated censor—in 1940 Joseph Breen—vetted all scripts submitted to him for salacious or offensive scenes or dialogue. If the writers changed the script according to the censor's recommendations, then the film received the Production Code's seal of approval. Since most exhibitors (in 1940 an estimated 95 per cent) refused to show films without a seal, the censor's approval was crucial to any film's financial viability. In the normal procedure scripts were submitted prior to production, but since *That Hamilton Woman* had been written as the film progressed, Korda did not have a final script to show Breen until the picture was almost completed. Korda expected no problems over the script and sent Sherriff along to see Breen.

But Korda had miscalculated. Even though the film was framed by a prologue and epilogue which showed the depths to which Emma Hamilton's adulterous life had led her (a drunken old hag thrown in jail for theft and assault), this was not enough 'retribution' to please the censor. Breen refused to approve the script until Korda and the writers made it explicit that they were not 'condoning the offence' of adultery.

Sherriff and Reisch came to Korda's rescue with an additional scene which satisfied the censor. In an encounter between Nelson and his clergyman father, Nelson is reprimanded for his affair with Emma. 'What you are doing is wrong,' says the father from his wheelchair. 'It is an evil thing that all right-minded people will condemn. It will do you great harm, and I beg of you to see no more of this woman.' [10] Ashamed, Nelson admits the wrongness of his actions, but states that he is simply too weak to give up Emma. The scene saved the production, but Korda was never happy with it and at a later date had it cut out of the film.*

*That Hamilton Woman* is the closest Korda ever came to recreating the spirit and success of *The Private Life of Henry VIII*. Designed as pure entertainment, albeit with a political punch, the film lacks the artistic pretensions of Korda's last directorial effort, *Rembrandt*, and since Korda was forced to economise on the production—the film was shot in black and white, and the sets were more spartan—he was unable to dwarf his actors with lavish production values. The result was that for the first time since 1933 Korda's emphasis was on the human potential of the story. The actors were able to create strong characterisations which in some ways surpassed the performances in *Henry VIII*. This was possible because *That Hamilton Woman* was not a comedy, and characters have more dimension when the film-maker can concentrate on their strengths as well as their weaknesses. Emma Hamilton, for example, may be a vain and at times silly creature who must be groomed to fit into the upper class society to which her husband Sir William elevates her, but she has a strong will and is able to cope with the misfortunes that befall her as she flouts conventional mores for love of Nelson.

Vivien Leigh's portrayal of Emma is as lively and sympathetic as Charles Laughton's Henry. She deftly captures the development of Emma's personality: the over-emotional, but charming young girl, whose response to the news of war with Napoleon is only distress that a 'witty and amusing' dinner guest must now be excluded from parties ('That's done it, bang goes the French Ambassador!'), becomes a

---

* The scene is not in the copy of *Lady Hamilton*—as it was titled in Britain—held by the National Film Archive in London. It is possible that it may remain in other prints of the film, for Korda may not have been able to excise it from all copies.

devoted wife and mother ready to sacrifice her happiness for the good of the country and to accept in shocked silence the news of Nelson's death. But unlike *Henry*, *That Hamilton Woman* does not rely so completely on one bravura performance. Alan Mowbray, as the culturally alive, emotionally dead Sir William, also creates a rounded character: harsh and cold in his treatment of Emma, ultimately pathetic in his old age as he sits envisaging art works around him which have long since been sold off. Sara Allgood makes Emma's endlessly chattering mother so genuine and appealing, despite all her 'gaucheness', that (as was planned) we resent the patronising glances of the Nelson household.

Unfortunately, the members of the Nelson family were not as fully fleshed out, and the players had to resort to one-dimensional, stereotyped characterisations. According to his biographer Felix Barker, Olivier 'reluctantly decided that for the purposes of this film it would have been a mistake to venture beyond the popular conception of a great naval hero'.[11] Consequently, Olivier's Nelson provides us with no insights into the man, and alongside the other performances, his appears too passionless and stagey. (He is not helped by the obvious ageing make-up more appropriate to an amateur theatrical production.) Halliwell Hobbes and Gladys Cooper bring some conviction to their roles as the Reverend Nelson and Lady Nelson, but their parts are all too brief. Of the supporting players, Henry Wilcoxon (as Captain Hardy) and Gilbert Emery (as Lord Spencer) both deserve special mention for their sympathetic cameo roles.

Although *That Hamilton Woman* does suffer from the same narrative fragmentation of Korda's other historical pictures, the time and place transitions are at least handled with more finesse by way of Emma's voice-over narration. The flashback structure works as a whole, but it might have been more successful if the prologue and epilogue sequences had been less heavy-handed. Sherriff and Reisch, more sophisticated scriptwriters than Lajos Biro and Arthur Wimperis, constructed the story without needless repetitions of scenes and dialogue and with a light, off-handed humour which lacks the coyness prevalent in earlier Korda works.

Since Korda is concerned with portraying Nelson and Emma as national heroes rather than as notorious lovers, the couple's passions have been played down, and sexual innuendoes are avoided, except for a passing reference to a bed large enough for six ('Why I've never tried'). There are several immediately recognisable Kordaesque touches: the farcical treatment of the family life of the King and Queen of Naples (Emma's comment that 'The real King of Naples is really the Queen' is pure Korda) and the use of a Romney portrait to give us our first impression of Emma. As we might expect, there is nothing subtle in the film's references to war and in Nelson's political speeches: Sir William explains to Emma, 'We must fight those who want to dictate to the world,' and later Nelson warns the Neapolitan court, 'We [England] can't protect all Europe.' The parallels were inescapable and perhaps too crudely made, but they did not fail to hit their target.

The film is not technically innovative, but at least the camera is trained on the actors this time. Close-ups and medium shots appear with more frequency than is normal for a Korda film, and camera movements are confined to following the actors, usually during an emotional scene (e.g. Emma's flight to Nelson on the balcony). Korda tends to shy away from dramatic cutting within a scene, preferring to let the camera record from only one or two set-ups. Although the exigencies of a tight shooting schedule may have necessitated this utilitarian camera coverage of sequences, it was not an uncharacteristic feature of Korda's overall directing style.

*That Hamilton Woman* was released in America in April 1941. It was a great success there, as it was to be in unlikely places such as South America and the Soviet Union. If its success did not reach the heights of *Henry VIII*, this is probably due to two factors: some American audiences balked at the political message of the film (which reviewers were quick to warn them about) and others were disappointed by Korda's chaste handling of the Nelson–Hamilton affair. The latter resented that the provocative spice of sex had not been added to the historical–political mixture, a fault which Korda had avoided in *Henry*. In Britain, of course, the film's success was assured. Its most enthusiastic supporter was Prime Minister Winston Churchill, who saw the film innumerable times (for the fifth time when he arranged for it to be screened on board the *Prince of Wales* as it took him to the Atlantic Conference in August 1941) and was, by all reports, emotionally moved at every screening. As Felix Barker reveals:

> Mr. Churchill's interest dated back to the time when it was first announced that the film was to be made. Within twenty-four hours he had cabled Korda in Hollywood with a suggestion for a title and this had been followed up by other cables with other suggestions. Korda, alive to the importance of security, kept very quiet about these cables, but when he returned to England in

January, 1942, Mr. Churchill invited him to Chequers for the weekend, and the first thing he asked was whether Korda had received them. Korda thanked him and said he had, and added that of course he had kept them absolutely secret for fear of vulgar publicity. Churchill looked at him quizzically. 'I *meant* them to be used,' he said. 'I sent them to put your stock up!' [12]

But *That Hamilton Woman*'s success only exacerbated the controversy which was to arise in America in the autumn of 1941. 'Propaganda,' Alex had told Laurence Olivier, 'can be bitter medicine. It needs sugar coating—and Lady Hamilton is a very thick coating of sugar indeed.' [13] As it happened, the sugar coating was not thick enough to protect Korda from those who found the medicine too hard to swallow.

During the years prior to American entry into the war, Hollywood film-makers had not been afraid to express their political sympathies, although certain precautions had been taken to ensure that these sympathies were tactfully exploited.

'. . . there was always a very strong pro-British feeling in Hollywood with producers and directors,' R. C. Sherriff explained to me in a letter, 'and I was on a Committee organised by the British Consul which was intended to watch over films that might have embarrassed the American Government as being too much against Germany before War was declared. Among these pictures was "Mrs. Miniver", and of course "Lady Hamilton". . . . I was never at any time conscious that our activities as British citizens in writing these pictures was under any Government suspicion, although clearly it would obviously have been wrong to emphasize their British bias.' [14]

Nevertheless, there were those, like the German Consul in Los Angeles and the isolationist Senators in Washington, who wanted to expose the 'complicity' of the British colony and the Hollywood community in making pro-British films. The pro-German and isolationist factions in America found added support from the British press which fanned the fires already started by continuing to question the presence in Hollywood of British 'deserters'. In June 1941 one of Korda's gestures precipitated the following attack in *Kinematograph Weekly*:

'Korda must think I'm starving,' writes a Sunday paper critic. And this because he received a parcel from Hollywood containing

butter, tea, sugar, coffee, bacon, ham, onion soup extract, choco-
lates, figs, dates and prunes.

'I feel grateful to my friend Korda for this luxury gift,' he continues. 'But I feel resentment for our propaganda people for letting
Hollywood think that I am so hungry that I need such a parcel of
food. . . .'

In order to open Hollywood's eyes, why don't our propaganda
people arrange for a deputation from Hollywood's British colony
to send over a complete food ship and deliver the parcels personally.[15]

By September 1941 suspicions were sufficiently aroused to prompt the
establishment of a Senate investigatory committee.

Korda and his scriptwriters may have honestly believed that they had
not over-emphasised British bias in *That Hamilton Woman*, but few on
the Senate Committee would have agreed. Korda had, in fact, blown
any chance to claim his neutrality by including in the film the following
speech by Nelson to the members of the British Admiralty:

> Lord Spencer, gentlemen—you're celebrating a peace with
> Napoleon Bonaparte—peace is a very beautiful word as long as
> the impulse of peace is behind it. But, gentlemen, you will never
> make peace with Napoleon. He doesn't mean peace to-day. He
> just wants to gain a little time to re-arm himself at sea and to make
> new alliances with Italy and Spain—all to one purpose. To destroy
> our Empire! Years ago I said the same thing at Naples. I begged
> them, I entreated them not to give way but they wouldn't listen
> to me, and they paid the price. But that was a little Kingdom miles
> away in the Mediterranean. But now it is England our own land.
> Napoleon can never be master of the world until he has smashed
> us up—and believe me, gentlemen, he means to be master of the
> world. You cannot make peace with dictators. You have to destroy
> them. Wipe them out! Gentlemen, I implore you—speak to the
> Prime Minister before it is too late. Do not ratify this peace!

Nelson's plea has such obvious Churchillian overtones that some have
suggested that Churchill must have himself written it, a possibility
which R. C. Sherriff has unequivocally denied. This speech was to become one of the main bases of the American Senate's attack on Alex
Korda.

During the first week of September a sub-committee of the Senate

Interstate Commerce Committee, under the chairmanship of Senator D. Worth Clark, began hearings to ascertain whether Hollywood film-makers could be charged with 'inciting to war'. The big Hollywood production companies, rather than individual directors like Korda, were the Senators' primary targets, and the Hollywood moguls intended to rebutt the charges as vehemently as possible and chose Wendell L. Willkie, the popular statesman who had unsuccessfully run against Roosevelt for the Presidency in 1940, as their defence counsel. Industry leaders like Harry Warner and Darryl F. Zanuck, both of whom rushed to testify, made no attempt to hide their contempt for Hitler and Nazism, but they all refused to admit that their films were intentional propaganda weapons. This, of course, did not stop the Senators from trotting out a list of those films which they considered suspect, among them Chaplin's *The Great Dictator* (1940),* Hitchcock's *Foreign Correspondent* (1940), and Korda's two productions, *The Spy in Black* (1939) and *The Lion Has Wings* (1939).

On the 20th of September John T. Flynn, an economist, writer, and director of the 'America First Committee', appeared before the investigators and read out aloud from the press books of certain films 'which he proposed the sub-committee investigate for propaganda content'.

> His reading of and comment on the suggestions to theater managers for promoting the pictures kept the crowded committee room in a gale of laughter. There was no doubt that the press book material on 'That Hamilton Woman' was never expected by its authors to be the subject of discourse by a man with a cutting sense of humor.[17]

Although Korda was undoubtedly offended by Flynn's attempt at public ridicule, he was probably more concerned with a more serious charge which had been brought the week before. Senator Gerald P. Nye, vocal Administration critic and instigator of the hearings, had 'asked an investigation to determine whether there are British agents operating "in any capacity" in the American industry'.[18]

* As Chaplin admits, Alex Korda was the first man to plant the idea of *The Great Dictator* in Chaplin's mind. 'Alexander Korda,' he wrote in his autobiography, 'in 1937 had suggested I should do a Hitler story based on mistaken identity, Hitler having the same moustache as the tramp: I could play both characters, he said. I did not think too much about the idea then. . . .'[16] Chaplin later reconsidered, but the film took two years to make, by which time the point of the satire was lost in the gravity of the international situation.

Although the Clark hearings were suspended in October (and postponed indefinitely soon after), Senator Nye's suggestion was taken up by the Senate Foreign Relations Committee which had for some time been investigating the status of possible 'foreign agents' in America. This Committee decided to scrutinise the activities of certain British film-makers then working in Hollywood, including Korda and Victor Saville, and the Senators planned to confront Korda with the charge that the American branch of his film company, Alexander Korda Films Inc., was a centre for pro-British propaganda. (There were, as we shall presently see, other grounds for their investigation of Korda.) In particular, they wanted to know if there was any historical justification for the inclusion in *That Hamilton Woman* of Nelson's speech to the Admiralty. If Korda's answers did not satisfy the Senators, he faced at best censure, and at worst expulsion from the country.

Some time in November, Korda received a subpoena to appear before the Committee on the 12th of December, a Friday. The Japanese attack on Pearl Harbor the previous Sunday and Roosevelt's subsequent declaration of war saved Korda from certain professional embarrassment and put a quick end to this fairly mild episode in the history of Government versus film industry relations in America.

In January 1942 no longer under the threat of a Senate subpoena, Alex Korda made his first trip back to England since June 1940. Legend has it that during this visit Winston Churchill told Alex (perhaps during his weekend stay at Chequers?) that he was to be knighted in the forthcoming Birthday Honours List. Korda's reaction is, sadly, unrecorded, but it seems likely that the significance of the honour and the title it conferred on him must have immensely pleased Korda. He had, after all, only been a British citizen for six years, and now, at a time when his loyalty was still being questioned in some quarters, he was to be the first film producer to receive a knighthood. Moreover, although he never was boorish about being 'Sir' Alexander Korda, the title must have appealed to his aristocratic pretensions. On the 11th of June Korda's knighthood was publicly announced; three months later Sir Alex and Lady Korda returned to London for the official ceremony at Buckingham Palace.

In the Honours List citation there is no mention of the services for which Korda was being honoured. 'For his contribution to the British film industry' was, and still is, the most often repeated explanation. While this was reason enough, there was more to the knighthood than most people realised. After all, 1942 was a rather critical year for the passing out of such congratulatory awards. Korda had, of course, served his country by producing two good propaganda films, but is it possible that Korda got his knighthood simply because Churchill was deeply moved by *Lady Hamilton*? Perhaps the fact that Korda was raising money in America through film re-issues (an estimated $7,000,000 gain for the British Treasury) influenced the decision, but there *were* other reasons, ones not related to Korda's film-making activities.

> The services for which he was so rewarded remain vague, but it is known that Korda was in close touch with the O.S.S. and his American office had been called a British espionage centre by isolationist senators. (*News Chronicle*, 22 October 1959)

> It is not generally known that Korda's recognition was not entirely for his work in British films. His important work during the war, of which I knew a great deal that I cannot, alas, disclose here, was much more the basic reason. (Herbert Wilcox) [19]

> London Films and its chief had done a certain amount of economic intelligence work before the war. (Paul Tabori) [20]

These comments force us to take another look at Korda's activities both before and during the war. This review unfortunately leads us on to the thin ice of rumour and speculation, for the exact nature and extent of Korda's political activities are still shrouded in mystery. None the less, it is necessary to examine the rumours as well as the facts, for they, too, have become vital parts of the Korda legend. Since most of the stories relate in some way to Winston Churchill, it is best to begin with a brief account of Korda's friendship and unusual partnership with one of Britain's foremost twentieth-century statesmen.

Although Korda had always been drawn to men with political power and influence, his attraction to British political figures, in contrast to similar alliances with Hungarian leaders like Karolyi and Kun, was a corollary of his social ambitions, not of any specific political commitment. In the early thirties Korda met Brendan Bracken through friends, and through Bracken he came to know Robert Vansittart, Winston Churchill, and other Conservative Party members. Korda's alignment with the Conservatives was understandable; he had long since abandoned the left-wing stance of his early days in Hungary, and his new aspirations—for power and social acceptance—could be better realised within the ranks of the Tory Party. Even though Winston Churchill, whose friendship Alex cultivated more than any other, was at that time out of favour even within his own party, it was because of this, rather than despite it, that Korda was able to establish a relationship with Churchill which was to be mutually beneficial.

Korda and Churchill were both dynamic and charismatic personalities, commanding conversationalists who shared similar tastes and pleasures. In addition, Churchill, unlike most other politicians, had a dilettante's fascination with the arts and was therefore receptive to Korda's encouragements that he should try his hand at film-making. In September 1934, at a meeting in an Isleworth pub arranged by Winston's son Randolph (who had been working in the London Films publicity department), Churchill agreed to sign a contract with Korda's company. His first assignment was to supervise a series of 'topical shorts' on subjects like 'Will Monarchies Return?', 'Unemployed', and 'Gold'. Korda took great pains to make sure that Churchill's first experiments would be successful. *Kinematograph Weekly* reported: 'London Films have engaged a special staff of technical experts in order to ensure that Mr. Churchill's ideas will be presented in the most vivid, novel and entertaining fashion.'[21] Filming on the series was to begin in January 1935, but for some reason, probably financial, none of the shorts were ever made.

A week after the 'Churchill shorts' were first arranged, however, another Churchill–Korda project was announced in the press. Churchill was to write the script for Korda's film commemorating the twenty-five-year reign of King George V, planned for release in 1936 to coincide with the Silver Jubilee celebrations. Anthony Asquith, the project's director, and Lajos Biro spent a fortnight at Chartwell giving Churchill instruction in the basics of script-writing, but this film, like the shorts, was abandoned in January 1935.* Seven months later, London Films announced that Churchill was to supervise some sequences of *Conquest of the Air*, which, as we already know, was another

---

* Two different explanations have been given for the abandonment of the Silver Jubilee film: one that Korda discovered it would be too difficult (too expensive?) to reconstruct the historical events of the King's reign and the other that British film-makers objected to a Hungarian being allowed to produce such a 'British' work and forced Korda to withdraw his project.

of Korda's ill-fated productions. The impression that Korda was simply making a welcome contribution to Churchill's finances was emerging, strengthened by the fact that Korda bought at this time the screen rights to at least one of Churchill's books—*Marlborough* for £10,000—with very little intention of actually filming it. (At some point Korda also bought the rights to Churchill's *History of the English-Speaking Peoples*.)

After 1937 or 1938, Korda's aid to Churchill took on an entirely different form. Sharing Churchill's growing concern with the Fascist regimes in Europe and having lost some of his enthusiasm for film production, Korda was ready to try a more exciting career.

Paul Tabori has tantalised us with his mention of the 'economic intelligence work' conducted by Korda and London Films prior to the war, but he has offered no elaboration on the point. It is, however, now known that in the years before 1939 Winston Churchill organised his own private group of 'secret agents'—businessmen in the main—who provided him with information concerning the German military build-up. Churchill then used their information in his attempts to urge the British Government to take measures to forearm the country for the war which he believed to be inevitable. It is reasonable to suggest that, with his many contacts abroad, Korda was in a position to render such information to Churchill. Nevertheless, Korda's pre-war work for Churchill remains unsubstantiated, something which does not hold true for his activities after 1939.

In 1940 one of Churchill's personal agents, William Stephenson, a Canadian businessman, was chosen to set up the British secret intelligence centre in America, which operated, until December 1941 clandestinely, from the Rockefeller Center in New York and which was known as BSC (British Security Co-ordination). This organisation worked successfully in the fields of espionage and counter-espionage and, before American entry into the war, helped to gain needed supplies for Britain and to promote a pro-British climate of opinion in the United States. In his book on Stephenson and the BSC, H. Montgomery Hyde states that Alexander Korda was one of Stephenson's 'willing helpers outside B.S.C., who put [his] own resources and facilities at his disposal'.[22]

Although Montgomery Hyde gives us no details regarding the nature of Korda's assistance to BSC, it is clear that Korda was closely connected with several men at BSC and at the OSS (Office of Strategic Services, the American counterpart to BSC which was formed in June

1941)* and that his undercover activities took two forms: acting personally as a secret courier between British and American intelligence centres and allowing his New York office in the Empire State Building to be used as a clearing house for intelligence information.

Robert Vas's 1968 television documentary on Korda carefully side-stepped the issue of Korda's wartime departure to Hollywood, but, according to one viewer, it created the impression that Korda had 'fled' the country. This one viewer was Korda's son Peter, who fired off an angry letter to *The Sunday Telegraph* in which he defended his father by disclosing what others had been (and still are) afraid to reveal:

> The B.B.C. alleged that my father left for America during the war and didn't return until peace was declared. [The programme does not, in fact, allege this.]
>
> Once again, this B.B.C.-organised suggestion of opportunism is totally false as in actual fact my father crossed the Atlantic over 16 times as a secret courier for a certain Government department controlled by the Foreign Office.
>
> He was an Anglophile and during the war worked for Sir Winston Churchill as a secret courier.[23]

In the ten years from 1935 to 1945 Korda did make twenty-four Atlantic crossings, but the majority of these trips—four in 1939 and at least twelve between 1940 and 1945—were undertaken just prior to or during the war, at a time when passage was not easy to arrange (Stephenson was responsible for arranging several of his trips) and the journeys were particularly hazardous. Korda made several crossings by boat and spent weeks waiting for the Yankee Clipper in Lisbon and for exit visas in Washington. 'More than once,' Ian Dalrymple has written, 'he flew over in an ordinary bomber on delivery to the Royal Air Force. Once his oxygen-tube became disconnected in his sleep, and he owed his life to the keen eye of Captain Hussey, R.N. . . .'[24] On this same flight Korda refused to wear the cumbersome life jacket which one of the crew tried to put on him.

* William Stephenson was himself involved in British film-making, for he owned Sound City Films Ltd, the company which operated Shepperton Studios and in which Korda bought a controlling interest after the war. The head of the Security Division of BSC was none other than Sir Connop Guthrie, Korda's 'angel' from the Prudential, and the playwright Robert Sherwood, who had often worked with Korda, became head of the Foreign Information Service of the OSS. Alex also became friends with General William Donovan who directed all of the OSS's activities.

In answer to his inquiry as to the purpose of this article of equipment, the officer said: 'It will keep you afloat for twenty hours,
sir!'

It was mid-winter, intensely cold and blowing a gale. Korda was
not impressed. 'But I do not want to be kept afloat for twenty
hours,' he remarked somewhat plaintively. . . .[25]

Cold, uncomfortable, and dangerous as these journeys were, they provided Korda with that 'sharing of danger' which he had talked about
as the 'greatest exhilaration' of his life.

Korda's profession and his business concerns on both sides of the
Atlantic offered a perfect cover for a man engaged in passing intelligence information, and yet his cover was almost exposed by the Senate
in 1941. It seems it was not Korda's numerous Atlantic crossings which
raised the Senators' suspicions, but rather some of the activities at his
New York headquarters, the questionable nature of which must have
somehow leaked out. Precisely how Korda's offices were being used is
not clear, but it is likely that at least some of his staff was involved in
receiving, copying, perhaps translating, and forwarding material passed
to them from BSC and later OSS agents. After 1941, of course, Korda's
espionage activities would have received top-level American Govern-
mental approval, and his 'resources and facilities' would have been
integrated into the whole BSC–OSS network.

Although we may never know the details regarding and thus the
importance of Korda's wartime undercover work, we can assume that
his knighthood in 1942 was in recognition of these services to the
British Government. There is, however, another explanation for his
knighthood, an explanation far more fantastic than the preceding ones.
I received it in a letter from the respected German journalist Hans
Habe. 'Although I heard about all this several times after the invasion,'
Habe writes, 'I heard it also from an immediate source, namely from a
friend, the late Marcel Vertès, the great Hungarian painter, who served
as a set-designer for Korda during the shooting of KING PAUSOLE.'
The letter begins:

> There have been consistent rumors as to the reasons why
> Alexander Korda was knighted in England.
>
> Although, because of obvious reasons, such rumors cannot be
> absolutely verified, they have an undeniably real basis.
>
> When, after Hitler's rise to power, war was approaching, the
> British Secret Service was convinced that Africa might become

one of the most important battlefields of the war. However, England did not possess the necessary information about Africa and particularly about the coast-lines, which were so important for any future military operation.

Sir Robert Vansittart, then Chief of all Intelligence Operations, belonged to the most intimate friends of Alexander Korda. He confined [sic] his worries to the great film-maker.

Korda had an idea. He proposed to make a film in Africa—a 'bogus-film', so to say, with the sole aim to procure film-material about North- and West-Africa and, more particularly, about the potential invasion coast. The idea instantly found the approval of Sir Robert.

Thus preparations for a French–British co-production of a film called KING PAUSOLE started. None of the participants—actors, technicians, cameramen—had the slightest knowledge, that this picture was not to be presented.

The picture—one of the most costly in the history of British film-making—was indeed made. Korda arranged all the 'shots' in such a manner that, for instance, dozens of lightly cled [sic] girls danced on the rocks of the coast, showing less their lines as the lines of the beaches.

As a result, Great-Britain and its American allies had a complete picture of the North- and West-African coast when the hour of invasion rang. The Korda-picture was shown to the officers planning the invasion.[26]

It is a remarkable tale which sounds more 'like Korda' than the other stories, but sadly no one I've spoken to, many of whom worked closely with Korda during this period, has ever heard of the fabulous *King Pausole*. Some find it quite plausible that Korda should produce such a film, while others, notably Roy Boulting who was involved with the Army Film Unit in the production of documentaries about the African invasion, consider the enterprise far-fetched, the ruse too elaborate and unnecessary for the purpose it might have served. Nevertheless, let us put aside for the moment our reservations about the story's validity and explore some possibly corroborative evidence.

First, Sir Robert Vansittart had, in fact, taken steps to organise 'war-time' film activities long before the outbreak of war. In *Documentary Diary*, in an entry on 27 April 1938, Paul Rotha recorded that 'so far [the] only practical move has been . . . to set up a Coordinating Committee for Propaganda under Sir Robert Vansittart, but I am not clear who or what it intends to coordinate'.[27] Second, according to Victor Saville the Government did make a general request to film-makers for footage from films already completed or in production which might show territory likely to be important in future invasions or battles. The Pausole story, however, probably ante-dated this official request. Third, there is a film in existence called *Les Aventures du roi Pausole* (1933), a French film obviously made too early to be a contender, but produced and directed by Alexis Granowsky, Korda's partner in many Anglo-French productions. The film was shown in London as *The Merry Monarch*, but was taken off after one day because of censorship problems (the story revolved around a king who kept a wife for every day of the year).* Since Korda bought and re-made or shelved several of Granowsky's films, it is not unreasonable to suggest that *The Merry Monarch* may have been one of them. If Vansittart and Korda wanted a film script to work from which would guarantee that the film was never shown, this film would have been the perfect choice. If the cast and crew were predominantly French, this might explain why none of Korda's regular staff had any knowledge of the film. But this is as far as we can go in our speculations, and it is unlikely that we will ever get any closer to the truth about *King Pausole*, for most of the people who were in a position to know about it—Vansittart, Churchill, Granowsky, Korda, and Vertès—are now dead.

In time, more stories will undoubtedly be added to the fact and fiction surrounding Korda's wartime work and the reasons for his knighthood. Some of the more fantastic tales were probably promoted by those who needed to believe that Korda's departure from Britain was not based on selfish motives and therefore grasped at all rumours, elaborating them into a vindication of Korda's actions. In the long run, what Korda actually contributed to the war effort, the little we know of it, has done that job for them.

1. Jympson Harman, ' "Alex": A Study of Korda', in *The British Film Yearbook 1949–50*, ed. Peter Noble, London, Skelton Robinson, 1949, p. 107.
2. Paul Holt, 'A Cabby Decided his Future', *Daily Herald*, 9 May 1953.
3. *Today's Cinema*, 19 January 1940, p. 1, (my emphasis).
4. *Ibid*, (Korda's emphasis).
5. Jympson Harman, *op cit*, p. 109.
6. All information from David Lampe, *The Last Ditch*, London, Cassell & Company, 1968, which includes a copy of the Arrest List.

* Stills from this film, incidentally, do show several scenes of 'lightly clad girls' cavorting on a beach.

7. *Variety*, 10 October 1940.
8. From BBC documentary, 'David Lean: A Self-Portrait', shown 16 August 1974.
9. R. C. Sherriff, *op cit*, p. 335.
10. *Ibid*, p. 337.
11. Felix Barker, *The Oliviers: a biography*, London, Hamish Hamilton, 1953, p. 220.
12. *Ibid*, p. 221.
13. *Ibid*, p. 215.
14. R. C. Sherriff in a letter to the author, 11 September 1973.
15. *Kinematograph Weekly*, 5 June 1941, p. 5.
16. Charles Chaplin, *My Autobiography*, London, The Bodley Head, 1964, pp. 424–5.
17. This and previous quote from *Motion Picture Herald*, 20 September 1941, p. 31.
18. *Motion Picture Herald*, 13 September 1941, p. 23.
19. Herbert Wilcox, *Twenty-Five Thousand Sunsets: the autobiography of Herbert Wilcox*, London, The Bodley Head, 1967, pp. 157–8.
20. Paul Tabori, *op cit*, p. 221.
21. *Kinematograph Weekly*, 27 September 1934.
22. H. Montgomery Hyde, *Room 3603: the story of the British Intelligence Center in New York during World War II*, New York, Farrar Straus & Co., 1962, p. 183.
23. *The Sunday Telegraph*, 29 December 1968.
24. Ian Dalrymple, 'Alex', *Journal of the British Film Academy*, Spring 1956, p. 13.
25. H. Montgomery Hyde, *op cit*, p. 184.
26. Letter to the author from Hans Habe.
27. Paul Rotha, *Documentary Diary*, London, Secker and Warburg, 1973, pp. 214–15.

PART FOUR

## *The Last Years*

# CHAPTER SEVENTEEN

# A Commercial Producer in Wartime

BETWEEN 1940 and 1945 Alex lived in two very different worlds. Despite the occasional hysteria caused by 'sightings' of Japanese submarines off the West Coast, Hollywood, like the rest of America, remained detached from the physical devastation and deprivation inflicted by the Second World War. In actual fact, the war had a beneficial effect on American business and on the film industry, for it triggered off a prosperity boom in most spheres of commercial life. Alex and Merle worked hard, but they had no cause to worry about their professional careers. Their social life likewise suffered little during the war. They went to and gave dinner parties, had friends over for an afternoon swim in their pool, employed a female chauffeur, and, in general, spared no expense in their entertainments. Korda played the role of a movie mogul, and he and Merle were accepted into the ranks of the Hollywood elite.

Korda had to face an entirely different situation during the months he stayed in England. Although he maintained the lifestyle of his prewar days, he could not avoid the physical and human drama which surrounded him: the black-outs, the bombings and fires, the anxieties and sufferings of the British people. His own home in St John's Wood had been shattered by a bomb in December 1940, and his son Peter had just managed to escape with minor injuries. Claridges became Korda's wartime residence, and to cope with his loneliness (Merle accompanied him to London only once), Korda invited many of his old friends to dinner there and welcomed the company of most of the hotel guests. Korda had little work to do, for during the first four years of the war he promoted only two 'new' productions in Britain, both of which had been initiated prior to his departure for Hollywood.

The first film, *Conquest of the Air* (1940), was far from new.* John Monk Saunders, the American scriptwriter responsible for *Wings* (1928) and *Dawn Patrol* (1930), was originally commissioned in 1934 or 1935 to write the screenplay for this feature-length documentary about the history of aviation. By 1936 Zoltan Korda, Lee Garmes, and William Cameron Menzies had already directed and photographed much of the film, although it wasn't until 1938 that the film was put together for the first time. Donald Taylor and Alexander Shaw undertook to complete a sixty-minute compilation of the material which incorporated new footage filmed by cameramen Wilkie Cooper, Hans Schneeberger, and George Noble and edited by Richard Q. MacNaughten. In January 1938 this version had a limited press showing, but it was shelved before it could be released.† Late in 1939 Charles Frend, the British editor and director, salvaged the film from Korda's vaults and added a narration and more documentary footage (including some shots of early wartime aviation and of Churchill). This seventy-one-minute version was trade shown in May 1940 and then presumably released, although there is no conclusive evidence to substantiate this or any other public screening of the film.

*Conquest*'s erratic production history is at once apparent in the final result, a 'scrappy' mixture of newsreel footage and reconstructed 'dramatic' scenes which star most of Korda's contract players in the key roles of aviation pioneers. With the exception of one stunning visual sequence—D'Annunzio's leaflet 'bombing' of Vienna—the film lacks imagination and inspiration and pales in comparison with the contemporary work done by British documentary film-makers and with present-day television documentaries. Its main virtue is the musical score which Arthur Bliss was persuaded to compose during the early stages of production and which, as a concert piece on its own, has since become dissociated from the film. The history of *Conquest of the Air*

* See pages 126 and 255.

†At some point Ned Mann, Korda's special effects superviser, devised several sequences showing the future of aviation, *à la Things to Come*. How far he got in his plans is unknown; these sequences do not appear in the 1940 version. The narration which Leslie Mitchell, the British commentator, recorded at an early stage in production was likewise scrapped.

was further complicated in 1944 when Key Films distributed it in a cut, forty-six-minute form which some reviewers found preferable to the 'original'.

Although filmed while Korda was in America and planned with little or no concern for international markets, *Old Bill and Son* (1941) is still considered a 'Korda' picture by its director, Ian Dalrymple. Alex's two associates, Josef Somlo and Harold Boxall, produced the film in Korda's absence, and all the technicians on the production were Korda regulars. The picture was a 'bread-and-butter' British film based on Bruce Bairnsfather's famous cartoon character. Dalrymple, who is self-effacing with regard to his own work, has condemned it as a badly cast 'horror', although the critics were much kinder. The film opened in London just as France fell—'So did the film,' says Dalrymple.[1]

Of course, these two minor works were not representative of Korda's wartime output, for his real energies were concentrated in Hollywood where he was trying to carry on the tradition of large-scale feature production which he had established before the war. *Lydia* (1941) and *Jungle Book* (1942), Korda's last two Hollywood films, bore the unmistakable Korda imprint.

For several years Korda had searched with little success for a starring vehicle for Merle Oberon. She had not played in a 'good' Korda film since 1934 (*The Scarlet Pimpernel*), and although she was at the peak of her career in 1940, her success had come from the parts she had played while on loan to other producers, like Samuel Goldwyn. Alex obviously wanted to correct this situation.

Julien Duvivier, the French director whose major works in France had been *Pépé le Moko* (1937) and *Carnet de bal* (1937), was in Hollywood during the war, and he and Korda decided that an adaptation of the latter film might provide the right showpiece for Merle. Since the plot centres around an ageing heroine's reminiscences about her many past suitors, Merle would be the main female character paired with four leading men: Alan Marshall, Joseph Cotten, Hans Yaray, and George Reeves. Vincent Korda was to design the sets, Lee Garmes was to photograph the picture, and, as further insurance, Korda hired one of Hollywood's best writers Ben Hecht—*The Front Page* (1931) and *Nothing Sacred* (1937)—to script the story. Hecht, working with his collaborator Charles MacArthur, had just finished *Wuthering Heights*, in which Merle had played Cathy, the best role of her career.

Korda had set up the film in order to surround his wife with the best available talent, but *Lydia* did not live up to expectations. The dialogue was better than usual for a Korda production, but the film was uneven both in structure and direction. Although the flashback scenes of each love story which Lydia narrates are explored with polish, humour, and delicacy, the 'reunion' sequence which opens the film and links the stories together is awkwardly filmed, the actors moving stiffly about, uncomfortable in their unconvincing 'ageing' make-up. If Alex wanted Merle to outshine the rest of the cast, he made a mistake in casting Hollywood veteran Edna May Oliver as 'Granny', for she simply walks away with every scene in which she appears. The less discerning critics praised the film, Merle's performance, and Duvivier's direction, but the more discerning audiences stayed away from the film. *Lydia* was only a moderate success at the box office— and, without any desire to encourage a direct correlation, it must be added that *Lydia* was Merle's last picture for Alex Korda.

Zoltan Korda's *Jungle Book* was also designed to exploit one star's popularity—this time Korda's most popular contract player and only 'child star': Sabu. Although Robert Flaherty had discovered the young Indian boy, it was Korda who groomed him for an international career by starring him in *The Drum* (1938) and *The Thief of Bagdad* (1940). Sabu stayed in Hollywood after *The Thief* was completed, and in *Jungle Book*, his last Korda picture, played his best screen role as Mowgli, the hero of Rudyard Kipling's *Jungle Book* stories.

Laurence Stallings, the American writer who had adapted his play *The Big Parade* into a film for King Vidor in 1925 and had since co-written several screenplays, faithfully adapted and combined several of the Kipling stories into one feature production. Stallings excepted, *Jungle Book* was a reunion of the talent which had gone into Korda's previous big productions: Zoltan and Vincent Korda, Lee Garmes, Lawrence Butler, William Hornbeck, Miklos Rozsa, and even Jack Okey, the man who had designed Denham Studios. With these men, an enormous budget (£250,000), and all of Hollywood's technical facilities at his disposal, Korda could hardly go wrong.

According to Zoltan's son David, however, there was a running battle between Zolly and Alex throughout the film's production. Zoltan wanted *Jungle Book* to be an adventure film with a realistic background, on the lines of *Elephant Boy*, while Alex saw it more as a follow-up to *The Thief of Bagdad*, in other words, as a fantasy epic. Zoltan's conception might have provided a more interesting approach to the original material, but the film became a fraternal compromise:

an adventure film with an unrealistic (conventional Hollywood) background in which the 'jungle' wins out over the 'book' every time.

The 'book' starts with a handicap, for Stallings tried to deal with too many of Kipling's tales. Included in the picture are the stories of how infant Mowgli leaves his village and comes to live with the wolf pack, how he is later captured and 'tamed' by the villagers and his real mother Messua (Rosemary De Camp), how he takes revenge on Shere Khan, the tiger who terrorises both the beasts of the jungle and the native inhabitants as well, how Mowgli discovers the treasures of a 'lost city' and then protects it from plunder by three thieving villagers (who play in Three Stooges comedy style), and how Mowgli saves the villagers and beasts from a devastating fire and then returns to the jungle. In addition, all these incidents are told within a flashback framework, for the stories are recounted by a narrator (Buldeo–Joseph Calleia—one of the thieves) for the benefit of an over-effusive young English traveller. Minus one episode, the film might have better held audience attention. As it is, the film is at least twenty minutes too long.

The book's other handicap is the Kipling–Korda dialogue, suitable for neither man nor beast. The over-emphasis on Mowgli's jungle-pidgeon English ('tooth' for 'knife' and so on) leads to some unintentionally embarrassing exchanges, but the beasts don't fare much better, as the *Time* magazine reviewer pointed out:

> When the animals are talking their own language and roaming their improvised jungle near Los Angeles, *Jungle Book* is as absorbing as a behind-the-scenes trip to the zoo. But when they converse in Kipling's English, the result is painful. The python sounds like Lionel Barrymore; the cobra, who is very long winded, like a wheezy crackerbox philosopher; a tough monkey like a Tammany ward heeler.[2]

Nevertheless, the beasts and their convincing Technicolor jungle do save the film.

Shere Khan (real name: Roger), Bagheera the slinky black panther, and Baloo the bear share with Sabu the honours for best acting in the film. The man-made beasts—Kaa, the enormous python, and the ancient white cobra—are less satisfactory; 'It can be remarked,' one critic wrote, 'that both reptiles are over-garrulous.'[3] All the animals, however, are preferable to the oddly well-dressed and made-up natives of Zoltan's Indian village, which has more in common with Korda's 'Bagdad' than Flaherty's 'India'. Alex's insistence on conventional cinematic glamourisation was regrettable, but consistent with his concept of cinema. Korda saw films in terms of make-believe entertainments designed to attract maximum international exposure, and for him, realism or authenticity held little value, except perhaps in the field of documentary (and even there—*The Lion Has Wings* and *Conquest of the Air*—Alex could never resist injecting star names as box-office insurance).

*Jungle Book* made effective use of Technicolor and wild-life photography, and its production values were of such quality as to earn it six Academy Award nominations: for photography, special effects, music, set design, sound, and art direction. The film was a commercial success and represents, for its weaknesses as well as its strengths, the typical Alexander Korda production. This is fitting, for it was also the last all-Korda production ever made, the last film on which the three brothers worked together. (Vincent continued to work with Alex in Britain, but Zoltan remained in Hollywood and only directed two more pictures for London Films, *Cry, the Beloved Country* in 1952 and *Storm Over the Nile* in 1955.) For this and other reasons which will become clear, *Jungle Book* signalled the end of an era in Korda's career.

In between trips to London and the production and promotion of his own films, Korda had been kept busy with business and personal matters. Korda's partnership in United Artists required most of his outside attention and diplomacy. In July 1940, Samuel Goldwyn, one of the other owner members, had filed suit against the company asserting, in part, that the special concessions granted to Korda—the right to make films for distributors other than UA—had invalidated Goldwyn's original contract. Korda was able to mollify Goldwyn, who dropped the litigation, but in February 1941 Goldwyn left the UA 'family'. Two months later Korda waged a successful campaign against a proposal that UA should abandon its policy of booking films singly.* In August Korda was appointed temporary head of United Artists, replacing Mary Pickford, but his dissatisfaction with the company and its members increased. There were constant rumours in the press that

---

* This proposal—to allow the block-booking of five UA films at a time—would have increased the exhibition potential of UA products (and worked to the advantage of the less distinguished UA films which would be 'tied' to better productions); but the idea contravened the UA constitution, and Korda probably defended it on general principle as much as to protect his own films from being sold with inferior features.

Korda was unable to keep up his payments on his original membership or that he was about to sell out (usually to David O. Selznick, already a UA partner). Although Korda strongly denied these stories, his association with UA was clearly causing more trouble than it was worth.*

Korda found himself faced with litigation in 1941 from what was perhaps an unexpected source. Although Alex had made an alimony settlement with his first wife early in that year, Maria Corda took him to court in August in the hope of having their divorce annulled. She claimed that they had lived together after the divorce had been final; but, as Paul Tabori reports, 'Korda denied this and pointed out that his ex-wife had in 1935 publicly announced her engagement to a Count Teleki; this she would have hardly done if she had still considered herself married to *him*.'[4] Maria lost this suit, the first round in a long series of legal battles which have still not been resolved.

Korda started to make plans to return to England during his September 1942 trip to receive his knighthood. The first rumours of his intended permanent departure from Hollywood appeared in December. Two months later, the *Hollywood Reporter* announced that Merle Oberon was to quit pictures after completing three more films: '[Korda's] return to England next week for a government propaganda post is the decisive factor in Miss Oberon's plan to retire.'[5] The 'government propaganda post' was never mentioned again, but it is clear that Korda's return posed certain problems for him, the gravest of which was that he no longer had a base of operations there. This was one problem which he quickly solved. Louis B. Mayer, head of MGM, was looking for someone to take over as manager of his MGM–British subsidiary. Alex negotiated with Mayer and the executives of Loew's, Inc., the parent company to the Hollywood studio, and in March 1943 it was reported that Korda's London Film Productions had merged with MGM–British and that Alex was returning to take charge of the new company. Merle still had contract obligations in Hollywood, so Alex came home alone in May 1943.

* In 1941 Korda also became involved in Ernst Lubitsch's film *To Be or Not To Be* (1942), a black comedy about an acting troupe's encounters with the Gestapo in occupied Warsaw, which starred Jack Benny and Carole Lombard. Although Korda apparently helped to set up the film, by securing $100,000 for Walter Wanger and Lubitsch, there is no evidence, either within the film or on its credits, to conclude that Korda played any creative role in the production. He certainly did not, as sources claim, 'produce' the picture, although some publicity hand-outs mention the ambiguous phrase 'presented by Alexander Korda'.

When the news of Korda's impending return reached Britain, the British press and film community found it difficult to muster up much enthusiasm for the first film knight's home-coming. The announcement generated instead a resurgence of criticism directed at those deserters or 'homing pigeons', as they were more charitably called, who had made a timely exit to Hollywood. The intensity of this response is hard to recapture today, since even the most embittered critics now view their chauvinistic outbursts with embarrassment. It took a writer like J. B. Priestley to recreate the deeply felt resentment of the time through a fictional scriptwriter's diatribe:

> ... some of us here in the film business can't help feeling rather bitter. Just look at it a minute. Our people here were up to the neck in the war, and half the time they lived like rats in holes, with anything that would explode or burn raining down on 'em. And if they found their way through the black-out to spend a shilling or two at the pictures—what did they see, only too often? The Sunset Boulevard notion of the war. The American Way of Life. Yanks winning the Battle for Democracy. The March of Time. And occasional films about London Taking it, a London full of dukes and toothless coster-mongers, films produced or directed often by Englishmen who'd hared across the Atlantic in thirty-nine and seemed to have forgotten what England was like.[6]

However sympathetic we are to the emotions behind this criticism, we must also accept that at least part of the reaction against Korda's return derived as much from threatened self-interest as it did from patriotic outrage. The situation was far more complex than the critics or the defenders appreciated, for Sir Alexander Korda was coming back to reclaim his place in the British film industry and to construct a new film empire which could only be built at the expense of Britain's other film-producing organisations. The suspicions of industry leaders were further confirmed when Alex sent a barrage of telegrams from Hollywood to key industry personnel in Britain offering them the chance to work, at a higher salary of course, for Korda's revitalised film company. His less than cordial welcome only added to Korda's determination to show the parochial British producers that the 'golden years' of Alexander Korda were not over.

Korda could easily cope with the lack of support of men who were now his rivals, and during his absence new industry leaders *had* appeared to fill the vacuum which he had left. Even the more familiar figures like Michael Balcon had reached new heights. In 1938 Balcon had joined Ealing, the company which was to make its name by presenting precisely the type of British subject matter deeply rooted in British life and humour which Korda usually avoided. Balcon and Korda shared a common goal—the desire to develop a vital British cinema—but their approaches couldn't have been more different. Balcon's insularity was a pole apart from Korda's vision of international films made in England for international audiences. These two men also shared the distinction of being the only top-flight film producers who were personally responsible for their own studio and staff and the films which emerged. Ealing, Denham, and later Shepperton all operated not as film factories, but as family businesses with Balcon and Korda playing the roles of clan patriarch.

A friendship did develop between Balcon and Korda in later years, but not before they had gone through several 'cold war' periods. The stormiest of these times was upon Korda's return. As Balcon recently revealed: 'There was bad feeling between us because whilst he was away a lampoon had circulated (it was at the time he was knighted) and he thought for a long time that I was author of it. Indeed, I was not.'[7] Misunderstandings were inevitable with two such dissimilar personalities. In his autobiography Balcon, now Sir Michael, aptly summed up these differences:

> He took many chances. I am much more canny. He had, I suppose, a brilliant if unconventional financial flair. I tend to orthodoxy in matters of finance. He was cosmopolitan in his outlook while I retain some of the influences of my provincial upbringing. He spoke and thought in four or five languages and altogether was a much more sophisticated character than I.[8]

In addition, Balcon's earnestness contrasted sharply with Korda's dry wit and more frivolous attitude towards his life and his work. 'But, Alex, you made a gentleman's agreement with me,' Balcon once argued. 'But, my dear Mick, it takes two gentlemen to make a gentleman's agreement,' replied Korda.[9]

Nevertheless, we might wonder what would have been the result of a film partnership between the two, a possibility which apparently was discussed in passing conversation 'more than once'. Perhaps a *Whisky Galore* starring Marlene Dietrich or *The Private Life of the Lavender Hill Mob?* It does leave the mind fairly reeling.

One of the new faces to appear on the British film scene during the immediate pre-war period was another Hungarian, Gabriel Pascal. A year younger than Korda, he had a career, both on the Continent and later making quota pictures for Paramount British, which paralleled Korda's own rise. Both men were renowned for their lively humour, financial extravagance, passion for cinematic detail, and their magician's ability to coax the birds out of the trees. In this latter attribute, 'Gabby' had the edge on Korda, for he had convinced the reluctant George Bernard Shaw to entrust him with the film rights to his plays. This was something which Hollywood, Wardour Street, and Alex Korda himself had been unable to accomplish.

By 1943, after *Pygmalion* (1938) and *Major Barbara* (1940), Pascal was set to film *Caesar and Cleopatra* (1945), the Rank-financed film which was destined to be the most expensive (close to £1,300,000) failure in British film history. When the film trade union initiated a censure motion against Gabby for the excess and waste in time, money, and studio space which *Caesar and Cleopatra* represented, Alex came to his defence. Alex's reaction was not a friendly gesture—the Pascal–Korda relationship was notoriously cool—but a response to an action which might set a dangerous precedent and inhibit large-scale production in Britain. His defence also came at a time when the press reported that Pascal and Korda were discussing a co-production deal to film *The Doctor's Dilemma*, a project which never materialised, to the relief of many in the industry.*

Without a doubt Pascal's attempt to carry on the Korda tradition never really convinced anyone; he had neither the business acumen nor the artistic discipline to bring it off. The Shaw 'conversion' was a significant coup, but it is all we now remember about Gabby. Pascal was not to remain a rival to Korda for very long. In 1947 he left Britain for Hollywood where he was to stay until his death.

An Italian émigré, Filippo Del Giudice, had also come to prominence during the war and was briefly considered Korda's heir apparent. A lawyer by profession, 'Del' was a madly extravagant, charismatic figure who could inspire film-makers by the sheer force of his persuasive personality. Del was himself exclusively a film promoter rather than a film-maker; he initiated or supported projects which were made by the men who worked for him and his Two Cities Films company. Del, like Korda, had an enchanting accent and a flair for living in the grand manner and for accumulating friends in high places, but whereas Korda gravitated to the political right, Del wooed the other side.

* *The Doctor's Dilemma* was finally filmed by Anthony Asquith in 1959.

Pascal had Shaw, Korda had Churchill, so it was only proper that Del should have his own patron in the person of Sir Stafford Cripps.

Del Giudice was brought into films by the same man who had helped Alex during the making of *Henry VIII*, Ludovico Toeplitz de Grand Ry. Del was legal adviser to Toeplitz and Bette Davis in that star's court battle with Warner Brothers in which Korda had appeared as a witness for the Hollywood opposition. Two Cities Films was formed in 1937 and became a part of the Rank Organisation five years later. Two Cities was responsible for some of Britain's finest wartime films; *French Without Tears* (1939), *In Which We Serve* (1942), *The Way Ahead* (1944), *Henry V* (1945), and *Blithe Spirit* (1945) were but five of the thirty-five films which Del promoted during his short tenure in the British cinema. Unfortunately, strife with the Rank hierarchy later put an end to the Two Cities association, and Del set up a new company, Pilgrim Pictures, in 1947. Although Del Giudice possessed an impresario's genius and charm and an artist's sensibilities, his financial naïvety coupled with ill health made it difficult for him to operate his own organisation. In 1949 Pilgrim Pictures folded, and Del left the country.

Korda's most serious rival, however, was J. Arthur Rank, flour millionaire, financial entrepreneur, and film magnate. These two men were to dominate British films during the post-war years. (That the name of J. Arthur Rank still dominates the film world in this country is a testament not to the longevity of a creative talent but rather to the indestructible fortress empire which he built.) Rank was not a film man; he didn't direct films, nor did he 'produce' them in the conventional studio sense. A devout Methodist, Rank was first attracted to the cinema by a desire to improve the quality of religious films by setting up his own company to make them. From there he went on to acquire major interests in studios—both Pinewood and Denham—distribution organisations, and exhibition chains, notably the Odeon circuit.

In his excellent biography *Mr Rank*, Alan Wood assures us that Rank's growing financial investment in the film industry was not motivated by greed. Rank considered it his Divine Mission: 'If I could relate to you some of my various adventures and experiences in the larger film world, you would not only be astonished, but it would, I think, be as plain to you as it is to me that I was being led by God.'[10] God, perhaps; a highly acute business sense, to be sure.

Rank was the consummate businessman, and compared to him,

Korda was the consummate artist. The rivalry which developed between them when they tried to out-prestige produce each other was a respectful one which they both enjoyed. They knew each other's limitations—as Rank put it: 'I've always told Alex that he should stick to making films. He's brilliant at anything to do with them ... but he should never have got tied up with this business of running companies ...,' while Alex retorted: 'I only wish I knew as much about finance as Arthur. But when it comes to films....'[11] Sadly, neither man heeded the advice of the other, and their comments were uncanny predictions of the problems which both men were to face in the late forties.

Balcon, Pascal, Del Giudice, and Rank—these were the men whom Korda was up against in his come-back bid. The cast of characters had a new look, but the industry itself had changed more radically. Close to seventy-five per cent of the film community was engaged in producing propaganda features or shorts, and commercial film-making was severely handicapped. The rationing of resources necessary for film production, the requisitioning of at least half of the available studio space, the shortage of film stock and trained technical staff and artistes, the new trade union regulations, all this Alex had to contend with both during the war and for several years afterwards. He had little idea just how difficult the coming years were to be.

From his penthouse suite at Claridges Korda began the job of taking over the MGM–British–London Films operation. The company's board of directors included Alex, Ben Goetz, Sam Eckman, Jnr, Sydney Wright, Harold Boxall, and Sir David Cunynghame. Once again shunning the Wardour Street milieu, Korda arranged for MGM to purchase, in August 1943, the lease on a five-storey, thirty-room mansion at 1, Belgrave Square, previously owned by Viscountess Harcourt. As Korda commented: 'This is our home for 14 hours a day. Why should it be too poky? In any case I hate Wardour Street offices.'[12] After minor alterations, which involved the construction of a projection room in the garage, the central offices were opened, and Alex was in business.

The MGM press boys immediately set out to explain the new image which the Korda merger would bring to MGM's British output. The company would, they promised, eventually parallel the vast MGM Culver City studio complex in Hollywood. They assured the industry that Korda was in complete control of this 'independent' subsidiary and that MGM would not countenance the making of quota pictures. Over the late summer and autumn of 1943 the two major issues which concerned Korda were to find a studio and to recruit the people to fill it. In typical Korda fashion the second problem was tackled first.

It took Alex six months to prepare his first programme announcement, but when it came out, it surpassed all his previous efforts. A two-fold manifesto, it was carefully divided into 'plans for 1944' and 'plans for the future'. With regard to 1944, Korda's company was to rent studio space at Denham until a proper home could be found, derequisitioned, and refitted. Four films would be made during the first year, their total budget being £1,200,000. The real 'meat' of the announcement related to Korda's future plans. He expected to produce ten to sixteen features each year at an annual cost of between three and four million pounds. Nine films were listed as on the drawing boards, the most ambitious of which was *War and Peace*.

During a wartime trip to Canada, Basil Wright had reason to go to New York, where he had dinner one night with Sidney Bernstein, Edmund Goulding, David O. Selznick, and Alex Korda.

> 'It was a fascinating evening,' Wright remembers, 'because being a documentary chap I hadn't been able to enjoy the seats of the mighty like this; and Selznick had a telephone put on the table, plugged in, and he kept ringing up Los Angeles.
>
> 'Korda charmed me into practical extinction—he was *so* marvellous, he talked *so* beautifully, and his description of how *he* would approach the problem of making Tolstoy's *War and Peace* was absolutely marvellous. I mean ... I'm a great Tolstoy fan, and we talked and talked for hours—or at least half an hour!—purely on this subject. And he really knew it—don't let's fool about Alex Korda, he *really* knew it. And of all the people who've done *War and Peace*, I think he'd have been the one who'd have done it best.'[13]

Korda's plans for *War and Peace* were certainly audacious. Budgeted at a conservative £500,000, it was to be co-produced by Orson Welles, who would also direct and star in it, presumably as Pierre.* Alex went so far as to get the Soviet Government's blessings on the project and permission for filming to be done in Smolensk. If Welles had directed

---

* Interesting to note that the Russian *War and Peace* (1967) was directed by Sergei Bondarchuk, who also starred as Pierre.

the film, it might well have been Korda's greatest achievement, although the idea of Lajos Biro as scriptwriter and Merle Oberon as Natasha raises certain misgivings about this. The project was abandoned, but we must agree with Korda's own admission: 'My greatest films are those I announced . . . and never made.'[14]

More mind-boggling than Korda's announcement of plans to make *The Hardy Family in England* and a set-in-England addition to the *Dr Kildare* series (both MGM staples) was the list of artistes whom Korda now had under contract. Besides the expected people it included the names of no fewer than eighteen writers, notably Enid Bagnold, James Bridie, Robert Graves, Graham Greene, James Hilton, A. E. W. Mason, Neville Shute, and Evelyn Waugh. To top off this surreal manifesto it was intimated that the new company's logo would be an amalgamation of the MGM and London Films trademarks. Leo the Lion roaring from out of the clock face of Big Ben?

From past history we can conclude that Korda didn't honestly expect to complete most of these films. As one journalist later remarked: '. . . it may be that this tall, sallow Hungarian with an iron-grey mane, a big cigar, a cynical fat-cat smile, and light tired eyes behind his horn-rims, doesn't take his own bubbling ideas too seriously'.[15] Korda had, at least on paper, proved the unimpaired power of his personality by attempting a talent monopoly to rival Rank's business monopoly. The press and the industry were, however, not as impressionable or gullible as they had been in the thirties. Korda was up to his old tricks—trying to build up industry confidence from planned 'projects' instead of finished 'products'—but he didn't understand that everyone already knew his game-plan. Small wonder that in a London stage revue of the time the news that a certain actress had been put under a seven-year contract to Korda elicited the response: 'That's a long time to be out of work.'[16]

Although Alex confided in 1946 that he was 'at a loss to explain' why he had joined MGM, he was fully aware of the reasons in 1943. The 'dollar drain' was a serious issue during the war. Parliament and the press almost daily criticised the amount of money spent on importing American films—then in the region of £26,500,000 a year ($80,000,000). As Robert Boothby said in a House of Commons debate, it was a question of deciding between 'Bogart and bacon', and the seriousness of this controversy was not lost on Korda. In his December 1943 manifesto he justified his MGM partnership in terms calculated to win industry support and to ease the crisis situation:

This contribution will have two national advantages of special importance. By arrangement between its American and British partners, the company will not only bring back to this country a substantial proportion of the world profits in foreign exchange, but will cause to be invested in sterling a large annual sum running into several millions which would otherwise be remitted to America.[17]

The MGM affiliation thus provided the type of financial backing which Korda personally required and which the industry as a whole urgently needed. Even with this sound financial superstructure Korda did not find the going easy.

Buried among these glowing plans was the announcement that Korda did not intend to direct any of these pictures himself. He revealed that he would act only as producer or executive producer for directors and producers like Ian Dalrymple, Carol Reed, Edward Black, and David McDonald—a relatively short list presumably owing to the 'employed' status of most of Britain's other film men.* For Korda film directing had become a tedious, time-consuming activity. 'I find that directing is like going down a mine,' Korda later admitted to David Lewin. 'These are days of darkness. You get up before the sun is shining and you go home at night. You never see the sun. I like the sun.'[19]

Given Alex's intention of abandoning direction, it does come as a surprise that the only film completed by MGM–British–London Films, *Perfect Strangers* (1945), was directed by him. In the original plans the film was to have been scripted by Arthur Wimperis, Esther McCracken, and Anthony Pelissier, produced by Ian Dalrymple, and directed by the American film director Wesley Ruggles. Unhappy with the scenario, Alex put most of his writing staff to work on writing or rewriting it. Nobody knew exactly what it was that Korda wanted out of the script, and it appears that Alex wasn't too clear on the matter himself. The second casualty was the director, for Ruggles 'threw up the job' early on, possibly out of frustration with the lack of organisation. In the late spring of 1944 Alex returned to Denham and personally took over the direction of the film.

* The limits to which Alex had gone to corral already employed film-makers is exemplified by the story that he offered the Boulting Brothers a retainer of $1,000 a week for the duration of the war in order to secure their post-war association with him. This offer, and perhaps many similar ones, was rejected.[18]

According to Ian Dalrymple, who received no final credit on the film, it was a 'nervy time': wartime conditions and the absence of proper guidance made everyone jumpy. Korda always weathered production confusion well,\* but it was more difficult for him to get used to the new regulations of the trade union. These specified that reasonable and regular hours of work had to be observed, but Korda, with his more easy-doing methods, found such regimentation unreasonable. 'My artistes cannot start making love at nine o'clock in the morning,' he proclaimed.[20] To make matters worse, the film was shot during the height of the flying-bomb attacks on London. Roger Manvell, the film critic and historian, described the difficulties encountered during the making of *Perfect Strangers*:

> Korda had his script torn to ribbons by jagged glass when a flying-bomb fell in the studio grounds and blasted the office block and dressing rooms. . . . Plywood for sets being no longer obtainable, set walls were constructed of composition board, often made from salvaged newspapers, or of paper pasted over old wooden frames. In addition, tons of plaster, cardboard, brown wrapping-paper, re-used timber and miles of wall-paper were all assembled into sets. Costumes and uniforms had to be borrowed; the Government's allowance of materials for costumes in films is scarcely sufficient. The unit however, gained greatly from assistance from the Admiralty, so that scenes were shot at Naval and W.R.N.S. establishments with the co-operation of naval personnel.[21]

Throughout the summer Alex worked under these conditions during the day, only to return to Claridges at night to 'relax' to the sound of more flying-bombs. He became increasingly moody and nervous. Lady Sarita Vansittart, who with her husband Sir Robert was a frequent dinner guest at Claridges, was struck by Korda's hypertensive state: 'He was especially worried about the possibility of flying glass from a bomb striking and damaging his eyes.'[22] Given his poor eyesight and his dependence on his visual sense, this over-protectiveness was understandable.

Despite all its production problems, *Perfect Strangers* turned out to be

---

\* An actor once complained to Korda: 'I'm sorry, Alex, but I can't play my role. I haven't received a complete script, and I have no idea how it's supposed to turn out.' With a reassuring pat on the back, Korda came out with his now legendary reply: 'That's all right, my dear boy. None of us know how it's going to end.'

a substantial little film about the effect of wartime service on a colourless English couple. The film divides, too neatly, into three 'acts'. We are first introduced to the couple: drab Cathy Wilson (Deborah Kerr) with her eternal sniffles and deferential manner is devoted to and dependent on her equally drab husband Robert (Robert Donat) whose shuffling gait and ineffectual personality suit his office clerk job. We watch a day in their life from breakfast in their dull flat to their trainside farewell as Robert goes off to join the Royal Navy. Shortly thereafter, Cathy joins the Wrens, thus giving way to the central portion of the film where in ping-pong fashion we are shown how the demands of war and their new friendships effect a parallel personality change. As their horizons broaden, each begins to worry about the timid spouse left behind. The mutually dreaded reunion (Act III) turns into a long night of bitching, followed by the first tentative step at reconciliation against a backdrop of bomb-devastated London.

For the most part the dialogue is genuine, biting, and funny, and the underlying psychology is well observed, if a bit over-stated. The studio-recreated picture of London during the black-outs is realistic in feeling, although not, I have been assured, totally accurate. Unfortunately, the repetitiveness of actions and dialogue, partially necessitated by the parallelism of the narrative, undermines the otherwise delicate structure of the satire. We get the feeling that the writers of the later parts of the script didn't know what the characters had already said, and perhaps they didn't. It is at the end of the over-burdened, cross-cut central portion, during the couple's reunion, that the film comes alive: Cathy and Robert ridiculing each other's pre-war habits and foibles. Cathy coyly reminds Robert of how he used to dither. He defends: 'I might have been just a little lacking in star quality, but I did *not* dither.'

Star quality was certainly not lacking in the film. Donat and Kerr make the transition in the characters both credible and fascinating to watch. Glynis Johns's Wren and Ann Todd's nurse are two finely drawn portraits, proof of Korda's ability to extract the most from his actresses. From the opening shot we are also aware of the star behind the camera, Georges Périnal, who creates the London world in the studio in the same way as he showed us the Parisian world in René Clair's *Sous les toits de Paris* (1930). Credit must also go to Vincent Korda for the superb sets, and as in *Henry VIII*, both men worked miracles with the slimmest resources.

In relation to Korda's other directorial efforts, *Perfect Strangers* stands up admirably. As a cohesive film with a progression in character development, it is, in fact, better than Korda's 'historical' endeavours which suffer from a lack of fluidity and from fixed characterisations. Korda should have perhaps attempted other 'contemporary' pieces, for he was a more assured director when exploring the strengths of modern people than when exposing the weaknesses of legendary figures. However, the script inevitably lets Korda and his actors down, and the heavy, parallel structure and editing of the film destroys the intimacy developed in the best scenes.

Korda had, of course, picked a timely subject; and the film benefited from its delayed release, for it was even more relevant in late 1945. *Perfect Strangers* was a commercial success in Britain and America, where it was retitled *Vacation from Marriage*, a telling comment on America's concept of wartime service.* The ironic twist—the sort that Korda appreciated—was that the film won for Clemence Dane an Academy Award for best original story.

Although Korda had returned to commercial film-making, he still contributed to the country's propaganda efforts. In 1943, probably some time after his request to be dropped into Hungary to help to organise the resistance movement there had been refused, Alex produced a fifteen-minute short, *The Biter Bit* (1943), for the Ministry of Information. Winston Churchill apparently suggested the idea for the film to Korda, and the title refers to Churchill's own phrase: 'The biter has bit.' The intention was to show how the Nazis had exploited film propaganda to their advantage and how the Allies were paying the Germans back in kind for their intense bombing raids on English cities.

The film starts with a reconstruction of a party for high-ranking officials in Oslo, during which the Nazis, as was their habit, screened extracts from *Baptism of Fire* (1940), the record of their blitzkrieg victory in Poland, in order to demonstrate the futility of further resistance to Hitler. The short then proceeds to show scenes from a 'phoney' German film prematurely prepared to show how the Nazis had 'conquered' England, and these sequences are compared with extracts from some British documentaries like *London Can Take It* (1940) which

* The MGM people in America were not, however, wholly to blame for this curious new title, for Korda *had* presented an over-glamorised 'Hollywood' portrait of the war similar to that in William Wyler's *Mrs Miniver* (1942), also produced by MGM.

present an altogether different picture of the situation. German footage of the bombing of London is accompanied by Churchill's 'Finest Hour' speech, and finally the British plans for retaliation are explained. A series of bombers take off from their English bases, and maps contrasting the bomb damage in certain British and German cities are compared. The film ends with footage from a night-time bombing raid on a German city.

For such a short film, it is a dramatic and effective piece of propaganda, with an appropriately straightforward narration by Ralph Richardson. Korda, however, kept his name off the credits, this unusual modesty perhaps prompted by Korda's desire to treat his wartime association with Churchill with the utmost discretion.

In the spring of 1944 two business transactions were completed which bolstered Korda's finances and the industry's confidence in his company's future. In April Korda finally disposed of his shares in United Artists, selling them to the American businessman David Copland for $900,000. In the same month MGM purchased, through the Prudential, Amalgamated Studios at Elstree and one hundred surrounding acres of land. The only problem with the latter deal was that the studios were still requisitioned, used as a supply depository. Once derequisitioned, they were to be renovated so that the Korda group could move in. Derequisitioning, however, took another eighteen months. Now able to afford philanthropic gestures, Korda, also in 1944, endowed ten £500 scholarships at the Royal Academy of Dramatic Arts, specifically for British men and women recently demobilised from the services, and he also sponsored (to the tune of £5,000) an Oxford University Commission's trip to the United States to study drama and film departments there in the hopes of setting up such a department at Oxford. (The Commission went to America in April 1945, but no action was taken on its findings.)

Alex went to New York with Ben Goetz in December 1944 to discuss with the head office their plans for the second MGM–London Films project. Rumours abounded that the MGM hierarchy was not happy about the money Alex was spending on contracts for people who had still not been used and for whom Alex had no immediate plans. From New York Korda travelled on to Hollywood.

In early January 1945 Merle Oberon announced that she had decided to obtain a divorce from Alex Korda. The reason given was that their separate careers had kept them apart and had made enormous demands on their marriage. She had denied rumours that they were splitting up in 1942, while admitting: 'If anything, I stood to lose by our marriage, professionally. Because Alex was in England then and it was definitely hurtful to my career; it was a real sacrifice on my part every time I left Hollywood to join him in England. For me, it would have been better if I had stayed here and got on with my job.'[23] Alex's return to Britain in 1943 intensified her predicament and precipitated her final decision. The marriage was dissolved in Mexico in June 1945.*

Alex had adored Merle, and the divorce upset him very deeply. On the 25th of January the tensions of the past year, and perhaps the recent emotional strain, caught up with him. He collapsed while at dinner at Romanoff's in Hollywood; and although the doctor who attended him at the restaurant diagnosed a heart attack and although Alex was taken to hospital, there was no further confirmation at that time that his condition was that serious.

Alex was in New York in September 1945 when MGM announced that Amalgamated Studios, finally derequisitioned, would be ready for production before the end of the year. Ironically, Korda never used the studios which he had worked so hard to get organised, for in late October Korda went to Hollywood to confer with Louis B. Mayer and, over the weekend of the 20th, decided to resign from MGM. Although their joint communiqué emphasised that Korda was resigning 'due to ill health' (thus lending credence to the reported 'heart attack'), the MGM–Korda association had not been a fruitful one. Korda chafed under the pressure of always being responsible to the head office, and the MGM executives in turn were increasingly displeased with Korda's needless extravagances. During Korda's two-year stint as head of MGM–British–London Films, the company had only produced one film, and the American company had lost £1,000,000. The dissolution of the partnership was undoubtedly welcomed by both parties.

The same old rumours again swept through the British film industry: Korda was not going to make films in England any more, he was moving to the Continent. Nothing could have been further from his

---

* By the end of that year Merle had married her second husband, the Hollywood cameraman Lucien Ballard who had worked on two of her latest pictures, *The Lodger* (1944) and *This Love of Ours* (1945). That marriage was dissolved in 1949, and in 1957 she married Bruno Pagliai, a Mexican industrialist. She spent most of the next ten years in semi-retirement, occasionally being persuaded to return to the screen (e.g. *Hotel*—1967). In 1972 she left Pagliai, and after starring in *Interval* (1972), which she also produced, edited, and partially financed, she announced her intention of returning to an active film career.

mind, and within a month of his resignation Korda put an end to all the rumours. He returned to Britain in November, made the final arrangements for his leave-taking from MGM and stated to the press that he was feeling 'the benefit from being away from the slings and arrows of top executive work'.[24] Few believed this meant his retirement, least of all Korda himself. The 'rest' that he had intended to take after his resignation lasted barely a month.

1. Interview with Ian Dalrymple conducted by the author, 24 July 1973.
2. *Time*, 13 April 1942.
3. *Hollywood Reporter*, 25 March 1942.
4. Paul Tabori, *op cit*, p. 228, (Tabori's emphasis).
5. *Hollywood Reporter*, 12 February 1943.
6. J. B. Priestley, *Bright Day*, London, William Heinemann, 1946, quote from the Penguin edition, p. 199.
7. From letter from Sir Michael Balcon to the author, 14 August 1973.
8. Sir Michael Balcon, *A Lifetime of Films*, London, Hutchinson, 1969, p. 94.
9. *Ibid*, p. 95.
10. *The Methodist Recorder*, 26 March 1942.
11. Both quotes from Alan Wood, *Mr Rank*, London, Hodder and Stoughton, 1952, p. 215.
12. Unmarked press cutting from Alexander Korda microfiche, BFI Information Department.
13. Interview with Basil Wright conducted by the author, 17 July 1973.
14. Unmarked press cutting from Alexander Korda microfiche, BFI Information Department.
15. E. M. Wood, 'Korda: Dreamer and Spellbinder', *Leader Magazine*, 24 May 1947, p. 15.
16. *Ibid*.
17. *Today's Cinema*, 17 December 1943, p. 11.
18. Interview with John and Roy Boulting conducted by the author, 23 August 1973.
19. David Lewin, 'The Man Who Made the Stars Shine', Chapter Five, *Daily Express*, 31 January 1956.
20. Alan Wood, *op cit*, p. 216.
21. Roger Manvell, 'Perfect Strangers', British Council Programme Note, 7 November 1945, duplicated typescript.
22. Interview with Lady Sarita Vansittart conducted by the author, 24 July 1973.
23. Merle Oberon, 'I Married My Boss', Hollywood fan magazine, 1942, no further details.
24. Unmarked press cutting from Alexander Korda microfiche, BFI Information Department.

# CHAPTER EIGHTEEN

# The Revival of London Films

IN 1919 political persecution had put an end to Korda's Hungarian career. Twenty years later, economic difficulties had finally terminated the most ambitious period of his British career and deprived Korda of his greatest ahievement, Denham Studios. He had made admirable recoveries after these crises, but in 1946 Korda was once again faced with the collapse of his latest film-making venture. Although he was fifty-two years old and had already accomplished enough to be able to retire gracefully into the background, Alex instead chose to embark on the fourth major phase of his film career by reviving London Film Productions as an independent company and by constructing, again from scratch, a large and influential film empire.

For once Korda had adequate financing to set his enterprise in motion. His wartime films had earned a substantial profit, as had the earlier London Films pictures which Korda had bought back from the Prudential in 1943 (for £42,500) and subsequently re-issued throughout the world with great success. These successful re-releases, as many were quick to point out, were not only a tribute to Korda's promotional abilities but also a vindication of his confidence in the economic viability, albeit long-term, of prestige British films. 'Old films,' Korda opined, 'are like having grandchildren to keep me in my old age.'[1] Korda had at first misjudged the value of certain commodities which he had maintained after the loss of Denham, for he now had at his disposal the money from his recent sale of United Artists shares and an additional £141,000 which the Rank Organisation paid him in March

1945 for controlling interest in Denham Laboratories. With this capital behind him Korda resurrected London Film Productions in January 1946 as a private company, all but two per cent of the shares of which were held by Alex or members of his family.

His distribution connection with United Artists severed, Korda knew that he had to make satifactory arrangements for film distribution both within Britain and in America as quickly as possible. Therefore, in January 1946 he also purchased controlling interest in British Lion Film Corporation, a film renting organisation which had been formed in November 1927 and which had managed to survive among the larger American and Rank-owned distribution companies due to its exclusive contract with Republic, one of Hollywood's minor studios. There was a reshuffle of the British Lion board of directors in which Korda took on the position of Production Adviser and General Manager of the studio, Arthur Jarratt (formerly at Gaumont British) became Managing Director and Deputy Chairman, and Hugh Quennell was made Chairman of the Board.* For the first time Korda controlled his own distribution organisation, although it only covered the home market.

Two months later Korda became involved in setting up Regina Films, a French production company, in association with Julien Duvivier, Marcel Carné, and René Clair, and Tricolore Films, Inc., a company which was to engage in distributing French and other foreign films in America. Since the re-establishment of a distribution link in the American market was all-important, Korda visited Hollywood in mid-1947, and in July it was announced that 20th Century-Fox (which owned the large Fox Film Theatre circuit) was henceforth to distribute Korda's films in America.

Korda, of course, needed a studio to 'manage', and even though Rank owned well over 50 per cent of all British studios at the time, the Korda group soon found a home of their own. In April 1946 Korda negotiated British Lion's purchase (for £380,000) of 74 per cent interest in Sound City (Films), Ltd, the production company which owned Shepperton Studios, then the second largest studio after Denham. British Lion already owned 50 per cent of the smaller Worton Hall Studios in Isleworth, and in May the remaining half was acquired by Korda's company. Both studio complexes needed certain

---

* Other members of the board included Sidney Myers, Harold Boxall, Sir David Cunynghame, A. J. Mitchell, Sir Claude Dansey, I. Charles Flower, and L. C. Sennitt.

expansions and renovations—which took nearly a year to complete—but 'with eight stages and 110,000 square feet of studio floor space available the new Group was in a position to become a powerful factor in British film production'.²

A company with such potential power also needed impressive headquarters. In March 1947 Korda surpassed all his previous efforts by purchasing for £50,000 the mansion at 144–145 Piccadilly, next door to the childhood home of Queen, then Princess, Elizabeth. His sumptuous offices, where 'beneath the glitter of crystal chandeliers, you walk on Aubusson and sit upon Gobelins',³ looked out over Hyde Park Corner, thereafter known by some as 'Hyde Park Korda'. Number 146 Piccadilly was eventually acquired as well, and the unused space was rented out to other film companies, such as 20th Century-Fox's British subsidiary. Number 144 became famous for its well-stocked cellar and its first floor private cinema which was used by the Royal Family. Ernest Betts, who was then working for the Fox subsidiary, describes the aura surrounding Korda's establishment:

> No. 144, with its well-kept window-boxes, always sent a bright splash of colour into Piccadilly and carried a suggestion of substance and ease which it was far from possessing in fact.
>
> But the illusion was pleasant. At the back of the house was a well-kept garden adjoining the one in which, before the war, the Royal Princesses had played.
>
> The garden contained a lily-pond and was well suited to the meditations of film executives and the posing of film stars for publicity purposes. Indeed, the house reminded me of one of those fashionable rendezvous described by Balzac or Maupassant. It was always peopled with beautiful women, glossy men, bright and shady financiers, film accountants, film directors, producers, playwrights, authors, and well-paid secretaries as glamorous as film stars.
>
> It seemed impossible that any serious work could be done here, yet the whole place buzzed with business and clattered with typewriters amid an inspiring atmosphere of artistic lunacy.⁴

These offices were to be Korda's real home for the next ten years.*

* All trace of Korda's Piccadilly mansions are now gone. Nos. 145 and 146 were torn down when Park Lane was widened, and 144 survived an invasion of demonstrating squatters in September 1969 (the event provided the story for film director Samuel Fuller's novel *144 Piccadilly*) only to be demolished in 1973 in order to make way for yet another London hotel complex.

To round off his property-buying spree Korda had purchased the Rialto Cinema in August 1946 as a West End showcase theatre for his films. This was putting the cart before the horse, for it wasn't until six months later that Korda had a film to release there, or anywhere. From the first three Korda–British Lion productions it is clear that Alex had learned the lessons which the Denham *débâcle* had offered. He knew that to maintain a large studio the stages had to be occupied all the time, with major *and* minor productions if necessary, and he finally accepted the fact that he could not personally produce every picture at the studio. These three films were all low-budget thrillers and were not wildly impressive in their own right. However, they represented the inauguration of a new, more rational studio policy which totally depended on, and received, the support of Britain's independent film-makers.*

Finding the personnel to fill his studio presented a major problem for Korda during these first years. Many of his pre-war technicians had since found 'homes' elsewhere, but others, notably Georges Périnal and Vincent Korda, remained loyal to Korda and began to build up their respective departments at Shepperton. Lajos Biro was still head scriptwriter, but his death in 1948 left Korda stranded. (Alex never found a suitable successor to Biro as 'studio dramaturge', the position he had held since 1932.) American Ned Mann returned to Britain after the war in order to help establish Shepperton's special effects department, but he didn't stay for long. French-born Percy (Pop) Day was to take charge of the studio's matte painting department, a post which he held until his retirement at the age of eighty-four. Editor William Hornbeck and costumer John Armstrong could not apparently be coaxed back, so their jobs went to other men. Music director Muir Mathieson and publicity man Johnny Myers were now

* The inaugural films were *The Shop at Sly Corner* (1947), *A Man About the House* (1947), and *Night Beat* (1948). They were produced, respectively, by George King, Ted Black, and Harold Huth, three of the first producers to associate themselves with Korda's company. King and Huth, both minor figures in the British film-making establishment, directed as well as produced their first (and last) British Lion–London Films pictures. Ted Black, whose successful partnership with British director Leslie Arliss at Gaumont British had resulted in such popular 'period' melodramas as *The Man in Grey* (1943) and *The Wicked Lady* (1945), emigrated from that Rank-owned company to Korda's MGM–British outfit in 1945 and then joined British Lion in March 1946, bringing Leslie Arliss with him. The Black–Arliss picture, *A Man About the House*, was marginally more successful than the other two films; it was the first post-war Korda film distributed in America, where it was well received.

under contract to Rank; Dr Hubert Clifford and Leslie Mitchell were to be their replacements. Mitchell, whose experience was in broadcasting not publicity, recalls his interview with Korda:

> Early in 1946 I was called to Korda's office and asked to create and build the biggest damn publicity department in Europe. I was to be given *carte blanche*. When I asked him why he picked me, he recited all the facets of my working life (some of which I had forgotten) and convinced me in a short time that not only was he a genius, but so was I. I asked him for time to think it over. This upset Alex as he had planned to take me with him to America in two weeks' time. I was told that I could have whatever salary I wanted. I suggested that I would rather have what I was now getting [at Movietone News] plus an expense account until I had proved myself in the job. But Alex couldn't stand a lack of confidence. He thought you were small-minded if you didn't think big financially and every other way.[5]

After discussing the job with his predecessor Myers, Mitchell decided to accept Korda's offer.* Although he had experienced the Korda 'charm', Mitchell was one of several men who were to witness the more malicious side of Korda's character.

As the London Films staff grew and while the studio was teething on those first low-budget pictures, Korda was himself occupied with his own project, *An Ideal Husband* (1947).

Alex Korda intended *An Ideal Husband* to be his last directorial effort, and many wondered why he had chosen Oscar Wilde's play for his 'swan song'. Korda had long believed in the selling advantages of films taken from popular literary sources and had produced a number of these—e.g. *The Scarlet Pimpernel*, *Things to Come*, and *The Four Feathers* —during his heyday. Yet in spite of his supposed dislike of original screenplays, he had usually preferred to *direct* films from scripts planned around historical figures but written expressly for the screen. His last literary adaptation had been *The Girl from Maxim's*, made fifteen years before. Why did he return to a literary adaptation for his 'last' film? Because *An Ideal Husband* offered Korda three things of which he was inordinately fond: a comic exposé of the eccentric British upper classes, a late Victorian setting which demanded ornate sets and lavish costumes

---

* Myers had given Mitchell some useful advice, two tips on how to get on with Korda: work hard, and treat him like a mistress you haven't yet made.[6]

and was perfect Technicolor material, and Wilde's sense of irony and humour which relied heavily on epigrammatic dialogue.

While Lajos Biro began working on this, his last script for Korda, Vincent Korda, Georges Périnal, and Cecil Beaton addressed themselves to the task of designing the film's visual appearance. Since the film was to be a condensed, but faithful adaptation of the play and was thus to depend more on 'acting' than on 'action', Korda decided to cast as many stage-experienced actors and actresses as he could. Diana Wynyard, Hugh Williams, Sir C. Aubrey Smith, Glynis Johns, and Constance Collier were therefore all enlisted for the major roles. Michael Wilding, who was then co-starring in a series of successful Herbert Wilcox–Anna Neagle pictures,★ was chosen to play the most Wilde-like of the characters, the debonair Viscount Goring. Korda had already engaged the American actress Paulette Goddard for a film project called *Carmen*, this picture was never made, but Goddard was given the lead role in *Ideal Husband* as the scheming Mrs Cheveley.

When the film was released in November 1947, the Fleet Street punsters had a field day: 'Wilde and Woolly' (*News Chronicle*), 'Korda Puts the Spangles on Wilde' (*Daily Express*), 'Witty, Wordy, but Wilde' (*Sunday Dispatch*), and 'The Unimportance of Being Oscar' (*Daily Mail*). As these headlines suggest, the critics were clearly divided in their response to Korda's first post-war super-production. Few had qualms with the adaptation *per se*. The telescoping of a four-act play into a ninety-six-minute film had led to the inevitable shortchanging of certain secondary characters; but the, admittedly thin, plot line— adventuress unsuccessfully attempts to blackmail a Parliamentary Under-Secretary with the exposure of a past political bribe in order to force him to make a speech favourable to her own financial schemes— is adhered to, as are the Wildean characterisations. On one level, the rigidly moral Lady Chiltern and her less than ideal husband Sir Robert are played off against the genuinely unscrupulous Mrs Cheveley, while on another level the frivolous younger generation, personified by Mabel Chiltern and Viscount Goring, are contrasted with their more serious elders.

Biro and Korda had made obvious attempts to open out the play. They added a prologue and epilogue of carriage outings in Hyde Park

★ Herbert Wilcox had also transferred his film-making activities to Korda's studio in 1946–7. *Spring in Park Lane* (1948) was the first of the Neagle–Wilding pictures (others had included *Piccadilly Incident*—1946 and *The Courtneys of Curzon Street*—1947) to be made under the British Lion banner.

and set some of the scenes in new locations, such as Sir Robert's Parliamentary office. The chronological shifting of other scenes is revealing, for it proves that Korda's primary concern was not Wilde's moral or his characters, but his dialogue. The first scene of the third act, for example, has been placed at the beginning of the film in order to exploit the following exchange between Viscount Goring and his butler Phipps:

Goring: You've got another buttonhole for me, Phipps?

Phipps: Yes, M'lord.

Goring: It's rather a distinguished thing, Phipps. I am the only person of the smallest importance in London at present who wears a buttonhole.

Phipps: Yes, M'lord. I have observed that.

Goring: You see, Phipps, fashion is what one wears oneself. What is unfashionable is what other people wear.

Phipps: Yes, M'lord.

Goring: Just as vulgarity is simply the conduct of other people.

Phipps: Yes, M'lord.

Goring: And falsehoods the truths of other people.

Phipps: Yes, M'lord.

Goring: Oh, other people are quite dreadful, Phipps. The only possible society is oneself.

Phipps: Yes, M'lord.

Goring: To love oneself is the beginning of a lifelong romance, Phipps.

Phipps: Yes, M'lord.

Goring: I'm not quite sure that I like this buttonhole, Phipps, it makes me look a little too old, almost in the prime of life, eh, Phipps?

Phipps: I have not observed any alteration in your lordship's appearance.

Goring: You haven't, Phipps?

Phipps: No, M'lord.

Goring: I am not so sure. No, for the future a more trivial buttonhole, Phipps, on Thursday evenings.

Phipps: I'll speak to the florist, M'lord. She has had a loss in her family lately, which perhaps accounts for the lack of triviality your lordship complains of in the buttonhole.

Goring: Extraordinary thing about the lower classes in England,
Phipps, they are always losing their relations.
Phipps: Yes, M'lord. They are extremely fortunate in that respect.

The fidelity to Wilde's actual dialogue, here and throughout the film,
is exemplary. There was no need for the usual Biro–Wimperis addi-
tions, for Korda had finally found an author whose concept of dialogue
and humour perfectly reflected his own. Sadly, Korda permitted his
fondness for the subject matter and dialogue to be subjugated to the
colour visualisation of the 'period' and the need for a box-office,
Hollywood 'star'.

Over the past ten years Korda had done much to promote colour
cinematography, in particular the Technicolor process, both in Britain
and abroad. Perhaps it was inevitable that Korda's exploitation of
colour would one day overwhelm the material which he was presenting,
and this is certainly what happened in *Ideal Husband*. Critic Leonard
Mosley remarked that 'the ball scene and some of the sequences in
Diana Wynyard's boudoir have such riotously coloured backgrounds
that the décor drowns out the dresses the women are wearing'.[7] It
drowns out the actors as well, for the players, photographed almost
exclusively in medium range, are lost in the midst of the Korda 'gilt'
and cannot possibly command our attention. Michael Wilding, Glynis
Johns (as Mabel Chiltern), and Constance Collier (as Lady Markby)
are able to make some impression because their roles and their performances contain the most vitality; the more staid characters like
Sir Robert (Hugh Williams) and Lady Chiltern (Diana Wynyard)
haven't a chance. A bigger disappointment, however, is the inadequacy
of the 'star' attraction. Paulette Goddard plays with some spirit and
much glamour, but she cannot handle the Wildean dialogue and is
outclassed by the stage-trained actors who surround her. One rather
cutting critic noted: 'As a distraction from Miss Goddard's attempts to
hold an over-loaded stage alone, my eye repeatedly fled to two paintings glowing through the ugly Technicolor. They are by Bellotto and
were lent to the film by Sir Alexander Korda. They are the one original
thing he put into the film.'[8]*

His career as a director in Britain had come full circle, for in dialogue,
subject matter, and execution his last London Films production was

* The film offers at least one other 'original': the emerald jewellery worn by
Paulette Goddard. When Ernest Betts asked Korda why she was given real
emeralds for her part, he replied with characteristic nonchalance: 'Because it
makes her feel better.'[9]

reminiscent of his first, *Wedding Rehearsal*. In the intervening years Korda's own films had grown in cost, cast, and technical and visual splendour, but his own talent had not progressed very far. He had stubbornly clung to the weak narratives, facile characterisations, unconvincing dialogue, and over-emphasised production values of his early films in an attempt to repeat the international success of *The Private Life of Henry VIII*, the one film which had made good in spite of these flaws. He never achieved this goal and once explained his failure after *Henry* with the remark: 'Maybe part of the trouble afterwards was that we all had too much money.'[10] Seduced by the money at his disposal and discouraged by the reception accorded his one 'artistic' endeavour (*Rembrandt*), Korda had preferred to maintain his own particular formula of large-scale productions even when their decreasing box-office returns might have suggested a needed re-evaluation of his policies. During the first two years of his post-war revival Korda continued to exploit his pre-war film-making concepts and was so concerned with re-instating his position in the film industry that he blinded himself to the changes in public taste which the war had brought about. Korda's final recognition of these new developments—in 1949—coincided, not surprisingly, with his further divorcement from the active side of film production.

In a time of widespread austerity *An Ideal Husband* had been a shallow testament to the glories of two bygone eras: the 1890s of the play and the mid-1930s of Korda's own career. The film fell flat commercially and was less favourably received in critical circles than *Mine Own Executioner* (1947), a small-budgeted film made at the same time at Shepperton.* Part of the film's financial failure can, however, be attributed to an event over which Alex Korda had no control: the Anglo-American Film War of 1947–8.

The British Government's wartime concern with the large amount of

---

* Anthony Kimmins, the British film-writer and director whose previous experience included several pictures starring the British music hall comedian George Formby, brought his own production company into the Korda fold in March 1946. He made six films for Korda over the next ten years, the first and best of which was *Mine Own Executioner*. Scripted by Nigel Balchin from his own novel, the film dealt with a psychologist (Burgess Meredith, then Paulette Goddard's husband) and his attempts to diagnose and treat a schizophrenic patient (Kieron Moore). The patient's deep-seated psychoses are nicely contrasted with the psychologist's own marital problems, and Kimmins and Balchin were brave enough to keep to the story's disturbing dénouement (the patient eventually murders his wife and commits suicide). The picture won much praise for its serious and intelligent handling of one of film-making's newer subjects.

money earned in Britain by imported American films and subsequently taken out of the country by American producers and distributors had led to a three-year restriction on the amount of sterling which could be remitted to the United States by these companies. This kept down the annual remittance to between £4·8 and £8·5 million, but when the restriction was lifted in 1944 the remittance figures immediately doubled. By 1947 Britain was losing in excess of £17 million ($70 million) a year on this one trade commodity. That summer the Government decided to act to redress the critical balance of payments deficit, and American film importation was one of several areas in which measures were taken. On the 8th of August 1947 the Treasury imposed a 75 per cent customs duty (equal to a 300 per cent *ad valorem* duty) on the value of all films imported into Britain. As the principal victim of this new duty, the American industry quickly countered with an effective film boycott: no more American films were to be sent to Britain until the duty was rescinded. Although American films already in the country continued to make profits, for eight months the British film industry was deprived of all new American products.*

The 'Dalton Duty' as it was called (after the then Chancellor of the Exchequer) had not been imposed in order to ensure protection of the home market for British films, but that is what in fact happened. Many looked on this crisis as a perfect opportunity for British film producers to prove that they alone could fill all the cinemas in Britain. It was a pipe dream, however, for it was completely impossible for British film-makers to produce enough feature films (over three hundred were needed) to supply the nation's cinemas. This did not stop the big producers like Rank and Korda from responding to the challenge, although in rather unexpected ways.

Despite the heavy production losses (£1,667,000 in 1945–6) which the Rank Organisation had recently suffered in its disastrous 'prestige' film-making venture,† Rank decided to go all-out to counteract the

---

* Although the boycott did not ostensibly extend to a closure of the American market to British films, pictures from Britain were more hostilely received than usual, and their distribution and thus their box-office takings were substantially lower during this eight-month period.

† During the war the Rank Organisation had embarked on a 'prestige experiment': an attempt to gain mass US distribution by producing expensive, export-oriented British films. Korda had tried this in the thirties, but had not succeeded. Rank failed to learn from Korda's example, and although he had enough money to bear the initial losses which were expected, he found the American market, except for the art house circuits, fiercely antagonistic to his experiment.

effects of the American embargo and announced in that 'Black Autumn' of 1947 a £9,250,000 ($40 million) programme for producing forty-seven films in 1948. Korda was, for once, more cautious. He refused to forsake his 'quality, not quantity' policy, even though the need for an increase in output seemed most desperate. Moreover, he warned Rank of the risk involved in producing so many films without sufficient creative and technical talent to back them up. For his own programme, Korda planned to spend £4,625,000 ($20 million) on thirteen feature films in 1948. If the first films were successful, Korda quipped, he intended to 'increase production to eight' so he could 'improve his product'.[11] He confidently stated to the press in November 1947: 'There exists no crisis in the British film-producing industry. . . . Twenty-four so-called A pictures are in active production in Hollywood . . . 20 in British studios. . . . So long as the British movie-maker retains his creative independence . . . he will win through.'[12]

By the end of 1948 Rank had produced thirty-two films and Korda only five, but both had spent too much money and had been left in an over-extended state when the American boycott was suspended in March 1948. The British Government had signed an agreement with the Americans which fixed the sum for annual US remittance to just over £4 million ($17 million) and allowed an additional remittance proportionate to the amount of dollars earned by British films in America. Although the Government had encouraged British film-makers to step up production, it could give them no immediate relief when the backlog of American films flooded the British market and British films again found 75–80 per cent of British screen time occupied by both 'old' and new American productions. With property and cinema holdings to offset some of his enormous losses, Rank was in a critical, but recoverable position; Korda, on the other hand, faced insurmountable financial difficulties. In the summer of 1948, the Government, whose shortsightedness the year before had compounded the industry's plight, was to awake finally to the seriousness of the situation and was to offer British film-makers the monetary assistance which they urgently needed.

Between 1946 and 1948 Korda had also become involved in several extra-curricular projects, some of which throw a decidedly dark shadow on his character. The one praiseworthy venture was his founding of the British Film Academy (now the Society of Film and Television

Arts) in 1947. Mrs P. J. Steele, secretary of the organisation since its establishment, explains how and why Korda set it up:

> . . . it really was Alex's idea from the start. He wanted to have an organisation where the top creative people in the film industry could get together and discuss the problems of the industry, new technical developments, and things of that kind. How it came about was he simply sat down . . . and wrote some seventy letters to the top people in the industry (and he wasn't only concerned with producers and directors, he had art directors, editors, cameramen). He invited them to a meeting in the penthouse at Claridges . . . to discuss the foundation of this thing. The idea was that it was going to be a highly select body . . . the members would meet twice a year at some super place and have a smashing dinner and discuss the British film industry.[13]

As it turned out, the Academy was simply patterned after Hollywood's Academy of Motion Picture Arts and Sciences (i.e. it promoted certain projects, but focused its attention on an annual awards ceremony, begun in 1948). Although always ready to support the Academy when financial troubles arose, Alex gradually dissociated himself from the running of the organisation. 'He was an initiator,' Mrs Steele observed. 'Having got it going, it became not of any great interest because there were other things to initiate.'[14]

In the same year Korda helped to initiate another project, one which the stage and film producer and director Basil Dean had been nurturing for some time. Dean's idea was to form an 'alliance' between stage producer and film producer for the sharing of performers. He presented the plan to Korda:

> 'He embraced it,' writes Dean, 'with modest enthusiasm, agreeing that when actors under contract to London Films were available they should be given opportunities to appear in the theatre under my direction, thus giving me the advantage of first-class acting talent while relieving Alex of some of his extravagance in the shape of paying actors for not working.
> 'With apparent good faith on either side, a company was formed, called Group Theatres Ltd., with Hugh Quennell, a City solicitor, then Alex's financial adviser, as chairman. I was not to be a member of the Board but employed as its artistic director at a nominal salary.'[15]

Dean took a year's lease on the St James's Theatre where several plays were performed over the winter of 1947–8. The plays were not commercially successful, and at one point the bank handling the Group Theatre account had refused to honour any more of Dean's cheques. Dean comments:

> I had accepted without question the financial arrangements that Hugh Quennell had made with the bank. An account had been opened in the name of Group Theatres Ltd., with Hugh Quennell acting as guarantor. . . . I assumed, quite wrongly, that Quennell was acting as nominee for Sir Alexander Korda. . . .
>
> Half-way through the season the bank informed me that the guarantee had already been much exceeded and that no more cheques would be honoured unless the guarantee were heavily increased. This information was also passed to Mr. Quennell who presumably held a board meeting. At all events he later assured me that he had increased the guarantee and the bank would now resume operations, which they did. But when the season came to an end I found myself confronted with a demand from the bank for the repayment of an overdraft exceeding £18,000.[16]

Dean had unwisely signed all the cheques with his own name, as he had been told to do. In 1948 the bank took the case to court, and Dean was eventually held responsible for some of the debt. Although Quennell was perhaps the villain in the story, Alex Korda made no attempt to help Dean. In fact, Dean later discovered that 'there had been a furious row between Quennell and Korda who resolutely refused any share in the responsibility for the equivocal guarantee'.[17] This was the second time in a year that Korda had left his supposed associates in the lurch.

In 1946 the British playwright Rodney Ackland and his friend Bill Gillette had formed Kinsmen Pictures 'in association with Sir Alexander Korda' in order to produce *Maria Chapdelaine*, a film about a French–Canadian peasant girl. Ackland was to write and direct the picture, and he was given an office in Korda's Piccadilly headquarters where he finished the script and chose the cast. He and Gillette then went to Canada to scout locations and await the arrival of cast and crew. The cast never arrived, and the only technical crew forthcoming from London was an assistant camera operator and a continuity girl. With this inadequate staff and a few locals as extras, Ackland began shooting exteriors. After much confusion and a flood of telegrams, Ackland was informed that Korda, disapproving of the script, had engaged another writer. The new script which was mailed to them bore no resemblance to the original. Ackland and Gillette saw no point in going ahead with their work, but were still surprised at the cable which their Korda liaison man wired the next day: 'Pack up and come home. Korda does not wish to continue with the film.'[18]

Distressed but undaunted, Ackland headed instead for the New York hotel where Korda was staying during a States-side trip.

> '[Korda] asked me to come and see him,' remembers Ackland, 'and when I did so and poured out my heart to him over "Maria Chapdelaine" he was perfectly charming. Of course it would make a beautiful film, he said—a film poem. "But . . . but why did you disapprove of my script, then?" I said. "What do you mean?" asked Korda. "I had a cable from London saying so," I assured him. "But I have never read your script!" cried he. "The story you have told me is beautiful. The film must be made. It would be madness to spend less than a year on it—in Canada. And, of course, Maria must be Michele Morgan [Ackland's first choice]." '[19]

Korda told Ackland to telephone him when they were both back in England. Ackland returned to London with revived hope and tried to contact Korda, who now refused to see him. In his book *The Celluloid Mistress* Ackland says that he never discovered why Korda had dropped the project, why in particular Korda had given him such encouragement in New York, but it is not unreasonable to assume a certain malicious intent on Korda's part.

During the war Rodney Ackland had given a lecture on 'The Future of the Cinema' in which he openly criticised Korda's work. As he relates it:

> What I had said about Alexander Korda's films was that they fulfilled the prophecy made by S. M. Eisenstein . . . in 1929. . . . The Cinema, he prognosticated, would inevitably go through a bad period in which fundamentally vulgar films, devoid of all cinematic qualities, would, because of their veneer of culture—borrowed from literature and the Stage —be acclaimed as works of art. This was the period we were now living through . . . and the best examples of these fundamentally vulgar works were the pictures of Alexander Korda and of Gabriel Pascal. I did concede, I believe, that Korda must have *something*: it took a certain kind of genius to be able to overlay a rousing cinematic subject like 'The

Scarlet Pimpernel' with so much borrowed 'culture' that the film left one about as limp with suspense and excitement as one would be after visiting an exhibition of Regency furniture.[20]

This was not the most tactful speech to make at a meeting of the Free Hungarians' Club, especially when a member of the audience happened to be Steven Pallos, one of Korda's oldest and closest friends. 'I went home,' Ackland concluded, 'with a distinct feeling that none of the Hungarians in the British film industry would ever want me to write or direct a film for them.'[21] That Korda was stringing Ackland along, that his dissatisfaction with *Maria Chapdelaine* revolved around Ackland is clear, for in 1950 British Lion promoted and distributed *The Naked Heart*, a film about Maria Chapdelaine which starred Michele Morgan and Kieron Moore and was directed by one of Korda's French associates Marc Allégret. It was little comfort to Ackland that this film was a complete flop.

Korda's charming exterior, his fierce loyalty to his friends, and his generosity towards untold numbers of Hungarians, those in Hungary and those resident in England,* concealed from the public and from unsuspecting 'associates' and employees the meanness and spite of which he was more than capable. It was easy to fall from Korda's graces and find yourself in the 'dog house', but more often than not, the unlucky person was at a loss to explain the capriciousness or inconstancy of Korda's behaviour. Certainly revenge was seldom the motivation; it was rather Korda's overwhelming need to establish his authority on the studio floor and in the company office. Anyone who questioned his authority or demanded more independence presented a threat, however mild, to Korda's power and received the requisite lesson in humility as punishment.† These lessons were, how-

---

* Over the years Korda sent much aid, financial and otherwise, to Hungarians living in Hungary either directly or through agencies like the Red Cross. His support of Hungarian émigrés in London usually took the form of disguised 'film work' which left the recipient with some dignity and for which Korda could bill his own company. According to one story, Korda's professed interest in a biographical film about Nijinsky was simply an excuse for paying Nijinsky's Hungarian wife Romola for a script which he had no intention of using. (He presumably financed the Nijinskys until the dancer's death in 1950.)

† After the initial 'bad start' at his interview with Korda in 1946, Leslie Mitchell gradually found out that his *'carte blanche'* as head of publicity had been revoked. Korda sent him to Hollywood early in 1947 'to learn the ropes' but had immediately cabled a disconcerting restriction on his activities there: 'PLEASE DO NOT MAKE ANY ANNOUNCEMENT OF ANY OF OUR PRODUCTION PLANS IN HOLLYWOOD.'

ever, usually not necessary, for Korda preferred to surround himself with deferential personnel rather than risk confrontations with high-powered employees who might challenge his judgements and his orders.

*Anna Karenina, The Fallen Idol, The Winslow Boy,* and *Bonnie Prince Charlie* were the four major Korda releases in 1948. All the money and talent that Korda had saved by not stepping up production during the film crisis had been put, with varying skill, into these expensive, quality efforts. Undeniably, *The Fallen Idol* and *The Winslow Boy* represent the best of the lot, and Alex Korda, not incoincidentally, played little part in their execution.

Korda *was* responsible, however, for conceiving the project which was to turn into *The Fallen Idol* (1948). It was he who first saw the cinematic possibilities of Graham Greene's 1935 short story *The Basement Room* and then had the inspiration to bring novelist Greene and director Carol Reed together to work on the film.* The Reed–Greene–Korda association was an auspicious one not only for British cinema but also for the men themselves. Their close personal friend-

---

On his trip back aboard the *Queen Elizabeth* Mitchell received another characteristic message: 'PAULETTE GODDARD TELLS ME THAT YOU ARE BRINGING WITH YOU HER PERSONAL PRESENTS TO ME IN THE FORM OF LOTS OF CIGARS STOP THEY ARE EVEN MORE WELCOME THAN YOURSELF STOP IF YOU HAVE NOT ENOUGH MONEY FOR DUTY CODRINGTON WILL AWAIT YOU WITH SUFFICIENT REGARDS ALEXANDER KORDA.' Then followed a series of fiascos during the promotion of *Ideal Husband* for which Mitchell was unjustly blamed. Finally, after working all night on some radio scripts for *Ideal* which Korda wanted to take to America, Mitchell presented them the next day to Alex who inexplicably tore them up in great anger. After only a year at London Films, Mitchell resigned. Why had Korda turned against Mitchell? One possible explanation relates to Mitchell's successful promotion campaign for *A Man About the House*. In the autumn of 1947 Mitchell had called in at Korda's office. 'Leslie,' Korda began, 'you are saying that I am not giving you sufficient control. I am giving you a black and white picture, a Ted Black picture, and you will keep my name out of it.' Both men knew that it was only a 'B' feature, but Mitchell designed an impressive campaign for the film, thanks to which it commercially surpassed all expectations. 'And I always had an uneasy feeling that I should not have kept Korda's name out of it,' says Mitchell.[22]

* With a track record which included *The Stars Look Down* (1939), *The Way Ahead* (1944), and *Odd Man Out* (1947), Carol Reed was a distinguished addition to the Korda group, to which he emigrated (from Rank) after financial wrangles over the *Odd Man Out* budget. He was the first major producing-directing talent to leave the Rank stable; others were to include Frank Launder and Sidney Gilliat, Michael Powell and Emeric Pressburger, and David Lean.

ship helped to establish a creative environment in which each could display his talent and Korda could without hesitation grant the kind of autonomy which he reserved for very few artists.

Left alone with Korda's brainstorm, Reed and Greene significantly refashioned the original story 'so that', Greene explains, 'the subject no longer concerned a small boy who unwittingly betrayed his best friend to the police, but dealt instead with a small boy who believed that his friend was a murderer and nearly procured his arrest by telling lies in his defence'.[23] The new script, Georges Périnal's effective, high-contrast black and white photography, Vincent Korda's uncluttered and expansive set designs, and, above all, Reed's sympathetic direction of Ralph Richardson (as Baines, the butler and supposed murderer), Michele Morgan (as his mistress), and Bobby Henrey (as the over-eager boy, Felipe) resulted in one of the best 'quiet' thrillers of all time, one in which scenes of great charm, innocence, and humour are expertly interwoven with moments of pure terror. It is a faultless film which stands up admirably to the work of the master thriller-maker, Alfred Hitchcock, and there is a nice Hitchcockian homage in the treatment of the villainess, Mrs Baines (played by Sonia Dresdel), so reminiscent of Judith Anderson's Mrs Danvers in *Rebecca* (1940).

*The Winslow Boy* (1948) was also the product of an expert film-making team. Unlike Reed and Greene, though, producer Anatole de Grunwald, director Anthony Asquith, and playwright Terence Rattigan had already successfully collaborated on two films: *French Without Tears* (1939) and *The Way to the Stars* (1945). After the war they transferred their combined activities (again from Rank) to Korda's company for this one film. Rattigan's play of the same name was the basis for the film, and the play, in turn, had derived from a famous court trial, the Archer–Shee case. With the assistance of cameramen Frederick Young and Osmond Borradaile and art director Andre Andrejew, the film-makers were able to create a convincing period (England, 1912) atmosphere and succeeded in making the story—a proud family sacrifices everything in order to exonerate the younger son, falsely charged with stealing a five-shilling postal order—more compelling than might have been expected. Margaret Leighton and Sir Cedric Hardwicke perform with great warmth their roles as the Winslow boy's sister and father, and in a difficult role Robert Donat acquits himself creditably as barrister Sir Robert Morton. Although as technically accomplished as *Fallen Idol*, *The Winslow Boy* is less satisfying in comparison. It lacks the former's gripping narrative, appears more dated because of its period setting, and is only half successful in coping with the cinematic translation of a stage play.

While these two teams were left to get on with their films, Korda was himself busy supervising two other productions. As we know, Korda had long planned to make *War and Peace*, and soon after that project fell through, he moved on to Tolstoy's other masterpiece, *Anna Karenina* (1948). Still hooked on his formula for 'international' films, Korda chose Julien Duvivier to direct this Russian subject, another Frenchman, Henri Alekan, to photograph it, and a third, dramatist Jean Anouilh, to write the script. When finished, Anouilh's treatment placed the Karenina story in France in the early 1900s; this, of course, was wholly unacceptable to Korda. He hired British writer Guy Morgan to work on a new script with Duvivier, and what ensued was a replay of the famous Korda story conferences of the thirties. Paul Tabori recounts:

> It began with a wonderful dinner, exquisite wines, brandy and cigars. Then Korda changed completely; he was no longer the charming host but the ice-cold, ruthless executive producer. He tore into the script, using colourful expletives and did not spare anybody's feelings. Duvivier would get angrier and angrier; until, in a towering rage, he would gather up his papers, announce that he would abandon the picture and return to Paris.
>
> Alex and the director would shout at each other from opposite sides of the room while Morgan would sit on the sofa, his head swivelling from one to another. Sometimes Korda's doctor would arrive, take him into the bathroom to give him an injection— but the argument continued through the open door. Every night Alex would let Duvivier get as far as the threshold—and there would stop him dead in his tracks with a subtly calculated final insult. The director would turn back, react, argue and forget about his decision to leave. In the end something constructive would be achieved—but next night the same scene would be repeated with slight variations.[24]

With production carried on in this manner, it is no wonder that the film took a year to make and cost £700,000 ($3,000,000).

For once the critics were unanimous: *Anna Karenina* was condemned as a 'big', 'beautiful', but ultimately 'boring' picture. Korda's decision to make an intelligent adaptation of Tolstoy's work had backfired. His serious approach had been applied only to the tragic plot—

the moral issues and themes raised by the author had been ignored—and this selectivity invalidated the film-makers' so-called 'thoughtful' interpretation of the book while robbing the actual story of all its passion and emotional depth. Vivien Leigh's subdued portrayal of Anna, for instance, may give us more insights into the character's mind, but it can't give us any measure of the uncontrollable passions which guide Anna's actions and lead to her eventual suicide. The lover Vronsky should be driven by equally powerful emotions, but Kieron Moore is so mis-cast as Vronsky that, as critic Dilys Powell noted, '[he] might be playing a professional dancing partner instead of a headstrong Tsarist officer'.[25] Anna's husband Karenin is the one restrained character in the story, and Ralph Richardson's outstanding performance does credit to the character and the film's approach.

The film is visually striking, but suffers, unlike *Fallen Idol* and *Winslow Boy*, from not being in Technicolor. Duvivier has captured some moments of cinematic beauty (e.g. Anna's somnambulant walk along a snow-covered train station platform), but he is unable to enliven material so weighted down by the script. The film invited obvious, unfavourable comparison with Clarence Brown's *Anna Karenina* (1935) which had starred Greta Garbo and Fredric March, Korda's version relates to Brown's in much the same way as *Catherine the Great* had to *The Scarlet Empress*, for in both cases the Hollywood films were intended to be nothing more than rousing, cinematic entertainments. For all his ambitions and pretensions, Korda deprived his films of being even that.

Korda reportedly 'lost a packet' on *Anna Karenina*. Although its overlength was wisely trimmed by sixteen minutes in Britain and by twenty-nine minutes for its American release, the film made no impression on either market. The blame for this was perhaps too conveniently placed on the repercussions of the Anglo-American film dispute. The blame for the failure of his last film of the year, however, was to fall directly on Korda's shoulders.

*Bonnie Prince Charlie* (1948) did not begin as a Korda project; producer Ted Black had initiated it, and Korda had been forced to take it over when Black died early in 1948. Presumably, too much money had already been spent for the production to be shelved, but besides the cast (including a reluctant David Niven loaned by Samuel Goldwyn for the starring part), little else was prepared at this stage. Leslie Arliss was to direct, and Clemence Dane to script; but before the production got fully under way Arliss had been replaced by Robert Stevenson, then Alex Korda, and finally Anthony Kimmins, and several writers had lent a hand in order to keep the script up to date with the filming. 'There was never a completed screenplay,' Niven remembers, 'and never at any time during the eight months we were shooting were the writers more than two days ahead of the actors. ... (Whenever we actors really started to breathe down the writers' necks, Korda ordered another battle to delay us for a few more days.)'[26] Everyone knew that the film was heading for a disastrous reception, and few were surprised by the venom of the majority of critics.

The critic for the *Manchester Guardian* wrote on the 30th of October:

> The worst of the film is not that it plays tricks with history, though it does this repeatedly. ... Nor is it most grave that the glens and mountains are emerald as picture-postcards and that every postcard scene is accompanied by enough chorus wailing of old Gaelic and Jacobite airs almost to turn the film into a slap-up musical. The great, the unforgivable fault is worse than all that; it is that the story has been made dull.
>
> To turn to dullness the most poignant and romantic episode in the last 250 years of British history was, in its way, a remarkable achievement. How and why it happened seems plain enough. It was because the director and producer—having, no doubt, less sense of the grandeur of their subject than of the value of the transatlantic box office—wanted to include everything; they wanted the battles, the colour, the singing, and, above all, they wanted Prince Charlie to spend a long time with Flora MacDonald.

*The Star*'s reviewer added that 'at times the characters seem to have no more animation than the mist-clad Highland peaks'.[27] Unexpectedly and ill-advisedly, Korda launched an attack on the London critics and an expensive publicity campaign to offset the antagonistic critical climate which threatened to ruin the film. In a two-page trade paper advertisement, he claimed: 'The Scottish critics, who should know, praise "Bonnie Prince Charlie" as a fine and exciting film. Some of the London critics have written about it not with a pen but with a hatchet. . . .'[28] Korda had not, it seems, read all the Scottish papers, for at least two Scottish critics were as appalled by the film as their London brethren:

> Considered even as a piece of fantasy, however, it will not do. It is a concentration of inspid hokum, in which the costumes are new and remain immaculate, and in which the tartans have a

primary brilliance that the vegetable dyes of the period could not have given them. The action is slow, the photography uninspired, and the accents are mixed. David Niven does not succeed in giving any impression of the subtle qualities in the character of the Prince who remains throughout boyish, clean and vapid. Indeed, the only part with any real life in it is that of Jack Hawkins as Lord George Murray. (*Glasgow Herald*, 27 October)

The start was almost unbelievably bad. Here was what was to be the film's most shocking deficiency—the inadequacy of the studio sets. (*Scotsman*, 27 October)

Almost unanimously, the performances of Margaret Leighton (as Flora MacDonald) and Jack Hawkins were judged the only redeeming features in the film. Korda's vain essay into critic-chastisement and self-justification had only added to an already costly mistake.

By the end of 1948 Korda and his company were reeling under the combined effect of audience disenchantment and critical disapprobation. He had been slow to realise the extent of post-war changes in the film-going public's tastes, changes which had much to do with the war and the wartime influence of documentary films. Ralph Bond noted in 1946:

> The drawing rooms and stately mansions, the vapid meanderings of the idle rich, the affected accents of the public schools had been left behind. . . . Real people, real situations and real instead of synthetic emotions became the rule and not the exception. British films found an integrity that the public at once responded to. Especially with themes connected with the war, their sincerity was in striking contrast to the synthetic values of the average Hollywood production.[29]

By continuing to ape Hollywood, Korda was fast losing touch with the British public. He finally began to take stock of the situation late in 1948 and reluctantly re-adjusted his sights. It was a wise move which prompted Peter Price's more hopeful comment in a *Sight and Sound* article two years later:

> . . . the talkies have come of age now, and the old showmanship of big stars and production value is ceasing to satisfy even the box office. Korda hasn't made a really significant contribution to the medium since the 'thirties—he makes the same sort of picture but it isn't news any more. Or perhaps we have yet to see.[30]

1. Unmarked press cutting, Alexander Korda microfiche, BFI Information Department.
2. *The British Film Industry*, PEP Report, London, 1952, p. 94.
3. E. M. Wood, *loc cit*.
4. Ernest Betts, *Inside Pictures*, London, Cresset, 1960, pp. 43–4.
5. Interview with Leslie Mitchell conducted by the author, 31 July 1973.
6. *Ibid.*
7. Leonard Mosley, 'Korda Puts the Spangles on Wilde', *Daily Express*, 14 November 1947.
8. Richard Winnington, 'Wilde and Woolly', *News Chronicle*, 15 November 1947.
9. Ernest Betts, *op cit*, p. 22.
10. David Lewin, *Daily Express*, 24 January 1956.
11. *Time*, 17 November 1947.
12. *Ibid.*
13. Interview with Mrs P. J. Steele conducted by the author, 10 July 1973.
14. *Ibid.*
15. Basil Dean, *Mind's Eye: an autobiography*, London, Hutchinson, 1973, p. 294.
16. *Ibid*, p. 303.
17. *Ibid.*
18. Rodney Ackland and Elspeth Grant, *The Celluloid Mistress*, London, Allan Wingate, 1954, p. 174.
19. *Ibid.*
20. *Ibid*, p. 153–4.
21. *Ibid*, p. 154.
22. Interview with Leslie Mitchell conducted by the author, 31 July 1973.
23. Graham Greene, preface to 'The Fallen Idol' in Penguin edition of *The Third Man and The Fallen Idol*, London, 1971, p. 123.
24. Paul Tabori, *op cit*, p. 262.
25. *Sunday Times*, 25 January 1948.
26. David Niven, *The Moon's a Balloon*, London, Coronet edition, 1973, pp. 258–9.
27. *The Star*, 29 October 1948.
28. *Manchester Guardian*, 12 November 1948.
29. Ralph Bond, *Monopoly: The Future of British Films*, London, ACT pamphlet, May 1946, p. 10.
30. Peter Price, 'The Impresario Urge', *Sight and Sound*, vol. 19 no. 7, November 1950, p. 292.

# CHAPTER NINETEEN

# British Lion and the £3,000,000 Loan

THE Anglo-American Film War had one beneficial effect: it precipitated a renewed series of Government enquiries into the economics of the British film industry, led by Harold Wilson, then President of the Board of Trade. Late in 1947 the National Film Production Council was formed under Wilson's chairmanship and including members of the production industry, and this Council was to examine ways in which British film-makers could 'achieve maximum output on a sound economic basis'.[1] After six months of preliminary investigations, the Council discovered that concepts like 'maximum output' were no longer operative, for almost the whole of the British film industry (Rank excepted) faced imminent collapse unless more working capital could be made available to the country's independent film producers. Investors in the City were asked to mount a salvage operation by making loans to beleaguered companies; but, having burned their fingers ten years before, they refused this time to come to the industry's assistance. It was finally left to the Government to intervene.

In the summer of 1948 an organising Committee began to consider how the Government should manage an official loan scheme and who the beneficiaries of the scheme should be. On the first of October 1948 this Committee evolved into the National Film Finance Company, an organisation which was 'empowered to borrow up to £2½ million from its bankers on Treasury Guarantee'.[2] At this point Sir Wilfrid Eady, Second Secretary of the Treasury, convinced his associates at the Treasury and the Board of Trade to make a special recommendation to the Company for the granting of immediate aid to Korda's British Lion. Although British Lion had shown a profit (£61,154) in 1946–7, it had since been brought to the verge of bankruptcy by heavy production losses (totalling £2,187,016 for the 1948 fiscal year). Eady and others argued that if British Lion, the second largest production-distribution company in the country, were allowed to collapse, the rest of the industry might well follow suit. On the 11th of November their recommendation was accepted, and Korda's company received a £2 million loan, with fixed 4 per cent interest, from the Government through the National Film Finance Company. This loan was subsequently increased to £3 million. In March 1949, Parliament passed the Cinematograph Film Production (Special Loans) Bill which sanctioned the loan scheme, established the National Film Finance Corporation, which was to take over the National Film Finance Company's work, and allocated £5 million (i.e. an additional £2½ million) for the five-year project. When the NFFC was set up in April 1949, it immediately inherited the Korda–British Lion loan.

The Government's action with regard to British Lion provoked much adverse criticism both within and outside the industry. Many people questioned why aid had been given to a distribution company rather than to the film producers themselves and further wondered whether Alex Korda, a film-maker closely connected with the British cinema's most extravagant days and ways, was the best choice as principal beneficiary. To understand the peculiar nature of the British Lion loan, however, two things had to be taken into account. First, the loan was an emergency rescue operation approved before the NFFC guidelines had been established. In order to expedite the injection of working capital into the independent sector, the Finance Company had decided, for better or worse, to give a blanket loan to British Lion, then home for a great many independent producers, rather than waste precious time assessing the merits of individual applications for assistance.* The

* When fully established, the NFFC did, in fact, operate under this second principle. Individual producers would apply to the Corporation for a loan before production had commenced, and each application would be examined with regard to the experience of the producer in question, the merits of the film's script or subject, the likelihood of finance being easily obtainable elsewhere, and the existence of a distribution guarantee. Not a charity foundation, the NFFC demanded certain prerequisites: the producer in most cases must have already found some capital of his own to spend and must have secured a distribution guarantee from a distributor upon which a bank loan for the rest of the 'front money' (approximately 70 per cent of the budget) could be raised. Once satisfied

assessment procedure was to be undertaken by the British Lion board itself, and it was assumed that they would use their discretion in allocating the Government loan to those producers who distributed through British Lion. Although it seemed at the time the most expeditious solution to the immediate problem, the NFFC was soon to regret the amount of control which had been conceded to the British Lion executive. Second, the loan was not given to Alexander Korda and London Film Productions, but to British Lion.* Many producers not directly affiliated with Korda worked at British Lion, and if in financial difficulty, they were all to have access to the Government money. Of course, in practice London Films, as the largest single unit functioning at the British Lion studios, consumed the biggest proportion of the loan and was to take the largest share of the blame when things started to go wrong.

A month before the NFFC loan was announced, Alex Korda had made an important declaration of his own. He told the press that his own name would no longer appear on the screen credits of his films. The removal of the 'Alexander Korda presents' credit from the screen symbolised Korda's almost complete withdrawal from active film-making. Having retired from film directing on the completion of *An Ideal Husband*, Korda now decided to put an end to his career as a film producer as well. After thirty-five years in the business Korda had finally lost his enthusiasm for the daily struggles and frustrations of film production and his drive to have authority over each and every film produced or presented by London Films. He still enjoyed promoting film projects, negotiating contracts and film rights, and arranging impressive business deals, but these activities were the domain of an executive producer or studio administrator. This was the role which Korda successfully played during his last seven years. Given the disrepute in which Korda's brand of film-making was then held and the increased administrative burdens which the NFFC loan placed on him,

---

with these conditions, the NFFC would then offer a loan to cover a percentage of the 'end money' without which the production could not be completed.

* To comply with the Government instruction that production and distribution spheres of an organisation receiving state aid should be separated, there were resignations from the British Lion Board of Directors of men (Harold Boxall, Hugh Quennell, and David Cunynghame) prominent in the London Films company. A City financier, Harold C. Drayton, was appointed chairman of British Lion, and Korda's position became that of 'production adviser'.

it was an opportune time for Korda to leave the studio floor for the company office.

Korda's decision was made easier because he for once had confidence in the men who were to take over the creative work at his studio. Between 1946 and 1955 almost a dozen of Britain's best film-makers were to migrate from the Rank Organisation to Korda's British Lion– London Films outfit. Men like Carol Reed, Michael Powell, Emeric Pressburger, Frank Launder, Sidney Gilliat, David Lean, Ian Dalrymple, John and Roy Boulting, and Laurence Olivier had all found the Rank Organisation a fairly congenial home. Rank had offered them great creative freedom, and they had produced some of their best works while at Rank. Why, then, did they leave? Some came back out of loyalty: Michael Powell and Emeric Pressburger, for instance, felt a special affinity for Korda because he had been responsible for the formation of their partnership. Some migrated because Korda offered more lucrative contracts. Almost all of them, however, switched allegiance because they found Korda a more sympathetic studio executive. The Rank Organisation was run by businessmen, like John Davis, who had no practical experience in film-making. Their ignorance of film production prevented them from interfering in the work of their employees, but it also meant that they were unable to provide any guidance or assistance, except in financial matters.* Korda, on the other hand, was an executive whose own film-making background created a bond of artistic sympathy and understanding between him and his associates. Directors and producers could draw on Korda's experience, in particular his knowledge of foreign markets, and could rely on his judgements and his suggestions. Korda was also able to inspire and encourage film-makers in a way that Rank couldn't. Films like *The Fallen Idol* and *The Third Man*, for example, would never have been made if it hadn't been for the impetus given to the projects by Korda himself.

Perhaps the best proof of the stimulating atmosphere which these film-makers encountered at Korda's studio is the number of films which were produced during that seven-year period. In the sixteen years between 1933 and 1948 Alex Korda had presented, produced, or directed fifty-eight feature films: between 1949 and 1955 he was

---

* At least five people who left Rank (Carol Reed, Sidney Gilliat and Frank Launder, Michael Powell and Emeric Pressburger), did so after having financial wrangles with Rank over their last films (*Odd Man Out*—1947, *The Blue Lagoon*— 1949, and *The Red Shoes*—1948).

'associated with' thirty-seven pictures. More important than the increase in productivity, however, is the fact that both periods fostered an almost equal number of distinguished pictures. The NFFC loan and Korda's reappraisal of his own position within the studio hierarchy made this post-1948 recovery possible. Although the Government's resuscitation of British Lion's fortunes was illusory, it at least postponed the company's collapse for six years, thus giving Korda time to prove his abilities as an executive producer.

A glance at the Korda–British Lion output during this period immediately prompts two correlative observations. First, the vast majority of the films have nothing in common with Korda's pre-war work. The pervasive Korda stamp which had ruined so many earlier productions has virtually disappeared. Second, the films' credits reveal a significant increase in the number of employed British producers, directors, technicians, and stars. Korda's studio was no longer the home for a foreign enclave making 'international' pictures; it was rather a film centre where British talent and, in most cases, British subjects were fostered. These changes were partially necessitated by the economic limitations of the time, but neither would have occurred if Korda had continued to take creative responsibility for all his films. The demise of the 'old Alexander Korda', therefore, not only promised freedom from interference for Korda's contracted artists, but also allowed London Films to contribute to the development of the national cinema in a new and different way. International markets were not ignored—Korda was to expend much of his own energy on securing better international distribution for these films—but 'internationalism' did not on the whole dominate studio policy as it had in the thirties.

The most prolific British writer-producer-director team to work under contract to Korda during these years was that of Sidney Gilliat and Frank Launder. Their successful film partnership (in which they alternately produced or directed for each other) had been forged in 1937 when they began co-writing film scripts. They formed Individual Pictures during the war and produced several films for Rank including *The Rake's Progress* (1945), *I See a Dark Stranger* (1946), and *The Blue Lagoon* (1949). Their transfer to Korda in 1949 inaugurated a series of Launder and Gilliat comedies which explored the kind of British humour which Korda could never quite understand or appreciate. Although some of their films—*The Happiest Days of Your Life* (1950), *Folly To Be Wise* (1953), *Belles of St Trinian's* (1954), and *The Constant*

312

*Husband* (1955)—were more successful than others, like *State Secret* (1950) and *Lady Godiva Rides Again* (1951), they only produced one box-office failure, *The Story of Gilbert and Sullivan* (1953).

This last film was a 'musical biopic' in which the lives of W. S. Gilbert (Robert Morley) and Arthur Sullivan (Maurice Evans) were to be interwoven with extracts from their popular operettas. The project offered great potential for a lavish Technicolor treatment, and perhaps for this reason (and despite his basic ignorance of things musical\*), Alex Korda decided to involve himself in this one Launder and Gilliat production. Both Alex and Vincent Korda sat in on the story conferences, discussing and arguing with Gilliat and writer Leslie Bailey the relative merits of the different operetta sequences under consideration.

The resulting film, not surprisingly, betrays the usual Kordaesque feature of overblown production values and overwhelmed story and acting. Even extensive retakes (perhaps initiated by Korda) and a big publicity campaign—the film was chosen to celebrate London Films' 21st Anniversary—could not save the picture. Although Sidney Gilliat had seen the Korda stamp in operation on his own work, he was one film-maker who later defended Korda from the charge of extravagance.

> 'He has often been called extravagant,' Gilliat wrote of Korda in 1956. 'But how difficult it must have been for a cosmopolitan of bounding imagination even to attempt to confine himself within the hundred and one restrictions—and crises—of film-making in this country, or to accommodate his bold (and at times reckless) temperament to the rigidity imposed by the inverted pyramid of the industry's structure here, where production has always been forced into a subordinate role, and where, as he always maintained, the rewards to the producer of a successful production are disproportionately small!
>
> 'It is a wonder that he ever stayed with us to go on trying, and almost a miracle that he so often succeeded.'⁴

As this comment and the success of their next two films (*Belles of St Trinian's* and *The Constant Husband*) prove, Launder and Gilliat had emerged unscathed from their one collaboration with Alex Korda.

\* With regard to Korda's limited musical sense, music director Muir Mathieson once quipped: 'He only knew it was *God Save the Queen* because the crowd stood up, other than that he hadn't got a clue.'³

Ten of the other British Lion films made between 1949 and 1955 were also the work of established British film-makers.* Jack Lee's now classic POW film *The Wooden Horse* (1950), the Boulting Brothers' thriller *Seven Days to Noon* (1950), and Anthony Kimmins's comedy *The Captain's Paradise* (1953) are the most outstanding productions in this group, but the rest—Kimmins's *Mr Denning Drives North* (1952) and *Who Goes There?* (1952), George More O'Ferrall's *The Heart of the Matter* (1954) and *The Holly and the Ivy* (1952), Leslie Arliss's *Saints and Sinners* (1949), Guy Hamilton's *The Ringer* (1953), and producer Ian Dalrymple's *Three Cases of Murder* (1955)—are certainly respectable, if modest-budgeted, efforts. All the films were enhanced by the talented cameramen, designers, and editors who were engaged by Korda, and these film-makers made good use of Korda's contracted artistes, in particular Ralph Richardson, Margaret Leighton, and Jack Hawkins. But Korda's actual participation in these films was negligible. He readily offered advice on request and almost always asked to see the pictures in rough-cut form in order to make suggestions for re-takes which might improve the final product's overseas marketability. None the less, to call these films 'Korda pictures' in anything but the widest sense would be a misnomer.

Alex Korda was more tangibly involved in the remaining thirteen films of this period. As a group these pictures could not have been more different, for three of them were directorial debuts and ten were the work of Britain's most celebrated and individualistic film-makers.

The NFFC–British Lion loan had given Korda an opportunity to encourage three of his favourite actors—Emlyn Williams, Robert

* Four foreign producers—the Russian Gregory Ratoff, the Germans Karl Hartl and Josef Somlo, and Zoltan Korda—were responsible for an additional seven films. Ratoff produced and directed *That Dangerous Age* (1949) and *My Daughter Joy* (1950). Hartl and Somlo, whose contracts were the result of their long friendship and working association with Korda, both produced two pictures. Hartl was the producer on *The Angel with the Trumpet* (1950) and *The Wonder Kid* (1951), which he also directed. Somlo produced for British directors Wendy Toye (*The Teckman Mystery*—1954) and Harold French (*The Man Who Loved Redheads* —1955). Zoltan Korda was also to reap the benefit of the more independent climate of his brother's post-war company. With *Cry, the Beloved Country* (1952), Zoltan was for once able to express his own feelings about Africa, in this case the plight of black South Africans. Assisted by Alan Paton's sympathetic script based on his novel and by the performances of Canada Lee and Sidney Poitier, Zoltan directed one of the cinema's finest statements about the necessity of racial under-standing.

Donat, and Ralph Richardson—to direct their first films.* Korda approved the scripts and the budgets (none were to cost more than £50,000), arranged for his actor-directors to be guided by more experienced producers and assistants, provided the technicians and casts largely from his own stable, and gave freely of his time and advice when problems arose. Emlyn Williams's *The Last Days of Dolwyn* (1949) was the first and best of this actor-turned-director series. The story revolves around the confusion which a dam construction project unleashes on the citizens of a small Welsh village, and Williams wrote the original screenplay as well as starring in and directing the picture. Despite the sympathetic direction and a fine cast headed by Dame Edith Evans, Hugh Griffith, and a young Welsh actor Richard Burton,† *Last Days*, as Williams and Korda expected, was not a commercial success.

Robert Donat's *The Cure for Love* (1950) also represented a British picture with a regional flavour, this time Yorkshire. Donat, Alexander Shaw, and Albert Fennell adapted the film from Walter Greenwood's play, but the stageyness of the adaptation and the sentimentality of the story undermined the warmth of the performances (notably those of Robert Donat, Renee Asherson, Marjorie Rhodes, and Dora Bryan). Ralph Richardson's *Home at Seven* (1952) was the first of four experiments in the economical shooting of recent stage plays. 'By rehearsing the script as thoroughly as a stage play for three weeks on the actual set at Shepperton Studios,' a *Daily Mail* journalist reported, 'the film was shot in 13½ days, as against eight weeks by normal production methods.' 5 The script (of R. C. Sherriff's play) was written by Anatole de Grunwald, and the well-rehearsed cast was led by Richardson, Margaret Leighton, and Jack Hawkins.‡ Although *Home at Seven* was a little 'thin' and looks today like a 'movie made for television', Korda was pleased with

* Actor Anthony Bushell was also allowed to make his directorial debut at this time. He directed a more characteristic Korda project: *Angel with the Trumpet* (1950), an English version of Karl Hartl's Austrian film *Der Engel mit der Posaune* (1948) which had starred Curt Jurgens and Maria Schell.

† Three years later Korda put Richard Burton under a five-year, £500-a-week contract and then promptly loaned him to 20th Century-Fox (for $150,000) for three pictures.

‡ Some ambiguous accounts of the making of *Home at Seven* leave the impression that Alex Korda directed at least part of the film himself. There is no evidence to substantiate this, although it was true that Korda carefully 'supervised' the project and at one point demanded re-takes (the first ten minutes of the film were re-shot in four hours).

the result and promoted three more similarly-conceived projects (the aforementioned *Who Goes There?*, *The Holly and the Ivy*, and *The Ringer*).

In the race to monopolise Britain's best film-making talent, Korda scored a decisive victory over Rank when Carol Reed, Michael Powell and Emeric Pressburger, and David Lean all decided to switch stables from Rank's South Street headquarters to Korda's Piccadilly mansions. Of these four men David Lean was the most unexpected addition to the London Films staff. In 1947, at the height of the public attacks on Rank's industry monopoly and the talent exodus from Rank, Lean had written an enthusiastic defence of Rank in which he described the great freedom which Rank allowed his film-makers and concluded that these conditions 'have at last given our films a style and nationality of their own'.[6] Lean's support was understandable, for his own distinguished career as a film director had been forged at Rank. Having started with *In Which We Serve* (1942) which he co-directed with Noël Coward, Lean went on to direct a series of immensely popular films: *This Happy Breed* (1944), *Blithe Spirit* (1945), *Brief Encounter* (1945), *Great Expectations* (1946), and *Oliver Twist* (1948). Lean's enthusiasm for Rank apparently cooled after he made two less successful pictures, *The Passionate Friends* (1949) and *Madeleine* (1950), and he joined Korda's group in August 1950.

A meticulous and slow-working director, Lean took two years over his first London Films production, *The Sound Barrier* (1952). The subject had appealed to Korda whose own fascination with aviation (*viz. Things to Come*, *The Lion Has Wings*, and *Conquest of the Air*) seemed limitless, and he wholeheartedly supported Lean throughout the film's difficult passage to the screen. The script, written by Terence Rattigan, presented the most problems, for Lean was concerned with more than just the drama of how the sound barrier was broken and wanted to explore the inner conflicts which accompany almost all technological advances. Ralph Richardson was so unimpressed by the script that he declined the leading role (opposite Ann Todd and Nigel Patrick) twice before Korda was able to wear down his resistance. Although a long time in production, the film cost comparatively little (£250,000) and easily made a profit both in England and America where it was well received.

To launch this rather low-key film Korda resorted to a real show-man's publicity stunt. Korda, Lean, Ann Todd, and others flew to Paris in a Comet performing aerial acrobatics over the Champs-Elysées on the way. Korda admitted to a French reporter that some of his friends considered this a vulgar idea. 'What did you reply?' asked the journalist. 'That given we live in a vulgar age, it is absolutely necessary to have vulgar ideas,' responded Korda.[7]

For Lean's next picture, *Hobson's Choice* (1954), Charles Laughton was coaxed back to London Films after a fourteen-year absence. Laughton starred as Henry Hobson, the egocentric and pleasantly vulgar boot-seller who prefers to keep his industrious daughters unmarried so they can work for him unpaid. The daughters who finally rebel by leaving home for husbands were beautifully portrayed by Daphne Anderson, Prunella Scales, and especially Brenda de Banzie, the eldest who marries her father's best bootmaker, Willie Mossop (John Mills), and sets up a rival shop. Although the film derived from a play, Lean and cameraman Jack Hildyard succeeded (where the inexperienced Robert Donat had failed in *Cure for Love*) in rendering the comedy in cinematic terms. *Hobson's Choice* was certainly the warmest and most charming of Korda's post-war productions.

Since their first collaboration on Korda's *The Spy in Black* in 1939, Michael Powell and Emeric Pressburger had produced ten feature films together, including *49th Parallel* (1941), *One of our Aircraft is Missing* (1942), *I Know Where I'm Going* (1945), and their four Technicolor extravaganzas for Rank: *The Life and Death of Colonel Blimp* (1943), *A Matter of Life and Death* (1946), *Black Narcissus* (1947), and *The Red Shoes* (1948). They had developed a highly distinctive, often exotic, always visually imaginative style, and their films, which after 1942 were produced by their own company (The Archers), had won for them an international reputation. Powell and Pressburger had intended to return to Korda in 1947, but the project they wanted to work on—*The Red Shoes*—no longer interested Korda.* They finally rejoined London Films after *The Red Shoes* and were contracted to make several pictures over the next few years.

Working in collaboration with the fine production team (cameraman Chris Challis, art director Hein Heckroth, editor Reginald Mills, and

---

* Before the war Alex had commissioned Emeric Pressburger to write a starring vehicle for Merle Oberon in which she was to play a ballerina and a double was to be used for the dancing. Korda paid Pressburger about £2,000 for the script, which was never used. In 1947 Powell and Pressburger decided to resurrect the script; but Korda, perhaps for understandable personal reasons, wasn't sympathetic to the project and, thinking he was making a great business deal, sold the script to them for £12,000. After much reworking of the idea, the Archers made the film for Rank, and it was a colossal artistic and financial success.

composer Brian Easdale) which Powell and Pressburger had established, the Archers produced and directed four features for Korda between 1949 and 1951. (Emeric Pressburger also made one film as solo director: *Twice Upon a Time*—1953.) Their first, *The Small Back Room* (1949), was a modest, but effective thriller taken from Nigel Balchin's novel. It dealt with a bomb disposal expert's attempts to unravel the mysteries of a new type of bomb which the Nazis were dropping on England, and Powell's gift for creating atmosphere and tension with the utmost economy of sound and image was well exploited in the film. Powell has stated that he considers *The Small Back Room* his 'best film'; unfortunately, audiences did not agree, and the film was a financial failure.

Their contract with Korda then led them into even deeper water. Powell admitted to interviewer Kevin Gough-Yates in 1970:

> There's something killing about a contract or maybe by this time we were just incapable of falling in with Korda's ideas. But of course his situation was that he had to get certain films made and we were there and could eventually be talked into anything. That's not the best way to make a film. Though we loved Alex and understood him very well, we did succeed in making several disastrous films together.[8]

It was Korda's wheeling-and-dealing which was to blame for the disasters which *Gone to Earth* (1950) and *The Elusive Pimpernel* (1950) represented.

In his search for more finance and better distribution Korda had made deals with both David O. Selznick and Samuel Goldwyn in which they were to loan talent and provide additional financing in exchange for some control over the projects advanced and distribution rights in the Western Hemisphere. Much impressed by Powell and Pressburger's recent work, Selznick wanted them to make a film with his wife, Jennifer Jones. After several ideas were scrapped, everyone agreed on an adaptation of Mary Webb's novel, *Gone to Earth*. Selznick was displeased with the results and tried to stop Korda from releasing the picture, ostensibly on the grounds that the original story had been 'distorted'.* Since Selznick did have control over the film's American

---

* Powell later recalled this exchange with Selznick over *Gone to Earth*:
Selznick: I'm going to sue on deviation from the script.
Powell: But we didn't deviate.
Selznick: That's what I'm going to sue you on.[9]
Selznick's objections, as it turned out, had more to do with his dissatisfaction over the inadequate amount of screen time preserved for Jennifer Jones's close-ups.

release, he held up distribution until Hollywood director Rouben Mamoulian had re-cut the film and added some new sequences which he had directed. This substantially different version was released in 1952 in America as *The Wild Heart*.

The Archers ran into similar problems with *The Elusive Pimpernel* for which Samuel Goldwyn had loaned the twice unlucky David Niven to star as Sir Percy Blakeney. Powell reluctantly accepted the project, but his proposal to turn it into a musical was rejected by Korda. 'It never went right,' Powell explains, 'because there were relics of the musical idea still in it. I'd given it a completely different story line but Alex and Samuel Goldwyn wanted a lot of the original story line put back again . . . if you're making a film between Goldwyn and Alex Korda . . . you get ground to powder.'[10] The picture had already cost £450,000, and the extensive re-takes added £27,000 (at least) to that figure. According to David Lewin in his *Daily Express* article, at a news conference Goldwyn and Korda were quizzed about the amount of money spent on re-takes for the film. 'How much?' one reporter bravely asked. 'Two per cent of the cost of the picture,' Korda replied. The reporter persisted: 'How much did the picture cost?' 'One hundred per cent,' Korda elusively responded.[11]

Both films ended in prolonged legal battles between Selznick and Korda and Goldwyn and Korda; furthermore, Powell and Pressburger were on the verge of breaking their contract. Korda's enthusiasm for their next project, *The Tales of Hoffman* (1951)—prompted perhaps by his guilt feelings over the last two—convinced them to stay. They brought together much the same team that had created *The Red Shoes* in order to give Offenbach's opera a similarly stylish treatment. Sir Thomas Beecham, who had suggested the project to Powell and Pressburger in the first place, worked with Powell on arranging and recording the entire score before the film was shot, and the famous choreographer Frederick Ashton was employed to design the ballet sequences. The talented cast, which included Moira Shearer, Robert Helpmann, Ludmilla Tcherina, Leonide Massine, Ann Ayars, and Robert Rounseville, spent several weeks in rehearsal, and their expertise plus Powell's careful preproduction work helped to keep the shooting schedule down to just over two months. Despite its opulence, which at times bordered on garishness, and the professionalism of its artists, *The Tales of Hoffman* was not well received. The public (and Alex Korda) found the film inaccessible and frequently boring, perhaps because, with its prologue and epilogue and three very different 'tales', the film lacked the continuity and focus of *The Red Shoes*. After *Hoffman*, the Archers amicably terminated their contract with Korda.

Of all the films with which Korda was associated during his last ten years in the British cinema, one stands head and shoulders above the rest, Carol Reed's *The Third Man* (1949). Like *The Fallen Idol* this film was made in collaboration with Graham Greene, and also like its predecessor the project derived from suggestions made by Alex Korda. Ever since the end of the war Korda had been gathering ideas for a film about the aftermath of war in a European city. At first he envisaged it as a comedy set in Vienna and starring Cary Grant. Then R. C. Sherriff was hired to adapt Paul Tabori's novel *Epitaph for Europe* with the prospects that Ian Dalrymple might produce and Spencer Tracy might play in the film. Finally, in 1948 Korda tried his ideas out on Reed and Greene one night over dinner. They agreed on the background—occupied Vienna—but needed a story. Greene offered one sentence which he had years before written on an envelope: 'I had paid my last farewell to Harry a week ago, when his coffin was lowered into the frozen February ground, so that it was with incredulity that I saw him pass by, without a sign of recognition, amongst the host of strangers in the Strand.'[12] On the basis of that sentence Korda sent Greene off to Italy to write the rest of the story. Two months later, he returned with *The Third Man*.

While Reed and Greene were left alone to fashion a script from Greene's treatment, Korda busied himself with finding the finance needed to pay for the big star names which the project obviously warranted. Korda's tie-up with Selznick had not yet gone sour so, again for American rights to the film, Korda received Joseph Cotten who was to play the hero Holly Martins and Italian actress Alida Valli who was to portray Anna, Harry Lime's Russian girlfriend. For the all-important though small role of Harry Lime, Korda hired Orson Welles, who was then in self-imposed exile from Hollywood following his production of *Macbeth* (1948). Although Greene and Reed were forced to 'consult' with David Selznick before production started (and received forty pages of suggestions on their departure from Southern California), they stood their ground and made the film their own way. Given the result, Selznick had no reason to complain.

Like *The Fallen Idol*, *The Third Man* is about the breaking down of an illusion; but whereas Philip in *Idol* readily *but mistakenly* accepts the new image of his hero as a murderer, here Holly Martins stubbornly clings to his illusion of Harry Lime until it is conclusively proven to him that his hero *is* a murderer. Shortly after his arrival in Vienna and his discovery that friend Harry has been killed in an accident, Martins, a naïve American writer of Western stories, becomes convinced that his 'idol' has been murdered. While he questions Lime's friends in an attempt to track down the killer—the 'third man' at the scene of the crime—the British police officer Major Calloway (Trevor Howard) tries to persuade him that his hero was an amoral black marketeer who is better off dead. Discovering that Harry is still alive, Martins's doubts begin to grow and are finally confirmed by the evidence which Calloway has accumulated against Harry. The illusion now broken, Martins co-operates with the police in trapping and eventually killing Lime.

This melodrama of corruption and disillusionment is enriched by being placed in the bombed-out ruins and empty streets of a divided city where phantoms like Lime commute through the sewers. Reed and Greene have embroidered this decaying canvas with black humour, pathos, and surprising comic touches and have purposely only sketched in some of the film's more mysterious figures, notably Harry's friends Anna (Valli), Kurtz (Ernst Deutsch), Popescu (Siegfried Breuer), and Dr Winkel (Erich Ponto). The exotic camera angles—photographer Robert Krasker won an Oscar for his work—Anton Karas's zither music, Oswald Hafenrichter's editing, and Reed's objective treatment reinforce the film's disturbing qualities: the false climaxes, the impenetrable emotions, the horrors left unseen, and the isolation of the city's trapped population. Above all, the acting is superlative. It is perhaps Joseph Cotten's best role: the simple, and not very talented, innocent abroad, delightfully pathetic in his drunken pursuit of Anna's affection, in his boring speech to a literary society, and in his search for justice. Trevor Howard is excellent as Martins's guide to the underworld, the major who has not become anaesthetised to the horrific deeds perpetrated in the city which he polices. Valli is cool and impassive as the estranged Anna; her understated performance, though condemned at the time, is perfectly attuned to the story's moods and themes. Orson Welles squeezes every possibility from his small but key appearance as Lime and encapsulates Lime's attitude with his own addition to Greene's witty dialogue: 'In Italy for thirty years under the Borgias, they had warfare, terror, murder, bloodshed—they produced Michelangelo, Leonardo da Vinci, and the Renaissance. In Switzerland they had brotherly love, five hundred years of democracy and peace, and what did that produce? The cuckoo clock.'

*The Third Man* was a colossal triumph for all who were involved in it. It is widely considered a classic of the thriller genre and is the most often revived production with which Korda was ever associated. Although Carol Reed's next two films made for Korda and without Greene—*Outcast of the Islands* (1952) from Joseph Conrad's novel and *The Man Between* (1953), a thriller which unevenly followed the lines of *Third Man*—were distinguished and under-rated efforts, neither of them conquered the international market as *The Third Man* had. Even though Korda took little credit for the part he had played in setting up *The Third Man*, he must have received great satisfaction from the knowledge that a British team had demonstrated to Hollywood and the world that the British cinema was alive and kicking, despite all rumours to the contrary.

Korda's disengagement from film-making provided his life with something it had always lacked: leisure time. Thriving as he did on the pressures and excitements of hard work, Korda found it difficult to adjust to a leisurely life away from the studio. His greatest outlet during the early fifties, however, was his yacht *Elsewhere*. 'I was born on the plains of Hungary,' Korda explained to *Daily Express* journalist David Lewin, 'so far from the sea that I did not have fish to eat until I was 30. . . . Now I love the sea, so I bought a yacht.'[13] During the summers Alex took his converted air-sea rescue boat—'with four private cabins, an observation lounge, a deck saloon, and a cocktail bar'[14]—around the Mediterranean, cruising the Greek Islands and often anchoring at Antibes or Nice. He was enormously proud of his yacht, especially of its seaworthiness.

> 'At night one time on the yacht,' Carol Reed, a frequent guest, remembers, 'it was so rough I kept being bounced out of my bunk.
> 'Everything was going round and up and down and the water was coming in and there was Alex on the bridge in the dry, telling me how well the ship was riding. "See how steady she is," he would say as I was being sick again.'[15]

Even while on vacation, Korda stayed in constant communication with London and kept a steady flow of guests aboard ship. The people who accompanied Alex on his cruises ranged from close friends and associates like Reed, Vivien Leigh and Laurence Olivier, Graham Greene, and Marcel Pagnol to illustrious guests like Margot Fonteyn, Ingrid Bergman, and Roberto Rossellini. During the summer 1953 cruise

Korda entertained a special guest, a twenty-five-year-old Canadian named Alexandra Boycun. On the 3rd of June, exactly fourteen years after his marriage to Merle Oberon at Antibes, Korda announced his engagement to the attractive blonde Alexa. Five days later they were married at Vence.

Born in Fort William, Ontario, Alexa Boycun had studied to be a dramatic soprano at the Toronto Conservatory and the New York College of Music and had continued her voice training in Munich and London. Korda met her at a party in London in 1952, and rumours of a possible marriage had been in circulation for some time. The match was very different from Korda's previous ones, for despite her training, Alexa had no career ambitions. Because of this she was able to provide Alex with the kind of 'real home life' (Korda's words) which he had never known. They settled in a house at 20 Kensington Palace Gardens (Millionaires' Row) and were extremely happy, although, according to some, Alexa had a hard time adapting to the glamorous Korda world.

The restless summer wanderings of *Elsewhere* were a manifest expression of Korda's own growing restlessness. He had begun to feel trapped by his own ambition. 'Sometimes I think of retiring,' he later admitted, 'but then I go to my desk again and know I cannot. When you have been on the treadmill as long as I have, it goes faster and faster and it is not possible to step off.'[16] Neither was it possible for Korda to accept his worsening physical condition. For several years he had suffered from a severe form of neuritis. In 1952 Korda was warned about the weakness of his circulatory system and told to cut back on his more luxurious habits.* Korda refused to slow down his pace even after he suffered his first major heart attack in the summer of 1954.

*Elsewhere* provided a needed respite from the troubles which Korda was facing at home. The NFFC loan had allowed British Lion to make a gradual recovery between 1949 and 1951. On his part Alex Korda had made a great effort to increase production and cut down on production costs. In addition, he had sought wider distribution for his films by securing agreements in America (with Selznick, Goldwyn, and a new partner Ilya Lopert), in Germany (with the formation of Deutsche London Films), in Canada (through Eagle-Lion), and South Africa.

---

* One colleague went into Korda's office and noticed a few cigars resting on the desk with white papers underneath them. Korda explained that he had been told to curtail his cigar-smoking and that the times written on the papers indicated the hour at which he could light up his next one.

Nevertheless, the budgets had not been pared down soon enough, and his films as a whole had not earned a large enough profit. The £3,000,000 Government loan and its repayment became the focal point of the last major crisis in Korda's career.

A chronology of the events best describes the story:

| | |
|---|---|
| April 1949 | British Lion announces that even with the loan the company expects to lose £700,000. |
| December 1949 | London Films owes £1,350,374 to British Lion. |
| March 1950 | London Films loses £127,000 in financial year 1949–50. |
| June 1950 | By transfer of assets and film rights, Korda repays money owed to British Lion by London Films. |
| | Eady Fund is established.* |
| April 1951 | NFFC announces improvements in film budgets at British Lion; Korda calculates that costs have been cut by 45 per cent. |
| May 1951 | London Films shows profit of £6,225 (March to August, 1950). |
| October 1951 | NFFC loan, due to be repaid, is extended with the expectation of added profits from the Eady Fund. |
| May 1952 | NFFC forecasts that £1,000,000 of the loan will never be recovered. |
| | Robert Dowling's City Investing Corporation of New York invests $500,000 in London Films.† |
| July 1952 | British Lion asks the Board of Trade for financial assistance in building more stages at Shepperton in order to increase production, and request is approved. |

* The British Film Production Fund, known as the 'Eady' Levy, Plan or Fund (after the Second Secretary of the Treasury, whose son David was subsequently to make two shorts at London Films), was a way of increasing the producers' receipts from their own films. Cinema exhibitors, in return for Entertainment Tax relief, were to pay a levy into this Fund upon which British film-makers, on a film-by-film basis, could draw. Confident that Korda would regain financial stability with the added revenue from the Fund, the Government held off calling in the loan for two and a half years. However, Eady Levy payments came in too slowly to be of any good to Korda and British Lion.

† Korda had met Dowling through film distributor Ilya Lopert.

September 1952   British Lion pays two years' arrears of preference share dividends.

October 1952   Korda loans London Films £50,000 to finance the re-issuing of earlier London Films successes.

November 1952   Debate in Parliament on Special Loans Bill is held, and the NFFC's choice of Korda as beneficiary is seriously called into question.

Korda receives a telegram of 'whole-hearted support and continued loyalty' from the staff at Shepperton.

March 1953   Additional stages at Shepperton are ready.

December 1953   British Lion's net loss for 1952–3 is disclosed as £150,330, thus making the total debit £2,217, 035 (over ⅔rds of the original loan).

June 1954   Government finally calls in the loan and applies to the courts for a receiver to be appointed.

Korda had spent nine years building up British Lion and six years trying to adjust his film-making activities to the requirements of the loan, fostering along the way many projects which were alien to him. When the axe fell on British Lion in June 1954 Korda saw all his work wiped out. People outside the industry shovelled the blame on Korda's mismanagement and extravagance; colleagues in the industry cursed the Government's hasty decision and claimed that films could not be expected to return a profit overnight and that given time British Lion would have recouped its losses. Both sides were right, for Korda (and the British Lion executive) had made some bad decisions, and the Government had never properly understood the mechanics of the industry. The loss of British Lion stunned Korda, who lost £500,000 of his own money in the ordeal. Korda believed that he had done his best, now wondered why he had gone back into film production at all, and came the closest he would ever come to retiring from the whole maddening business.

1. Harold Wilson, *Board of Trade Journal*, 3 January 1948.
2. *The British Film Industry*, PEP Report, London, 1952, p. 257.
3. Interview with Muir Mathieson conducted by the author, 17 July 1973.
4. Sidney Gilliat and others, *loc cit*.
5. *Daily Mail*, 5 December 1951.
6. David Lean, *Penguin Film Review*, no. 4, October 1947.
7. Press cutting dated October 1952, Alexander Korda microfiche, BFI Information Department.

8. Kevin Gough-Yates, *Michael Powell in collaboration with Emeric Pressburger*, London, British Film Institute, 1971.
9. Speech by Michael Powell at the Cinema City Exhibition, The Roundhouse, London, 30 September 1970.
10. Kevin Gough-Yates, *loc cit*.
11. David Lewin, *op cit*, Chapter Two, 27 January 1956.
12. Graham Greene, Preface to The Third Man, in *The Third Man and The Fallen Idol*, London, Penguin, 1971, p. 9.
13. David Lewin, *op cit*, Chapter Four, 30 January 1956.
14. *Ibid.*
15. *Ibid.*
16. David Lewin, *Daily Express*, 24 January 1956.

# CHAPTER TWENTY

# 'I Don't Grow on Trees'

THE Government's intervention in the affairs of British Lion had been a mixed blessing for Korda. It had kept his company afloat and had allowed him time to establish himself in the congenial role of executive producer. It had also put a strait-jacket on Korda's more ambitious and extravagant nature, forcing him to practise the opposite of what he preached. Although he had had to cut production costs drastically, he still maintained that 'a film that costs £400,000, and earns £600,000, is the sort of extravagance I like'. 'A film that costs £100,000, and loses £90,000,' he continued, 'that is an economy I cannot afford.'[1] He had increased London Films' average yearly output by 50 per cent, but quantity in film production meant little to Korda. In 1952 he reiterated his stance: 'To my mind, the British industry is not here to release a hundred productions each year but to present very few of very high quality. The English cinema must give the world the Rolls Royce and not the Ford. Mind you, Fords are excellent cars.'[2]

Korda was obviously not the right man to run a state-financed British Lion, but who was? That was the question one of the newly appointed directors of British Lion put to Korda shortly after he had resigned as 'production adviser'. Korda's reply was classic: 'That is a very difficult question for me to answer. You see . . . I don't grow on trees.'

For a few days or perhaps only a few hours after the loss of British Lion, Korda considered retirement. Although he was sixty, and looked and probably felt a lot older, the prospect of stepping off the treadmill, perhaps to join the leisure world in the South of France, did not appeal to him. Within a week of the British Lion collapse, Korda announced that London Films was to continue producing films under his guidance.

Since Korda needed working capital but had exhausted his credit with City bankers and the Government, he turned once again to a film patron. This time it was an American property investor, Robert Dowling, who was persuaded to invest £5,000,000 ($15,000,000) in London Films. Dowling's City Investing Corporation of New York had come to Korda's assistance twice before,★ and Dowling was an ideal patron for Korda, one who wasn't the least upset by British Lion's recent losses. Dowling explained: 'Property isn't so safe. You can lose millions in it too if you buy at the wrong time or the wrong price. I know about the losses on British Lion. That is too bad. But it doesn't deter me. . . . Korda has the talent for the films I am interested in. I don't want the ordinary routine films at the rate of 10 or 20 a year. I like a few artistic pictures of special merit.'³

John Woolf, son of C. M. Woolf (one of the leading figures in the British industry's early days), also became associated with London Films at this time, and he invested £500,000 ($1·5 million) on a four-picture tie-up with Korda and Dowling. Since the new British Lion continued as a film distributing company, Korda could still depend on that company for releasing his films in the home market. More importantly, Korda maintained his international distribution agreements with 20th Century-Fox and Lopert Films. These latter connections were vital to his new, and final, programme, for Korda intended to return to the field of 'international' British film-making which he had pioneered and promoted.

Korda's financial come-back was as impressive as the films which comprise his last programme. They were ambitiously conceived colour presentations, and the technical staff and stars, as well as five of the six directors, were all previous Korda associates who remained loyal to him.

Despite his initial reluctance, Korda financed Carol Reed's fantasy *A Kid for Two Farthings* (1955) which was set in London's East End and

★ In 1950 Dowling and his friend Ilya Lopert had formed a distribution company (Lopert Films Distributing Corporation) with Korda in order to promote better worldwide distribution for selected British and American films. This company provided Korda with production money in return for certain distribution rights, chiefly in America. In 1952 Dowling's City Investing Corporation of New York had invested a further £166,000 ($500,000) in Korda's company.

was scripted by Wolf Mankowitz from his own novel. More to Korda's taste was David Lean's *Summer Madness* (1955) in which Katharine Hepburn played the spinster school teacher on holiday in Venice opposite leading man Rossano Brazzi. Brother Zoltan was coaxed back from Hollywood to produce a remake of his *Four Feathers, Storm Over the Nile* (1955), which was directed by Terence Young and which used much action footage from the earlier film.\* In 1949 Korda had encouraged Laurence Olivier to set up his own production company, and this company, in association with London Films, produced Olivier's *Richard III* (1956), a worthy successor to Olivier's two other Shakespearian films, *Henry V* (1945) and *Hamlet* (1949). Korda's interest in producing films in foreign locations—he had plans at one time to go into production in India—was manifest in Anthony Kimmins's film *Smiley* (1956) which was shot entirely on location in Australia. The only newcomer to the Korda fold was Russian-born director Anatole Litvak whose Hollywood work had included *Tovarich* (1938), *Confessions of a Nazi Spy* (1939) and more recent psychological thrillers like *The Snake Pit* (1948) and *Sorry, Wrong Number* (1948). Litvak was hired to direct *The Deep Blue Sea* (1955) from Terence Rattigan's adaptation of his play.

As a whole the programme was enormously successful, and it looked as if Korda's new patron was to be the first one *not* to lose money on Korda's films. The auspicious box-office returns of these pictures indicated that Korda's 'Internationalism' was a viable proposition, but only as long as the films themselves were executed by men other than Korda. Not satisfied with sitting back and watching others prove his long-held views, Korda was himself busy charting totally new ground. He was, for instance, the first British producer to respond to the technical challenge which the wide screen revolution had presented. Three of his last six pictures were filmed in CinemaScope, the process which 20th Century-Fox had developed, and one (*Richard III*) tried out Paramount's rival system, VistaVision. Korda had also examined the potential of '3-D' cinema and Cinerama, judging that the first was as yet too crude, but marking that the second was 'as big a thing as the coming of talkies'.[4] He actually bought the Eastern Hemisphere rights to the Cinerama system, although any plans he may have had for using it were abandoned.

\* Since the remake was in CinemaScope, the old footage had to be blown up to size, a fact which is obvious in at least one scene where the moon takes on a decidedly un-moon-like shape.

While seemingly quick to jump on the bandwagon with other film producers who were determined to use wide screen film-making as a weapon in their battle with the new medium of television, Korda did not share their pessimistic views on the television threat to film production. In May 1953 he prophesied:

> I am sure there will be some sort of marriage between films and television. In time we will come to it. The gramophone did not kill orchestras; films did not kill the theatre; and TV will never kill films. Maybe fewer films will be made. I hope so, because too many were, at one time, made. Maybe there will be fewer cinemas. There is, after all, much redundancy, but this is a great industry and it will outface any changes it may have to.[5]

In his last years Korda did much to bring this mass media 'marriage'. His most unusual and successful deal stemmed from his convictions that American television opened up a whole new market for British films and that exposure on the small screen did not necessarily hurt a film's larger screen prospects. Although he had already sold some of his previous films to American television companies, in 1955 Korda negotiated with the American network NBC for the US premiere showing of two of his latest features, *The Constant Husband* and *Richard III*. For the March 1956 airing of *Richard*, Korda was paid $500,000 (over £165,000), thus demonstrating that this type of deal could promise advance receipts for a film in production. Another ambitious undertaking with NBC—London Films was to produce twenty-six features at £65,000 each for immediate release on American TV—came to nothing; but it was certainly a clever and forward-looking idea, one which was to save many Hollywood companies during the next two decades.

Korda also planned to enter television production itself. In June 1955 he signed a contract with Zenith Radio Corporation, a Chicago-based company which had developed a system, Phonevision, for subscription television. A press release stated: 'Armed with a broad gauge contract covering use of Zenith Phonevision, and the technical know-how of the Chicago company, Korda plans to seek permission of his government to broadcast subscription TV programs and make manufacturing arrangements to produce the necessary devices for the system.'[6] In October Korda registered two new companies, London Films (Television Services) Ltd, and Big Ben (Television Services) Ltd; and although it was rumoured that Korda had only taken this move as a precaution (to preserve the London Films trademark for the new medium), he did have concrete plans to begin several television series. Korda had bought the television rights to several properties, including some of Somerset Maugham's short stories, and up until the week before his death he was arranging for some 'pilots' to be made.

All of these plans, revolutionary as they were, were never realised because of Korda's death. If he had lived longer, he might well have become one of the leaders of the British television industry.

Korda's involvement in these new business ventures did not preclude him from pursuing his more established forms of film-trading. He was still, for example, buying and selling film rights at an impressive rate. In 1953 Korda's property-buying instincts had proven quite profitable. Paying only £1,000 for a play by an unknown British dramatist, Frederick Knotts, Korda turned around and sold it for £30,000 to Warner Brothers, and Alfred Hitchcock was then able to direct *Dial M for Murder* (1954). One of Korda's last deals involved British writer L. P. Hartley's novel *The Go-Between*, which was finally filmed in 1971 by Joseph Losey from a script by Harold Pinter. In an interview in *The Guardian* (16 March 1971), Hartley explained: 'You know, Korda never meant to make a film of the book; that's what annoyed me. He just bought it to keep as a property, thinking it might go up in market value. I was so annoyed when I learned this that I put a curse upon him, and he died, almost the next morning.' Another project which was left in limbo upon Korda's death was his intended adaptation of Bernard Shaw's *Arms and the Man*. Alec Guinness and Claire Bloom, who were then under contract to Korda, were to star in the production, Oliver Messel had already designed the costumes, but although several writers had attempted treatments of the story, Korda was displeased with their efforts. He called one of the writers into his office:

'Sit down, have a cigar,' he invited. 'You know, there is bad news—Guinness doesn't like the script.'

'Oh,' said the writer.

'Claire Bloom doesn't like it, too,' Korda said. 'And the director, *he* doesn't like it.'

'Ha, ha,' said the writer, unconvincingly. 'That makes it unanimous, Sir Alex.'

Korda leaned forward affably and smacked him on the back. 'It's more than unanimous,' he said. '*I* don't like it.'[7]

In 1955 Alex had reluctantly given in to the suggestions of his wife, and perhaps his doctor, and had sold his yacht. In its place Korda bought a £50,000 villa—'*Le domaine des orangers*'—at Biot near Antibes and told the French press: 'I have always wanted to be rich. When I used to take the Metro in Paris, I dreamed of being able to pay for taxis. When I was able to do that, I wanted a particular model of car, with chauffeur, then a yacht . . . Now I have a chateau and a wife. I have worked hard all my life. Now all I want is happiness without fuss.'[8] This final wish was one which Korda was to be denied, for in November he underwent a physical examination and immediately afterwards made out his will. Although he kept on working through the new year, near midnight on the 22nd of January, a few days before he was scheduled to leave for his villa, Korda suffered a severe heart attack and died eight hours later.

At Alexa's request Korda's funeral was a quiet and private one; as the London Films publicity head remarked: 'We did not want it to look like another premiere. . . .'[9] Four days later, however, a memorial service was held at St Martin-in-the-Fields and over four hundred stars, filmmakers, and friends heard Laurence Olivier pay a final tribute to the irreplaceable Alexander Korda. Korda's death did leave a vacuum in the industry, and it was clear to everyone that, as the *New York Times* put it, there was 'no one man available in the industry who shapes up as an obvious candidate for the Korda chair'.[10] Either realising this in advance or simply unwilling to have the show go on without him, Korda had so written his will that London Films as a production company could not continue after his death.

If Korda had retired in 1954 he might well have salvaged a few more years. He didn't because he desperately wanted to end his career as a success. All the ideas, plans, and productions of those last eighteen months were attempts to put the British Lion fiasco behind him so that Korda could leave the industry in honour and glory. He had sacrificed his health and ultimately his life, but he had achieved this final vindication.

A film mogul who had always dealt in seven-figure finance, Korda left a surprisingly small estate: £385,684 (£158,160 after death duties had been paid). Alex's brothers, David Cunynghame, and Harold Boxall were named as executors and were instructed to pay £10,000 to Korda's son Peter, £2,000 to his first wife Maria, and £500 to his chauffeur. A quarter of the remainder of the estate and all Korda's personal belongings were to go to Alexa. Maria Corda and their son were never happy with the settlement: Maria still claimed that she was

Korda's only legal wife and insisted that Korda had millions 'scattered throughout the world in secret bank accounts, real estate, and such property as a solid platinum door built into his yacht'.[11]* The two contested the will in regular intervals over the next years, only succeeding in prolonging the final execution of the will. (As of 1973 the estate had not yet been settled.)

'We are in the show business now,' Korda told reporter David Lewin shortly before his death, 'and we come from the fairground and the fairground barker. The barkers may have worn checked coats and crude colours while we are more elegant; but never forget we are the same. We are in the show business—and we should make a good show.'[12] For forty years Alex Korda tried to do just that. In the process he encountered more crises and setbacks than most people ever have to contend with, but he also made the kind of impressive recoveries of which few people are capable. Of all the qualities which Korda had in abundance, the most valuable was his resilience. It was the resilience of a self-educated and ambitious man who yearned for culture and power and cared little for money or ephemeral success, of a self-confident man who kept his goal in sight (if not in reach) and never under-rated his own capabilities, of a highly strung man who seemed to crave the excitement of a crisis, and of a clever man who knew he could always depend on his magician's charm to create new film empires out of thin air.

Korda's amazing recoveries should not obscure the fact that the crises which necessitated them were by and large of his own making. The main problem was Korda's inability to work within his financial means, to produce a programme of films which earned more than it cost. Although the niche which best suited him was that of executive producer, he tried too often to run a one-man show, interfering in the work of other film-makers and thus wasting the talent of men whom he was genius enough to hire in the first place. He was impulsive, and this led him to make many mistakes. His abilities could not keep pace with his

* Korda had, in fact, left Alexa with at least one very valuable possession: his art collection. Alexa, who married a Lloyds broker David Metcalfe in March 1957 (divorced him in 1963 and died from poisoning in 1966), sold this collection of works by Maillol, Degas, Bonnard, Cézanne, Gauguin, Van Gogh, Renoir, Soutine, and Monet at Sotheby's in 1962. The auction netted £464,470 and some adverse comments in the press, for some considered it unseemly that Korda should have died owing the taxpayers £3 million (i.e. the British Lion Loan) while owning masterpieces worth almost £500,000.

ambitions, and this resulted in some of the most famous unrealised projects of all time. More importantly, Korda could not resist the temptation to manipulate vast sums of money or to embark on another colossal film deal. If there was a conflict between the artist in Korda and the businessman, the businessman almost always won out. Since Korda was one of the finest salesmen in the international industry and since his talent as a film-maker was limited, this need not have been a bad thing. Disaster came only when Korda tried, as he often did in the thirties, to play both roles.

As a film-maker and as a man Alex Korda represented an enigma. He was a movie mogul who came to films not (as so many of his Hollywood counterparts had) because he wanted to diversify his business interests, but rather because he loved the cinema. Therefore, unlike the Hollywood czars, Korda had begun by directing pictures himself and continued to direct for over thirty years. He was a film-maker whose own works were heavily flawed, and yet he could still inspire other directors to be (in Michael Powell's words) 'storytellers in the grand manner'. His more flamboyant attitudes with regard to film-making were only partially based on his eccentric and unorthodox nature, for he often used them as a smokescreen to hide some of his shrewd practices. His generosity was so widely acclaimed that few expected the ruthlessness and rudeness which he could just as easily exhibit. Korda enjoyed the professional limelight and shunned personal publicity. Physically lethargic and mentally hyperactive, Korda disguised his personal unhappiness with a hedonistic veneer, and only his love of paradox and irony betrayed this carefully constructed artifice. He was a fascinating blend of con-man and connoisseur, bohemian and conservative, a man with artistic pretensions and a showman's vulgarity. Finally, although honours did come to him and he was not one to feign humility, Korda never took credit for the work which had won him his knighthood.

Alexander Korda was the only film producer in Britain who consistently tried to match swords with Hollywood. It was his very foreignness which allowed him to fight a losing battle for so long. The Italian journalist and author Luigi Barzini once wrote: 'The foreigner, or the man who is almost foreign, has perhaps the cold decisiveness of a surgeon operating on another's flesh, the convert's fanaticism and illusions, and a confused misunderstanding of the national character that distorts and simplifies faults and virtues, real and imaginary possibilities, and often helps him make ambitious plans for the country he lives in, and to envisage a great destiny for it which he would not dare if he saw things in sharp focus.'[13] The miracles which Korda worked in film financing ultimately turned sour; the American market conquest which he attempted was, with few exceptions, a failure; and the international films that he stood for have since been ignored in the rush to proclaim the more national movements of the war years and the early sixties. Nevertheless, Alex Korda was for twenty-five years the most imaginative and courageous man to work in the British film industry, and for that reason alone his name and his films deserve to be remembered in the history of the British cinema.

1. Campbell Dixon, 'Sir Alexander Korda', *Films in 1951, Sight and Sound* supplement, p. 6.
2. Press cutting *c.* 1952, Alexander Korda microfiche, BFI Information Department.
3. David Lewin, 'Korda Finds New "Angel" to Back Him', *Daily Express*, 1 July 1954.
4. *Evening News*, 22 March 1952.
5. *Kinematograph Weekly*, 14 May 1953.
6. Press release dated 3 June 1955, Alexander Korda file, Academy of Motion Picture Arts and Sciences, Hollywood.
7. *News Chronicle*, 28 February 1956.
8. Unmarked obituary, Alexander Korda microfiche, BFI Information Department.
9. *Daily Sketch*, 31 January 1956.
10. *New York Times*, 19 February 1956.
11. *Los Angeles Times*, 29 January 1956.
12. David Lewin, 'The Man Who Made the Stars Shine', *Daily Express*, Chapter Five, 31 January 1956.
13. Luigi Barzini, *From Caesar to the Mafia: sketches of Italian life*, London, Hamish Hamilton, 1971, p. 41.

# Filmography

THIS filmography is divided into three sections: the films actually directed by Alexander Korda comprise Part I, Part II includes those films produced by, or associated with him, and Part III is a list of Korda projects announced, but never completed. The year which follows each film title is the year of the picture's first public showing in its country of origin. Parentheses after a title indicate a translation, whereas square brackets signify other titles under which the film was released. The roles played by cast members are put, when available, in parentheses; names in square brackets are other names under which the people may be known. Abbreviations used throughout the filmography are as follows:

*adapt:* adaptation
*add:* additional
*adv:* adviser
*arch:* architect
*assoc:* associate
*asst:* assistant
*cam op:* camera operator
*co:* company
*cons:* consultant
*cont:* continuity
*cos:* costume designer
*des:* art director
*dial:* dialogue
*dir:* director
*dist:* distributor
*ed:* editor
*exec:* executive
*ext:* exterior or location
*Fr:* French
*Ger:* German
*GB:* Great Britain
*hist:* historical

*loc:* location
*man:* manager
*mus:* music composer
*mus dir:* music director
*ph:* photography
*prem:* premiere
*pres:* presented by
*prod:* production or producer
*rec:* recording
*rel:* release date
*rt:* running time
*scr:* scriptwriter
*shot:* dates in production
*spec:* special
*sound:* for Hollywood films, sound system; thereafter, sound technicians
*sup:* supervising or superviser
*tech:* technician or technical
*ts:* trade show
*US:* United States

337

# I. FILMS DIRECTED BY ALEXANDER KORDA
## HUNGARY (1914-1919)

1. *A becsapott újságíró* (The Duped Journalist)—1914
*prod co:* Tricolor for Pedagogical Film Studio, Budapest; *dir:* Sándor Korda and Gyula Zilahy; *ph:* Béla Zsitkovszky; *cast:* Ibolya Nagy, Margit Lánczy, Gyula Zilahy, Alajos Mészáros, Gyula Gozón, Gyula Szöreghy [Julius Szöreghi], and Gyula Fehér.

(In 1914 Gyula Zilahy directed another film for Tricolor, *Őrház a Kárpátokban* (Watchhouse in the Carpathians). Since Zilahy never worked without a co-director, it is likely that Korda co-directed this film, although his name does not appear in the trade paper which announced the production.)

2. *Tutyu és Totyo* (Tutyu and Totyo)—1914
*prod co:* Tricolor for Pedagogical Film Studio, Budapest; *dir:* Sándor Korda and Gyula Zilahy; *ph:* Béla Zsitkovszky; *cast:* Gyula Zilahy, Jenő Horváth, Gyula Szöreghy [Julius Szöreghi], Anna Hadrik, Gusztáv Vándory, Irén O. Keczeri, Hedda Lencz, and Alajos Mészáros.

3. *Lyon Lea* (Lea Lyon)—1915
*prod co:* Nemzeti; *dir:* Sándor Korda and Miklós Pásztory; *scr:* Sándor Bródy; *ph:* Béla Zsitkovszky; *cast:* Emil Fenyvessy, Amáliá Jákó, Márton Rátkai, Sándor Viranyi, Mari K. Demjén, Oszkár Fodor, Péter Andorffy; *rt:* 1,500 metres.

4. *A tiszti kardbojt* (The Officer's Swordknot)—1915
*prod co:* Korona; *dir* and *scr:* Sándor Korda (under the name of József Neumann); *ph:* Béla Zsitkovszky; *cast:* Gábor Rajnay, Mici Haraszti, Ödön Pajor, Irén Gombaszögi, Jenő Horváth, Lajos Szöke, Ili Vörbös, and Gyula Fehér; *rt:* 1,150 metres.

5. *Fehér éjszakák* or *Fedora* (White Nights or Fedora)—1916
*prod co:* Corvin; *dir* and *scr:* Sándor Korda; adapted from Victorien Sardou's *Fedora; cast:* Lili Berky, György Kürthy, Kálmán Körmendy, Andor Szakács, Rezső Harsányi, Valéria Berlányi, Aranka Laczkó, and József Berky.

(Korda's films for Jenő Janovics's Corvin—nos. 5 to 11—were probably photographed by either Mihály Fekete or Árpád Virágh, and Janovics undoubtedly produced and co-scripted most of the films, if not all of them.)

6. *A nagymama* (The Grandmother)—1916
*prod co:* Corvin; *dir* and *scr:* Sándor Korda; adapted from the play by Gergely Csiky (1891); *cast:* Lujza Blaha, Imre Szirmai, Mihály Várkonyi [Victor Varconi], Annuska Fényes, Erzsi Ághy, Alajos Mészáros, József Hajdu, Adél Marosi, and László Gábányi.

7. *Mesék az írógépről* (Tales of the Typewriter)—1916
*prod co:* Corvin; *dir* and *scr:* Sándor Korda; adapted from the novel by István Szomaházy (1905); *cast:* Lili Berky, György Kürthy.

8. *A kétszívű férfi* (The Man with Two Hearts)—1916
*prod co:* Corvin; *dir:* Sándor Korda; *cast:* Árpád Ódry, Lili Berky, Flóra Fáy, and György Kürthy.

9. *Az egymillió fontos bankó* (The One Million Pound Note)—1916
   *prod co:* Corvin; *dir* and *scr:* Sándor Korda; adapted from the story by Mark Twain; *ph:* Árpád Virágh; *cast:* Lajos Ujváry, Gyula Nagy, and Aladár Ihász.

10. *Ciklámen* (Cyclamen)—1916
    *prod co:* Corvin; *dir:* Sándor Korda; *scr:* Jenő Janovics; *story:* Andor Gábor; *cast:* Ella Kertész [Mrs Góth] and Sándor Góth.

11. *Vergődő szívek* (Struggling Hearts)—1916
    *prod co:* Corvin; *dir:* Sándor Korda; *story:* Soma Guthi; *cast:* Lili Berky, Gyula Gál, Alajos Mészáros, Márton Garas, Aranka Laczkó, Flóra Fáy, Andor Szakács, and Gyula Kozma; *rt:* 1,400 metres; *dist:* Transylvania.

12. *A nevető Szaszkia* (The Laughing Saskia)—1916
    *prod co:* Unió; *dir:* Sándor Korda; *ph:* Béla Zsitkovszky; *des:* János Tábor; *cast:* Sari Kőrmendy, Desző Kertész, Gyula Fehér, and László Békeffy; *rt:* 1,400 metres.

13. *Mágnás Miska* (Miska the Magnate)—1916
    *dir:* Sándor Korda; *scr:* Jenő Janovics from the play by Károly Bakonyi and Andor Gábor; *cast:* Lili Berky, Alajos Mészáros, Mihály Várkonyi [Victor Varconi], Imre Szirmai, Lajos Kemenes, and Amáliá Jákó. (The film was probably completed, although there is no proof of this.)

(Korda probably produced as well as directed all the remaining Hungarian films. The cameraman at Korda's Corvin was Gusztáv Kovács, the art director László Márkus, so they presumably worked on most of the films between 1917 and 1919.)

14. *Szent Péter esernyője* (St Peter's Umbrella)—1917
    *prod co:* Corvin; *dir:* Sándor Korda; *scr:* unknown; adapted from Kálmán Mikszáth's novel (1895); *ph:* Gusztáv Kovács; *cast:* Márton Rátkai, Mihály Várkonyi [Victor Varconi], Ica Lenkeffy, Károly Huszár [Charles Puffy], József Kürti, József Hajdu, Károly Lajthay, Marcsa Simon, Gyula Bartos, and Mari K. Demjén; *rel:* 29 October 1917.

15. *A gólyakalifa* (The Stork Caliph)—1917
    *prod co:* Corvin; *dir:* Sándor Korda; *scr:* Frigyes Karinthy; adapted from Mihály Babits' novel (1916); *cast:* Oszkár Beregi [Oscar Beregi], Judit Bánky, Gyula Bartos, and Alajos Mészáros; *dist:* Uránia; *rel:* October 1917.

16. *Mágia* (Magic)—1917
    *prod co:* Corvin; *dir:* Sándor Korda; *scr:* Frigyes Karinthy and Kálmán Sztrókay; *cast:* Juci Lábass, Mihály Várkonyi [Victor Varconi], Magda Nagy, and Antal Nyáray; *dist:* Corso; *rel:* October 1917.

17. *Harrison és Barrison* (Harrison and Barrison)—1917
    *prod co:* Corvin; *dir:* Sándor Korda; *scr:* Gyula Kőváry and Richárd Falk; *cast:* Nusi Somogyi, Dezső Gyárfás, Márton Rátkai, Manci Dobos, Károly Lajthay, Ilona Bánhidy, Árpád Latabár, and Lajos Szalkay; *dist:* Omnia; *rel:* 12 November 1917.

18. *Faun*—1918
    *prod co:* Corvin; *dir:* Sándor Korda; *scr:* László Vajda and Richárd Falk from the play by Edward Knoblock; *des:* László Márkus; *cast:* Gábor Rajnay, Dezső Gyárfás, Artur Somlay, Ica Lenkeffy, Paula Horváth, Erzsi Ághy, János Ducret, Jenő Horváth, Gyula Bartos, József Hajdu.

19. *Az aranyember* (The Man with the Golden Touch)—1918
*prod co:* Corvin; *dir:* Sándor Korda; *scr:* László Vajda; adapted from the novel
by Mór Jókai (1873); *des:* László Márkus; *cast:* Oszkár Beregi [Oscar Beregi],
Lili Berky, Gábor Rajnay, Ica Lenkeffy, Margit Makay, Jenő Horváth, and
Gyula Szöreghy [Julius Szöreghi].

20. *Mary Ann*—1918
*prod co:* Corvin; *dir:* Sándor Korda; *scr:* László Vajda; adapted from the nove
by Israel Zangwill; *cast:* Ica Lenkeffy, Tivadar Uray, Dezső Gyárfás, Hermin
Haraszti, Nusi Somogyi, and Gyula Szöreghy [Julius Szöreghi].

21. *Ave Caesar!*—1919
(Councils' Republic); *dir:* Sándor Korda; *scr:* László Vajda; *des:* László
Márkus; *cast:* Gábor Rajnay, Antónia Farkas [Maria Corda], Oszkár Beregi
[Oscar Beregi].

22. *Fehér rózsa* (White Rose)—1919
(Councils' Republic); *dir:* Sándor Korda; *scr:* László Vajda; adapted from
Mór Jókai's novel (1853); *ph:* Gusztáv Kovács; *des:* László Márkus and István
Lhotka Szirontai; *cast:* Antónia Farkas [Maria Corda] (Gül-Bejaze), Gyula
Bartos, Emil Fenyvessy, Ilona Mattyasovszky, Gyula Szöreghy [Julius
Szöreghi], Nusi Somogyi, Márton Rátkai, Mihály Várkonyi [Victor Varconi],
Mari K. Demjén.

23. *Yamata*—1919
(Councils' Republic); *dir:* Sándor Korda; *scr:* László Vajda; *des:* László
Márkus; *cast:* Gábor Rajnay, Ila Lóth, Emil Fenyvessy, and Gusztáv Vándory.

24. *Se ki, se be* (Neither In Nor Out)—1919
*prod co:* Corvin; *dir:* Sándor Korda; *story:* Dezső Gyárfás; *scr:* László Vajda;
*cast:* Lajos Ujváry, Hermin Haraszti, László Molnár, Antónia Farkas [Maria
Corda], Nusi Somogyi, Gusztáv Vándory, Tivadar Uray, Janka Csatay,
and Dezső Gyárfás.

25. *A 111-es* (Number 111)—1919
*prod co:* Corvin; *dir:* Sándor Korda; *scr:* László Vajda; adapted from a novel
by Jenő Heltai; *cast:* Gábor Rajnay, Antónia Farkas [Maria Corda], Dezső
Kertész, Jenő Balassa, and Bäby Becker.

# VIENNA (1920-1922)

26. *Seine Majestät das Bettelkind* [Also in Austria: *Prinz und Bettelknabe;* GB: *The
Prince and the Pauper*]—1920
*prod co:* Sascha-Film; *prod:* Count Alexander Kolowrat; *dir:* Alexander
Korda; *scr:* Lajos Biro; adapted from Mark Twain's novel; *asst dir* and *ed:*
Karl Hartl; *des:* Artur Berger; *cos:* Lambert Hofer; *cast:* Tibi Lubinsky
(Prince Edward and Tom Canty), Franz Everth (Miles Hendon), Wilhelm
Schmidt (Hugh Hendon), Franz Herterich (John Canty), Ditta Ninjan (Lady
Edith), Lilly Lubin (Isabel, the Spanish Infanta), Alfred Schreiber (Henry
VIII), A. D. Weisse (Lord Chancellor); *Austrian rel:* 19 November 1920; *rt:*
2,400 metres: *GB rel:* 21 April 1924; *GB rt:* 75 minutes; *dist:* Adria; *GB dist:*
Pathé.

27. *Herren der Meere* (Masters of the Sea)—1922
    *prod co:* Sascha-Film; *prod:* Arnold Pressburger; *dir:* Alexander Korda; *scr:* Ernst Vajda from his novel *The Pirates*; *ph:* Hans Theyer; *asst dir:* Karl Hartl and Herr Arnold; *ed:* Karl Hartl; *des:* Artur Berger and Julius Borsody; *cos:* Lambert Hofer; *cast:* Maria Palma [Maria Corda?], Max Devrient, Michael Varkonyi [Victor Varconi], Count Ludi Salm, Gert Lubbers, Tibi Lubinsky, Reinhold Häussermann, Paul Pranger, Alfred Schreiber, Harry de Loon, Julius Szöreghi [Gyula Szöreghy]; *Austrian rel:* 3 February 1922; *rt:* 2,300 metres; *dist:* Adria.

28. *Eine Versunkene Welt* [Ger: *Die Tragödie eines Verschollenen Fürstensohnes*] (A Vanished World)—1922
    *prod co:* Sascha-Film; *prod:* Leo Mandl; *dir:* Alexander Korda; *scr:* Lajos Biro from his novel *Serpoletto; ph:* Hans Theyer; *asst dir:* Karl Hartl and Herr Arnold; *ed:* Karl Hartl; *des:* Alexander Ferenczy, Max H. Joli, and Emil Stepanek; *cos:* Lambert Hofer; *cast:* Alberto Capozzi (Peter Herzog), Karl Baumgartner (Gross Herzog), Olga Lewinsky (Mother Herzog), Maria Palma [Maria Corda?] (Anny Lind), Harry de Loon (Adjutant Ridarsky), Max Devrient (Kammerdiener Bartel), Michael Varkonyi [Victor Varconi] (Matrose Vannoni), Julius Szöreghi [Gyula Szöreghy], Paul Lukacs, Tibi Lubinsky, Count Ludi Salm, Reinhold Häussermann, and Ernst Arndt; *Austrian rel:* 23 February 1922; *rt:* 2,200 metres; *dist:* Adria and Dalmatien; *prize:* Gold Medal for best dramatic film at Milan International Cinema Concourse.

29. *Samson und Delila; der Roman einer opernsängerin* [GB: *Samson and Delilah*]— 1922
    *prod co:* Corda Film Consortium-Vita Konzern; *prod:* N. Szücs; *dir:* Alexander Korda; *scr:* Ernst Vajda and Alexander Korda; *ph:* Nikolaus Farkas; *asst ph:* Maurice Armand Mondet and Josef Zeitlinger; *ed:* Karl Hartl; *des:* Alexander Ferenczy, Julius Borsody; *cos:* Alexander Konia, Remigius Geyling, and Lambert Hofer; *spec effects:* Otto Wannenmacher; *prod asst:* Karl Hartl, Mihály Kertész [Michael Curtiz](?); *cast:* Maria Corda (Delila, a dual role), Alfredo Galoar (Samson), Franz Herterich (Khan), Ernst Arndt, Paul Lukacs, Franz Hauenstein, Oskar Hugelmann, and 400 extras; *Austrian rel:* 25 March 1922; *rt:* 2,250 metres; *dist:* Adria; *GB rel:* 29 October 1923; *GB dist:* Stoll Film Company Ltd.


## BERLIN (*1923–1926*)

30. *Das unbekannte Morgen* [GB: *The Unknown To-morrow*]—1923
    *prod co:* Korda-Film Gmbh, Berlin; *prod* & *dir:* Alexander Korda; *scr:* Alexander Korda and Ernst Vajda; *ph:* E. Wango; *asst dir* & *ed:* Karl Hartl; *des:* Alexander Ferenczy; *cos:* Lambert Hofer; *cast:* Maria Corda (Stella Manners), Werner Krauss (Marc Muradock), Olga Limburg (maid), Carl Ebert (Gordon Manners), Louis Ralph (Muradock's accomplice), and Friedrich Kühne (Raorama Singh); *German rel:* late 1923; *German rt:* 2,280 metres; *GB dist:* Stoll Film Company Ltd; *GB rt:* approx. 90 minutes; *GB titles* (& editing?): Challis N. Sanderson.

341

31. *Jedermanns Frau* [Austria: *Jedermanns Weib*] (Everybody's Woman)—1924
    *prod co:* Ufa-Dreamland Studio, Vienna co-production; *dir:* Alexander
    Korda; *scr:* probably by Korda based on *Pygmalion; des:* Julius Borsody; *asst
    dir:* Karl Hartl (?); *cast:* Maria Corda, May Hanbury, Jeffrey Bernard, Harry
    Nestor, Arthur Somlay, Otto Schmöle, and A. D. Weisse; *Austrian rel:*
    9 January 1924; *rt:* 2,420 metres; *dist:* Adria (Since there was a Ufa and Stoll
    Film Company connection, both may have distributed as well.)

32. *Tragödie im Hause Habsburg* [Alternate Ger title: *Das Drama von Mayerling;*
    Austria: *Der Prinz der Legende*] (Tragedy in the House of Hapsburg)—1924
    *prod co:* Korda-Film, Berlin; *prod & dir:* Alexander Korda; *scr:* Lajos Biro;
    *ph:* Nikolaus Farkas; *asst dir & ed:* Karl Hartl; *des:* Heinrich Richter, Hans
    Fleming, Alexander Ferenczy; *cos:* Kaufmann; *cast:* Maria Corda (Baroness
    Vetsera), Koloman Zatony (Crown Prince Rudolf), Emil Fenyvessy (Kaiser
    Franz Josef), Werner Schott (Lt Corradini), Mathilde Sussin, Friedrich
    Kayssler, Jacob Tiedtke, Ferdinand von Alten, Louis Ralph, Arthur Bergen,
    Hans Brausewetter; *German rel:* 30 May 1924; *rt:* 3,057 metres; *dist:* Hansa-
    Ufa.

33. *Der Tänzer meiner Frau* [GB: *Dancing Mad*]—1925
    *prod co:* Felsom-Ufa; *prod:* Josef Somlo; *dir:* Alexander Korda; *scr:* Adolf
    Lantz and Alexander Korda from a play by Armont and Bousquet; *ph:*
    Nikolaus Farkas; *des:* Paul Leni; *cast:* Maria Corda, Willy Fritsch, Victor
    Varkonyi [Victor Varconi], Livio Pavanelli, Lea Seidl, Hans Junkermann,
    Olga Limburg, Hermann Thimig; *German rel:* 6 November 1925; *shot:*
    April–June 1925; *rt:* 2,207 metres; *dist:* Ufa; *GB rel:* 23 January 1928; *GB
    dist:* W & F Film Service; *GB titles:* G. A. Atkinson.

34. *Madame wünscht keine Kinder* [US: *Madame Wants No Children*]—1926
    *prod co:* Deutsche Fox-Decla; *prod:* Karl Freund; *dir:* Alexander Korda; *scr:*
    Béla Balázs and Adolf Lantz from novel by Clément Vautel; *ph:* Theodor
    Sparkuhl and Robert Baberske; *des:* O. F. Werndorff; *prod asst:* Rudolf
    Sieber; *mus:* Schmidt-Gentner; *cast:* Maria Corda (Elyane Parizot), Harry
    Liedtke (Paul), Maria Paudler (Louise Bonvin), Trude Hesterberg (Elyane's
    mother), Dina Gralla (Lulu), Camilla von Hollay (Maid), Hermann Vallentin
    (Paul's uncle), Olga Mannel (Cook), Ellen Müller (Elyane's maid), Marlene
    Dietrich and John Loder (dress extras); *shot:* Tempelhof Oct–Nov 1926;
    *Ger rel:* 14 December 1926; *rt:* 2,166 metres; *dist:* Deutsche Fox; *US rel:* 12
    June 1927.

35. *Eine Dubarry von heute* [GB: *A Modern Dubarry*]—1927
    *prod co:* Felsom-Ufa; *prod :*Josef Somlo; *dir:* Alexander Korda; *scr:* Lajos
    Biro from an original story idea; *ph:* Fritz Arno Wagner; *des:* O. F. Wern-
    dorff; *mus:* Werner Heymann; *cast:* Maria Corda (Toinette), Jean Bradin
    (King Sandor), Hans Albers (Toinette's first lover), Alfred Abel, Julius
    Szöreghi [Gyula Szöreghy], Friedrich Kayssler, Alfred Gerasch, Albert
    Paulig, Hans Wassmann, Karl Platen, Eugen Burg, Marlene Dietrich, Hilde
    Radney, Julia Serda, Hedwig Wangel, and Lotte Lorring; *shot:* Tempelhof
    April–August 1926; *German rel:* 24 January 1927; *rt:* 3,004 metres; *dist:*
    Parufamet; *GB dist:* W & F Film Service; *GB rel:* 5 September 1927; *US
    ed & titles:* James O. Spearing; *US rel:* 19 March 1928.

# HOLLYWOOD (1927–1930)

36. *The Stolen Bride*—1927

*prod co:* First National; *pres:* Richard A. Rowland; *prod & scr:* Carey Wilson; *dir:* Alexander Korda; *ph:* Robert Kurrle; *cos:* Max Ree; *cast:* Billie Dove (Sari, Countess Thurzo), Lloyd Hughes (Franz Pless), Armand Kaliz (Capt., The Baron von Heimberg), Frank Beal (Count Thurzo), Lilyan Tashman (Ilona Taznadi), Cleve Moore (Lt Kiss), Otto Hoffman (Papa Pless), Charles Wellesley (The Regiment Pater), and Bert Sprotte (The Sergeant); *US rt:* 7,179 feet; *dist:* First National; *US rel:* 14 August 1927; *GB rel:* 28 May 1928.

37. *The Private Life of Helen of Troy*—1927

*prod co:* First National; *pres:* Richard A. Rowland; *prod & adapt & scr:* Carey Wilson; *dir:* Alexander Korda; adapted from John Erskine's book of the same title (1925), and Robert Sherwood's 1927 play *The Road to Rome*; *ph:* Lee Garmes and Sid Hickox; *ed:* Harold Young; *mus:* Carl Edouarde; *cos:* Max Ree; *titles:* Ralph Spence, Gerald Duffy, and Casey Robinson; *cast:* Maria Corda (Helen of Troy), Lewis Stone (Menelaus), Ricardo Cortez (Paris), George Fawcett (Eteoneus), Charles Puffy [Károly Huszár] (Malapokitora-toreadetos), Alice White (Adraste), Gordon Elliott (Telemachus), Tom O'Brien (Ulysses), Bert Sprotte (Achilles), Mario Carillo (Ajax), George Kotsonaros (Hector), Constantine Romanoff (Aeneas), Emilio Borgato (Sarpedon), Alice Adair (Aphrodite), Helen Fairweather (Athena), Virginia Thomas (Hera), and Gus Partos (Ajax); *rt:* 7,694 feet; *dist:* First National; *US prem:* 9 December 1927; *US rel:* 8 January 1928; *GB dist:* First National-Pathé; *GB rel:* 7 January 1929.

38. *Yellow Lily*—1928

*prod co:* First National; *pres:* Richard A. Rowland; *prod:* Ned Marin; *dir:* Alexander Korda; *scr & story:* Lajos Biro; *ph:* Lee Garmes; *ed:* Harold Young; *des:* Max Parker; *cos:* Max Ree; *titles:* Garrett Graham; *cont:* Bess Meredyth; *cast:* Billie Dove (Judith Peredy), Clive Brook (Archduke Alexander), Gustav von Seyffertitz (Kinkelin), Nicholas Soussanin (Dr Eugene Peredy), Marc MacDermott (Archduke Peter), Eugenie Besserer (Archduchess), Charles Puffy [Károly Huszár] (Mayor of Tarna); *rt:* 7,187 feet (approx. 65 minutes); *dist:* First National; *US rel:* 20 May 1928; *GB dist:* First National-Pathé; *GB rel:* 29 April 1929.

39. *Night Watch*—1928

*prod co:* First National; *pres:* Richard A. Rowland; *prod:* Ned Marin; *dir:* Alexander Korda; *scr:* Lajos Biro; adapted from Michael Morton's 1921 play *In the Night Watch;* *ph:* Karl Struss; *ed:* George McGuire; *titles:* Dwinelle Benthall and Rufus McCosh; *cast:* Billie Dove (Yvonne Corlaix), Paul Lukas (Capt. Corlaix), Donald Reed (Lt D'Artelle), Nicholas Soussanin (Officer Brambourg), Nicholas Bela (Leduc), George Periolat (Fargasson), William Tooker (Mobrayne), Gus Partos (Dagorne), and Anita Garvin (Ann); *rt:* 6,676 feet; *dist:* First National; *sound effects & musical score:* Vitaphone; *US rel:* 9 September 1928; *GB dist:* First National-Pathé; *GB rel:* 1930 or 1931.

40. *Love and the Devil*—1929

*prod co:* First National; *pres:* Richard A. Rowland; *prod:* Ned Marin; *dir:*

Alexander Korda; *scr:* Josef Laszlo, Leo Birinski; *ph:* Lee Garmes; *ed:* John Rawlins; *titles:* Paul Perez and Walter Anthony; *cast:* Milton Sills (Lord Dryan), Maria Corda (Giovanna), Ben Bard (Barotti), Nellie Bly Baker (Maid), Amber Norman (Street walker); *rt:* 6,370 feet (silent) and 6,588 feet (sound); *sound effects & music score:* Vitaphone; *dist:* First National; *US rel:* 24 March 1929; *GB dist:* First National-Pathé; *GB rel:* 5 June 1929.

41. *The Squall*—1929

*prod co:* First National; *pres:* Richard A. Rowland; *dir:* Alexander Korda; *scr & dial:* Bradley King; adapted from Jean Bart's drama, *The Squall; ph:* John Seitz; *ed:* Edward Schroeder; *titles:* Paul Perez; *mus:* Leo Forbstein; *song:* 'Gypsy Charmer' by Grant Clarke and Harry Akst; *sound:* Vitaphone; *cast:* Myrna Loy (Nubi), Richard Tucker (Josef Lajos), Alice Joyce (Maria Lajos), Carroll Nye (Paul), Loretta Young (Irma), Harry Cording (Peter), ZaSu Pitts (Lena), Nicholas Soussanin (El Moro), Knute Erickson (Uncle Dani), and George Hackathorne (Niki); *prem:* 9 May 1929; *US rel:* May 1929; *dist* First National; *rt:* 9,456 feet (sound); also released silent (23 June 1929) at 7,085 feet: *GB dist:* First National-Pathé; *GB rel:* 10 July 1929.

42. *Her Private Life*—1929

*prod co:* First National; *pres:* Richard A. Rowland; *prod:* Ned Marin; *dir:* Alexander Korda; *scr & titles & dial:* Forrest Halsey, adapted from Zöe Akins' play *Déclassée* (1923); *ph:* John Seitz; *ed:* Harold Young; *song:* 'Love is Like a Rose' by Al Bryan and George W. Meyer; *sound:* Vitaphone; *cast:* Billie Dove (Lady Helen Haden), Walter Pidgeon (Ned Thayer), Holmes Herbert (Rudolph Solomon), Montagu Love (Sir Bruce Haden), Thelma Todd (Mrs Leslie), Roland Young (Charteris), Mary Forbes (Lady Wildering), Brandon Hurst (Sir Emmett Wildering), ZaSu Pitts (Timmins); *rt:* 6,488 feet (sound) and 5,815 feet (silent); *US rel:* 25 August or 8 September 1929 (sound) and 6 October 1929 (silent); *dist:* First National; *GB rel:* 16 October 1929. (A remake of the 1925 film *Déclassée* directed by Robert Vignola and starring Corinne Griffith and Clive Brook, also a First National production.)

43. *Lilies of the Field*—1930

*prod co:* First National; *prod:* Walter Morosco; *dir:* Alexander Korda; *scr & dial:* John F. Goodrich, adapted from William Hurlbut's novel *Lilies of the Field* (1921); *ph:* Lee Garmes; *song* 'I'd Like to Be a Gypsy' by Ned Washington, Herb Magidson, and Michael H. Cleary; *dance dir:* Roy Mack; *sound:* Vitaphone; *cast:* Corinne Griffith (Mildred Harker), Ralph Forbes (Ted Willing), John Loder (Walter Harker), Eve Southern (Pink), Jean Bary (Gertie), Tyler Brooke (Bert Miller), Freeman Wood (Lewis Conroy), Ann Schaeffer (first maid), Clarissa Selwynne (second maid), Patsy Page (baby), Andre Beranger (Barber), Douglas Gerrard (Headwaiter), Rita Le Roy (Florette), Betty Boyd (Joyce), May Boley (Maizie), Virginia Bruce (Doris), Charles Mailes (Judge), Ray Largay (Harker's lawyer), Joe Bernard (Mildred's lawyer), Tenen Holtz (Paymaster), Wilfred Noy (Butler), and Alice Moe (Third Maid); *rt:* 5,979 feet; *US rel:* 5 January 1930 (also released silent); *dist:* First National; *GB dist:* First National-Pathé; *GB rel:* 6 October 1930. (A remake of the 1924 film of the same title directed by John Francis Dillon and starring Corinne Griffith.)

44. *Women Everywhere*—1930
    *prod co:* Fox Film Corp.; *pres:* William Fox; *assoc prod:* Ned Marin; *dir:* Alexander Korda; *scr & dial:* Harlan Thompson and Lajos Biro; *story:* George Grossmith and Zoltan Korda; *asst dir:* Edwin Marin; *ph:* Ernest Palmer; *ed:* Harold Schuster; *des:* William Darling; *songs:* 'Women Everywhere,' 'Beware of Love,' 'One Day,' 'Good Time Fifi,' 'Bon Jour,' 'Marching Song by William Kernell, 'All the Family' by William Kernell and George Grossmith, 'Smile, Legionnaire' by William Kernell and Charles Wakefield Cadman; *sound:* Movietone; *sound rec:* Arthur L. von Kirbach; *cos:* Sophie Wachner; *cast:* J. Harold Murray (Charles Jackson), Fifi Dorsay (Lili La Fleur), George Grossmith (Aristide Brown), Clyde Cook (Sam Jones), Ralph Kellard (Michel Kopulos), Rose Dione (Zephyrine), and Walter McGrail (Legionnaire); *rt:* 7,500 feet; *dist:* Fox; *US rel:* 1 June 1930; *GB rel:* 3 December 1930; *working title: Hell's Belles.*

45. *The Princess and the Plumber*—1930
    *prod co:* Fox Film Corp; *assoc prod:* Al Rockett; *dir:* Alexander Korda; *scr & dial:* Howard J. Green, adapted from Alice Duer Miller's story of same title serialised in *Saturday Evening Post*, December 1929; *ph:* L. William O'Connell and Dave Ragin; *ed:* Margaret V. Clancey; *des:* Stephen Goosson; *asst dir:* Ewing Scott; *cos:* Sophie Wachner; *mus dir:* Arthur Kay; *sound:* Movietone; *sound rec:* Arthur L. von Kirbach; *cast:* Charles Farrell (Charlie Peters), Maureen O'Sullivan (Princess Louise), H. B. Warner (Prince Conrad of Daritzia), Joseph Cawthorn (Merkl), Bert Roach (Albert Bowers), Lucien Prival (Baron von Kemper), Murray Kinnell (Worthing), Louise Closser Hale (Miss Eden), and Arnold Lucy; *rt:* 6,480 feet; *dist:* Fox; *US rel:* 21 December 1930; *GB rel:* 8 January 1931. John Blystone directed one scene.

## PARIS (*1931*)

46. *Die Manner um Lucie*—1931
    *prod co:* Paramount; *prod:* Alexander Korda (?); *dir:* Alexander Korda; *scr:* Benno Vigny; *ph:* Harry Stradling; *ed:* Harold Young; *mus:* G. Zoka, Paul Barnaby, Ray Noble, Paul Maye, and Jane Bos; *cast:* Liane Haid. Walter Rilla, Oskar Karlweis, Trude Hesterberg, Lien Deyers, Ernst Stahl-Nachbaur, Karl Huszar-Puffy [Károly Huszár/Charles Puffy], Jaro Furth, Eugen Jensen; *dist:* Paramount-Film AG. (The German version of *Laughter* (1930), an American film directed by Harry D'Arrast for Paramount.)

47. *Rive Gauche* [French version of *Die Manner um Lucie*]—1931
    Attempts to find credits have failed (except for two cast members: Henri Garat and Meg Lemonvier); most would be same as No. 46.

48. *Marius*—1931
    *prod co:* Marcel Pagnol-Paramount Publix Corporation; *prod:* Marcel Pagnol; *dir:* Alexander Korda; *scr:* Marcel Pagnol from his play; *ph:* Ted Pahle; *des:* Alfred Junge and Vincent Korda; *ed:* Roger Spiri Mercanton; *mus:* Francis Gromon; *cast:* Raimu (César), Orane Demazis (Fanny), Pierre Fresnay (Marius), Charpin (Panisse), Alida Rouffe (Honorine), Robert Vattier (M Brun), Paul Dulac (Escartefigue), Mihalesco (Piquoiseau), Edouard Delmont (Second Mate), Milly Mathis (Claudine), Callamand (Le Goelec), Maupi (Stoker), V. Ribe (a customer), Oueret (Félicité), Vassy (Arab); *rt:* 120 mins;

*dist:* Paramount; *Fr rel:* October 1931; *shot:* Joinville Studios, June to August 1931; *US rel:* 14 April 1933; *GB rel:* 1949.

49. *Zum Goldenen Anker* [German version of *Marius*]—1931

Same credits as above, with these changes; *scr:* Marcel Pagnol and Alfred Polgar; *cast:* Albert Basserman (César), Ursula Grabley (Fanny), Mathias Wieman (Marius), Jacob Tiedtke (Panisse), Lucie Höflich (Honorine), Karl Ettlinger (M Brun), Ludwig Stoessel, Rolf Müller, Karl Plater, Jaro Furth; *dist:* Paramount-Film AG; *Ger rel:* 23 November 1931.

## GREAT BRITAIN (1932–33)

50. *Service for Ladies* [US: *Reserved for Ladies*]—1932

*prod co:* Paramount British; *prod & dir:* Alexander Korda; *scr:* Eliot Crawshay-Williams and Lajos Biro from Ernest Vajda's novel *The Head Waiter; asst dir:* Stephen Harrison; *ed:* Harold Young; *des:* Alfred Junge; *mus:* Percival Mackey; *cast:* Leslie Howard (Max Tracey), Benita Hume (Countess Riccardi), Elizabeth Allan (Sylvia Robertson), Morton Selten (Mr Robertson), Cyril Ritchard (Sir William Carter), Ben Field (Breslmeyer), Annie Esmond (Duchess), Martita Hunt (Aline), Gilbert Davis (Chef), and Merle Oberon (?); *dist:* Paramount; *GB rt:* 93 mins.; *GB ts:* 14 January 1932; *GB rel:* 13 June 1932; *US rt:* 90 mins.; *US rel:* 20 June 1932; *working title:* The Head Waiter. (A remake of Harry D'Arrast's Paramount film *Service for Ladies*—1927. In 1932 Korda did pre-production work on Arthur Rosson's *Women Who Play*.

51. *Wedding Rehearsal*—1933

*prod co:* London Film Productions; *prod & dir:* Alexander Korda; *scr:* Helen Gardom from a story by Lajos Biro and George Grossmith; *dial:* Arthur Wimperis; *ph:* L. Rowson; *des:* O. F. Werndorff and Vincent Korda; *asst des:* J. Wills; *ed:* Harold Young; *mus:* Kurt Schroeder; *sound:* George Burgess; *cast:* Roland Young ('Reggie', Marquis of Buckminster), George Grossmith (Lord Stokeshire), Lady Tree (Lady Stokeshire), Wendy Barrie (Lady Mary Rose Roxbury), Joan Gardner (Lady Rosemary Roxbury), Merle Oberon (Miss Hutchinson), Maurice Evans ('Tootles'), John Loder ('Bimbo'), Kate Cutler (Dowager Marchioness of Buckminster), Morton Selten (Major Harry Roxbury), Diana Napier (Mrs Dryden), Edmund Breon (Lord Fleet), Lawrence Hanray (News editor) and Rodolfo Mele; *dist:* Ideal Films; *rt:* 84 mins; *GB rel:* 30 January 1933.

52. *The Private Life of Henry VIII*—1933

*prod co:* London Film Productions; *prod:* Alexander Korda; *dir:* Alexander Korda; *asst dir:* Geoffrey Boothby; *scr:* Arthur Wimperis; *story* and *dial:* Lajos Biro and Arthur Wimperis; *ph:* Georges Périnal; *cam op:* Osmond Borradaile; *des:* Vincent Korda; *sup ed:* Harold Young; *ed:* Stephen Harrison; *mus dir:* Kurt Schroeder; *song:* 'What Shall I Do for Love' by King Henry VIII, sung by Binnie Barnes; *sound:* A. W. Watkins; *hist cons:* Philip Lindsay; *cos:* John Armstrong; *prod man:* David Cunynghame; *cast:* Charles Laughton (Henry VIII), Robert Donat (Culpeper), Lady Tree (Henry's Old Nurse), Binnie Barnes (Katherine Howard), Elsa Lanchester (Anne of Cleves), Merle Oberon (Anne Boleyn), Wendy Barrie (Jane Seymour), Everley Gregg (Katherine Parr), Franklyn Dyall (Cromwell), Miles Mander (Wriothesly),

Claude Allister (Cornell), John Loder (Thomas Peynell), Lawrence Hanray (Cranmer), William Austin (Duke of Cleves), John Turnbull (Holbein), Frederick Culley (Duke of Norfolk), Gibb McLaughlin (French Executioner), Sam Livesey (English Executioner), Judy Kelly (Lady Rochford); *dist:* United Artists; *rt:* 96 mins; *GB prem:* 17 August 1933; *GB rel:* 24 October 1933; *US rel:* 12 October 1933; *prizes:* Academy Award to Charles Laughton.

## PARIS (1932)

53. *The Girl from Maxim's*—1933
*prod co:* London Film Productions; *prod:* Alexander Korda and Ludovico Toeplitz; *dir:* Alexander Korda; *scr:* Capt. Harry Graham from the play by Georges Feydeau; *dial:* Capt. Harry Graham and Arthur Wimperis; *des:* Vincent Korda; *ph:* Georges Périnal; *ed:* Harold Young and R. Bettinson; *mus:* Kurt Schroeder; *cos:* Jean Oberle; *cast:* Frances Day ('La Mome'), Leslie Henson (Dr Petypon), Lady Tree (Mme Petypon), George Grossmith (The General), Stanley Holloway (Mongicourt), Evan Thomas (Corignon), Gertrude Musgrove (Clementine), Desmond Jeans (Etienne); *dist:* United Artists; *rt:* 79 mins; *GB prem:* 18 August 1933; *GB rel:* 8 January 1934; *US rel:* 14 September 1936; *US dist:* J. H. Hoffberg; *US rt:* 67 minutes; *shot:* 1932.
54. *La Dame de Chez Maxim*—1934
Credits same as above, with these exceptions; *scr:* Henri Jeanson from the Georges Feydeau play; *ed:* Jean-Paul Le Chanois; *cast:* Odette Florelle ('La Mome'), André Lefaur (Dr Petypon), Madeleine Ozeray (Mme Petypon), Alerme (Le Général), Ginette Leclerc (Clementine); *rt:* 83 mins; *Fr rel:* January 1934; *shot:* 1932.

## GREAT BRITAIN (1934-1940)

55. *The Private Life of Don Juan*—1934
*prod co:* London Film Productions; *prod & dir:* Alexander Korda; *scr:* Frederick Lonsdale and Lajos Biro [ostensibly] from a play by Henri Bataille; *dial:* Arthur Wimperis; *ph:* Georges Périnal; *asst ph:* Robert Krasker; *cam op:* Osmond Borradaile; *des:* Vincent Korda; *cos:* Oliver Messel; *ed:* Harold Young; *asst ed:* Stephen Harrison; *mus:* Ernst Toch and Michael [Mischa] Spoliansky, Don Juan Serenade, sung by John Brownlee; *mus dir:* Muir Mathieson; *tech adv:* Marquis de Portago; *cast:* Douglas Fairbanks, Snr (Don Juan), Benita Hume (Dolores), Melville Cooper (Leporello), Merle Oberon (Antonita), Binnie Barnes (Rosita), Owen Nares (Actor playing Don Juan), Patricia Hilliard (Girl in Castle), Clifford Heatherley (Pedro), Gina Malo (Pepita), Joan Gardner (Carmen), Barry MacKay (Roderigo), Heather Thatcher (Actress), Claude Allister (Duke), Diana Napier (lady of Seville), Lawrence Grossmith (Guardian), Bruce Winston (Cafe Manager), Edmund Willard (Prisoner), Athene Seyler (Theresa), Gibson Gowland (Don Ascanio), Edmund Breon (Play's Author), Hindle Edgar (Husband), Florence Wood (Cook), Annie Esmond (Dolores' Duenna), Morland Graham (Don Juan's Cook), Hay Petrie ('Golden Pheasant' manager), William Heughan, Natalie Lelong (2nd Wife), Natalie Paley (First Wife), Veronica Brady (Mistress), Betty Hamilton, Toto Koopman, and Virginia Bradford (Actresses); *dist:* United Artists; *GB rt:* 89 minutes; *GB rel:* 10 September 1934; *US rt:* 80

minutes; *US rel:* 30 November 1934; *world prem:* 28 August 1934 at Venice Film Festival; *working title: Exit Don Juan.*

56. *Rembrandt*—1936

*prod co:* London Film Productions; *prod & dir:* Alexander Korda; *scr:* Carl Zuckmayer, Lajos Biro, and June Head; *dial:* Arthur Wimperis; *ph:* Georges Périnal and Richard Angst; *cam op:* Robert Krasker; *des:* Vincent Korda; *asst des:* H. M. Waller; *cos:* John Armstrong; *sup ed:* William Hornbeck; *ed:* Francis Lyon; *asst ed:* Eric Hodges; *spec effects:* Ned Mann; *mus:* Geoffrey Toye; *mus dir:* Muir Mathieson; *sound rec:* A. W. Watkins and A. Fischer; *prod man:* David Cunynghame; *tech adv:* Johan de Meester; *unit man:* Geoffrey Boothby; *cast:* Charles Laughton (Rembrandt van Rijn), Gertrude Lawrence (Geertje Dirx), Elsa Lanchester (Hendrickje Stoffels), Edward Chapman (Fabrizius), Walter Hudd (Banning Cocq), Roger Livesey (Beggar/Saul), John Bryning (Titus van Rijn), Allan Jeayes (Dr Tulp), John Clements (Gavaert Flink), Raymond Huntley (Ludwick), Abraham Sofaer (Dr Menasseh), Lawrence Hanray (Heertsbeeke), Austin Trevor (Marquis), Henry Hewitt (Jan Six), Gertrude Musgrove (Agelintje), Basil Gill (Adriaen), Edmund Willard (Van Zeeland), Marius Goring (Baron Leivens), Richard Gofe (Titus, as child), Meinhart Maur (Ornia), George Merritt (Church Warden), John Turnbull (Minister), Sam Livesey (Auctioneer), William Fagan (Burgomaster), Lewis Broughton and Frederick Burtwell (Saskia's brothers), Baroness Barany (Waitress), Barry Livesey (Peasant), Herbert Lomas (Rembrandt's father), Jack Livesey (Journeyman), Quintin McPherson (Official), James Carney (Peasant), Roger Wellesley (Burgomaster's Secretary), Byron Webber and Bellenden Powell (Court Members), Charles Paton, Hector Abbas, and Leonard Sharpe (Burgers at Auction), George Pughe and Jerrold Robert Shaw (Museum Directors), and Evelyn Ankers; *dist:* United Artists; *GB rt:* 85 minutes; *GB rel:* 6 November 1936; *US rt:* 83 minutes; *US rel:* 21 November 1936.

## *HOLLYWOOD (1940–1943)*

57. *That Hamilton Woman* [GB: *Lady Hamilton*]—1941

*prod co:* Alexander Korda Films, Inc.; *prod & dir:* Alexander Korda; *asst dir:* Walter Mayo; *scr:* Walter Reisch and R. C. Sherriff; *ph:* Rudolph Maté *asst ph:* Edward Linden; *spec effects:* Lawrence Butler; *des:* Vincent Korda; *associate des:* Lyle Reynolds Wheeler; *sets:* Julia Heron; *cos:* René Hubert; *ed:* William Hornbeck; *mus & mus dir:* Miklos Rozsa; *sound rec:* William H. Wilmartin; *prod asst:* André De Toth; *cast:* Vivien Leigh (Emma Hamilton), Laurence Olivier (Lord Nelson), Alan Mowbray (Sir William Hamilton), Sara Allgood (Mrs Cadogan-Lyon), Gladys Cooper (Lady Nelson), Henry Wilcoxon (Captain Hardy), Heather Angel (Street Girl), Halliwell Hobbes (Reverend Nelson), Gilbert Emery (Lord Spencer), Miles Mander (Lord Keith), Ronald Sinclair (Josiah), Luis Alberni (King of Naples), Norma Drury (Queen of Naples); George Renavent (Hotel Manager), Leonard Carey (Orderly), Alec Craig (Gendarme), and George Davis; *dist:* United Artists; *US rel:* 30 April 1941; *US rt:* 128 mins.; *GB rel:* 11 June 1941; *GB rt:* 125 mins; *prize:* Academy Award for Sound Recording.

348

# GREAT BRITAIN (1943-1947)

58. *Perfect Strangers* [US: *Vacation from Marriage*]—1945
*prod co:* MGM-London Film Productions; *prod & dir:* Alexander Korda; *asst dir:* Phil Brandon; *scr:* Clemence Dane and Anthony Pelissier from the story by Clemence Dane; *ph:* Georges Périnal; *asst ph:* Laurie Freedman; *des:* Vincent Korda; *asst des:* Ferdinand Bellan and Joseph Bato; *ed:* E. B. Jarvis; *mus:* Clifton Parker; *mus dir:* Muir Mathieson; *sound rec:* A. W. Watkins; *cast:* Robert Donat (Robert Wilson), Deborah Kerr (Catherine Wilson), Glynis Johns (Dizzy Clayton), Ann Todd (Elena), Roland Culver (Richard), Elliot Mason (Mrs Hemmings), Eliot Mareham (Mr Staines), Brefni O'Rorke (Mr Hargrove), Edward Rigby (Charlie), Muriel George (Minnie), Allan Jeayes (Commander), Ivor Barnard (Chemist), Henry B. Longhurst (Petty Officer), Bill Shine (Webster), Billy Thatcher (Essex), Brian Weske (Gordon), Rosamund Taylor (Irene), Harry Ross (Bill), Vincent Holman (ARP Warden), Leslie Dwyer (Strupey), Caven Watson (Scotty), Jeanine Carre (Jeannie), Molly Munks (Meg); *dist:* MGM; *GB rel:* 15 October 1945; *GB rt:* 102 mins.; *US rel:* November/December 1945; *US rt:* 94 mins.; *prize:* Academy Award for Best Original Story.

59. *An Ideal Husband*—1947
*prod co:* London Film Productions; *prod & dir:* Alexander Korda; *assoc prod:* Phil Brandon and Hugh Stewart; *asst dir:* Bluey Hill; *scr:* Lajos Biro from the play by Oscar Wilde; *ph* (Technicolor): Georges Périnal; *cam op:* Denys Coop; *spec effects:* W. Percy Day; *des:* Vincent Korda; *assoc des:* Joseph Bato; *cos:* Cecil Beaton; *fabric des:* Scott Slimon; *ed:* Oswald Hafenrichter; *mus:* Arthur Benjamin; *mus dir:* Dr Hubert Clifford; *prod man:* Jack Clayton; *sound:* John Cox, Leo Wilkins, Red Law; *Technicolor dir:* Natalie Kalmus; *assoc:* Joan Bridges; *cont:* Peggy McClafferty; *make-up:* U. P. Hutchinson and Dorrie Hamilton; *hair:* Gladys Weston; *cast:* Paulette Goddard (Mrs Cheveley), Michael Wilding (Viscount Goring), Diana Wynyard (Lady Chiltern), Hugh Williams (Sir Robert Chiltern), Sir C. Aubrey Smith (Earl of Caversham), Glynis Johns (Mabel Chiltern), Constance Collier (Lady Markby), Christine Norden (Mrs Marchmont), Harriette Johns (Countess of Basildon), Michael Medwin (Duke of Nonsuch), Michael Anthony (Vicomte de Nanjac), Fred Groves (Phipps), Peter Hobbes (Mr Montford), Johns Clifford (Mr Mason), Michael Ward (Mr Trafford); *GB dist:* British Lion; *GB rel:* 14 November 1947; *rt:* 96 mins.; *US dist:* 20th Century-Fox; *US rel:* 17 November 1947.

# II. FILMS PRODUCED BY, OR ASSOCIATED WITH, ALEXANDER KORDA
# GREAT BRITAIN (1933-41)

1. *Men of To-morrow*—1933
*prod co:* London Film Productions; *prod:* Alexander Korda; *dir:* Leontine Sagan and Zoltan Korda; *scr:* Arthur Wimperis and Anthony Gibbs, from the novel *Young Apollo* by Anthony Gibbs; *ph:* Bernard Browne; *des:* Vincent Korda; *ed:* Leontine Sagan; *sound:* A. W. Watkins and Robert A. Smith;

*cast:* Maurice Braddell (Allan Shepherd), Joan Gardner (Jane Anderson), Merle Oberon (Ysobel d'Aunay), Emlyn Williams ('Horners'), Robert Donat (Julian Angell), John Traynor (Mr Waters), Esther Kiss (Maggie), Annie Esmond (Mrs Oliphant), Charles Carson (Senior Proctor), Gerald Cooper (Tutor), Patric Knowles; *GB dist:* Paramount; *GB rt:* 88 minutes; *GB rel:* 20 March 1933; *US dist:* Mundus; *US rt:* 45 minutes; *US rel:* 16 April 1935.

2. *That Night in London* [US: *Overnight*]—1933
   *prod co:* London Film Productions; *prod:* Alexander Korda; *dir:* Rowland V. Lee; *scr:* Dorothy Greenhill and Arthur Wimperis, from a story by Dorothy Greenhill; *ph:* Robert Martin; *mus:* Peter Mendoza; *ed:* Stephen Harrison; *sound:* A. W. Watkins; *cast:* Robert Donat (Dick Warren), Pearl Argyle (Eve Desborough), Miles Mander (Harry Tresham), Lawrence Hanray (Ribbles), Roy Emmerton (Captain Paulson), Graham Soutten (Bert), James Knight (Inspector Brody), Eugene Leahy (Bank Manager), James Bucton (Inspector Ryan), the Max Rivers Girls; *dist:* Paramount; *rt:* 78 minutes; *GB rel:* 10 April 1933; *US rel:* 1934.

3. *Strange Evidence*—1933
   *prod co:* London Film Productions; *prod:* Alexander Korda; *dir:* Robert Milton; *scr:* Miles Malleson; *ph:* Robert Martin; *ed:* Stephen Harrison; *sound:* A. W. Watkins; *cast:* Leslie Banks (Francis Relf), Carol Goodner (Barbara Relf/Marie), Frank Vosper (Andrew Relf), Diana Napier (Jean), George Curzon (Stephen Relf), Norah Baring (Clare Relf), Haidee Wright (Mrs Relf) Lyonel Watts (Henry Relf), Lewis Shaw (Larry); *dist:* Paramount; *rt:* 71 minutes; *rel:* 10 July 1933.

4. *Counsel's Opinion*—1933
   *prod co:* London Film Productions; *prod:* Alexander Korda; *dir:* Allan Dwan; *scr:* Arthur Wimperis and Dorothy Greenhill, from the play by Gilbert Wakefield; *ph:* Phil Tannura; *asst ph:* Bernard Browne; *des:* Holmes-Paul; *ed:* Harold Young; *sound:* A. W. Watkins; *cast:* Henry Kendall (Logan), Binnie Barnes (Leslie), Cyril Maude (Willock), Lawrence Grossmith (Lord Rockburn), Harry Tate (Taxi-driver), Francis Lister (James Govan), Mary Charles (Stella Marston), Margaret Baird (Saunders), J. Fisher White (Judge), C. Denier Warren (Manager), Stanley Lathbury (George); *dist:* Paramount; *rt:* 76 minutes; *rel:* 22 August 1933. (Remade in 1938 as *The Divorce of Lady X;* see no. 30.)

5. *Cash* [US: *For Love or Money*]—1933
   *prod co:* London Film Productions; *prod:* Alexander Korda; *dir:* Zoltan Korda; *scr:* Arthur Wimperis, from a story by Anthony Gibbs and Dorothy Greenhill; *ph:* Robert Martin; *ed:* Stephen Harrison; *sound:* A. W. Watkins; *cast:* Edmund Gwenn (Edmund Gilbert), Wendy Barrie (Lilian Gilbert), Robert Donat (Paul Martin), Morris Harvey (Meyer), Lawrence Grossmith (Joseph), Hugh E. Wright (Jordan), Clifford Heatherley (Hunt), Anthony Holles (Inspector); *dist:* Paramount; *rt:* 73 minutes; *GB rel:* 9 October 1933; *US rel:* 26 July 1934.

6. *The Rise of Catherine the Great* [US: *Catherine the Great*]—1934
   *prod co:* London Film Productions; *prod:* Alexander Korda; *dir:* Paul Czinner; *asst dir:* Geoffrey Boothby; *scr:* Marjorie Deans and Arthur Wimperis, from

the play *The Czarina* by Lajos Biro and Melchior Lengyel; *dial:* Lajos Biro, Arthur Wimperis and Melchior Lengyel; *ph:* Georges Périnal; *cam op:* Robert LaPresle, Bernard Browne; *asst cam op:* Robert Krasker; *des:* Vincent Korda; *arch:* Francis Hallam; *mus dir:* Muir Mathieson; *sup ed:* Harold Young; *ed:* Stephen Harrison; *cos:* John Armstrong; *prod man:* David Cunynghame; *sound:* A. W. Watkins; *cast:* Douglas Fairbanks Jnr (Grand Duke/Czar Peter), Elisabeth Bergner (Catherine), Flora Robson (Empress Elizabeth), Gerald du Maurier (Lecocq), Irene Vanbrugh (Princess Anhalt-Zerbst), Joan Gardner (Katushienka), Dorothy Hale (Countess Olga), Diana Napier (Countess Vorontzova), Griffith Jones (Grigory Orlov), Gibb MacLaughlin (Bestujhev), Clifford Heatherley (Ogarev), Lawrence Hanray (Goudovitch), Allan Jeayes (Colonel Karnilov); *dist:* United Artists; *rt:* 95 minutes; *prem:* 9 February 1934; *GB rel:* 27 February 1934; *Us rel:* 13 April 1934. (Alexander Korda also directed numerous sequences of the film, without credit.)

7. *The Private Life of the Gannets*—1934

*prod co:* London Film Productions; *prod & dir:* Julian Huxley; *asst dir:* Ronald Lockley; *ph:* Osmond Borradaile and John Grierson; *mus dir:* Muir Mathieson (music based on *The Skye Boat Song*); *ed:* Philip Charlot; *commentary:* spoken by Julian Huxley; *rt:* 15 minutes; *rel:* late 1934; *prizes:* Academy Award for best short subject (one-reel), 1937.

8. *The Scarlet Pimpernel*—1934

*prod co:* London Film Productions; *prod:* Alexander Korda; *dir:* Harold Young; *asst dir:* Geoffrey Boothby; *scr:* S. N. Behrman, Robert Sherwood, Arthur Wimperis and Lajos Biro, from the novel by Baroness Orczy [and the play by Orczy and Montague Barstow?]; *ph:* Harold Rosson; *asst ph:* Osmond Borradaile and Bernard Browne; *spec effects:* Ned Mann; *des:* Vincent Korda; *arch:* Francis Hallam; *mus:* Arthur Benjamin; *mus dir:* Muir Mathieson; *ed:* William Hornbeck; *cos:* John Armstrong and Oliver Messel; *prod man:* David Cunynghame; *sound:* A. W. Watkins; *cast:* Leslie Howard (Sir Percy Blakeney), Merle Oberon (Lady Marguerite Blakeney), Raymond Massey (Chauvelin), Nigel Bruce (The Prince of Wales), Bramwell Fletcher (The Priest), Anthony Bushell (Sir Andrew Ffoulkes), Joan Gardner (Suzanne de Tournay), Walter Rilla (Armand St Just), Mabel Terry-Lewis (Countess de Tournay), O. B. Clarence (Count de Tournay), Ernest Milton (Robespierre), Edmund Breon (Colonel Winterbottom), Melville Cooper (Romney), Gibb McLaughlin (The Barber), Morland Graham (Treadle), John Turnbull (Jellyband), Gertrude Musgrove (Jellyband's daughter, Sally), Allan Jeayes (Lord Grenville), Bromley Davenport (French Innkeeper), Hindle Edgar (Lord Hastings), William Freshman (Lord Wilmot), Lawrence Hanray (Burke), Bruce Belfrage (Pitt), Edmund Willard (Bibot), Roy Meredith (Viscount de Tournay), Billy Shine (An Aristocrat), Brember Wills (Doman), Kenneth Kove ('Codlin', a fisherman), Renee Macredy (Lady Q), Philip Strange, Carl Harbord, Philip Desborough, Hugh Dempster, Peter Evan Thomas, Derrick de Marney (Members of the Pimpernel League), Harry Terry ('Renad'), Douglas Stewart ('Merieres'), Arthur Hambling (Captain of the Guard); *dist:* United Artists; *GB rt:* 98 minutes; *GB rel:* 23 December 1934; *US rt:* 95 minutes; *US rel:* 8 February 1935. (Rowland Brown and Alexander Korda also directed sequences for the film, neither receiving credit for this. Two later Korda films derive from the same subject: *The Return of the Scarlet Pimpernel* (1938) and *The Elusive Pimpernel* (1950), see nos. 28 and 71.)

9. *Sanders of the River* [US: *Bosambo*]—1935
*prod co:* London Film Productions; *prod:* Alexander Korda; *dir:* Zoltan Korda; *asst dir:* Stanley Irving; *scr:* Lajos Biro and Jeffrey Dell, from the novel by Edgar Wallace; *ph:* Georges Périnal; *cam op:* Bernard Browne; *ext ph:* Osmond Borradaile, Louis Page, and Ernst Udet; *des:* Vincent Korda; *mus:* Michael [Mischa] Spoliansky; *lyrics:* Arthur Wimperis; *mus dir:* Muir Mathieson; *sup ed:* William Hornbeck; *ed:* Charles Crichton; *asst ed:* Compton Bennett; *prod man:* G. E. T. Grossmith; *sound:* A. W. Watkins; *sound tech:* L. Fisher, D. Field and J. Paddon; *tech advisers:* C. O. Lemon ('Squash'), Cecil Gross and Major C. Wallace; *cast:* Leslie Banks (Sanders), Paul Robeson (Bosambo), Nina Mae McKinney (Lilongo), Robert Cochran (Tibbets), Martin Walker (Ferguson), Richard Grey (Hamilton), Tony Wane (King Mofolaba), Marquis de Portago (Farini), Eric Maturin (Smith), Allan Jeayes (Father O'Leary), Charles Carson (Governor of the Territory), Oboja (Chief of the Acholi Tribe), Orlando Martins (K'Lova), Luao and Kilongalonga (Chiefs of the Wagenia Tribe), Bertrand Frazer (Makara), Anthony Popafio (Bosambo's son), Beresford Gale (Topolaka), James Solomons (Kaluba), John Thomas (Obiboo), Members of the Acholi, Sesi, Tefik, Juruba, Mendi and Kroo Tribes; *dist:* United Artists; *GB rt:* 98 minutes; *GB rel:* 8 April 1935; *US rt:* 95 minutes; *US rel:* 4 July 1935; *working title: Kongo Raid.*

10. *Wharves and Strays*—1935
*prod co:* London Film Productions; *dir:* Bernard Browne; *ph:* Bernard Browne; *mus:* Arthur Benjamin; *mus dir:* Muir Mathieson; *dist:* United Artists; *rt:* 20 minutes; *rel:* 9 April 1935.

11. *The Ghost Goes West*—1935
*prod co:* London Film Productions; *prod:* Alexander Korda; *dir:* René Clair; *asst dir:* Imlay Watts and Albert Valentin; *scr:* Robert E. Sherwood, René Clair and Geoffrey Kerr, from the story *Sir Tristram Goes West* in *Punch* by Eric Keown; *ph:* Harold Rosson; *cam op:* Bernard Browne; *spec effects:* Ned Mann; *des:* Vincent Korda; *assoc des:* John Bryan; *mus:* Michael [Mischa] Spoliansky; *mus dir:* Muir Mathieson; *sup ed:* William Hornbeck; *ed:* Harold Earle-Fischbacher and Henry Cornelius; *cos:* René Hubert and John Armstrong; *prod man:* David Cunynghame; *sound:* A. W. Watkins; *cast:* Robert Donat (Murdoch/Donald Glourie), Jean Parker (Peggy Martin), Eugene Pallette (Joe Martin), Elsa Lanchester (Lady Shepperton), Ralph Bunker (Ed Bigelow), Patricia Hilliard (Shepherdess), Everley Gregg (Gladys Martin), Morton Selten (Gavin Glourie), Chili Bouchier (Cleopatra), Mark Daly (Groom), Herbert Lomas (Fergus), Elliot Mason (Mrs McNiff), Jack Lambert, Colin Leslie, Richard Mackie, J. Neil More, Neil Lester (Sons of MacLaggan), Hay Petrie (The MacLaggan), Quintin McPherson (MacKaye), Arthur Seaton and David Keir (Creditors); *dist:* United Artists; *GB rt:* 90 minutes; *prem:* 17 December 1935; *GB rel:* 22 December 1935; *US rt:* 85 minutes; *US rel:* 7 February 1936. (Alex Korda re-shot and/or re-shaped some of Clair's material.)

12. *Miss Bracegirdle Does Her Duty*—1936
   *prod co:* London Film Productions; *prod:* Alexander Korda; *dir:* Lee Garmes;
   *scr:* Stacy Aumonier; *ph:* Bernard Browne and Lee Garmes; *cast:* Elsa
   Lanchester (Miss Bracegirdle); *dist:* London Film Productions; *rt:* 20 minutes;
   *rel:* January 1936.

13. *The Fox Hunt*—1936
   *prod co:* London Film Productions; *dir:* Hector Hoppin and Anthony Gross;
   *dist:* United Artists; *rt:* 8 minutes. (A Technicolor cartoon.)

14. *Things to Come*—1936
   *prod co:* London Film Productions; *prod:* Alexander Korda; *dir:* William
   Cameron Menzies; *asst dir:* Geoffrey Boothby; *scr:* H. G. Wells from his
   novel; *ph:* Georges Périnal; *cam op:* Robert Krasker and Bernard Browne;
   *spec effects:* Ned Mann, Lawrence Butler, Edward Cohen, Harry Zech,
   Wally Vaevers, and Ross Jacklin; *des:* Vincent Korda; *assoc des:* John Bryan,
   William Cameron Menzies and Frederick Pusey; *asst des:* Frank Wells;
   *mus:* Arthur Bliss; *mus dir:* Muir Mathieson; *sup ed:* William Hornbeck; *ed:*
   Charles Crichton and Francis Lyon; *cos:* John Armstrong, René Hubert and
   the Marchioness of Queensberry; *prod man:* David Cunynghame; *sound:* A.
   W. Watkins; *tech adviser:* Nigel Tangye; *cast:* Raymond Massey (John
   Cabal/Oswald Cabal), Edward Chapman (Pippa Passworthy/Raymond
   Passworthy), Ralph Richardson (The Boss), Margaretta Scott (Roxana/
   Rowena), Cedric Hardwicke (Theotocopulos), Maurice Braddell (Dr
   Harding), Sophie Stewart (Mrs Cabal), Derrick de Marney (Richard Gordon),
   Ann Todd (Mary Gordon), Pearl Argyle (Catherine Cabal), Kenneth Villiers
   (Maurice Passworthy), Ivan Brandt (Morden Mitani), Anne McLaren (The
   Child), John Clements (The Airman), Abraham Sofaer (The Jew), Patricia
   Hilliard (Janet Gordon), Charles Carson (Great Grandfather), Patrick Barr
   (World Transport Official), Anthony Holles (Simon Burton), Allan Jeayes
   (Mr Cabal) and Paul O'Brien; *dist:* United Artists; *rt:* 100 minutes; *GB rel:*
   22 February 1936; *US rel:* 24 April 1936; *working title: Whither, Mankind?*
   and *One Hundred Years to Come.*

15. *Moscow Nights* [US: *I Stand Condemned*]—1936
   *prod co:* Denham Productions in association with London Film Productions-
   Capitol; *exec prod:* Alexander Korda; *prod:* Alexis Granowsky and Max
   Schach; *dir:* Anthony Asquith; *asst dir:* Teddy Baird; *scr:* Anthony Asquith
   and Eric Siepmann from a novel by Pierre Benoît; *ph:* Philip Tannura; *des:*
   Vincent Korda; *mus dir:* Muir Mathieson; *sup ed:* William Hornbeck; *ed:*
   Francis Lyon; *cos:* John Armstrong; *sound:* A. W. Watkins; *cast:* Harry Baur
   (Brioukow), Laurence Olivier (Captain Ignatoff), Penelope Dudley Ward
   (Natasha), Robert Cochran (Polonsky), Morton Selten (Kovrin), Athene
   Seyler (Mme Sabline), Walter Hudd (Doctor), Kate Cutler (Mme Kovrin),
   C. M. Hallard (President), Edmund Willard (Prosecution), Charles Carson
   (Defence), Morland Graham (Servant), Hay Petrie (Spy), Richard Webster
   (Second Servant); *dist:* General Film Distributors; *rt:* 74 minutes; *GB rel:*
   16 April 1936; *US rel:* 2 July 1936. (An English remake of *Les Nuits de
   Moscou* (1934) directed by Alexis Granowsky.)

16. *Men Are Not Gods*—1936
   *prod co:* London Film Productions; *prod:* Alexander Korda; *dir:* Walter

Reisch; *scr:* Walter Reisch, G. B. Stern, and Iris Wright; *ph:* Charles Rosher; *cam op:* Robert Krasker; *spec effects:* Ned Mann; *des:* Vincent Korda; *asst des:* Arthur Cornwall; *cos:* René Hubert; *mus:* Geoffrey Toye; *mus dir:* Muir Mathieson; *sup ed:* William Hornbeck; *ed:* Henry Cornelius; *sound:* A. W. Watkins; *sound tech:* R. Hobbs; *prod man:* David Cunynghame; *unit man:* Imlay Watts; *cast:* Miriam Hopkins (Ann Williams), Gertrude Lawrence (Barbara Halford), Sebastian Shaw (Edmond Davey), Rex Harrison (Tommy Stapleton), A. E. Matthews (Skeates), Val Gielgud (Producer), Laura Smithson (Katherine), Lawrence Grossmith (Stanley), Sybil Grove (Painter), Wally Patch (Attendant), Winifred Willard (Mrs Williams), James Harcourt (Porter), Noel Howlett (Cashier), Rosamund Greenwood (Pianist), Paddy Morgan (Kitty), Nicholas Nadejin (Iago), Michael Hogarth (Cassio); *dist:* United Artists; *GB rt:* 90 minutes; *GB rel:* 27 November 1936; *US rt:* 82 minutes; *US rel:* 22 January 1937.

17. *Forget-me-not* [US: *Forever Yours*]—1936
*prod co:* London Film Productions; *prod:* Alexander Korda and Alberto Giacalone; *dir:* Zoltan Korda; *asst dir:* Stanley Irving; *scr:* Hugh Gray and Arthur Wimperis; *ph:* Hans Schneeberger; *cam op:* Robert Krasker; *mus:* Michael [Mischa] Spoliansky; *mus dir:* Muir Mathieson; *ed:* Henry Cornelius; *sound:* A. W. Watkins; *cast:* Beniamino Gigli (Enzo Curti), Joan Gardner (Helen Carlton), Ivan Brandt (Hugh Anderson), Hugh Wakefield (Jackson), Jeanne Stuart (Irene Desbrough), Allan Jeayes (London Manager), Hay Petrie (New York Manager), Charles Carson (George Arnold), Richard Gofe (Benvenuto); *GB dist:* Grand National; *GB rel:* 21 December 1936; *rt:* 72 minutes; *US dist:* United Artists; *US rel:* 15 May 1937.

18. *The Man Who Could Work Miracles*—1937
*prod co:* London Film Productions; *prod:* Alexander Korda; *dir:* Lothar Mendes; *asst dir:* Imlay Watts; *scr:* H. G. Wells (credited), Lajos Biro (uncredited), from the short story by H. G. Wells; *ph:* Harold Rosson; *cam op:* Maurice Forde, Bernard Browne, and Robert Krasker; *spec effects:* Ned Mann, Lawrence Butler, and Edward Cohen; *des:* Vincent Korda; *mus:* Michael [Mischa] Spoliansky; *mus dir:* Muir Mathieson; *sup ed:* William Hornbeck; *ed:* Philip Charlot; *prod man:* David Cunynghame; *sound:* A. W. Watkins; *cast:* Roland Young (George McWhirter Fotheringay), Ralph Richardson (Colonel Winstanley), Edward Chapman (Major Grigsby), Ernest Thesiger (Mr Maydig), Joan Gardner (Ada Price), Sophie Stewart (Maggie Hooper), Robert Cochran (Bill Stoker), Lawrence Hanray (Mr Bamfylde), George Zucco (Moody), Wallace Lupino (P. C. Winch), Lady Tree (Housekeeper), Joan Hickson (Effie Brickman), Wally Patch (Superintendent Smithells), Bernard Nedell (Reporter), Bruce Winston (Cox), George Sanders (Indifference), Ivan Brandt (Player), Torin Thatcher (Observer), Mark Daly (Toddy Beamish); *dist:* United Artists; *rt:* 82 minutes; *GB rel:* 8 February 1937; *US rel:* 19 February 1937.

19. *Fire Over England*—1937
*prod co:* Pendennis, for London Film Productions; *pres:* Alexander Korda; *prod:* Erich Pommer; *dir:* William K. Howard; *asst dir:* W. O'Kelly; *scr:* Clemence Dane and Sergei Nolbandov, from the novel by A. E. W. Mason; *ph:* James Wong Howe; *cam:* Paul Barralet; *cam op:* Wilkie Cooper; *spec*

*effects:* Ned Mann, Lawrence Butler, and Edward Cohen; *des:* Lazare Meerson; *asst des:* Frank Wells; *mus:* Richard Addinsell; *mus dir:* Muir Mathieson; *ed:* Jack Dennis; *cos:* René Hubert; *sound:* A. W. Watkins and Jack Rogerson; *prod man:* Roland Gillett; *cast:* Flora Robson (Queen Elizabeth I), Laurence Olivier (Michael Ingolby), Vivien Leigh (Cynthia), Leslie Banks (Earl of Leicester), Raymond Massey (Philip of Spain), Morton Selten (Burleigh), Tamara Desni (Elena), James Mason (Hillary Vane), Herbert Lomas (Richard Ingolby), Robert Newton (Don Pedro), Robert Rendell (Don Miguel), Charles Carson (Admiral Valdez), Henry Oscar (Spanish Ambassador), Lawrence Hanray (French Ambassador), Roy Russell (Cooper), Howard Douglas (Lord Amberley), Cecil Mainwaring (Illingworth), Francis de Wolfe (Tarleton), Graham Cheswright (Maddison), George Thirlwell (Gregory), A. Corney Grain (Hatton), Donald Calthrop (Don Escobal), Lyn Harding (Sir Richard); *dist:* United Artists; *rt:* 91 minutes; *prem:* Paris, February 1937; *GB rel:* March 1937; *US rel:* 4 March 1937; *prizes:* Gold Medal of the *Comité international pour la diffusion artistique et littéraire pour le cinéma.*

20. *I, Claudius*—1937

*prod co:* London Film Productions; *prod:* Alexander Korda; *dir:* Josef von Sternberg; *asst dir:* Geoffrey Boothby; *scr:* Josef von Sternberg, Lajos Biro, Carl Zuckmayer, Arthur Wimperis, Lester Cohen, and Robert Graves, from the novel by Robert Graves; *ph:* Georges Périnal; *cam op:* Robert Krasker; *des:* Vincent Korda; *cos:* John Armstrong; *choreography:* Agnes De Mille; *tech adviser:* Professor Ashmole; *cast:* Charles Laughton (Tiberius Claudius Drusus), Merle Oberon (Messalina), Flora Robson (Livia), Emlyn Williams (Caligula), Robert Newton, John Clements, Basil Gill, Everley Gregg. (Never completed; see text.)

21. *Dark Journey* (reissued as *The Anxious Years* in 1953)—1937

*prod co:* Victor Saville Productions, for London Film Productions; *prod:* Alexander Korda; *dir:* Victor Saville; *scr:* Arthur Wimperis from a story by Lajos Biro; *ph:* Georges Périnal; *add ph:* Harry Stradling; *spec effects:* Ned Mann, Lawrence Butler, and Edward Cohen; *des:* Andre Andrejew and Ferdinand Bellan; *mus:* Richard Addinsell; *mus dir:* Muir Mathieson; *sup ed:* William Hornbeck; *ed:* Hugh Stewart and Lionel Hoare; *cos:* René Hubert; *tech adv:* L. Stackell; *sound:* A. W. Watkins and Charles Tasto; *cast:* Conrad Veidt (Baron Karl von Marwitz), Vivien Leigh (Madeleine Godard), Joan Gardner (Lupita), Anthony Bushell (Bob Carter), Ursula Jeans (Gertrude), Eliot Makeham (Anatole), Margery Pickard (Colette), Austin Trevor (Dr Muller), Sam Livesey (Major Schaffer), Cecil Parker (Captain), Edmund Willard (German Intelligence Officer), Charles Carson (Fifth Bureau Man), William Dewhurst (Killer), Henry Oscar (Magistrate), Reginald Tate (Mate), Robert Newton (Officer), Philip Ray (Faber), Lawrence Hanray (Cottin), Percy Walsh (Captain of the Swedish Packet), Laidman Browne (Rügge), Martin Harvey (Bohlan), Anthony Holles (Dutch Man); *dist:* United Artists; *rt:* 77 minutes; *GB rel:* 2 April 1937; *US rel:* 2 July 1937.

22. *Elephant Boy*—1937

*prod co:* London Film Productions; *prod:* Alexander Korda; *dir:* Robert Flaherty and Zoltan Korda; *asst dir:* David Flaherty; *scr:* John Collier, Akos Tolnay, and Marcia de Silva from the novel *Toomai of the Elephants* by Rudyard

355

Kipling; *ph:* Osmond Borradaile; *des:* Vincent Korda; *mus:* John Greenwood; *mus dir:* Muir Mathieson; *sup ed:* William Hornbeck; *ed:* Charles Crichton; *prod asst:* André de Toth; *sound:* A. W. Watkins and H. G. Cape; *cast:* Sabu (Toomai), Walter Hudd (Petersen), Allan Jeayes (Machua Appa), W. E. Holloway (Father), Bruce Gordon (Rham Lahl), D. J. Williams (Hunter), Wilfrid Hyde-White (Commissioner); *dist:* United Artists; *rt:* 80 minutes; *GB rel:* 9 April 1937; *US rel:* 23 April 1937; *shot:* 1935–1936.

23. *Farewell Again* [US: *Troopship*]—1937

*prod co:* Pendennis, for London Film Productions; *prod:* Erich Pommer; *dir:* Tim Whelan; *asst dir:* F. Penrose Tennyson; *scr:* Clemence Dane and Patrick Kirwan from a story by Wolfgang Wilhelm; *ph:* James Wong Howe (interiors) and Hans Schneeberger (exteriors); *cam op:* Wilkie Cooper; *des:* Frederick Pusey; *mus:* Richard Addinsell; *mus dir:* Muir Mathieson; *ed:* Jack Dennis; *asst ed:* John Guthrie; *sound:* A. W. Watkins and Jack Rogerson; *prod man:* W. H. Burnside; *cast:* Flora Robson (Lucy Blair), Leslie Banks (Colonel Harry Blair), Patricia Hilliard (Ann Harrison), Sebastian Shaw (Captain Gilbert Reed), Robert Cochran (Carlisle), Leonora Corbett (Lady Joan), Rene Ray (Elsie Wainwright), Anthony Bushell (Roddy Hammond), Robert Newton (Jim Carter), Edward Lexy (Sergeant Brough), Edmund Willard (Private Withers), Alf Goddard (Private Bulger), Wally Patch (Sergeant-Major Billings), Jerry Verno (Private Judd), Martita Hunt (Adela Swayle), Maire O'Neill (Mrs Brough), John Laurie (Private McAllister), Eliot Makeham (Major Swayle), David Horne (John Carlisle), J. H. Roberts (Dr Pearson), Gertrude Musgrove (Lily Toff), Margaret Moffat (Mrs Billings), Billy Shine (Corporal Edrich), Edie Martin (Mrs Bulger), Phil Ray (Moore), Janet Burnell (Mrs Moore); *dist:* United Artists; *rt:* 85 minutes; *GB rel:* 15 May 1937; *US rel:* 8 November 1937.

24. *Storm in a Teacup*—1937

*prod co:* Victor Saville Productions, for London Film Productions; *prod:* Victor Saville; *assoc prod:* Stanley Haynes; *dir:* Victor Saville and Ian Dalrymple; *scr:* Ian Dalrymple and Donald Bull, from James Bridie's adaptation of the play *Sturm im Wasserglas* by Bruno Frank; *ph:* Mutz Greenbaum [Max Greene]; *spec effects:* Ned Mann and Edward Cohen; *cam op:* D. Gallai-Hatchard; *des:* Andre Andrejew; *mus:* Frederic Lewis; *mus dir:* Muir Mathieson; *sup ed:* William Hornbeck; *ed:* Hugh Stewart and Cyril Randell; *sound:* A. W. Watkins and Charles Tasto; *prod man:* D. Wright; *cast:* Vivien Leigh (Victoria Gow), Rex Harrison (Frank Burdon), Sara Allgood (Mrs Hegarty), Cecil Parker (Provost Gow), Ursula Jeans (Lisbet Skirving), Gus McNaughton (Horace Skirving), Arthur Wontner (Fiscal), Edgar K. Bruce (McKellar), Robert Hale (Lord Skerryvore), Quintin McPherson (Baillie Callender), Eliot Makeham (Sheriff), Ivor Barnard (Watkins), W. G. Fay (Cassidy), George Pughe (Menzies), Arthur Seaton (Police Sergeant), Cecil Mannering (Police Constable), Cyril Smith (Councillor), Scruffy the dog; *dist:* United Artists; *rt:* 87 minutes; *GB rel:* 12 June 1937; *US rel:* 22 November 1937.

25. *Action for Slander*—1937

*prod co:* Victor Saville Productions, for London Film Productions; *prod:* Victor Saville; *assoc prod:* Stanley Haynes; *dir:* Tim Whelan; *scr:* Miles

Malleson, from the novel by Mary Borden; *add dial:* Ian Dalrymple; *ph:* Harry Stradling; *cam op:* D. Gallai-Hatchard; *des:* Vincent Korda and Frederick Pusey; *mus dir:* Muir Mathieson; *sup ed:* Jack Dennis; *ed:* Hugh Stewart; *prod man:* Dora Wright; *sound:* A. W. Watkins and Jack Rogerson; *cast:* Clive Brook (Major George Daviot), Ann Todd (Ann Daviot), Margaretta Scott (Josie Bradford), Arthur Margetson (Captain Bradford), Ronald Squire (Charles Cinderford), Athole Stewart (Lord Pontefract), Percy Marmont (William Cowbit), Frank Cellier (Sir Bernard Roper), Morton Selten (Judge Trotter), Gus McNaughton (Tandy), Francis L. Sullivan (Sir Quinton Jessops), Anthony Holles (Grant), Enid Stamp-Taylor (Jenny), Kate Cutler (Dowager), Felix Aylmer (Sir Eustace Cunningham), Lawrence Hanray (Clerk of the Court), Albert Whelan (Butler), Allan Jeayes (Colonel), Googie Withers (Mary); *dist:* United Artists; *rt:* 83 minutes; *GB rel:* 3 September 1937; *US rel:* 24 January 1938.

26. *Knight Without Armour*—1937

*prod co:* London Film Productions; *prod:* Alexander Korda; *dir:* Jacques Feyder; *asst dir:* Imlay Watts and Adam Dawson; *scr:* Lajos Biro and Arthur Wimperis, from Frances Marion's adaptation of the novel by James Hilton; *ph:* Harry Stradling; *asst ph:* Bernard Browne; *cam op:* Jack Cardiff; *spec effects:* Ned Mann; *des:* Lazare Meerson; *asst des:* Halfdan Waller; *mus:* Miklos Rozsa; *mus dir:* Muir Mathieson; *sup ed:* William Hornbeck; *ed:* Francis Lyon; *asst ed:* Eric Hodges; *cos:* Georges Benda; *assoc dial dir:* Maxwell Wray; *prod man:* David Cunynghame; *sound:* A. W. Watkins; *sound tech:* M. Paggi; *tech adviser:* Roman Goul and Col Zinovieff; *cast:* Marlene Dietrich (Alexandra Vladinoff), Robert Donat (Ainsley Fothergill), Irene Vanbrugh (Duchess of Zorin), Herbert Lomas (General Gregor Vladinoff), Austin Trevor (Colonel Adraxine), Basil Gill (Axelstein), John Clements (Poushkoff), Miles Malleson (Drunken Soldier), Hay Petrie (Station Master), David Tree (Alexis Maronin), Lyn Harding (Bargee), Frederick Culley (Stanfield) Lawrence Hanray (Forrester), Lisa d'Esterre (Czarina), Franklin Kelsey (Tomsky), Allan Jeayes and Raymond Huntley (White Officers), Lawrence Baskcomb (Commissar), Dorice Fordred (Maid); and Paul O'Brien; *dist:* United Artists; *rt:* 108 minutes; *GB ts:* 1 June 1937; *GB rel:* 8 October 1937; *US rel:* 23 July 1937.

27. *The Squeaker* [US: *Murder on Diamond Row*]—1937

*prod co:* Denham Productions; *prod:* Alexander Korda; *dir:* William K. Howard; *asst dir:* Wilfred O'Kelly; *scr:* Edward O. Berkman and Bryan Wallace, from the novel by Edgar Wallace; *ph:* Georges Périnal; *cam op:* Robert Krasker; *des:* Vincent Korda; *asst des:* Arthur Cornwall; *mus:* Miklos Rozsa; *mus dir:* Muir Mathieson; *sup ed:* Jack Dennis; *ed:* Russell Lloyd; *prod man:* David Cunynghame; *sound:* A. W. Watkins; *songs:* William Kernell and Edward O. Berkman; *cast:* Edmund Lowe (Inspector Barrabal), Sebastian Shaw (Frank Sutton), Ann Todd (Carol Stedman), Tamara Desni (Tamara), Robert Newton (Larry Graeme), Allan Jeayes (Inspector Elford), Alastair Sim (Joshua Collie), Stewart Rome (Supt Marshall), Mabel Terry-Lewis (Mrs Stedman), Gordon McLeod (Mr Field); *dist:* United Artists; *rt:* 77 minutes; *GB rel:* 6 November 1937; *US rel:* 10 December 1937.

28. *The Return of the Scarlet Pimpernel*—1937
    *prod co:* London Film Productions; *exec prod:* Alexander Korda; *prod:* Arnold Pressburger; *assoc prod:* Adrian Brunel; *dir:* Hans Schwartz; *asst dir:* Oswald Skilbeck; *scr:* Lajos Biro, Arthur Wimperis, and Adrian Brunel, from the novel by Baroness Orczy; *ph:* Mutz Greenbaum; *des:* Lazare Meerson; *mus:* Arthur Benjamin; *mus dir:* Muir Mathieson; *ed:* Philip Charlot; *asst ed:* John Guthrie; *sound:* Jack Rogerson; *cast:* Barry K. Barnes (Sir Percy Blakeney), Sophie Stewart (Marguerite Blakeney), Margaretta Scott (Theresa Cabarrus), James Mason (Jean Tallien), Francis Lister (Chauvelin), Anthony Bushell (Sir Andrew Ffoulkes), Patrick Barr (Lord Hastings), David Tree (Lord Denning), Henry Oscar (Robespierre), Hugh Miller (de Calmet), Allan Jeayes (Judge), O. B. Clarence (de Marre), George Merritt (Chief of Police), Evelyn Roberts (Prince of Wales), Esme Percy (Richard Sheridan), Edmund Breon (Colonel Winterbottom), Frank Allenby (Professor Wilkins), John Counsell (Sir John Selton), Torin Thatcher; *dist:* United Artists; *GB rt:* 94 minutes; *GB rel:* 20 December 1937; *US rt:* 88 minutes; *US rel:* 29 April 1938.

29. *Paradise for Two* [US: *The Gaiety Girls*]—1937
    *prod co:* Denham Productions; for London Film Productions; *prod:* Gunther Stapenhorst; *dir:* Thornton Freeland; *asst dir:* Donald Wilson; *scr:* Robert Stevenson and Arthur Macrae; *ph:* Gunther Krampf; *cam op:* Jack Asher; *des:* Vincent Korda and Shamoon Nadir; *mus:* Michael [Mischa] Spoliansky; *mus dir:* Muir Mathieson; *lyrics:* William Kernell; *sup ed:* William Hornbeck; *ed:* E. B. Jarvis; *cos:* René Hubert; *dance dir:* Jack Donohue and Philip Buchel; *unit man:* William Boyle; *sound:* A. W. Watkins; *cast:* Jack Hulbert (René Martin), Patricia Ellis (Jeanette), Arthur Riscoe (Jasques Thibaud), Googie Withers (Miki), Sydney Fairbrother (Miss Clare), Wylie Watson (Clarence), David Tree (Marcel), Cecil Bevan (Renaud), Anthony Holles (Brand), Roland Culver (Paul Duval), H. F. Maltby (Director), Finlay Currie (Creditor); *dist:* United Artists; *GB rt:* 77 minutes; *GB rel:* 22 December 1937; *US rt:* 73 minutes; *US rel:* 18 March 1938.

30. *The Divorce of Lady X*—1938
    *prod co:* London Film Productions; *prod:* Alexander Korda; *dir:* Tim Whelan; *asst dir:* Philip Brandon; *scr:* Ian Dalrymple and Arthur Wimperis, from Lajos Biro's adaptation of the play *Counsel's Opinion* by Gilbert Wakefield; *ph* (Technicolor: Harry Stradling; *cam op:* Jack Hildyard; *spec effects:* Ned Mann; *des:* Lazare Meerson; *asst des:* P. Sherriff and A. Waugh; *mus:* Miklos Rosza; *mus dir:* Muir Mathieson; *Technicolor dir:* Natalie Kalmus; *Technicolor ph adv:* William V. Skall; *sup ed:* William Hornbeck; *ed:* L. J. W. Stockviss; *cos:* René Hubert; *sound:* A. W. Watkins; *sound tech:* Charles Tasto; *prod man:* David Cunynghame; *unit man:* Wilfred O'Kelly; *cast:* Merle Oberon (Leslie), Laurence Olivier (Logan), Binnie Barnes (Lady Mere), Ralph Richardson (Lord Mere), Morton Selten (Lord Steele), J. H. Roberts (Slade), Gus McNaughton (Waiter), Gertrude Musgrove (Saunders), Hugh McDermott, H. B. Hallam (Jefferies), Eileen Peel (Mrs Johnson); *dist:* United Artists; *rt:* 92 minutes; *GB rel:* 15 January 1938; *US rel:* 15 April 1938. (Remake of the 1932 *Counsel's Opinion*, directed by Allan Dwan; see no. 4)

31. *The Drum* [US: *Drums*]—1938
    *prod co:* London Film Productions; *prod:* Alexander Korda; *dir:* Zoltan

Korda; *scr:* Arthur Wimperis, Patrick Kirwan, and Hugh Gray, from Lajos Biro's adaptation of the novel by A. E. W. Mason; *ph* (Technicolor): Georges Périnal; *ext ph:* Osmond Borradaile; *cam op:* Robert Krasker; *spec effects:* Edward Colman [Cohen]; *colour tech:* Christopher Challis and Geoffrey Unsworth; *Technicolor dir:* Natalie Kalmus; *des:* Vincent Korda and Ferdinand Bellan; *mus:* John Greenwood and Miklos Rozsa; *mus dir:* Muir Mathieson; *sup ed:* William Hornbeck; *ed:* Henry Cornelius; *asst ed:* Maurice Harley; *prod man:* David Cunynghame; *prod asst:* André de Toth; *sound:* A. W. Watkins; *tech adv:* Brigadier Hector Campbell and Lt. Col. F. D. Henslowe; *cast:* Sabu (Prince Azim), Raymond Massey (Prince Ghul), Valerie Hobson (Mrs Carruthers), Roger Livesey (Captain Carruthers), Desmond Tester (Bill Holder), Martin Walker (Herrick), David Tree (Lieutenant Escott), Francis L. Sullivan (Governor), Roy Emmerton (Wafadar), Edward Lexy (Sergeant-Major Kernel), Julien Mitchell (Sergeant), Amid Taftazani (Mohammed Khan), Archibald Batty (Major Bond), Frederick Culley (Dr Murphy), Charles Oliver (Rajab), Alf Goddard (Private Kelly), Ronald Adam (Major Gregoff), Lawrence Baskcomb (Zarrulah), Michael Martin Harvey (Mullah); *dist:* United Artists; *GB rt:* 104 minutes; *GB rel:* 9 April 1938; *US rt:* 96 minutes; *US rel:* 30 September 1938.

32. *South Riding*—1938

*prod co:* Victor Saville Productions, for London Film Productions; *pres:* Alexander Korda; *prod:* Victor Saville; *assoc prod:* Stanley Haynes; *dir:* Victor Saville; *scr:* Ian Dalrymple and Donald Bull, from the novel by Winifred Holtby; *ph:* Harry Stradling; *cam op:* D. Gallai-Hatchard; *spec effects:* Lawrence Butler and Edward Cohen; *des:* Lazare Meerson; *mus:* Richard Addinsell; *mus dir:* Muir Mathieson; *sup ed:* Jack Dennis; *ed:* Hugh Stewart; *prod man:* Dora Wright; *sound:* A. W. Watkins and Charles Tasto; *cast:* Edna Best (Sarah Burton), Ralph Richardson (Robert Carne), Edmund Gwenn (Alfred Huggins), Ann Todd (Madge Carne), John Clements (Astell), Marie Lohr (Mrs Beddows), Milton Rosmer (Alderman Snaith), Glynis Johns (Midge Carne), Joan Ellum (Lydia Holly), Herbert Lomas (Castle), Peggy Novak (Bessie Warbuckle), Gus McNaughton (Tedman), Lewis Casson (Lord Sedgmire), Felix Aylmer (Chairman of Council), Jean Cadell (Miss Dry), Skelton Knaggs (Reg Aythorne), Edward Lexy (Mr Holly), Josephine Wilson (Mrs Holly), Laura Smithson (Mrs Brimsley), Florence Grosson (Mrs Malton); *dist:* United Artists; *rt:* 91 minutes; *GB rel:* 28 April 1938; *US rel:* 1 July 1938.

33. *The Challenge*—1938

*prod co:* Denham Productions, for London Film Productions; *exec prod:* Alexander Korda; *prod:* Gunther Stapenhorst; *dir:* Milton Rosmer and Luis Trenker; *scr:* Emeric Pressburger, from a scenario by Patrick Kirwan and Milton Rosmer; *ph:* Georges Périnal and Albert Benitz; *cam op:* Robert Krasker; *des:* Vincent Korda and Frederick Pusey; *mus:* Allan Gray; *mus dir:* Muir Mathieson; *ed:* E. B. Jarvis; *sound:* A. W. Watkins; *cast:* Robert Douglas (Edward Whymper), Frank Birch (Rev. Charles Hudson), Geoffrey Wardell (Lord Francis Douglas), Moran Caplat (Hadow), Lyonel Watts (Morris), Luis Trenker (Jean Antoine Carrel), Mary Clare (His Mother), Fred Groves (Favre), Joan Gardner (Felicitas), Lawrence Baskcomb (The

Podestà), Ralph Truman (Giordano), Reginald Jarman (Minister Sella), Tony Sympson (Luc Meynet), Cyril Smith (Customs Officer), Lloyd Pearson (Seiler), Violet Howard (Mrs Seiler), Babita Soren (Mrs Croz), Luis Gerald (Croz), Max Holzboer (Elder Guide), Emeric Albert (Younger guide), Howard Douglas (Ropemaker), D. J. Williams, Bernard Miles, Tarva Penna (Peasants); *dist:* United Artists; *rt:* 75 minutes; *rel:* 14 May 1938.

34. *Prison Without Bars*—1938

*prod co:* London Film Productions; *exec prod:* Alexander Korda; *prod:* Arnold Pressburger; *assoc prod:* Irving Asher; *dir:* Brian Desmond Hurst; *scr:* Arthur Wimperis, from Hans Wilhelm's adaptation of the play *Prison sans Barreaux* by Gina Kaus, E. and O. Eis and Hilde Koveloff; *dial:* Margaret Kennedy; *ph:* Georges Périnal; *cam op:* Bernard Browne; *des:* Vincent Korda; *mus:* John Greenwood; *mus dir:* Muir Mathieson; *ed:* Charles Crichton; *asst ed:* John Guthrie; *prod asst:* Terence Young; *cast:* Corinne Luchaire (Susanne), Edna Best (Yvonne Chanel), Barry K. Barnes (Georges Maréchal), Mary Morris (Renée), Lorraine Clewes (Alice), Sally Wisher (Julie), Martita Hunt (Mme Appel), Margaret Yarde (Mme Artemise), Elsie Shelton (Mme Rémy), Glynis Johns (Nina), Phyllis Morris (Mlle Pauline), Nancy Roberts (Mlle, Dupont), Enid Lindsey (Mlle Renard); *dist:* United Artists; *rt:* 80 minutes; *GB rel:* 19 Sept 1938; *US rel:* 10 March 1939. (English remake of *Prison sans barreaux* (1933), directed by Léonide Moguy.)

35. *Q Planes* [US: *Clouds over Europe*]—1939

*prod co:* Harefield; *exec prod:* Alexander Korda; *prod:* Irving Asher; *dir:* Tim Whelan; *scr:* Ian Dalrymple, from a story by Brook Williams, Jack Whittingham and Arthur Wimperis; *ph:* Harry Stradling; *des:* Vincent Korda; *asst des:* Frederick Pusey; *mus dir:* Muir Mathieson; *sup ed:* William Hornbeck; *ed:* Hugh Stewart; *sound:* A. W. Watkins; *cast:* Laurence Olivier (Tony McVane), Ralph Richardson (Major Hammond), Valerie Hobson (Kay Hammond), George Curzon (Jenkins), George Merritt (Barrett), Gus McNaughton (Blenkinsop), David Tree (Mackenzie), Sandra Storme (Daphne), Hay Petrie (Stage Door Keeper), Frank Fox (Karl), George Butler (Air Marshall Gosport), Gordon McLeod (The Baron), John Longden (Peters), Reginald Purdell (Pilot), John Laurie (Editor), Pat Aherne (Officer); *dist:* Columbia; *GB rt:* 82 Minutes; *GB rel:* 2 March 1939; *US rt:* 79 minutes; *US rel:* 20 June 1939.

36. *The Four Feathers*—1939

*prod co:* London Film Productions; *prod:* Alexander Korda; *assoc prod:* Irving Asher; *dir:* Zoltan Korda; *scr:* R. C. Sherriff, from the novel by A. E. W. Mason; *add dial:* Lajos Biro and Arthur Wimperis; *ph* (Technicolor): Georges Périnal; *cam op:* Robert Krasker; *ext ph:* Osmond Borradaile and Jack Cardiff; *Technicolor dir:* Natalie Kalmus; *des:* Vincent Korda; *asst des:* Frederick Pusey and Ferdinand Bellan; *mus:* Miklos Rozsa; *mus dir:* Muir Mathieson; *sup ed:* William Hornbeck; *ed:* Henry Cornelius; *cos:* Godfrey Brennan and René Hubert; *prod man:* David Cunynghame; *prod asst:* André de Toth; *prod asst (Sudan):* Charles David; *second unit dir:* Geoffrey Boothby; *sound:* A. W. Watkins; *tech and military advisers:* Captain Donald Anderson and Lt-Col Stirling, DSO, MC; *cast:* John Clements (Harry Faversham), Ralph Richardson (Captain John Durrance), Sir C. Aubrey Smith (General Burroughs), June Duprez (Ethne Burroughs), Allan Jeayes (General Faversham), Jack Allen (Lt Willoughby), Donald Gray (Peter Burroughs), Frederick Culley (Dr Sutton), Amid Taftazani (Karaga Pasha), Henry Oscar (Dr Harraz), John Laurie (Khalifa), Robert Rendel (Colonel), Hal Walters (Joe), Clive Baxter (Harry as a child), Archibald Batty (Adjutant), Derek Elphinstone (Lt Parker), Norman Pierce (Sgt Brown); *dist:* United Artists; *rt:* 130 minutes; *GB rel:* 20 April 1939; *US rel:* 4 August 1939. (Remade as *Storm Over the Nile* in 1955; see no. 100.)

37. *The Rebel Son*—1939
*prod co:* Omnia, for London Film Productions; *prod:* E. C. Molinier and Charles David; *dir:* Alexis Granowsky and Adrian Brunel; *add dir:* Albert de Courville; *scr:* Adrian Brunel from a story by Nicholas Gogol; *ph:* Franz Planer and Bernard Browne; *sup ed:* William Hornbeck; *ed:* Pat Wooley and Lionel Hoare; *sound:* A. W. Watkins; *dial dir:* Jeffrey Dell; *cast:* Harry Baur (Tarass Boulba), Anthony Bushell (Andrew Boulba), Roger Livesey (Peter Boulba), Patricia Roc (Marina), Joan Gardner (Galka), Frederick Culley (Prince Zammitsky), Joseph Cunningham (Sachka), Stafford Hilliard (Stutterer), Bernard Miles (Polish Prisoner), Charles Farrell (Tovkatch), Ann Wemyss (Selima); *dist:* United Artists; *rt:* 80 minutes; *GB rel:* 28 July 1939; *US rel:* floating 1944. (Includes footage from Alexis Granowsky's 1936 French film *Tarass Boulba.*)

38. *The Spy in Black* [US: *U-Boat 29*]—1939
*prod co:* Harefield; *pres:* Alexander Korda; *prod:* Irving Asher; *dir:* Michael Powell; *scr:* Emeric Pressburger from Roland Pertwee's adaptation of a novel by J. Storer Clouston; *ph:* Bernard Browne; *sup des:* Vincent Korda; *des:* Frederick Pusey; *sup ed:* William Hornbeck; *ed:* Hugh Stewart; *asst ed:* John Guthrie; *mus:* Miklos Rozsa; *mus dir:* Muir Mathieson; *sound:* A. W. Watkins; *cast:* Conrad Veidt (Captain Hardt), Valerie Hobson (The Schoolmistress), Sebastian Shaw (Lt Ashington), Marius Goring (Lt Schuster), June Duprez (Anne Burnett), Athole Stewart (Rev. Hector Matthews), Agnes Langhlin (Mrs Matthews), Helen Haye (Mrs Sedley), Cyril Raymond (Rev. John Harris), Hay Petrie (Engineer), Grant Sutherland (Bob Bratt), Robert Rendel (Admiral), Mary Morris (Chauffeuse), George Summers (Captain Ratter), Margaret Moffatt (Kate), Kenneth Warrington (Cdr Denis), Torin Thatcher (Submarine Officer), and Bernard Miles, Esma Cannon, and Skelton Knaggs; *dist:* Columbia; *rt:* 82 minutes; *GB rel:* 12 August 1939; *US rel:* 7 October 1939.

39. *The Lion Has Wings*—1939
*prod co:* London Film Productions; *prod:* Alexander Korda; *assoc prod:* Ian Dalrymple; *dir:* Michael Powell, Brian Desmond Hurst, and Adrian Brunel; *scr:* Adrian Brunel and E. V. H. Emmett from a story by Ian Dalrymple; *ph:* Harry Stradling; *ext ph:* Osmond Borradaile; *cam op:* Bernard Browne; *des:* Vincent Korda; *sup ed:* William Hornbeck; *ed:* Henry Cornelius and Charles Frend; *mus:* Richard Addinsell; *mus dir:* Muir Mathieson; *sound:* A. W. Watkins; *tech adv:* Squadron Leader H. M. S. Wright; *prod man:* David Cunynghame; *cast:* Merle Oberon (Mrs Richardson), Ralph Richardson (WC Richardson), June Duprez (June), Robert Douglas (Briefing Officer), Anthony Bushell (Pilot), Derrick de Marney (Bill), Brian Worth (Bobby), Austin Trevor (Schulemburg), Ivan Brandt (Officer), G. H. Mulcaster

(Controller), Herbert Lomas (Holveg), Milton Rosmer (Head of Observer Corps), Robert Rendel (Chief of Air Staff), E. V. H. Emmett (Narrator), Lowell Thomas (Narrator US version), Archibald Batty (Air Officer), Ronald Adam, John Longden, Ian Fleming, Miles Malleson, Bernard Miles, Charles Carson, John Penrose, Frank Tickle, John Robinson, Carl Jaffe, Gerald Case, and Torin Thatcher; *dist:* United Artists; *rt:* 76 minutes; *GB rel:* 3 November 1939; *US rel:* 19 January 1940 (Includes footage from *Fire Over England;* see no. 19. Alexander Korda directed some sequences.

40. *Over the Moon*—1940
*prod co:* London Film Productions, Denham Productions; *prod:* Alexander Korda; *dir:* Thornton Freeland and William K. Howard; *scr:* Anthony Pelissier and Alec Coppel from a story by Robert E. Sherwood and Lajos Biro; *dial:* Arthur Wimperis; *ph* (Technicolor): Harry Stradling; *ext ph:* Robert Krasker; *des:* Vincent Korda; *ed:* Pat Wooley; *asst ed:* John Guthrie and Russell Lloyd; *cos:* René Hubert; *mus:* Mischa Spoliansky; *mus dir:* Muir Mathieson; *lyrics:* Desmond Carter; *sound:* A. W. Watkins; *cast:* Merle Oberon (June Benson), Rex Harrison (Dr Freddie Jarvis), Ursula Jeans (Lady Millie Parsmill), Robert Douglas (John Flight), Louis Borell (Count Pietro d'Altamura), Zena Dare (Julie Deethorpe), Peter Haddon (Lord Petcliffe), David Tree (Journalist), MacKenzie Ward (Lord Guy Carstairs), Carl Jaffe (Michel), Elizabeth Welch (Singer), Herbert Lomas (Ladbrooke), Wilfred Shine (Frude), Gerald Nodin (Cartwright), Bruce Winston, Lewis Gilbert, and Evelyn Ankers; *dist:* United Artists; *rt:* 78 minutes; *GB rel:* 19 February 1940; *US rel:* 29 March 1940; *shot:* 1937–38.

41. *Twenty-One Days* [US: *21 Days Together*]—1940
*prod co:* London Film Productions, Denham Productions; *prod:* Alexander Korda; *assoc prod & dir:* Basil Dean; *scr:* Graham Greene and Basil Dean from the play *The First and the Last* by John Galsworthy; *ph:* Jan Stallich; *des:* Vincent Korda; *asst des:* Frederick Pusey; *sup ed:* William Hornbeck; *ed:* Charles Crichton; *asst ed:* John Guthrie; *mus:* John Greenwood; *mus dir:* Muir Mathieson; *sound:* A. W. Watkins; *cast:* Vivien Leigh (Wanda), Laurence Olivier (Larry Durrant), Leslie Banks (Keith Durrant), Francis L. Sullivan (Mander), Hay Petrie (John Aloysius Evans), Esme Percy (Henry Walenn), Robert Newton (Tolly), Victor Rietti (Antonio), Morris Harvey (Alexander Macpherson), Meinhart Maur (Carl Grunlich), Lawrence Hanray (Solicitor), David Horne (Beavis), Wallace Lupino (Father), Muriel George (Mother), William Dewhurst (Lord Chief Justice), Frederick Lloyd (Swinton), Elliot Mason (Frau Grunlich), Arthur Young (Asher), Fred Groves (Barnes), and Aubrey Mallalieu (Magistrate); *working title: The First and the Last; dist:* Columbia; *rt:* 75 minutes; *GB rel:* 29 April 1940; *US rel:* 16 May 1940; *shot:* 1937. (Alex Korda directed one sequence.)

42. *Conquest of the Air*—1940
*prod co:* London Film Productions; *prod:* Alexander Korda; *assoc prod & tech adv:* Nigel Tangye; *dir:* [all uncredited] Zoltan Korda, Alexander Esway, Donald Taylor, Alexander Shaw, John Monk Saunders, William Cameron Menzies; *scr:* Hugh Gray and Peter Bezencenet, from stories by John Monk Saunders and St Exupery; *ph:* Wilkie Cooper, Hans Schneeberger, and George Noble; *des:* Vincent Korda and John Bryan; *ed:* Charles Frend and

Peter Bezencenet; *asst ed:* Adam Dawson; *mus:* Arthur Bliss; *mus dir:* Muir Mathieson; *sound:* A. W. Watkins; *prod sup:* John J. Croydon; *cast:* Charles Frend (Narrator), Laurence Olivier (Vincent Lunardi), Franklyn Dyall (Jerome de Ascoli), Henry Victor (Otto Lilienthal), Hay Petrie (Tiberius Cavallo), John Turnbull (Von Zeppelin), Charles Lefaux (Louis Blériot), Bryan Powley (Sir George Cayley), Frederick Culley (Roger Bacon), Alan Wheatley (Borelli), John Abott (De Rozier), Ben Webster (Leonardo da Vinci), Percy Marmont (Wilbur Wright), Dick Vernon (Simon the Magician), Denville Bond (Oliver the Monk), Charles Hickman (Orville Wright), Margaretta Scott (Isobella d'Este), David Horne and Michael Rennie; *dist:* United Artists; *rt:* 71 minutes; *GB ts:* 20 May 1940; *shot:* 1936–1938. (Lee Garmes (*ph*) and William Hornbeck (*ed*) worked on early filming. Leslie Mitchell recorded a commentary, perhaps for the 60-minute version edited by Richard Q. MacNaughten which was press-shown in 1938, but never released. In 1944, Key Films was distributing the film in a cut, 46-minute version.)

43. *The Thief of Bagdad*—1940
*prod co:* London Film Productions; *prod:* Alexander Korda; *assoc prod:* Zoltan Korda and William Cameron Menzies; *dir:* Ludwig Berger, Michael Powell, and Tim Whelan, and [uncredited] Zoltan Korda, William Cameron Menzies and Alexander Korda; *assoc dir:* Geoffrey Boothby and Charles David; *scr:* Lajos Biro; *screenplay and dial:* Miles Malleson; *ph* (Technicolor): Georges Périnal; *ext ph:* Osmond Borradaile; *cam op:* Robert Krasker; *spec effects:* Lawrence Butler and [uncredited] Tom Howard and Johnny Mills; *Technicolor dir:* Natalie Kalmus; *des:* Vincent Korda; *assoc des:* W. Percy Day, William Cameron Menzies, Frederick Pusey, and Ferdinand Bellan; *sup ed:* William Hornbeck; *ed:* Charles Crichton; *cos:* Oliver Messel, John Armstrong, and Marcel Vertes; *mus:* Miklos Rozsa; *mus dir:* Muir Mathieson; *sound:* A. W. Watkins; *prod man:* David Cunynghame; *prod asst:* André de Toth; *cast:* Conrad Veidt (Jaffar), Sabu (Abu), June Duprez (Princess), John Justin (Ahmad), Rex Ingram (Djinni), Miles Malleson (Sultan), Morton Selten (King), Mary Morris (Halima), Bruce Winston (Merchant), Hay Petrie (Astrologer), Roy Emmerton (Jailer), Allan Jeayes (Storyteller), and Adelaide Hall (Singer); *dist:* United Artists; *rt:* 106 minutes; *GB rel:* 25 December 1940; *US rel:* 25 December 1940; *prize:* Academy Awards for Color Cinematography, Color Art Direction, and Special Effects.

44. *Old Bill and Son*—1941
*prod co:* Legeran Films for London Film Productions; *prod:* Josef Somlo and Harold Boxall; *dir:* Ian Dalrymple; *assoc dir:* Geoffrey Boothby; *scr:* Bruce Bairnsfather and Ian Dalrymple from cartoons by Bruce Bairnsfather; *add dial:* Arthur Wimperis; *ph:* Georges Périnal; *des:* Vincent Korda; *ed:* Charles Crichton; *asst ed:* John Guthrie; *mus dir:* Muir Mathieson; *sound:* A. W. Watkins; *cast:* Morland Graham (Old Bill Busby), John Mills (Young Bill Busby), Mary Clare (Maggie Busby), Renee Houston (Stella Malloy), Rene Ray (Sally), Janine Darcey (Francoise), Roland Culver (Colonel), Gus McNaughton (Alf), Ronald Shiner (Bert), Manning Whiley (Chimp), Nicholas Phipps (Commentator), Donald Stuart (Canuck), Allan Jeayes (Willoughby), and Percy Walsh (Gustave); *dist:* General Film Distributors; *rt:* 96 minutes; *GB rel:* 3 March 1941.

# UNITED STATES (1941-42)

### 45. *Lydia*—1941

*prod co:* Alexander Korda Films, Inc.; *prod:* Alexander Korda; *assoc prod:* Lee Garmes; *dir:* Julien Duvivier; *asst dir:* Horace Hough; *scr:* Ben Hecht and Sam Hoffenstein; *story:* Julien Duvivier and L. Bush Fekete; *ph:* Lee Garmes; *spec effects:* Lawrence Butler; *des:* Vincent Korda; *assoc des:* Jack Okey and Julia Heron; *ed:* William Hornbeck; *cos:* Marcel Vertes and Walter Plunkett; *mus:* Miklos Rozsa; *sound:* William H. Wilmartin; *prod asst:* André de Toth; *prod man:* Walter Mayo; *cast:* Merle Oberon (Lydia MacMillan), Edna May Oliver (Granny), Alan Marshall (Richard), Joseph Cotten (Michael), Hans Yaray (Frank), George Reeves (Bob), John Halliday (Butler), Sara Allgood (Johnny's Mother), Billy Ray (Johnny), and Frank Conlan (Old Ned); *dist:* United Artists; *US rel:* 26 September 1941; *US rt:* 104 minutes; *GB rel:* 16 February 1942; *GB rt:* 98 minutes.

### 46. *To Be Or Not To Be*—1942

*prod co:* Romaine Film Productions; *pres:* Alexander Korda; *prod & dir:* Ernst Lubitsch; *asst dir:* William Tummel and William McGarry; *scr:* Edwin Justus Mayer; *story:* Ernst Lubitsch and Melchior Lengyel; *ph:* Rudolph Maté; *des:* Vincent Korda; *assoc des:* J. MacMillan Johnson and Julia Heron; *ed:* Dorothy Spencer; *cos:* Irene (Miss Lombard's costumes) and Walter Plunkett (others); *mus:* Miklos Rozsa; *mus dir:* Werner Heyman; *spec effects:* Lawrence Butler; *prod man:* Walter Mayo; *tech sup:* Richard Ordynski; *sound:* Frank Mahar; *cast:* Carole Lombard (Maria Tura), Jack Benny (Joseph Tura), Robert Stack (Lt Stanislav Sobinski), Felix Bressart (Greenberg), Lionel Atwill (Rawitch), Stanley Ridges (Prof. Siletzky), Sig Ruman (Col Ehrhardt), Tom Dugan (Bronski), Charles Halton (Producer Dobosh), George Lynn (Actor-Adjutant), Henry Victor (Capt. Schultz), Maude Eburne (Anna), Armand Wright (Makeup Man), Erno Verebes (Stage Manager), Halliwell Hobbes (General Armstrong), Miles Mander (Major Cunningham), Leslie Dennison (Captain), Frank Reicher (Polish Official), Peter Caldwell (William Kunze), Wolfgang Zilzer (Man in Bookstore), Olaf Hytten (Polonius in Warsaw), Charles Irwin (Reporter), Leland Hodgson (2nd Reporter), Alec Craig (Scotch Farmer), James Finlayson (2nd Scotch Farmer), Edgar Licho (Prompter), Robert O. Davis (Gestapo Sergeant), John Meredith (English Wireless Operator), Roland Varno (Pilot), Helmut Dantine and Otto Reichow (Co-Pilots), Maurice Murphy, Gene Rizzi, Paul Barrett, James Gillette, and John Kellogg (Polish RAF Flyers); *dist:* United Artists; *US rel:* 6 March 1942; *rt:* 99 minutes; *GB rel:* 3 May 1942

### 47. *Jungle Book*—1942

*prod co:* Alexander Korda Films, Inc.; *prod:* Alexander Korda; *dir:* Zoltan Korda; *second unit dir:* André de Toth; *asst dir:* Lowell Farrell; *scr:* Laurence Stallings from the stories by Rudyard Kipling; *ph* (Technicolor): Lee Garmes; *assoc ph:* W. Howard Greene; *spec effects:* Lawrence Butler; *prod designer:* Vincent Korda; *des:* Jack Okey, J. MacMillan Johnson and Julia Heron; *ed:* William Hornbeck; *mus:* Miklos Rozsa; *sound:* William H. Wilmartin; *prod man:* Walter Mayo; *Technicolor dir:* Natalie Kalmus; *prod asst:* Charles David; *cast:* Sabu (Mowgli), Joseph Calleia (Buldeo), John Qualen (The

Barber), Frank Puglia (The Pundit), Rosemary De Camp (Messua), Patricia O'Rourke (Mahala), Ralph Byrd (Durga), John Mather (Rao), Faith Brook (English Girl), and Noble Johnson (Sikh); *dist:* United Artists; *rt:* 109 minutes; *US rel:* 3 April 1942; *GB rel:* 5 June 1942.

## GREAT BRITAIN (1943–56)

48. *The Biter Bit*—1943
*prod co:* Coombe Productions; *prod:* Alexander Korda; *commentary:* Ralph Richardson; *rt:* 14 minutes. (A propaganda short made for the Ministry of Information presumably at the suggestion of Winston Churchill.)

49. *The Shop at Sly Corner*—1947
*prod co:* George King Productions for London Film Productions; *prod & dir:* George King; *scr:* Katherine Strueby, after the play by Edward Percy; *ph:* Hone Glendenning; *mus:* George Melachrino; *cast:* Oscar Homolka (Descius Heiss), Derek Farr (Robert Graham), Muriel Pavlow (Margaret Heiss), Manning Whiley (Corder Morris), Kenneth Griffith (Archie Fellowes), Diana Dors (Mildred), Garry Marsh (Major Elliot), and Kathleen Harrison, Jan Van Loewen, Irene Handl, and Johnnie Schofield; *GB dist:* British Lion; *GB rel:* 10 March 1947; *rt:* 91 minutes.

50. *A Man about the House*—1947
*prod co:* British Lion Productions for London Film Productions; *prod:* Edward Black; *dir:* Leslie Arliss; *asst dir:* Vincent Permane; *scr:* Leslie Arliss and J. B. Williams from the novel by Francis Brett Young and play by John Perry; *ph:* Georges Périnal; *cam op:* Tony Day; *des:* Andre Andrejew; *ed:* Russell Lloyd; *cos:* G. K. Benda; *mus:* Nicholas Brodsky; *mus dir:* Philip Green; *cast:* Margaret Johnston (Agnes Isit), Dulcie Gray (Ellen Isit), Kieron Moore (Salvatore), Guy Middleton (Sir Benjamin Dench), Felix Aylmer (Richard Sanctuary), Lilian Braithwaite (Mrs Armitage), Jane Salinas (Maria), Maria Fimiani (Assunta), Reginald Purdell (Higgs), Fulvia de Priamo (Gita), Nicola Esposito (Antonina), Wilfred Caithness (Solicitor), Victor Rietti and Andrea Malandrinos (Peasants); *GB dist:* British Lion; *GB rel:* 3 October 1947; *GB rt:* 99 minutes; *US dist:* 20th Century-Fox; *US rel:* October 1947; *US rt:* 93 minutes.

51. *Mine Own Executioner*—1947
*prod co:* Harefield Productions for London Film Productions; *pres:* Alexander Korda; *prod:* Anthony Kimmins and Jack Kitchin; *dir:* Anthony Kimmins; *asst dir:* William Kirby; *scr:* Nigel Balchin from his novel; *ph:* Wilkie Cooper; *cam op:* Freddie Francis; *spec effects:* Percy Day; *des:* William C. Andrews; *ed:* Richard Best; *cos:* Alan Haines; *mus:* Benjamin Frankel; *mus dir:* Dr Hubert Clifford; *cast:* Burgess Meredith (Felix Milne), Dulcie Gray (Patricia Milne), Kieron Moore (Adam Lucian), Barbara White (Molly Lucian), Christine Norden (Barbara Edge), John Laurie (Dr James Garsten), Michael Shepley (Peter Edge), Lawrence Hanray (Dr Lefage), Walter Fitzgerald (Dr Norris Pile), Martin Miller (Dr Hans Tautz), Jack Raine (Inspector Pierce), Helen Haye (Lady Maresfield), John Stuart (Dr John Hayling), Edgar Norfolk (Sir George Freethorne), Clive Morton (Robert Paston), Joss Ambler (Julian Briant), Ronald Simpson (Mr Grandison), Gwynne Whitby

(Miss English), and Malcolm Dalmayne (Charlie Oakes); *GB dist:* British Lion; *GB rel:* 22 November 1947; *GB rt:* 108 minutes; *US dist:* 20th Century-Fox; *US rel:* 12 July 1948; *US rt:* 103 minutes.

52. *Night Beat*—1948
*prod co:* British Lion Productions for London Film Productions; *pres:* Alexander Korda; *prod & dir:* Harold Huth; *asst dir:* John Bremer; *scr:* J. J. Morrison from a story by Guy Morgan with additional material by Roland Pertwee; *ph:* Vacklav Vich; *des:* Ferdinand Bellan; *ed:* Grace Garland; *mus:* Benjamin Frankel; *mus dir:* Dr Hubert Clifford; *cast:* Anne Crawford (Julie Kendall), Maxwell Reed (Felix Fenton), Ronald Howard (Andy Kendall), Christine Norden (Jackie), Hector Ross (Don Brady), Fred Groves (PC Kendall), Sidney James (Nixon), Nicholas Stuart (Rocky), Frederick Leister (Magistrate), and Michael Medwin (Spider); *dist:* British Lion; *rt:* 91 minutes; *GB rel:* 15 January 1948; *working title: West End Central.*

53. *Anna Karenina*—1948
*prod co:* London Film Productions; *prod:* Alexander Korda; *assoc prod:* Herbert Mason; *dir:* Julien Duvivier; *asst dir:* Mickey Delamar; *scr:* Julien Duvivier, Guy Morgan and Jean Anouilh from Tolstoy's novel; *ph:* Henri Alekan; *cam op:* Robert Walker; *spec effects:* W. Percy Day and Cliff Richardson; *des:* Andre Andrejew; *ed:* Russell Lloyd; *cos:* Cecil Beaton; *mus:* Constant Lambert; *mus dir:* Dr Hubert Clifford; *sound:* John Cox; *cast:* Vivien Leigh (Anna Karenina), Ralph Richardson (Alexei Karenin), Kieron Moore (Count Vronsky), Sally Ann Howes (Kitty Scherbatsky), Niall MacGinnis (Levin), Martita Hunt (Princess Betty Tversky), Marie Lohr (Princess Scherbatsky), Michael Gough (Nicholai), Hugh Dempster (Stefan Oblonsky), Mary Kerridge (Dolly Oblonsky), Heather Thatcher (Countess Lydia Ivanova), Helen Haye (Countess Vronsky), Austin Trevor (Colonel Vronsky), Ruby Miller (Countess Meskov), John Longden (General Serpuhousky), Leslie Bradley (Korsunsky), Michael Medwin (Doctor), Jeremy Spenser (Giuseppe), Gino Cervi (Enrico), Frank Tickle (Prince Scherbatsky), Mary Martlew (Princess Nathalia), Ann South (Princess Sorokina), Guy Verney (Prince Makhotin), Beckett Bould (Matvey), Judith Nelmes (Miss Hull), Valentina Murch (Annushka), Theresa Giehse (Marietta), John Salew (Lawyer), and Patrick Skipwith (Sergei); *GB dist:* British Lion; *GB rel:* 22 January 1948; *GB rt:* 123 minutes; *US dist:* 20th Century-Fox; *US rel:* 1 May 1948; *US rt:* 110 minutes.

54. *The Winslow Boy*—1948
*prod co:* Anatole de Grunwald Productions for London Film Productions; *prod:* Anatole de Grunwald; *assoc prod:* Teddy Baird; *dir:* Anthony Asquith; *asst dir:* Pat Jenkins; *scr:* Anthony Asquith, Terence Rattigan, and Anatole de Grunwald from the play by Terence Rattigan; *ph:* Freddie Young and Osmond Borradaile; *cam op:* John Wilcox; *des:* Andre Andrejew; *ed:* Gerald Turney-Smith; *cos:* William Chappell; *mus:* William Alwyn; *mus dir:* Dr Hubert Clifford; *cast:* Robert Donat (Sir Robert Morton), Margaret Leighton (Catherine Winslow), Cedric Hardwicke (Arthur Winslow), Basil Radford (Esmond Curry), Kathleen Harrison (Violet), Francis L. Sullivan (Attorney General), Marie Lohr (Grace Winslow), Jack Watling (Dickie Winslow), Frank Lawton (John Watherstone), Neil North (Ronnie

Winslow), Walter Fitzgerald (First Lord), Wilfrid Hyde-White (Wilkinson),
P. Knyaston Reeves (Lord Chief Justice), Ernest Thesiger (Mr Ridgeley-
Pearce), Lewis Casson (Admiral Springfield), Stanley Holloway and Cyril
Richard (Comedians), Nicholas Hannen (Colonel Watherstone), Evelyn
Roberts (Hamilton), Billy Shine (Fred), Anthony Bird (First Lord's P.P.S.),
Barry Briggs (Sir Robert's P.P.S.), Cecil Bevan (Speaker), Wilfred Caithness
(Minister), Lambert Enson (Mr Williams), Hugh Dempster (Agricultural
Member), Philip Ray (First Speaking Member), Archibald Batty, Edward
Lexy, and Gordon McLeod (Elderly Members), W. A. Kelley (Brian
O'Rourke), George Bishop (Usher), Charles Groves (Clerk of the Court),
Ian Colin (Mr Saunders), Ivan Samson (Commander Flower), Dandy
Nichols (Miss Hawkins), Vera Cook (Violet's Friend), Jane Gill Davies
(Mrs Curry), Frank Tickle (Mr Gunn), Honor Blake (Edwina Gunn),
Margaret Withers (Mrs Jordan), Noel Howlett (Mr Williams), Aubrey
Mallalieu (Mr Roberts), Mary Hinton (Mrs Elliott), Nicholas Hawtrey
(Charles Elliott, Jnr), Beatrice Marsden (Cook), Hilary Pritchard (Dr
Anstruther), Mona Washbourne (Miss Barnes); *GB dist:* British Lion; *GB
rel:* 24 September 1948; *GB rt:* 117 minutes; *US dist:* Eagle Lion; *US rel:*
11 May 1950; *US rt:* 97 minutes.

55. *The Fallen Idol—1948*
*prod co:* London Film Productions; *pres:* David O. Selznick and Alexander
Korda; *prod:* David O. Selznick and Carol Reed; *assoc prod:* Phil Brandon;
*dir:* Carol Reed; *asst dir:* Guy Hamilton; *scr:* Graham Greene from his story
'The Basement Room'; *add dial:* Lesley Storm and William Templeton;
*ph:* Georges Périnal; *cam op:* Denys Coop; *spec effects:* W. Percy Day; *des:*
Vincent Korda and James Sawyer; *asst des:* John Hawkesworth; *ed:* Oswald
Hafenrichter; *mus:* William Alwyn; *mus dir:* Dr Hubert Clifford; *sound:*
John Cox; *prod man:* Hugh Perceval; *cast:* Ralph Richardson (Baines),
Michele Morgan (Julie), Sonia Dresdel (Mrs Baines), Bobby Henrey (Felipe),
Dennis O'Dea (Inspector Crowe), Jack Hawkins (Detective Ames), Dora
Bryan (Rose), Walter Fitzgerald (Dr Fenton), Bernard Lee (Detective Hart),
Karel Stepanek (Secretary), Joan Young (Mrs Barrow), Geoffrey Keen
(Detective Davis), James Hayter (Perry), Hay Petrie (Clockwinder), John
Ruddock (Dr Wilson), Torin Thatcher (Policeman 'A'), George Woodbridge
(Police Sergeant), Dandy Nichols (Mrs Patterson), Gerard Heinz (Ambas-
sador), Nora Gordon (Waitress), Ethel Coleridge (Housekeeper), Ralph
Norman and James Swan (Policemen); *GB dist:* British Lion; *GB rel:* 30
September 1948; *rt:* 95 minutes; *US dist:* Selznick Releasing Organization;
*US rel:* 15 September 1949; *prize:* British Film Academy, Best British Film
(1948); *working title: The Lost Illusion.*

56. *Bonnie Prince Charlie—1948*
*prod co:* London Film Productions; *pres:* Alexander Korda; *prod:* Edward
Black; *dir:* Anthony Kimmins; *asst dir:* Bluey Hill; *scr:* Clemence Dane;
*ph* (Technicolor): Robert Krasker; *assoc ph:* Hone Glendinning; *ext ph:*
Osmond Borradaile; *cam op:* Ted Scaife; *des:* Vincent Korda, Wilfred
Shingleton, and Joseph Bato; *ed:* Grace Garland; *mus:* Ian Whyte; *mus dir:*
Dr Hubert Clifford; *cast:* David Niven (Bonnie Prince Charlie), Margaret
Leighton (Flora MacDonald), Judy Campbell (Clementine Walkinshaw),

Jack Hawkins (Lord George Murray), Morland Graham (Donald), Finlay Currie (Marquis of Tullibardine), Elwyn Brook-Jones (Duke of Cumberland), John Laurie (Blind Jamie), Hector Ross (Glenalandale), Hugh Kelly (Lt Ingleby), Charles Goldner (Captain Ferguson), Henry Oscar (James II), Martin Miller (George II), Franklyn Dyall (Macdonald), Herbert Lomas (Kinloch Moidart), Ronald Adam (Macloed), John Longden (Capt. O'Sullivan), James Hayter (Kingsburgh), Julien Mitchell (General Cope), Guy Lefeuve (Cameron of Lochiel), Stuart Lindsdell (MacDonald of Apridale), Simon Luck (Young Alan of Moidart), Tommy Duggan (Clanranald), G. H. Mulcaster (Duke of Newcastle), Kenneth Warrington (Staff Officer), Nell Ballantyne (Mrs Kingsburgh), Patricia Fox (Annie Kingsburgh), Molly Rankin (Lady Margaret MacDonald), John Rae (Duncan), Lola Duncan (Effie), John Forrest (Neil), Jane Gill Davies (Lady Graham), Louise Gainsborough (Madame d'Epoiles), Edward Lexy (Lachlan), Bruce Seton (Allan Macrae), Anthony Holles (Colonel Warren), Mark Daly (Ian MacQueen), Jean Stuart (Elspeth Patterson), Blanche Fothergill (Mary MacQueen), Margaret Gibson (Mysie), Alan Judd (Stewart of Ardshiel), Fred Hearn (Aeneas MacDonald), Bill Allison (Sir Francis Strickland), Charles Cullum (Sir John MacDonald), Norman Maitland (John Murray), and Harry Schofield (Rev. George Kelly); *GB dist:* British Lion; *GB rel:* 26 October 1948; *rt:* 136 minutes; *US dist:* Snader Productions; *US rel:* 29 January 1952. (Alex Korda directed some sequences of this film, prior to the hiring of Anthony Kimmins.)

57. *The Small Back Room*—1949

*prod co:* The Archers for London Film Productions; *prod:* Michael Powell and Emeric Pressburger; *dir:* Michael Powell and Emeric Pressburger; *asst dir:* Sydney Streeter; *scr:* Michael Powell, Emeric Pressburger, and Nigel Balchin from a novel by Nigel Balchin; *ph:* Christopher Challis; *cam op:* Freddie Francis; *prod designer:* Hein Heckroth; *des:* John Hoesli; *ed:* Reginald Mills and Clifford Turner; *mus:* Brian Easdale; *sound:* Alan Allen; *night club scene music:* Ted Heath's Kenny Baker Swing Group and Fred Lewis; *cast:* David Farrar (Sammy Rice), Kathleen Byron (Susan), Jack Hawkins (R. B. Waring), Leslie Banks (Colonel Holland), Cyril Cusack (Corporal Taylor), Robert Morley (Minister), Emrys Jones (Joe), Renee Asherson (ATS Corporal), Walter Fitzgerald (Brine), Anthony Bushell (Colonel Strang), Milton Rosmer (Professor Mair), Michael Gough (Captain Stewart), Michael Goodliffe (Till), Henry Caine (Sgt-Major Rose), James Dale (Brigadier), Sam Kydd (Crowhurst), Elwyn Brook-Jones (Gladwin), June Elvin (Gillian), David Hutcheson (Norval), Sidney James (Knucksie), Roderick Lovell (Pearson), James Carney (Sergeant Graves), Roddy Hughes (Welsh Doctor), Geoffrey Keen (Pinker), Bryan Forbes (Dying Gunner); *GB dist:* British Lion; *GB rel:* 21 February 1949; *rt:* 108 minutes; *US dist:* Snader Productions; *US rel:* 23 February 1952.

58. *That Dangerous Age* [US: *If This Be Sin*]—1949

*prod co:* London Film Productions; *prod & dir:* Gregory Ratoff; *assoc prod:* Phil Brandon; *asst dir:* John Moxey; *scr:* Gene Markey from Margaret Kennedy's adaptation of Ilya Surgutchoff's play *Autumn*; *ph:* Georges Périnal; *ext ph:* Anchise Bizzi; *cam op:* Denys Coop; *des:* Andre Andrejew; *ed:* Gerald Turney-Smith; *mus:* Mischa Spoliansky; *mus dir:* Dr Hubert Clifford; *cast:*

Myrna Loy (Lady Cathy Brooke), Roger Livesey (Sir Brian Brooke), Peggy Cummins (Monica Brooke), Richard Greene (Michael Barclaigh), Elizabeth Allan (Lady Sybil), Gerard Heinz (Dr Thorvald), Jean Cadell (Nannie), G. H. Mulcaster (Simmons), Margaret Withers (May Drummond), Robert Atkins (George Drummond), Barry Jones (Arnold Cane), George Curzon (Selby), Wilfrid Hyde-White (Mr Potts), Phyllis Stanley (Jane), Ronald Adam (Prosecutor), Henry Caine (Mr Nyburg), Patrick Waddington (Risley), Edith Sharpe (Angela Cane), Daphne Arthur (Margot), Martin Case (John), Louise Lord (Ellen), Nicholas Bruce (Charles), William Mervyn (Nicky); *GB dist:* British Lion; *GB rel:* 13 April 1949; *GB rt:* 98 minutes; *US dist:* United Artists; *US rel:* 8 September 1950; *US rt:* 72 minutes.

59. *The Last Days of Dolwyn* [US: *Woman of Dolwyn*]—1949

*prod co:* London Film Productions; *prod:* Anatole de Grunwald; *assoc prod:* Teddy Baird; *dir & scr:* Emlyn Williams; *assoc dir:* Russell Lloyd; *ph:* Otto Heller; *cam op:* Gus Drisse; *des:* Wilfred Shingleton; *ed:* Maurice Rootes; *cos:* Michael Weight; *mus:* John Greenwood; *cast:* Dame Edith Evans (Merri), Emlyn Williams (Rob), Richard Burton (Gareth), Anthony James (Dafydd), Barbara Couper (Lady Dolwyn), Alan Aynesworth (Lord Lancashire), Andrea Lea (Margaret), Hugh Griffith (Minister), Roddy Hughes (Caradoc), David Davies (Septimus), Edward Rees (Gruffyd), Tom Jones (John Henry), Sam Hinton (Idris), Prysor Williams (Old Tal), Kenneth Evans (Jabbez), Maurice Browning (Huw), Pat Glyn (Dorcas), Joan Griffiths (Eira), Betty Stanley (Nurse Pugh), Dudley Jones (Hughes), Aubrey Richards (Ellis), Madoline Thomas (Mrs Thomas), Dorothy Langley (Lizzie), Doreen Richards (Mrs Septimus), Bryan V. Thomas (Alwyn), Frank Dunlop (Ephrain), Daffyd Howard (Will), Eileen Dale (Mrs Ellis), Betty Humphries (Mrs John Henry), Rita Crailey (Hen Ann), Emrys Leyshon (Watkins), Constance Lewis (Mrs Richards), and Hywel Wood (Hywel); *GB dist:* British Lion; *GB rel:* 18 July 1949; *rt:* 95 minutes; *US dist:* Lopert Films; *US rel:* floating 1949.

60. *Saints and Sinners*—1949

*prod co:* London Film Productions; *prod & dir:* Leslie Arliss; *assoc prod:* Tom Connachie; *asst dir:* Bluey Hill; *scr:* Leslie Arliss and Paul Vincent Carroll; *add dial:* Mabbie Poole; *ph:* Osmond Borradaile; *cam op:* L. B. Young; *des:* Wilfred Shingleton; *ed:* David Newhouse; *cos:* Honoria Plesch; *mus:* Philip Green; *mus dir:* Dr Hubert Clifford; *cast:* Kieron Moore (Michael Kissane), Christine Norden (Blanche), Sheila Manahan (Sheila Flaherty), Michael Dolan (Canon), Maire O'Neill (Ma Murnaghan), Tom Dillon (O'Brien), Noel Purcell (Flaherty), Pamela Arliss (Betty), Tony Quinn (Berry), Eddie Byrne (Morreys), Liam Redmond (O'Driscoll), Eric Gorman (Madigan), Cecilia McKevitt (Maeve), Austin Meldon (Auctioneer), Minnie McKittrick (Brigid Madden), Godfrey Quigley (Colin), Edward Byrne (Barney Downey), Sheila Ward (Clothing Woman), Joe Kennedy (Guard), Dave Crowley (Barman), Vincent Ellis (Paddy), Gabrielle Daye (Maeve's Mother), Harry Hutchinson (Doctor), James Neylin, Sam Kydd, Glenville Darling, and Vic Hagan (Men in Bar), Maurice Keary (Flaherty's Hotel Barman), and Maureen Delaney (Postmistress); *GB dist:* British Lion; *GB rel:* 15 August 1949; *rt:* 85 minutes; *US dist:* Lopert Films; *US rel:* floating 1949.

61. *The Third Man*—1949
*prod co:* London Film Productions; *pres:* David O. Selznick and Alexander Korda; *prod & dir:* Carol Reed; *assoc prod:* Hugh Perceval; *asst dir:* Guy Hamilton; *scr:* Graham Greene; *ph:* Robert Krasker; *add ph:* John Wilcox and Stan Pavey; *cam op:* Denys Coop and Ted Scaife; *des:* Vincent Korda, Joseph Bato, and John Hawkesworth; *assoc des:* Ferdinand Bellan and James Sawyer; *ed:* Oswald Hafenrichter; *mus:* Anton Karas; *sound:* John Cox; *sound rec:* Bert Ross and Red Law; *cont:* Peggy McClafferty; *cast:* Joseph Cotten (Holly Martins), Orson Welles (Harry Lime), Alida Valli (Anna Schmidt), Trevor Howard (Major Calloway), Paul Hoerbiger (Porter), Ernst Deutsch (Baron Kurtz), Erich Ponto (Dr Winkel), Siegfried Breuer (Popescu), Bernard Lee (Sergeant Paine), Geoffrey Keen (British Policeman), Hedwig Bleibtreu (Anna's 'Old Woman'), Annie Rosar (Porter's Wife), Harbut Helbek (Hansl), Alexis Chesnakov (Brodsky), Wilfrid Hyde-White (Crabbin), Paul Hardtmuth (Hall Porter), and Eric Pohlmann; *GB dist:* British Lion; *GB rel:* 3 September 1949; *rt:* 104 minutes; *US dist:* Selznick Releasing Organization; *US rel:* 4 February 1950; *prizes:* Academy Award for Black and White Cinematography, British Film Academy Award for Best British Film of 1949, Cannes Grand Prix 1949.

62. *The Cure for Love*—1950
*prod co:* Island Productions, London Film Productions; *exec prod:* Albert Fennell; *prod & dir:* Robert Donat; *asst dir:* D. Johnson; *scr:* Robert Donat, Alexander Shaw, and Albert Fennell from the play by Walter Greenwood; *add dial:* Walter Greenwood; *ph:* Jack Cox; *cam op:* H. Gillam; *des:* Wilfred Shingleton; *ed:* Bert Bates; *mus:* William Alwyn; *mus dir:* Muir Mathieson; *cast:* Robert Donat (Jack Hardacre), Renee Asherson (Milly), Marjorie Rhodes (Mrs Hardacre), Charles Victor (Henry), Dora Bryan (Jenny Jenkins), Thora Hird (Mrs Dorbell), Gladys Henson (Mrs Jenkins), John Stratton (Sam), Francis Wignall (Claude), Norman Partridge (Vicar), Edna Morris (Mrs Harrison), Michael Dear (Albert), Tonie MacMillan (Mrs Donald), Lilian Stanley (Mrs Small), Margot Bryant (Mrs Hooley), Lucille Gray (Tough Girl), Jack Howarth (Hunter), Sam Kydd (Charlie Fox), Jack Rodney (Eddie), Reginald Green (Douglas), Johnnie Catcher (Canadian Soldier), and Jan Conrad (Polish Soldier); *GB dist:* British Lion; *GB rel:* 6 February 1950; *rt:* 98 minutes; *US dist:* Associated Artists; *US rel:* November 1955.

63. *The Happiest Days of Your Life*—1950
*prod co:* Individual Productions; *prod:* Frank Launder and Sidney Gilliat; *dir:* Frank Launder; *scr:* Frank Launder and John Dighton from a play by John Dighton; *ph:* Stan Pavey; *des:* Joseph Bato; *ed:* Oswald Hafenrichter; *mus:* Mischa Spoliansky; *cast:* Margaret Rutherford (Miss Whitchurch), Alastair Sim (Wetherby Pond), Joyce Grenfell (Miss Gossage), Edward Rigby (Rainbow), Guy Middleton (Victor Hyde-Brown), John Bentley (Richard Tassell), Bernadette O'Farrell (Miss Harper), Muriel Aked (Miss Jezzard), John Turnbull (Conrad Matthews), Richard Wattis (Arnold Billings), Arthur Howard (Anthony Ramsden), Millicent Wolf (Miss Curtis), Myrette Morven (Miss Chappell), Russell Waters (Mr West), and John Boxer; *GB dist:* British Lion; *GB rel:* 8 March 1950; *rt:* 81 minutes; *US dist:* Pacemaker Pictures; *US rel:* floating 1952.

64. *The Angel with the Trumpet*—1950
   *prod co:* London Film Productions; *prod:* Karl Hartl; *dir:* Anthony Bushell; *asst dir:* Guy Hamilton; *scr:* Karl Hartl, Franz Tassie and Clemence Dane from the novel *Der Engel mit der Posaune* by Ernst Lothar; *ph:* Robert Krasker; *des:* Andre Andrejew; *ed:* Reginald Beck; *cos:* Roger Furze; *mus:* Willy Schmidt-Gentner; *cast:* Eileen Herlie (Henrietta Stein), Norman Wooland (Prince Rudolf), Basil Sydney (Francis Alt), Maria Schell (Anna Linden), Olga Edwardes (Monica Alt), John Justin (Paul Alt), Andrew Cruickshank (Otto Alt), Oskar Werner (Herman Alt), Anthony Bushell (Baron Hugo Traun), Wilfrid Hyde-White (Simmerl), Campbell Cotts (General Paskiewicz), Dorothy Batley (Pauline Drauffer), John Van Eyssen (Albert Drauffer), Jane Henderson (Gretel Paskiewicz), Jill Gibbs (Monica Alt as a child), Brian Crown (Paul Alt as a child), Allan Woolston (Herman Alt as a child), John Corbett (Francis Alt II), Titia Brookes (Henrietta Alt II), Anton Edthofer (Emperor Franz Joseph), Alfred Neugebauer (Magistrate), Joan Schofield (Governess), Meadows White (Czerny), Jack Faint (Hausmann), David Davies (Nazi Leader), Nigel Neilson and Derrick Penley (Nazis), Olive Gregg (Flower Shop Assistant), and Marc Anthony ('Freddie'); *GB dist:* British Lion; *GB rel:* 20 March 1950; *rt:* 98 minutes; *US dist:* Snader Productions; *US rel:* floating 1952. (English-language remake of Karl Hartl's *Der Engel mit der Posaune* 1948.)
65. *The Bridge of Time*—1950
   *prod co:* London Film Productions; *dir:* David Eady and Geoffrey Boothby; *scr:* David Eady and Geoffrey Boothby; *ph:* Georges Périnal; *mus:* Dr Hubert Clifford; *narrator:* Anthony Bushell; *dist:* British Lion; *rt:* 15 minutes; *GB rel:* 12 June 1950. (A documentary.)
66. *My Daughter Joy* [US: *Operation X*]—1950
   *prod co:* London Film Productions; *prod:* & *dir:* Gregory Ratoff; *assoc prod:* Phil Brandon; *asst dir:* Cliff Brandon; *scr:* Robert Theoren and William Rose from the novel *David Golder* by Irene Nemirowsky; *ph:* Georges Périnal; *ext ph:* Andre Bac; *cam op:* Denys Coop; *des:* Andre Andrejew; *ed:* Ray Poulton; *mus:* R. Gallois-Montbrun; *mus dir:* Dr Hubert Clifford; *cast:* Edward G. Robinson (George Constantin), Peggy Cummins (Georgette Constantin), Richard Greene (Larry), Nora Swinburne (Ava Constantin), Walter Rilla (Andrews), Finlay Currie (Sir Thomas MacTavish), James Robertson Justice (Professor Keval), Ronald Adam (Colonel Fogarty), David Hutcheson (Annix), Peter Illing (Sultan), Ronald Ward (Dr Schindler), Don Nehan (Polato), Roberto Villa (Prince Alzar), and Harry Lane (Barboza); *GB dist:* British Lion; *GB rel:* 21 August 1950; *GB rt:* 81 minutes; *US dist:* Columbia; *US rel:* February 1951; *US rt:* 79 minutes.
67. *State Secret* [US: *The Great Manhunt*]—1950
   *prod co:* London Film Productions; *prod:* Frank Launder and Sidney Gilliat; *dir:* Sidney Gilliat; *asst dir:* Guy Hamilton; *scr:* Sidney Gilliat from Roy Huggins's novel *Appointment with Fear; ph:* Robert Krasker and John Wilcox; *cam op:* Ted Scaife; *des:* Wilfred Shingleton; *ed:* Thelma Myers; *mus:* William Alwyn; *mus dir:* Muir Mathieson; *cast:* Douglas Fairbanks, Jnr (Dr John Marlowe), Glynis Johns (Lisa), Jack Hawkins (Colonel Galcon), Herbert Lom (Karl Theodor), Walter Rilla (General Niva), Karel Stepanek

(Dr Revo), Carl Jaffe (Janovik Prada), Gerard Heinz (Bendel), Hans Moser (Sigrist), Gerik Schjelderup (Bartorek), Guido Lorraine (Lt Prachi), Anton Diffring (Policeman), Peter Illing (Macco), Olga Lowe (Baba), Therese Van Kye (Theresa), Leonard Sachs (Dr Poldoi), Robert Ayres (Buckman), Martin Boddey, Russell Waters, Howard Douglas, and Arthur Howard (Clubmen), Leslie Linder (Andre), Leo Bieber (Man at Phone), Nelly Arno (Shop Assistant), Paul Demel (Barber), Arthur Reynolds (Compere), Richard Molinas (Red Nose), Eric Pohlmann (Cable-Car Conductor), Louis Wiechert (Christian), Henrik Jacobsen (Mountain Soldier); *GB dist:* British Lion; *GB rel:* 11 September 1950; *GB rt:* 104 minutes; *US dist:* Columbia; *US rel:* December 1950; *US rt:* 97 minutes.

68. *The Wooden Horse*—1950

*prod co:* Wessex Productions; *prod:* Ian Dalrymple; *dir:* Jack Lee; *asst dir:* Phil Shipway; *scr:* Eric Williams from his book; *ph:* G. Pennington-Richards; *cam op:* Robert Day; *des:* William Kellner; *ed:* John Seabourne; *mus:* Clifton Parker; *mus dir:* Muir Mathieson; *cast:* Leo Genn (Peter), David Tomlinson (Phil), Anthony Steel (John), David Greene (Bennett), Peter Burton (Nigel), Patrick Waddington (C.O.), Michael Goodliffe (Robbie), Anthony Dawson (Pomfret), Bryan Forbes (Paul), Franz Schaftheitlin (Commandant), Hans Meyer (Charles), Jacques Brunius (Andre), Peter Finch (The Australian), Dan Cunningham (David), Russell Waters ('Wings' Cameron), Ralph Ward (Adjutant), Herbert Kilitz (Camp Guard), Lis Lovert (Kamma), Helge Ericksen (Sigmund), Walter Hertner (German Policeman), Meinhart Maur (Hotel Proprietor), Walter Gotell (The Follower), and Philip Dale; *GB dist:* British Lion; *GB rel:* 16 October 1950; *rt:* 101 minutes; *US dist:* Snader Productions; *US rel:* floating 1952.

69. *Seven Days to Noon*—1950

*prod co:* Boulting Brothers Productions for London Film Productions; *prod:* Roy Boulting; *assoc prod:* Peter de Sarigny; *dir:* John Boulting; *asst dir:* Mike Johnson; *scr:* Roy Boulting and Frank Harvey from a story by Paul Dehn and James Bernard; *ph:* Gilbert Taylor; *assoc ph:* Ray Sturgess; *cam op:* Bob Huke, Gerald Moss and Denis Fox; *des:* John Elphick; *ed:* Roy Boulting; *mus:* John Addison; *mus dir:* Dr Hubert Clifford; *sound:* Bert Ross; *sound ed:* Bert Eggleton; *prod man:* John Palmer; *asst:* Ann Chegwidden; *cast:* Barry Jones (Professor Willingdon), Olive Sloane (Goldie), Andre Morell (Superintendent Folland), Sheila Manahan (Ann Willingdon), Hugh Cross (Stephen Lane), Joan Hickson (Mrs Peckett), Ronald Adam (Prime Minister), Marie Ney (Mrs Willingdon), Merrill Mueller (American Commentator), Geoffrey Keen, Russell Waters, Wyndham Goldie, Martin Boddey, Frederick Allen, and Victor Maddern; *GB dist:* British Lion; *GB rel:* 30 October 1950; *rt:* 94 minutes; *US dist:* Mayer-Kingsley; *US rel:* 20 December 1950; *prize:* Academy Award for Best Original Story.

70. *Gone to Earth* [US: *The Wild Heart*]—1950

*prod co:* London Film Productions, Vanguard Productions; *pres:* Alexander Korda and David O. Selznick; *prod.* David O. Selznick; *assoc prod:* George R. Busby; *dir:* Michael Powell and Emeric Pressburger; *asst dir:* Sydney Streeter; *scr:* Michael Powell and Emeric Pressburger from a novel by Mary Webb; *ph* (Technicolor): Christopher Challis; *prod design:* Hein Heckroth;

*des:* Arthur Lawson; *ed:* Reginald Mills; *mus:* Brian Easdale; *cast:* Jennifer Jones (Hazel Woodus), David Farrar (Jack Reddin), Cyril Cusack (Edward Marston), Sybil Thorndyke (Mrs Marston), Edward Chapman (Mr James), Esmond Knight (Abel Woodus), Hugh Griffith (Andrew Vessons), George Cole (Albert), Beatrice Varley (Aunt Prowde), Frances Clare (Amelia Comber), Raymond Rollett (Landlord), Gerald Lawson (Roadmender), Bartlett Mullins and Arthur Reynolds (Chapel Elders), Ann Tetheradge (Miss James), Peter Dunlop (Cornet Player), Louis Phillip (Policeman), Valentine Dunn (Martha), Richmond Nairne (Mathias Booker), and Joseph Cotten (Narrator), *GB dist:* British Lion; *GB rel:* 6 November 1950; *GB rt:* 110 minutes; *US dist:* RKO Radio; *US rel:* July 1952; *US rt:* 82 minutes. (US version is substantially different; Rouben Mamoulian directed additional sequences for it.)

71. *The Elusive Pimpernel* [US: *The Fighting Pimpernel*]—1951
*prod co:* The Archers for London Film Productions; *prod:* Samuel Goldwyn and Alexander Korda; *assoc prod:* George R. Busby; *dir:* Michael Powell and Emeric Pressburger; *asst dir:* Sydney Streeter; *scr:* Michael Powell and Emeric Pressburger from the novel by Baroness Orczy; *ph* (Technicolor): Christopher Challis; *cam op:* Freddie Francis; *spec effects:* W. Percy Day; *prod design:* Hein Heckroth; *des:* Arthur Lawson and Joseph Bato; *ed:* Reginald Mills; *mus:* Brian Easdale; *sound:* Charles Poulton and Red Law; *cast:* David Niven (Sir Percy Blakeney), Margaret Leighton (Marguerite Blakeney), Jack Hawkins (Prince of Wales), Cyril Cusack (Chauvelin), Robert Coote (Sir Andrew Ffoulkes), Edmond Audran (Armand St Juste), Danielle Godet (Suzanne de Tournai), Arlette Marchal (Comtesse de Tournai), Gerard Nery (Phillipe de Tournai), Charles Victor (Colonel Winterbottom), David Hutcheson (Lord Anthony Dewhurst), Eugene Deckers (Captain Merieres), John Longden (The Abbot), Arthur Wontner (Lord Grenville), David Oxley (Captain Duroc), Raymond Rollett (Bibot), Philip Stainton (Jellyband), Robert Griffiths (Trubshaw), George de Warfaz (Baron), Jane Gill Davies (Lady Grenville), Richard George (Sir John Coke), Cherry Cottrell (Lady Coke), John Fitzgerald (Sir Michael Travers), Patrick Macnee (Hon. John Bristow), Terence Alexander (Duke of Dorset), Tommy Duggan (Earl of Sligo), John Fitchen (Nigel Seymour), John Hewitt (Major Pretty), Hugh Kelly (Mr Fitzdrummond), and Richmond Nairne (Beau Pepys); *GB dist:* British Lion; *GB rel:* 1 January 1951; *rt:* 109 minutes; *US dist:* Carroll Pictures; *US rel:* floating 1955.

72. *The Tales of Hoffman*—1951
*prod co:* The Archers for London Film Productions; *prod:* Michael Powell and Emeric Pressburger; *assoc prod:* George R. Busby; *dir:* Michael Powell and Emeric Pressburger; *asst dir:* Sydney Streeter; *scr:* Michael Powell and Emeric Pressburger from Dennis Arundell's adaptation of the opera by Offenbach; *ph* (Technicolor): Christopher Challis; *decor & cos:* Hein Heckroth; *des:* Arthur Lawson; *ed:* Reginald Mills; *mus:* Offenbach; *mus dir:* Sir Thomas Beecham; *choreography:* Frederick Ashton; *cast:*
*Prologue and Epilogue:* Moira Shearer (Stella), Robert Rounseville (Hoffman), Robert Helpmann (Lindorff), Pamela Brown (Nicklaus), Frederick Ashton (Kleinzack), Meinhart Maur (Luther), Edmond Audran (Cancer).

*The Tale of Olympia:* Moira Shearer (Olympia), Robert Helpmann (Coppelius), Leonide Massine (Spalanzani).
*The Tale of Giulietta:* Ludmilla Tcherina (Giulietta), Robert Helpmann (Dapertutto), Leonide Massine (Schlemiel).
*The Tale of Antonia:* Ann Ayars (Antonia), Robert Helpmann (Dr Miracle), Leonide Massine (Franz).
and the voices of Owen Brannigan, Monica Sinclair, René Soames, Bruce Darvaget, Dorothy Bond, Margherita Grandi, and Grahame Clifford; *GB dist:* British Lion; *GB rel:* May 1951; *rt:* 127 minutes; *US dist:* United Artists; *US rel:* 13 June 1952.

73. *Lady Godiva Rides Again*—1951
*prod co:* London Film Productions; *prod:* Frank Launder and Sidney Gilliat; *dir:* Frank Launder; *asst dir:* Percy Hermes; *scr:* Frank Launder and Val Valentine; *ph:* Wilkie Cooper; *cam op:* Denys Coop; *des:* Joseph Bato; *ed:* Thelma Connell; *cos:* Anna Duse; *mus:* William Alwyn; *mus dir:* Muir Mathieson; *cast:* Dennis Price (Simon Abbott), John McCallum (Larry Burns), Stanley Holloway (Mr Clark), Pauline Stroud (Marjorie Clark), Gladys Henson (Mrs Clark), Bernadette O'Farrell (Janie), George Cole (Johnny), Diana Dors (Dolores August), Eddie Byrne (Eddie Mooney), Kay Kendall (Sylvie), Renee Houston (Beattie), Dora Bryan (Publicity Woman), Sidney James (Lew Beeson), Dagmar Wynter (Myrtle Shaw), Tommy Duggan (Compere), Eddie Leslie (Comic), Walford Hyden (Conductor), Edward Forsyth and Lisa Lee (Singers), Cyril Chamberlain (Harry), Lyn Evans (Vic Kennedy), Peter Martyn (Photographer), Fred Berger (Mr Green), Henry Longhurst (Soap Director), Felix Felton, Arthur Brander, and Sidney Vivian (Councillors), Arthur Howard, Clive Baxter, and Paul Connell (Soap Publicity Men), John Harry (Buller), Rowena Gregory (Waitress), Tom Gill (Receptionist), Patricia Goddard (Susan), Richard Wattis (Casting Director), Michael Ripper (Stage Manager), Charlotte Mitchell (Lucille), Toke Townley (Lucille's Husband); *GB dist:* British Lion; *GB rel:* 25 October 1951; *rt:* 90 minutes; *US dist:* Carroll Pictures; *US rel:* floating 1955.

74. *The Wonder Kid* [Ger: *Entfuhrung ins Gluck*]—1951
*prod co:* London Film Productions; *prod & dir:* Karl Hartl; *asst dir:* Jack Causey; *scr:* Gene Markey from a story by Karl Hartl; *ph:* Robert Krasker and Gunther Anders; *cam op:* Denys Coop; *des:* Joseph Bato and Werner Schlighting; *ed:* Reginald Beck; *mus:* W. Schmidt-Gentner; *mus dir:* Dr Hubert Clifford; *cast:* Bobby Henrey (Sebastian Giro), Robert Shackleton (Rocks Cooley), Christa Winter (Anni), Muriel Aked (Miss Frisbie), Elwyn Brook-Jones (Mr Gorik), Paul Hardtmuth (Professor Bindl), Oskar Werner (Rudi), Sebastian Cabot (Pizzo), June Elvin (Miss Kirsch), Klaus Birsch (Nik), and Lowe the dog; *dubbed voices for German version:* Mario Doerner (Sebastian), Margarete Hagen (Miss Frisbie), Ralph Lothar (Mr Gorik), Hilde Volk (Anni), Karl Hellmer (Professor Bindl), Karl Meixner (Rudi), Axel Monje (Rocks); *GB dist:* British Lion; *GB rel:* 18 November 1951; *rt:* 85 minutes; *Ger dist:* Deutsche London Film Verleiom GMBH; *Ger rel:* December 1951; *US rel:* 29 December 1951.

75. *Mr Denning Drives North*—1952
*prod co:* London Film Productions; *prod:* Anthony Kimmins and Stephen

Mitchell; *dir:* Anthony Kimmins; *asst dir:* John Bremer; *scr:* Alec Coppel from his novel; *ph:* John Wilcox; *cam op:* Robert Day; *des:* John Elphick; *ed:* Gerald Turney-Smith; *mus:* Benjamin Frankel; *cast:* John Mills (Tom Denning), Phyllis Calvert (Kay Denning), Sam Wanamaker (Chick Eddowes), Herbert Lom (Mados), Eileen Moore (Liz Denning), Raymond Huntley (Wright), Bernard Lee (Inspector Dodds), Wilfrid Hyde-White (Woods), Freda Jackson (Ma Smith), Sheila Shand Gibbs (Matilda), Trader Faulkner (Ted Smith), Russell Waters (Harry Stoper), Michael Shepley (Chairman), John Stuart (Wilson), Ronald Adam (Coroner), Hugh Morton (Inspector Snell), David Davies (Chauffeur), Ambrosine Philpotts (Mrs Blade), Herbert Walton (Yardley), John Stevens and Edward Evans (Policemen), Lyn Evans (Mr Fisher), John Warren (Mr Ash), and Raymond Francis (Clerk of the Court); *GB dist:* British Lion; *GB rel:* 21 January 1952; *rt:* 93 minutes; *US dist:* Carroll Pictures; *US rel:* floating 1954.

76. *Outcast of the Islands*—1952
*prod co:* London Film Productions; *prod & dir:* Carol Reed; *assoc prod:* Hugh Perceval; *asst dir:* Guy Hamilton; *scr:* William Fairchild from the novel by Joseph Conrad; *ph:* Ted Scaife and John Wilcox; *cam op:* Freddie Francis and Ted Moore; *spec effects:* Percy Day; *des:* Vincent Korda; *ed:* Bert Bates; *mus:* Brian Easdale; *sound:* John Cox; *dancing:* T. Ranjana and K. Gurunanse; *cast:* Ralph Richardson (Captain Lingard), Trevor Howard (Peter Willens), Robert Morley (Mr Almayer), Wendy Hiller (Mrs Almayer), Kerima (Aissa), George Coulouris (Babalatchi), Wilfrid Hyde-White (Vinck), Frederick Valk (Hudig), Betty Ann Davies (Mrs Willens), Peter Illing (Alagapjan), James Kenney (Ramsey), A. V. Bramble (Badavi), Dharma Emmanuel (Ali), Annabel Morley (Nina Almayer), and Marne Maitland (Mate); *GB dist:* British Lion; *GB rel:* 25 February 1952; *GB rt:* 102 mins; *US dist:* United Artists; *US rel:* 11 July 1953; *US rt:* 93 minutes.

77. *Home at Seven* [US: *Murder on Monday*]—1952
*prod co:* London Film Productions; *prod:* Maurice Cowan; *assoc prod:* Hugh Perceval; *dir:* Ralph Richardson; *scr:* Anatole de Grunwald from the play by R. C. Sherriff; *ph:* Jack Hildyard and Ted Scaife; *cam op:* Denys Coop and Robert Day; *des:* Vincent Korda and Frederick Pusey; *ed:* Bert Bates; *cos:* Ivy Baker; *sound:* John Cox; *mus:* Malcolm Arnold; *mus dir:* Muir Mathieson; *prod man:* Jack Swinburne; *cast:* Ralph Richardson (David Preston), Margaret Leighton (Janet Preston), Jack Hawkins (Dr Sparling), Campbell Singer (Inspector Hemingway), Frederick Piper (Mr Petherbridge), Diana Beaumont (Ellen), Meriel Forbes (Peggy Dobson), Michael Shepley (Major Watson), Margaret Withers (Mrs Watson), and Gerald Case (Sergeant Evans); *dist:* British Lion, *rt.* 85 minutes; *GB rel:* 17 March 1952; *US rel:* floating 1953.

78. *Who Goes There?* [US: *The Passionate Sentry*]—1952
*prod co:* London Film Productions; *prod & dir:* Anthony Kimmins; *assoc prod:* Hugh Perceval; *asst dir:* Adrian Pryce-Jones; *scr:* John Dighton from his play; *ph:* Ted Scaife and John Wilcox; *cam op:* Robert Day; *des:* Wilfred Shingleton; *ed:* Gerald Turney-Smith; *mus dir:* Muir Mathieson; *cast:* Nigel Patrick (Miles Cornwall), Peggy Cummins (Christine Deed), Valerie Hobson (Alex Cornwall), George Cole (Arthur Crisp), A. E. Matthews (Sir Arthur Cornwall), Anthony Bushell (Major Guy Ashley), and Joss Ambler (Guide);

*GB dist:* British Lion; *GB rel:* 30 June 1952; *rt:* 85 minutes; *US dist:* Fine Arts Films; *US rel:* floating 1953.

79. *Cry, the Beloved Country* [US: *African Fury*]—1952
*prod co:* Zoltan Korda–Alan Paton Production for London Film Productions; *prod & dir:* Zoltan Korda; *asst dir:* John Bremer; *scr:* Alan Paton from his novel; *ph:* Robert Krasker; *cam op:* G. Massy-Collier; *second unit:* David Millen and Peter Lang; *des:* Wilfred Shingleton; *cos:* Maisie Kelly; *ed:* David Eady; *asst ed:* Valerie Leslie; *mus:* R. Gallois-Montbrun; *mus dir:* Dr Hubert Clifford; *sound:* John Mitchell and Red Law; *dubbing:* Lee Doig; *prod man:* Jack Swinburne; *adv:* Frank Rogaly; *makeup:* Peter Evans; *cast:* Canada Lee (Stephen Kumalo), Charles Carson (James Jarvis), Sidney Poitier (Rev. Maimangu), Joyce Carey (Margaret Jarvis), Edric Connor (John Kumalo), Geoffrey Keen (Father Vincent), Vivien Clinton (Mary), Michael Goodliffe (Masters), Albertina Temba (Mrs Kumalo), Lionel Ngakane (Absalom), Charles MacRae (Kumalo's Friend), Henry Blumenthal (Arthur Jarvis), Ribbon Dhlamini (Gertrude Kumalo), Cyril Kwaza (Matthew Kumalo), Max Dhlemini (Father Thomas), Shayiaw Riba (Father Tisa), Evelyn Nayati (Mrs Lithebe), Jsepo Gugusha (Gertrude's child), Reginald Ngcobo (Taxi Driver), Emily Pooe (Mrs Ndela), Bruce Meredith Smith (Captain Jaarsveldt), Bruce Anderson (Farmer Smith), Berdine Grunewald (Mary Jarvis), Cecil Cartwright (Harrison, Snr), Andrew Kay (Harrison, Jnr) Danie Adrewmah (Young Man), Clement McCallin (First Reporter), Michael Golden (Second Reporter), Stanley Van Beers (Judge), John Arnatt (Prison Warden), and Scott Harrold (Police Superintendent); *GB dist:* British Lion; *GB rel:* 10 August 1952; *GB rt:* 103 minutes; *US dist:* United Artists; *US rel:* 22 August 1952; *US rt:* 96 minutes; *prize:* British Film Academy United Nations Award 1952, Silver Laurel Award 1952.

80. *Edinburgh*—1952
*prod co:* London Film Productions; *dir & scr:* David Eady; *ph* (Technicolor): Stanley Grant and Jack Hildyard; *mus:* Dr Hubert Clifford; *narrator:* Rt. Hon. Walter Elliott; *GB dist:* British Lion; *GB rel:* 18 August 1952. (An 18-minute documentary.)

81. *Road to Canterbury*—1952
*prod co:* London Film Productions; *dir & scr:* David Eady; *ph* (Technicolor): Stanley Grant, John Wilcox and Cedric Williams; *ed:* Audrey Bennett; *mus:* Dr Hubert Clifford; *sound:* Red Law; *narrator:* Anthony Bushell; *GB dist:* British Lion; *rt:* 23 minutes. (Documentary.)

82. *The Sound Barrier* [US: *Breaking the Sound Barrier*]—1952
*prod co:* London Film Productions; *prod & dir:* David Lean; *assoc prod:* Norman Spencer; *dir aerial sequences:* Anthony Squire; *asst dir:* Adrian Pryce-Jones; *scr:* Terence Rattigan; *ph:* Jack Hildyard; *cam op:* Denys Coop; *aerial ph:* John Wilcox, Jo Jago, and Peter Newbrook; *des:* Joseph Bato and John Hawkesworth; *sets:* Vincent Korda; *ed:* Geoffrey Foot; *cos:* Elizabeth Hemmings; *mus:* Malcolm Arnold; *mus dir:* Muir Mathieson; *sound:* John Cox and Bert Ross; *cast:* Ralph Richardson (John Ridgefield), Ann Todd (Susan Garthwaite), Nigel Patrick (Tony Garthwaite), John Justin (Philip Peel), Dinah Sheridan (Jess Peel), Joseph Tomelty (Will Sparks), Denholm Elliott (Chris Ridgefield), Jack Allen (Windy Williams), Ralph Michael

(Fletcher), Leslie Phillips and Douglas Muir (Controllers), Jolyon Jackley (Baby), Donald Harron (ATA Officer), Vincent Holman (Factor), Robert Brookes Turner (Test Bed Operator), and Anthony Snell (Peter Makepeace); *GB dist:* British Lion; *GB rel:* 13 October 1952; *GB rt:* 118 minutes; *US dist:* United Artists; *US rel:* 21 December 1952; *US rt:* 115 minutes; *prize:* Academy Award for Sound Recording.

83. *The Holly and the Ivy*—1952

*prod co:* London Film Productions; *prod:* Anatole de Grunwald; *assoc prod:* Hugh Perceval; *dir:* George More O'Ferrall; *asst dir:* Edwin Cotton; *scr:* Anatole de Grunwald from the play by Wynyard Browne; *ph:* Ted Scaife; *cam op:* Robert Day; *sets:* Vincent Korda and Frederick Pusey; *ed:* Bert Bates; *cos:* Ivy Baker; *mus:* Malcolm Arnold; *mus dir:* Muir Mathieson; *cast:* Ralph Richardson (Rev. Martin Gregory), Celia Johnson (Jenny Gregory), Margaret Leighton (Margaret Gregory), Denholm Elliott (Michael Gregory), John Gregson (David Patterson), Hugh Williams (Richard Wyndham), William Hartnell (C.S.M.), Robert Flemyng (Major), Roland Culver (Lord B), Margaret Halstan (Aunt Lydia), Maureen Delaney (Aunt Bridget), John Barry (Clubman), and Dandy Nichols (Neighbour); *GB dist:* British Lion; *GB rel:* 22 December 1952; *GB rt:* 83 minutes; *US dist:* Pacemaker Prods.; *US rel:* 14 February 1954; *US rt:* 80 minutes.

84. *The Ringer*—1953

*prod co:* London Film Productions; *prod:* Hugh Perceval; *dir:* Guy Hamilton; *asst dir:* Edwin Cotton; *scr:* Val Valentine from the play by Edgar Wallace; *add dial:* Lesley Storm; *ph:* Ted Scaife; *cam op:* Robert Day; *des:* Joseph Bato and W. E. Hutchinson; *ed:* Bert Bates; *mus:* Malcolm Arnold; *mus dir:* Muir Mathieson; *cast:* Herbert Lomas (Maurice Meister), Donald Wolfit (Dr Lomond), Mai Zetterling (Lisa), Greta Gynt (Cora Ann Milton), William Hartnell (Sam Hackett), Norman Wooland (Inspector Bliss), Denholm Elliott (John Lemley), Dora Bryan (Mrs Hackett), Charles Victor (Inspector Wembury), Walter Fitzgerald (Commissioner), John Stuart (Gardener), John Slater (Bell), and Campbell Singer (Station Sergeant Carter); *GB dist:* British Lion; *GB rel:* 12 January 1953; *rt:* 78 minutes; *US dist:* Ellis Films; *US rel:* floating 1953.

85. *Folly To Be Wise*—1953

*prod co:* London Film Productions; *prod:* Frank Launder and Sidney Gilliat; *dir:* Frank Launder; *asst dir:* Sydney Streeter; *scr:* Frank Launder and John Dighton from the James Bridie play *It Depends What You Mean; ph:* Jack Hildyard; *cam op:* Peter Newbrook; *des:* Arthur Lawson; *cos:* Anna Duse; *ed:* Thelma Connell; *mus:* Temple Abady; *mus dir:* Ryalton Kisch; *cast:* Alastair Sim (Captain Paris), Roland Culver (George Prout), Elizabeth Allan (Angela Prout), Martita Hunt (Lady Dodds), Colin Gordon (Professor James Mutch), Janet Brown (Private Jessie Killigrew), Miles Malleson (Dr Hector McAdam), Edward Chapman (Joseph Byres), Peter Martyn (Walter), Robin Bailey (Intellectual), George Cole (Private), Clement McCallin (Colonel), Michael Ripper (Corporal), Leslie Weston (Landlord), Michael Kelly (Staff Sergeant), George Hurst (Bus Conductor), Cyril Chamberlain (Drill Sergeant), Jo Powell, Catherine Finn, Enid McCall, and Ann Valery (WRACs), and Myrette Morven (WRAC Officer); *GB dist:* British Lion; *GB rel:* 19

January 1953; *rt:* 91 minutes; *US dist:* Fine Arts Films; *US rel:* floating 1953

86. *Twice Upon a Time*—1953

*prod co:* London Film Productions; *prod & dir:* Emeric Pressburger; *assoc prod:* George R. Busby; *asst dir:* Sydney Streeter; *scr:* Emeric Pressburger from Erich Kastner's novel *Das Doppelte Lottchen; ph:* Christopher Challis; *cam op:* Freddie Francis; *des:* Arthur Lawson; *ed:* Reginald Beck; *mus:* Johannes Brahms and Carl Maria von Weber; *sound:* John Cox; *cast:* Hugh Williams (James Turner), Elizabeth Allan (Carol-Anne Bailey), Jack Hawkins (Dr Matthews), Yolande Larthe (Carol Turner), Charmaine Larthe (Anne Bailey), Violette Elvin (Florence la Roche), Isabel Dean (Miss Burke), Michael Gough (Mr Lloyd), Walter Fitzgerald (Professor Reynolds), Eileen Elton (Ballet Dancer), Kenneth Melville (Ballet Dancer), Nora Gordon (Emma), Isabel George (Molly), Cecily Walger (Mrs Maybridge), Molly Terraine (Miss Wellington), Martin Miller (Eipeldauer), Lily Kann (Mrs Eipeldauer), Jean Stuart (Mrs Jamieson), Margaret Boyd (Mrs Kinnaird), Myrette Morven (Miss Rupert), Jack Lambert (Mr Buchan), Archie Duncan (Doorman), Colin Wilcox (Ian), Pat Baker (Sonia), Monica Thomson (Thelma), Margaret McCourt (Wendy), Alanna Boyce (Susie), and Ilsa Richardson (Hilary); *GB dist:* British Lion; *GB rel:* 6 July 1953; *rt:* 75 minutes; *US dist:* Fine Arts Films, Inc.; *US rel:* floating 1953/54.

87. *The Captain's Paradise*—1953

*prod co:* London Film Productions; *prod & dir:* Anthony Kimmins; *scr:* Alec Coppel and Nicholas Phipps from Anthony Kimmins's adaptation of a story by Alec Coppel; *ph:* Ted Scaife; *cam op:* Denys Coop; *des:* Paul Sheriff; *ed:* Gerald Turney-Smith; *mus:* Malcolm Arnold; *mus dir:* Muir Mathieson; *cast:* Alec Guinness (Captain Henry St James), Yvonne De Carlo (Nita St James), Celia Johnson (Maud St James), Charles Goldner (Ricco), Miles Malleson (Lawrence St James), Bill Fraser (Absalom), Walter Crisham (Bob), Ferdy Mayne (Sheik), Nicholas Phipps (Major), Sebastian Cabot (Ali), Claudia Gray (Susan Dailey), George Benson (Salmon), Joss Ambler (Professor Ebbart), Joyce Barbour (Mrs Reid), Peter Bull (Kalikan Officer), Ann Heffernan (Daphne Bligh), Arthur Gomez (Chief Steward), Michael Balfour, Victor Fairley, and Robert Adair (Custom Officials), Jacinta Dicks (Flower Seller), Alejandro Martinez (Guitarist), Tutte Lemkow (Principal Dancer), Andrea Malandrinos (Maitre d'Hotel), Amando Guinle (Chief Engineer), Paul Armstrong (Deck Officer), Roy Purcell (Officer of the Watch), Raymond Hoole (Storekeeper), Henry Longhurst (Professor Killick), Bernard Rebel (Mr Wheeler), Ambrosine Philpotts (Marjorie), Catherina Ferraz (Shopkeeper), Roger Delgado (Kalikan Policeman); *GB dist:* British Lion; *GB rel:* 8 August 1953; *GB rt:* 93 minutes; *US dist:* United Artists; *US rel:* 18 December 1953; *US rt:* 77 minutes.

88. *The Story of Gilbert and Sullivan* [US: *The Great Gilbert and Sullivan*]—1953

*prod co:* London Film Productions; *prod:* Frank Launder and Sidney Gilliat; *assoc prod:* Leslie Gilliat; *dir:* Sidney Gilliat; *asst dir:* Percy Hermes; *scr:* Leslie Bailey, Sidney Gilliat, and Vincent Korda from Leslie Bailey's *The Gilbert and Sullivan Book; ph* (Technicolor): Christopher Challis; *prod designer:* Hein Heckroth; *des:* Joseph Bato; *ed:* Gerald Turney-Smith; *mus:* Gilbert and Sullivan; *mus dir:* Sir Malcolm Sargent; *asst mus dir:* Muir Mathieson; *cast:*

Robert Morley (W. S. Gilbert), Maurice Evans (Arthur Sullivan), Eileen Herlie (Helen Lenoir), Martyn Green (George Grossmith), Peter Finch (Richard D'Oyley Carte), Dinah Sheridan (Grace Marston), Isabel Dean (Mrs Gilbert), Wilfrid Hyde-White (Mr Marston), Muriel Aked (Queen Victoria), Michael Ripper (Louis), Bernadette O'Farrell (Jessie Bond), Ann Hanslip (Bride), Eric Berry (Rutland Barrington), Yvonne Marsh (Second Bride), Lloyd Lamble (Joseph Bennett), Ian Wallace (Captain), Owen Brannigan (Principal Bass Baritone), Richard Warner (Cellier), Perlita Neilson (Lettie), Charlotte Mitchell (Charlotte), Kenneth Downey (Counsel for the Plaintiff in 'Trial by Jury'), Sylvia Clarke (Gianetta in 'The Gondoliers' and Peep-Bo in 'The Mikado'), Stella Riley (Millicent), Leonard Sachs (Smythe), Philip Ray (Theatre Manager), John Rae (Ferguson), George Cross (Stage Manager), George Woodbridge (Reporter), Robert Brookes Turner (Doorman), Anthony Green (Office Boy), Gron Davies (The Ancestral Ghost in 'Ruddigore'), Arthur Howard (Usher in 'Trial by Jury'), John Banks (Strephon in 'Iolanthe'), John Hughes (Train Bearer in 'Iolanthe'), Thomas Round (Defender in 'Trial by Jury'; Nanki-Poo in 'The Mikado'), Harold Williams (Judge in 'Trial by Jury'), Muriel Brunskill (Principal Contralto), Harold Lang, Jennifer Vyvyan, Joan Gillingham, Gordon Clinton, John Cameron, Marjorie Thomas, and Webster Booth (Singers); *GB dist:* British Lion; *GB rel:* 7 September 1953; *GB rt:* 109 minutes; *US dist:* United Artists; *US rel:* 18 January 1954; *US rt:* 105 minutes.

89. *The Man Between*—1953
*prod co:* London Film Productions; *prod & dir:* Carol Reed; *assoc prod:* Hugh Perceval; *asst dir:* Adrian Pryce-Jones; *scr:* Harry Kurnitz and Eric Linklater from the novel *Susanne in Berlin* by Walter Ebert; *ph:* Desmond Dickinson; *cam op:* Denys Coop and Robert Day; *des:* Andre Andrejew; *ed:* Bert Bates; *mus:* John Addison; *mus dir:* Muir Mathieson; *sound:* John Cox; *cos:* Bridget Sellers; *cont:* Olga Brook; *cast:* James Mason (Ivo Kern), Claire Bloom (Susan Mallinson), Geoffrey Toone (Martin Mallinson), Hildegarde Neff (Bettina Mallinson), Albert Waescher (Haladar), Ernst Schroeder (Kastner), Karl John (Inspector Kleiber), Dieter Krause (Horst), and Hilde Sessak (Lizzi); *GB dist:* British Lion; *GB rel:* 2 November 1953; *rt:* 101 minutes; *US dist:* United Artists; *US rel:* 18 February 1954.

90. *The Heart of the Matter*—1954
*prod co:* London Film Productions; *prod:* Ian Dalrymple; *dir:* George More O'Ferrall; *loc dir:* Anthony Squire; *asst dir:* Adrian Pryce-Jones; *scr:* Ian Dalrymple from Lesley Storm's adaptation of the novel by Graham Greene; *ph:* Jack Hildyard; *des:* Joseph Bato; *ed:* Sidney Stone; *cos:* Julia Squire; *cast:* Trevor Howard (Harry Scobie), Elizabeth Allan (Louise Scobie), Maria Schell (Helen Rolt), Denholm Elliott (Wilson), Gerard Oury (Yusef), Peter Finch (Father Rank), Earl Cameron (Ali), Michael Hordern (Commissioner), Colin Gordon (Secretary), Cyril Raymond (Carter), Orlando Martins (Rev. Clay), Evelyn Roberts (Colonel Wright), Gillian Lind (Mrs Carter), George Coulouris (Portuguese Captain), John Rae (Loder), Peter Burton (Perrot), Eileen Thorndike (Mrs Bowles), Anthony Snell (Doctor), Jane Henderson (Miss Malcott), Stanley Lunin (Forbes), Eugene Leahy (Newall), Chris

Rhodes (French Officer), Judith Furze (Dr Sykes), Ewan Roberts (Druce), Jack Allen (RNVR Lieutenant), John Akar (Negro Servant), John Glyn-Jones (Harris), Assany Kamara Wilson (African Sergeant), Saidu Fofana and Errol John (African Policemen); *GB dist:* British Lion; *GB rel:* 8 February 1954; *GB rt:* 105 minutes; *US dist:* Associated Artists; *US rel:* 21 November 1954; *US rt:* 100 minutes.

91. *Hobson's Choice*—1954
*prod co:* London Film Productions; *prod & dir:* David Lean; *asst prod:* Norman Spencer; *asst dir:* Adrian Pryce-Jones; *scr:* David Lean, Wynard Browne and Norman Spencer from the play by Harold Brighouse; *ph:* Jack Hildyard; *cam op:* Peter Newbrook; *des:* Wilfred Shingleton; *cos:* John Armstrong; *ed:* Peter Taylor; *mus:* Malcolm Arnold; *mus dir:* Muir Mathieson; *sound:* John Cox; *sound rec:* Buster Ambler and Red Law; *prod man:* John Palmer; *cast:* Charles Laughton (Henry Hobson), John Mills (Willie Mossup), Brenda de Banzie (Maggie Hobson), Daphne Anderson (Alice Hobson), Prunella Scales (Vicky Hobson), Richard Wattis (Albert Prosser), Derek Blomfield (Freddy Breenstock), Helen Haye (Mrs Hepworth), Joseph Tomelty (Jim Heeler), Julien Mitchell (Sam Minns), Gibb McLaughlin (Tudsbury), Dorothy Gordon (Ada Figgins), John Laurie (Dr MacFarlane), Raymond Huntley (Nathaniel Breenstock), Jack Howarth (Tubby Wadlow), Philip Stainton (Denton), Madge Brindley (Mrs Figgins), and Herbert C. Walton (Printer); *GB dist:* British Lion; *GB rel:* 19 April 1954; *rt:* 107 minutes; *US dist:* United Artists: *US rel:* 11 June 1954.

92. *Belles of St Trinian's*—1954
*prod co:* Frank Launder and Sidney Gilliat Productions for London Film Productions; *prod:* Sidney Gilliat; *dir:* Frank Launder; *scr:* Frank Launder, Sidney Gilliat, and Val Valentine, inspired by Roland Searle's drawings; *ph:* Stanley Pavey; *des:* Joseph Bato; *ed:* Thelma Connell; *mus:* Malcolm Arnold; *cast:* Alastair Sim (Millicent and Clarence Fritton), Joyce Grenfell (Policewoman Ruby Gates), George Cole (Flash Harry), Beryl Reid (Miss Wilson), Hermione Baddeley (Miss Drownder), Betty Ann Davies (Miss Waters), Renee Houston (Miss Brinner), Irene Handl (Miss Gale), Mary Merrall (Miss Buckland), Joan Sims (Miss Dawn), Balbina (Mlle de St Emilion), Vivienne Martin (Arabella), Guy Middleton (Eric Rowbotham-Smith), Jane Henderson (Miss Holland), Diana Day (Jackie), Jill Braidwood (Florrie), Annabelle Covey (Maudie), Jauline Drewett (Celia), Jean Langston (Rosie), and Lloyd Lamble, Richard Wattis, and Eric Pohlmann; *GB dist:* British Lion; *GB rel:* 1 October 1954; *rt:* 91 minutes; *US dist:* Associated Artists; *US rel:* 5 January 1955.

93. *The Teckman Mystery*—1954
*prod co:* Corona, for London Film Productions; *prod:* Josef Somlo; *dir:* Wendy Toye; *asst dir:* Adrian Pryce-Jones and Peter Maxwell; *scr:* Francis Durbridge and James Matthews from a TV serial by Francis Durbridge; *ph:* Jack Hildyard; *cam op:* Peter Newbrook; *des:* William Kellner; *ed:* Albert Rule; *mus:* Clifton Parker; *mus dir:* Muir Mathieson; *cast:* Margaret Leighton (Margaret Teckman), John Justin (Philip Chance), Roland Culver (Inspector Harris), Michael Medwin (Martin Teckman), George Coulouris (Garvin), Duncan Lamont (Inspector Hilton), Raymond Huntley (Maurice Miller),

Jane Wenham (Ruth Wade), Meier Tzelniker (John Rice), Harry Locke (Leonard), Frances Rowe (Eileen Miller), Barbara Murray (Girl in Plane), Warwick Ashton (Sergeant Blair), Irene Lister (Waitress), Gwen Nelson (Duty Woman), Mary Crant (BEA Clerk), Andrea Malandrinos (Waiter), Dan Cressey (Drake), Peter Taylor (Leroy), Ben Williams and Frank Webster (Beefeaters), Peter Augustine (Man with Pipe), Maurice Lane (GPO Messenger), Mollie Palmer (Air Hostess), Bruce Beeby (Wallace), and Gordon Morrison (Boris); *GB dist:* British Lion; *GB rel:* 27 October 1954; *rt:* 90 minutes; *US dist:* Associated Artists; *US rel:* 28 April 1955.

94. *The Man Who Loved Redheads*—1955
*prod co:* British Lion, London Film Productions; *prod:* Josef Somlo; *assoc prod:* Hugh Perceval; *dir:* Harold French; *asst dir:* Robert Lynn; *scr:* Terence Rattigan from his play *Who Is Sylvia?; ph* (Eastman Colour): Georges Périnal; *cam op:* Denys Coop; *des:* Paul Sheriff; *ed:* Bert Bates; *mus:* Benjamin Frankel; *sound:* John Cox; *cast:* Moira Shearer (Sylvia/Daphne/Olga/Colette), John Justin (Mark St Neots), Ronald Culver (Oscar), Gladys Cooper (Caroline), Denholm Elliott (Dennis), Harry Andrews (Williams), Patricia Cutts (Bubbles), Moyra Fraser (Ethel), John Hart (Sergei), Jeremy Spenser (Young Mark), Melvyn Hayes (Sydney), and Joan Benham (Chloe); *GB dist:* British Lion; *GB rel:* 7 February 1955; *rt:* 90 minutes; *US dist:* United Artists; *US rel:* 10 July 1955.

95. *Three Cases of Murder*—1955
*prod co:* Wessex Films, for London Film Productions: *prod:* Ian Dalrymple, Alexander Paal, and Hugh Perceval; *ph:* Georges Périnal; *des:* Paul Sheriff; *ed:* Gerald Turney-Smith; *mus:* Doreen Carwithen; *GB dist:* British Lion; *GB rel:* 12 May 1955; *rt:* 99 minutes; *US dist:* Associated Artists; *US rel:* 1955.
*Lord Mountdrago sequence*
*dir:* George More O'Ferrall; *scr:* Ian Dalrymple from a story by Somerset Maugham; *cast:* Orson Welles (Lord Mountdrago), Alan Badel (Owen), Helen Cherry (Lady Mountdrago), and Andre Morell (Dr Audlin).
*You Killed Elizabeth sequence*
*dir:* David Eady; *scr:* Sidney Carroll from a story by Brett Halliday; *cast:* Elizabeth Sellars (Elizabeth), John Gregson (Edgar Curtain), Emrys Jones (George Wheeler), and Jack Lambert (Inspector Acheson).
*In The Picture sequence*
*dir:* Wendy Toye; *scr:* Donald Wilson from a story by Roderick Wilkinson; *cast:* Alan Badel (Mr X), Hugh Pryse (Jarvis), Leueen McGrath (The Woman), Eddie Byrne (Snyder), and John Salew (Rooke).

96. *The Constant Husband*—1955
*prod co:* Individual Productions, for London Film Productions; *prod:* Frank Launder and Sidney Gilliat; *dir:* Sidney Gilliat; *assoc prod:* E. M. Smedley-Aston; *asst dir:* Percy Hermes; *scr:* Sidney Gilliat and Val Valentine; *ph* (Technicolor): Ted Scaife; *cam op:* Robert Day; *des:* Wilfred Shingleton; *ed:* Gerald Turney-Smith; *mus:* Malcolm Arnold; *mus dir:* Muir Mathieson; *sound:* John Cox; *cast:* Rex Harrison (Charles Hathaway), Margaret Leighton (Miss Chesterman), Kay Kendall (Monica), Cecil Parker (Llewllyn), Nicole Maurey (Lola), George Cole (Luigi Sopranelli), Raymond Huntley (J. F.

Hassett), Michael Hordern (Judge), Robert Coote (Jack Carter), Eric Pohlmann (Papa Sopranelli), Valerie French (Bridget), Jill Adams (Miss Brent), Muriel Young (Clara), John Robinson (Secretary), Marie Burke (Mama Sopranelli), Eric Berry (Prosecuting Counsel), Arthur Howard (Clerk of the Court), Charles Lloyd Pack (Solicitor), Derek Sydney (Giorgio Sopranelli), Guy Deghy (Stromboli), Ursula Howells (Miss Pargiter), Roma Dunville (Sixth Wife), Stephen Vecoe (Dr Thompson), Sally Lahee (Nurse), Nora Gordon (Housekeeper), Noel Hood (Gladys), Pat Kenyon and Doreen Dawn (Models), Myrette Morven (Miss Prosser), Sam Kydd (Adelphi Barman), Paul Connell (Cardiff Barman), Nicholas Tannar (Usher), Graham Stuart (Government Messenger), Jill Melford (Monica's Golf Partner), Enid McCall (Welsh Chambermaid), Janette Richer (Typist), Michael Ripper (Left Luggage Attendant), Alfred Burke (Porter), David Yates, Robert Sydney (Detectives), Monica Stevenson (Olwen), Stuart Saunders (Policeman), Joe Clark, George Woodbridge, and Frank Webster (Old Bailey Warders), Arthur Cortez (Luigi's driver), Peter Edwards and Evie Lloyd (Fishermen), Paul Whitsun Jones (Welsh Farmer), Arnold Diamond (Car Loan Manager), Olive Kirby (Car Loan Assistant), Geoffrey Lovat (Commissionaire), Leslie Weston (Prison Jailer), and George Thorne (Horrocks); *dist:* British Lion; *rt:* 88 minutes; *GB rel:* 16 May 1955; *US rel:* 6 November 1955 (on NBC-TV).

97. *A Kid for Two Farthings*—1955
*prod co:* London Film Productions; *prod & dir:* Carol Reed; *asst dir:* John Bremer; *scr:* Wolf Mankowitz from his own novel; *ph* (Eastman Colour): Ted Scaife; *cam op:* Robert Day; *des:* Wilfred Shingleton; *ed:* A. S. Bates; *mus:* Benjamin Frankel; *cast:* Celia Johnson (Joanne), Diana Dors (Sonia), David Kossoff (Kadinsky), Joe Robinson (Sam), Jonathan Ashmore (Joe), Brenda de Banzie (Ruby), Vera Day (Mimi), Primo Carnera (Python Macklin), Sidney Tafler (Madam Rita), Sidney James (Ince Berg), Daphne Anderson (Dora), Lou Jacobi (Blackie Isaacs), Harold Berens (Oliver), Danny Green (Bason), Irene Handl (Mrs Abramowitz), Alfie Bass (Alf), Eddie Byrne (Sylvester), Joseph Tomelty (Vagrant), Rosalind Boxall (Mrs Alf), Harry Purvis (Champ), Harry Baird (Jamaica), Lily Kann (Mrs Kramm), Arthur Lovegrove (Postman), Madge Brindley (Mrs Quinn), Harold Goodwin (Chick Man), George Hurst, Eddie Malin, Peter Taylor (Dog Men), Derek Sydney (Fortune Teller), Ashr Day (Indian Girl), Nora Gordon and Max Denne (Customers), James Lomas (Sandwich Board Man), Bart Alison (Auctioneer), Arthur Skinner and Norman Mitchell (Stallholders), Marigold Russell (Third Customer), Judith Nelmes (Alf's Customer), Meier Leibovitch (Mendel), Locarno (Pigeon Man), Mollie Palmer, Barbara Denney, Barbara Archer, Ann Chaplin, and Anita Arley (Workroom girls), Raymond Rollett (Breakaway China Stallholder), Bruce Beeby (Policeman), Lew Marco (Referee), Frank Blake (M.C.), Ray Hunter and Charlie Green (Wrestlers); *GB dist:* British Lion; *GB rt:* 96 minutes; *GB rel:* 15 August 1955; *US dist:* Lopert Films; *US rt:* 91 minutes; *US rel:* 14 April 1956.

98. *The Deep Blue Sea*—1955
*prod co:* London Film Productions; *pres:* Alexander Korda; *prod & dir:* Anatole Litvak; *assoc prod:* Hugh Perceval; *asst dir:* Adrian Pryce-Jones; *scr:* Terence Rattigan from his play; *ph* (Eastman Colour; CinemaScope):

Jack Hildyard; *des:* Vincent Korda; *cos:* Anna Duse; *ed:* A. S. Bates; *mus:* Malcolm Arnold; *mus dir:* Muir Mathieson; *cast:* Vivien Leigh (Hester Collyer), Kenneth More (Freddie Page), Eric Portman (Miller), Emlyn Williams (Sir William Collyer), Moira Lister (Dawn Maxwell), Arthur Hill (Jackie Jackson), Dandy Nichols (Mrs Elton), Alex McCowen (Ken Thompson), Jimmy Hanley (Dicer Durston), Miriam Karlin (Barmaid), Heather Thatcher (Lady Dawson), Bill Shine (Golfer), Sidney James (Man), Gibb McLaughlin (Clerk), Brian Oulton (Drunk); *dist:* 20th Century-Fox *GB rel:* 17 October 1955; *rt:* 99 minutes; *US rel:* 20 November 1955.

99. *Summer Madness* [US: *Summertime*]—1955
*prod co:* London Film Productions and Lopert Productions; *prod:* Ilya Lopert; *assoc prod:* Norman Spencer; *dir:* David Lean; *asst dir:* Adrian Pryce-Jones and Alberto Cardone; *scr:* David Lean and H. E. Bates from the play *A Time of the Cuckoo* by Arthur Laurents; *ph* (Eastman Colour): Jack Hildyard; *cam op:* Peter Newbrook; *des:* Vincent Korda; *asst des:* Bill Hutchinson and Ferdinand Bellan; *ed:* Peter Taylor; *mus:* Alessandro Cicognini; *sound:* Winston Ryder and Jacqueline Thiedot; *cast:* Katharine Hepburn (Jane Hudson), Rossano Brazzi (Renato de Rossi), Isa Miranda (signora Fiorini), Darren McGavin (Eddie Yaegar), Mari Aldon (Phyl Yaegar), Jane Rose (Mrs McIlhenny), MacDonald Parke (Mr McIlhenny), Jeremy Spenser (Vito de Rossi), Gaetano Auterio (Mauro), Virginia Simeon (Giovanna), and Andre Morell (Englishman); *GB dist:* British Lion; *GB rel:* 7 November 1955; *rt:* 99 minutes; *US dist:* United Artists; *US rel:* 11 June 1955.

100. *Storm Over the Nile*—1955
*prod co:* London Film Productions; *prod:* Zoltan Korda; *dir:* Zoltan Korda and Terence Young; *scr:* R. C. Sherriff from the novel *The Four Feathers* by A. E. W. Mason; *add dial:* Lajos Biro and Arthur Wimperis; *ph* (Technicolor; Scope): Ted Scaife; *ext ph:* Osmond Borradaile; *des:* Wilfred Shingleton; *ed:* Raymond Poulton; *mus:* Benjamin Frankel; *sound:* John Cox; *cast:* Anthony Steel (Harry Faversham), Laurence Harvey (John Durrance), James Robertson Justice (General Burroughs), Mary Ure (Mary Burroughs), Ronald Lewis (Peter Burroughs), Geoffrey Keen (Dr Sutton), Ian Carmichael (Tom Willoughby), Michael Hordern (General Faversham), Jack Lambert (Colonel), Christopher Lee (Karaga Pasha), Ferdy Mayne (Dr Harraz), and Sam Kydd (Joe); *GB dist:* Independent Film Distributors in association with British Lion; *GB rel:* 26 December 1955; *rt:* 107 minutes; *US dist:* Columbia; *US rel:* 11 June 1956. (A remake of *The Four Feathers*—1939, directed by Zoltan Korda, see no. 36—which incorporates footage from the earlier film.)

101. *Richard III*—1956
*prod co:* London Film Productions; *prod & dir:* Laurence Olivier; *asst dir:* Anthony Bushell and Gerry O'Hara; *scr:* Alan Dent from the play by William Shakespeare; *ph* (Technicolor; VistaVision): Otto Heller; *asst ph:* Denys Coop; *des:* Carmen Dillon; *prod design:* Roger Furse; *ed:* Helga Cranston; *mus:* Sir William Walton; *mus dir:* Muir Mathieson; *sound:* John Cox; *cast:* Laurence Olivier (Richard III), John Gielgud (Clarence), Claire Bloom (Lady Anne), Ralph Richardson (Buckingham), Alec Clunes (Hastings), Sir Cedric Hardwicke (Edward IV), Stanley Baker (Henry Tudor), Laurence Naismith (Stanley), Norman Wooland (Catesby), Mary

Kerridge (Queen Elizabeth), Pamela Brown (Jane Shore), Helen Haye (Duchess of York), John Laurie (Lovel), Esmond Knight (Ratcliffe), Michael Gough (Dighton), Andrew Cruickshank (Brakenbury), Clive Morton (Rivers), Nicholas Hannen (Archbishop), Russell Thorndike (Priest), Paul Huson (Prince of Wales), Stewart Allen (Page), Wally Bascoe and Norman Fisher (Monks), Terence Greenridge (Scrivener), Dan Cunningham (Grey), Douglas Wilmer (Dorset), Michael Ripper (2nd Murderer), Andy Shine (Young Duke of York), Roy Russell (Abbot), George Woodbridge (Lord Mayor of London), Peter Williams (Messenger to Hastings), Timothy Bateson (Ostler), Willoughby Gray (Second Priest), Anne Wilton (Scrubwoman), Bill Shine (Beadle), Derek Prentice and Deering Wells (Clergymen), Richard Bennett (George Stanley), Patrick Troughton (Tyrell), John Phillips (Norfolk), Brian Nissen, Alexander Davion, Lane Meddick, and Robert Bishop (Messengers to Richard); *dist:* London Films International; *GB rel:* 16 April 1956; *GB rt:* 161 mins.; *US dist:* Lopert Film; *US rel:* May 1956; *US rt:* 155 mins.

102. *Smiley—1956*

*prod co:* London Film Productions; *prod & dir:* Anthony Kimmins; *scr:* Anthony Kimmins and Moore Raymond from the novel by Moore Raymond; *ph* (DeLuxe Color; Scope); Ted Scaife; *asst ph:* R. Wood; *ed:* Gerald Turney-Smith; *des:* Stan Woolveridge; *mus:* William Alwyn; *mus dir:* Muir Mathieson; *cast:* Ralph Richardson (Rev. Lambeth), John McCallum (Rankin), Chips Rafferty (Sgt Flaxman), Colin Petersen (Smiley Greevins), Bruce Archer (Joey), Jocelyn Hernfield (Miss Waterman), Charles Tingwell (Stevens), Margaret Christense (Mrs Greevins), Guy Doleman (Rider), Reg Lye (Pa Greevins), Marion Johns (Mrs Stevens), William Rees (Johnson), Gavin Davies (Fred Stevens), Chow Sing (Ah too), Bob Sunin (King Billy), and Reggie Weigand (Jackie); *dist:* 20th Century-Fox; *GB rel:* 23 July 1956; *GB rt:* 97 mins.; *US rel:* 14 January 1957; *US rt:* 91 mins.

# III. PROJECTS ANNOUNCED BY ALEXANDER KORDA

1. 'Mór Jókai series'—1919
Only two films of the planned
series were made: *Az aranyember*
and *Féher rózsa.*
2. 'Notre Dame'—1919
3. 'Faust'—1919
4. 'Rip Van Winkle'—1919
5. 'The Bells of Corneville'—1919
6. 'Walter Scott film'—1919
7. 'The Venice of Dreams'—1920
Korda to direct, Corda to star.
8. 'The Light That Failed'—1932
Korda to direct for Paramount
British.
9. 'Dance of the Witches'—1932
Robert Milton to direct, Leslie
Banks to star for London Films.
10. 'A Gust of Wind'—1933
Charles Laughton and Elsa
Lanchester to star.
11. 'The Field of the Cloth of Gold'—
1933
Charles Laughton to star, sequel
to *Henry VIII.*
12. 'Breach of Promise'—1933
13. 'Night Boat Express'—1933
14. 'Z'—1934
The 'private life' of Zorro, Korda
to direct, Douglas Fairbanks Snr
and Jnr to star.
15. 'The Marshal'—1934
Maurice Chevalier to star.
16. 'Hamlet'—1935
John Barrymore to star.
17. 'Nijinsky'—1935
Korda bought Romola Nijinsky's
biography, Charles Laughton to
play Diaghilev.
18. 'Marco Polo'—1935
Douglas Fairbanks Snr to co-
produce and star.
19. 'Joseph and His Brothers'—1935
20. 'Young Mr Disraeli'—1935
21. 'Marlborough'—1935
Korda bought film rights to

Winston Churchill's book for
£10,000.
22. '25 Years of the Reign of George
V'—1935
Anthony Asquith to direct from
script by Winston Churchill.
23. 'The Broken Road'—1935
from A. E. W. Mason work.
24. 'Mary Read'—1935
from A. E. W. Mason, Robert
Donat to star.
25. 'A Bicycle Built for Two' or
'Tandem'—1935
R. C. Sherriff script, René Clair
to direct, cast at times to include
Laurence Olivier, Vivien Leigh,
Binnie Barnes.
26. 'King of the Jews'—1935
Victor Sjöström to direct.
27. 'Franz Liszt'—1935
Conrad Veidt to star.
28. 'Lawrence of Arabia', later 'Revolt
in the Desert'—1935 and later.
For about four years Korda
intended to film T. E. Lawrence's
life. Walter Hudd was to star
originally, later Leslie Howard or
John Clements. Brian Desmond
Hurst wrote a script and was set to
direct in late 1937.
29. 'Hamlet'—1936
Robert Donat to star.
30. 'Nelson'—1936
Robert Donat to star, rights
bought to Hodson's book.
31. 'Precious Bane'—1936
Robert Donat to star.
32. 'Cyrano de Bergerac'—1936
Humbert Wolfe to script, Vivien
Leigh and Charles Laughton to star.
33. 'I, Claudius'—1936–7
see text; planned 1935 as 'Claudius
the God'.
34. 'Tempest Within'—1937
Merle Oberon to star.

35. 'Lunt and Fontanne film'—1937
36. 'Lovelies from America'—1937
Evelyn Waugh to script.
37. 'Calcutta'—1937
A. E. W. Mason story, Michael
Powell to direct, Sabu to star.
38. 'The Life of Charles II'—1937
Noel Coward and R. C. Sherriff to
script, Coward to produce and
star.
39. 'Tamara'—1937
Lester Cohen to script.
40. 'War and Peace'—1937
First plans: Merle Oberon and
Laurence Olivier to star, Lajos
Biro to script. Project announced
repeatedly over next few years.
41. 'Burmese Silver'—1937–8
Sir Robert Vansittart to script,
Michael Powell to direct.
42. 'The King's Messenger'—1938
R. C. Sherriff to script.
43. 'Irving Berlin–Robert Sherwood
musical'—1938
44. 'Elizabeth of Austria'—1939
Merle Oberon to star.
45. 'Pocahontas'—1939
Merle Oberon to star.
46. 'Manon Lescaut'—1940
Merle Oberon to star, Alex
Korda to direct, later Julien Duvivier to direct.
47. 'The Hunting of the U Boats'—
1940
48. 'New Wine'—1940
biopic of Franz Schubert, Ilona
Massey to star.
49. 'I Have Been Here Before'—1940
Alex Korda to script, Merle
Oberon to star.
50. 'Cyrano de Bergerac'—1940
Laurence Olivier to star.
51. 'War and Peace'—1943–5
Second plans: for MGM–London
Films, Orson Welles to co-
produce, direct, and star, Merle
Oberon to star, Lajos Biro to
script.

52. 'The Hardy Family in England'—
1944
The MGM Andy Hardy family
cast to film in London.
53. 'Dr Kildare film'—1944
The MGM cast for this series to
come over from Hollywood.
54. 'Lottie Dundas'—1944–5
Wolfgang Wilhelm to script
(from Enid Bagnold play), Vivien
Leigh to star.
55. 'Greenmantle'—1944
Edward Black to produce, adapted
from John Buchan's book, Ralph
Richardson to star.
56. 'Life of Robert Louis Stevenson' or
'Velvet Coat'—1944–5
G. B. Stern script, Robert Donat
and Merle Oberon to star.
57. 'London Revue of 1944'
58. 'Old Wives' Tale'—1944–5
adaptation of Arnold Bennett by
Lajos Biro, Edward Black to
produce.
59. 'An Habitation Enforced'—1944–5
Valentine Williams's script from
Kipling original, R. C. Sherriff to
produce, Merle Oberon to star.
60. 'Mr Chips' Boys'—1944
Sequel to Goodbye, Mr Chips,
script by James Hilton.
61. 'Gibraltar'—1944
Zoltan Korda to direct, script by
Eric Linklater.
62. 'Target Island'—1944–5
Story about Malta by John Brophy,
script by Anthony Gibbs.
63. 'Clemence Dane historical film'—
1944
64. 'James Bridie satirical comedy'—
1944
65. 'Return of a Warrior'—1945
R. C. Sherriff to script from Bricks
Upon Dust by Paul Tabori.
66. 'Pastoral'—1945
from Nevil Shute's book.
67. 'Pickwick Papers'—1945
Edward Black to produce from

script by Arthur Wimperis and J. B. Williams.

68. 'Heart of Gold'—1945
Pat Kirkwood to star in a musical tribute to the British variety stage.

69. 'In the Queen's Service'—1945
Anthony Gibbs to script from A. E. W. Mason's *Walsingham*.

70. 'Four Roads to Paradise'—1945
Maurice Collis to script.

71. 'The Wrecker'—1945
H. E. Bates to script from south seas story by Stevenson and Lloyd Osbourne.

72. 'Friday's Child'—1945
from Georgette Heyer.

73. 'Round the World'—mid-40s
From Jules Verne, Orson Welles to star.

74. 'The Eternal City'—mid-40s
from Hall Caine.

75. 'The King's General'—1946
from DuMaurier novel, James Mason to star.

76. 'The Doctor's Dilemma'—1946
Gabriel Pascal–Alex Korda project.

77. 'The True Story of Carmen'—1947
Paul Tabori and Lajos Biro to script, Paulette Goddard to star.

78. 'Salome'—1947
Orson Welles project, Welles and Eileen Herlie to star.

79. 'Cyrano de Bergerac'—1947
Orson Welles project.

80. 'The Angel and the Devil'—1947
Carol Reed to direct, Cary Grant to star.

81. 'The Promotion of the Admiral'—1947
Michael Powell–Emeric Pressburger project.

82. 'Korda–Runyon–Crosby film'—1947
Damon Runyon to script, Bing Crosby to star.

83. 'Modern Faust'—1948
Paul Tabori to script.

84. 'Spearhead'—1949
Boulting Brothers film to be made in South Africa.

85. 'Taj Mahal film'—1953
David Lean to direct.

86. 'The Long Hop'—1954
Kenneth More to star.

87. 'The Year of the Lion'—1954

88. 'The Admirable Crichton'—1955
Kenneth More, Robert Morley to star.

89. 'Arms and the Man'—1955
Alec Guinness to star.

90. 'Macbeth'—1955
Laurence Olivier to star.

91. 'The Go-Between'—1955
L. P. Hartley novel, Margaret Leighton or Deborah Kerr to star, Nancy Mitford to script.

92. 'Father, Dear Father'—1955
To be written by Ludwig Bemelmans, to star Alec Guinness.

93. 'Helen of Troy' (probably in the mid-thirties)
Remake of Hollywood film with Charles Laughton.

94. 'The Iliad'—(?)
To be scripted by Graham Greene, Laurence Olivier, and Vivien Leigh to star.

# Bibliography

ONLY three works of substantial length have been written about Alexander Korda:

Cowie, Peter, *Korda*, Paris, Anthologie du Cinéma, no. 6, 1965.

Dalrymple, Ian, 'Alex', *Journal of the British Film Academy*, Spring 1956, pp. 5–15. (Reprinted in *Quarterly of Film, Radio and Television*, vol. 11, no. 3, Spring 1957, pp. 294–309.)

Tabori, Paul, *Alexander Korda*, London, Oldbourne, 1959.

Other pertinent books and articles are listed below.

## I. ARTICLES BY ALEXANDER KORDA

'Korda Hits Back', *Film Pictorial*, 2 November 1935, p. 12.

'Fifty Million Questions—and only one Answer', *Daily Express Film Book*, ed. Ernest Betts, London, 1935, pp. 37–8.

'British Films: To-day and To-morrow', *Footnotes to The Film*, ed. Charles Davy, London, Lovat Dickson, 1937, pp. 162–71.

'What's *Right* with British Films', *The Evening News*, 25 January 1938.

'Plain Words About These Stars', press cutting dated 23 May 1938, Alexander Korda microfiche, BFI Information Department.

'Foreword', *British Film Yearbook 1946*, ed. Peter Noble, p. 5.

'The Future and the Film', *Winchester's Screen Encyclopedia*, ed. Maud M. Miller, London, Winchester Publishing, 1948, pp. 7–10.

'The First Talking Pictures', *Radio Times*, 25 December 1953, p. 5.

## II. SOURCES CONTAINING CAREER AND BIOGRAPHICAL INFORMATION ON KORDA

*Books and pamphlets*

Ackland, Rodney, and Grant, Elspeth, *The Celluloid Mistress*, London, Allan Wingate, 1954.

BIBLIOGRAPHY

Balcon, Michael, and others, *Twenty Years of British Film, 1925–45*, London, Falcon Press, 1947.

Balcon, Sir Michael, *A Lifetime of Films*, London, Hutchinson, 1969.

Barker, Felix, *The Oliviers: a biography*, London, Hamish Hamilton, 1953.

Behrman, S. N., *People in a Diary: a memoir*, Boston, Little, Brown & Co., 1972.

Betts, Ernest, *Inside Pictures*, London, The Cresset Press, 1960.

Brunel, Adrian, *Nice Work: the story of thirty years in British film production*, London, Forbes Robertson, 1949.

Burrows, Michael, *Charles Laughton and Fredric March*, St Austell, Primestyle Ltd, 1969. (Formative Films Series no. 1)

Calder-Marshall, Arthur, *The Innocent Eye: the life of Robert Flaherty*, London, W. H. Allen, 1963.

Capra, Frank, *The Name Above the Title: an autobiography*, New York, Macmillan, 1971.

Chaplin, Charles, *My Autobiography*, London, Bodley Head, 1964.

Connell, Brian, *Knight Errant: a biography of Douglas Fairbanks Jr.*, London, Hodder and Stoughton, 1955.

Davis, Bette, *The Lonely Life: an autobiography*, New York, C. P. Putnam's Sons, 1962; London, Macdonald, 1963.

Dean, Basil, *Mind's Eye: an autobiography*, London, Hutchinson, 1973.

Dent, Alan, *Vivien Leigh: a bouquet*, London, Hamish Hamilton, 1969.

Dunbar, Janet, *Flora Robson*, London, Harrap, 1960.

Fraenkel, Heinrich, *Unsterblicher Film*, München, Kindler Verlag, 1956 & 1957, (2 vols).

Frewin, Leslie, *Dietrich*, London, Leslie Frewin, 1967.

Gough-Yates, Kevin, compiler, *Michael Powell in collaboration with Emeric Pressburger*, London, British Film Institute, 1971.

——, *Michael Powell*, Brussels, Royal Film Archive of Belgium, October 1973.

Griffith, Richard, *The World of Robert Flaherty*, London, Gollancz, 1953.

Harman, Jympson, ' "Alex": a study of Korda', in *British Film Yearbook 1949–50*, ed. Peter Noble, London, Skelton Robinson, 1949.

Howard, Leslie Ruth, *A Quite Remarkable Father*, London, Longmans, 1959.

Huxley, Julian, *Memories*, London, Allen and Unwin, 1970.

Lanchester, Elsa, *Charles Laughton and I*, London, Faber and Faber, 1938.

Minney, R. J., *Puffin Asquith*, London, Leslie Frewin, 1973.

Montgomery Hyde, H., *Room 3603: the story of the British Intelligence Center in New York during World War II*, New York, Farrar Straus and Company, 1962.

More, Kenneth, *Happy Go Lucky*, London, Robert Hale, 1959.

Nemeskürty, István, *Word and Image: a history of the Hungarian Cinema*, Budapest, Corvina Press, 1968.

Niven, David, *The Moon's a Balloon: reminiscences*, London, Hamish Hamilton, 1971.

Noble, Peter, 'The Post-War Period' in *British Film Yearbook 1946*, pp. 44–7.

Norton, Richard Henry Brinsley, 6th Baron Grantley, *Silver Spoon, being extracts from the random reminiscences of Lord Grantley*, edited by Mary and Alan Wood, London, Hutchinson, 1954.

Oakley, C. A., *Where We Came In: seventy years of the British film industry*, London, Allen and Unwin, 1964.

Robyns, Gwen, *Light of a Star*, London, Leslie Frewin, 1968.
Seton, Marie, *Paul Robeson*, London, Dennis Dobson, 1958.
Sherriff, R. C., *No Leading Lady: an autobiography*, London, Gollancz, 1968.
Trewin, J. C., *Robert Donat: a biography*, London, Heinemann, 1968.
von Sternberg, Josef, *Fun in a Chinese Laundry*, New York, Macmillan, 1965; London, Secker and Warburg, 1966.
Wilcox, Herbert, *Twenty-Five Thousand Sunsets: the autobiography of Herbert Wilcox*, London, Bodley Head, 1967.
Wood, Alan, *Mr Rank: a study of J. Arthur Rank and British Films*, London, Hodder and Stoughton, 1952.

*Periodical and newspaper articles*

Atkinson, G. A., 'That Amazing Mr Korda', *Answers*, 14 May 1938.
Baldwin, Oliver, 'Korda and Company', *Picturegoer*, 10 August 1935, pp. 8–9, and 17 August 1935, pp. 16–17.
Boase, Allen, 'The Extravagant Empire of Korda', *Journal of the Federation of Victorian Film Societies*, Melbourne, Australia, no. 50, Winter 1966, pp. 71–94.
Courtney, W. B., 'New Worlds for Alexander', *Collier's*, 15 February 1936.
Dixon, Campbell, 'Sir Alexander Korda', *Films in 1951*, Sight and Sound, supplement.
Ermans, Marcel, '*Alexandre le magnifique*', translated and commented on in *World Film News*, vol. 2 no. 3, June 1937, pp. 6–7.
Gilliat, Sidney, and others, 'Sir Alexander Korda', *Sight and Sound*, vol. 25 no. 4, Spring 1956, pp. 214–15.
Holt, Paul, 'A Cabby Decided His Future', *Daily Herald*, 9 May 1953.
Johnson, Philip, 'The Creed of Korda', *The Star*, 9 March 1936.
Lejeune, C. A., 'Alexander Korda: A Sketch', *Sight and Sound*, vol. 4, no. 13, Spring, 1935, pp. 5–6.
——, 'The Five-Year Plan by Alexander Korda', *Picturegoer*, 26 January 1935, pp. 16–17.
——, 'The Private Lives of London Films', *Nash's Magazine*, September 1936, pp. 78–85.
Leni, Lore, 'The Private Life of Alex the Great', *Picturegoer*, 18 January 1936, pp. 12–13.
Lewin, David, 'The Man Who Made the Stars Shine', *Daily Express*, 26–31 January 1956.
Lockhart, Freda Bruce, 'Is He Really Alexander Korda the Great', *Film Pictorial*, 26 October 1935.
Oberon, Merle, 'How I Broke Into the Movies', *Los Angeles Daily News*, 19 May 1953.
Pánczél, György, 'Korda Sándor és a Magyar Némafilm', *Filmvilag*, no. 20, 1963, pp. 28–9.
Price, Peter, 'The Impresario Urge', *Sight and Sound*, vol. 19 no. 7, November 1950, pp. 290–3.
Raymond, Moore, 'Korda's Secret', *Sunday Dispatch*, 29 January 1956.
Seaman, H. W., two articles, *Sunday Chronicle*, 7 and 14 March 1937.
Sherwood, Lydia, 'Alexander Korda: Man of Destiny', *Vogue*, September 1936, pp. 91, 134–5.

Thompson, Herbert, 'Korda the Dreamer', *Film Weekly*, 20 June 1936.

Wallace, Leonard, 'Korda's Castles in the Air', *Film Weekly*, 20 June 1936, pp. 8–9.

Watts, Stephen, 'Alexander Korda and the International Film', *Cinema Quarterly*, vol. 2 no. 1, Autumn, 1933, pp. 12–15.

Wimperis, Arthur, 'Why Film Authors Are Not Stars', *Picturegoer*, 24 March 1934, p. 11.

Wood, E. M., 'Korda: Dreamer and Spellbinder', *Leader Magazine*, 24 May 1947.

*Miscellaneous*

Vas, Robert, *The Golden Years of Alexander Korda*, BBC Television documentary, originally shown 25 December 1968.

III. Sources containing information or critical analyses of the films of Alexander Korda

*Books and pamphlets*

Betts, Ernest, editor, *The Private Life of Henry VIII*, London, Methuen, 1934. (Script)

Charensol, Georges, and Régent, R., *Un Maître du Cinéma: René Clair*, Paris, La Table Ronde, 1952. (*The Ghost Goes West*)

Comité National Jacques Feyder, *Jacques Feyder ou le cinéma concret*, Brussels, Comité National Jacques Feyder, 1949. (*Knight Without Armour*)

Cooke, Alistair, editor, *Garbo and the Night Watchmen*, revised edition, London, Secker and Warburg, 1971.

Flaherty, Frances Hubbard, *Elephant Dance*, London, Faber and Faber, 1937. (*Elephant Boy*)

——, and Leacock, Ursula, *Sabu: the elephant boy*, London, Dent, 1937.

Greene, Graham, *The Pleasure Dome: the collected film criticism 1935–40*, edited by John Russell Taylor, London, Secker and Warburg, 1972.

——, *The Third Man*, London, Lorrimer, 1968. (Script)

Grierson, John, *Grierson on Documentary*, edited by Forsyth Hardy, revised edition, London, Faber and Faber, 1966. (*Things to Come*)

Higham, Charles, *Hollywood Cameramen: sources of light*, London, Thames and Hudson, 1970.

McClelland, Doug, *The Unkindest Cuts: the scissors and the cinema*, New Jersey, Thomas Yoseloff, 1972;

Margrave, Seton, *Successful Film Writing: as illustrated by 'The Ghost Goes West'*, London, Methuen, 1936.

Noble, Peter, editor, *Anthony Asquith*, London, British Film Institute, 1952. (New Index Series no. 5.) (*Moscow Nights* and *The Winslow Boy*)

Steinbrunner, Chris, and Goldblatt, Burt, *Cinema of the Fantastic*, New York, Saturday Review Press, 1972. (*Things to Come* and *The Thief of Bagdad*)

Wells, H. G., *The Man Who Could Work Miracles*, London, The Cresset Press, 1936.

——, *Things to Come*, London, The Cresset Press, 1935.

*Periodical and newspaper articles*

Asherman, Allan, 'Things to Come', *L'Incroyable Cinema*, no. 3, 1970, pp. 6–24.

Beard, Charles R., 'Why Get It Wrong?', *Sight and Sound*, vol. 2 no. 8, Winter 1933/4, pp. 124–5. (*The Private Life of Henry VIII*)

Borde, Raymond, 'Alerte aux Indes', *Image et Son*, no. 143 bis, Summer 1961, p. 9. (*The Drum*)

——, 'Lady Hamilton', *Image et Son*, no. 143, July 1961, pp. 33–4.

Bowen, Elizabeth, 'Things to Come: a critical appreciation', *Sight and Sound*, vol. 5 no. 17, Spring 1936, pp. 10–11.

E. G. C., 'Making Films in Paris', *Picturegoer*, 17 December 1932, pp. 12–13. (*The Girl from Maxim's*)

Catherine, B., 'Fantôme à vendre', *Image et Son*, no. 75/6, October 1954, pp. 21–2. (*The Ghost Goes West*)

——, 'Première Disillusion', *Image et Son*, no. 75/6, October 1954, pp. 45–6. (*The Fallen Idol*)

Dyer, Peter John, 'The Epic That Never Was', *Sight and Sound*, vol. 35 no. 1, Winter 1965/6, p. 45. (*I, Claudius*)

Ford, Charles, 'Marcel Pagnol', *Films in Review*, vol. XXI no. 4, April 1970, pp. 197–203. (*Marius*)

Grierson, John, 'The Finest Eyes in Cinema', *World Film News*, vol. 1 no. 12, March 1937, p. 5. (*Elephant Boy*)

R. H., 'Sagan's New Film', *Close-Up*, vol. 9 no. 4, December 1932, pp. 296–7. (*Men of To-morrow*)

Klingender, F. D., 'From Sarah Bernhardt to Flora Robson: The Cinema's Pageant of History', *World Film News*, vol. 2 no. 1, April 1937, pp. 8–11. (*The Private Life of Henry VIII*)

Lefevre, Raymond, 'La vie privée d'Henry VIII', *Image et Son*, no. 143, July 1961, p. 54.

Legay, Guy, 'Le livre de la jungle', *Image et Son*, no. 143 bis, Summer 1961, pp. 33–4. (*Jungle Book*)

O.R.O.L.E.I.S. de Toulouse, 'Elephant Boy', *Image et Son*, no. 143, July 1961, pp. 15–16.

Sherriff, R. C., 'Writing for the Films', *Uncommon Pleasures*, Contact Publications, 1949. (*Lady Hamilton*)

Williams, J. Danvers, ' "I Wrote This Film For Your Enjoyment" says H. G. Wells', *Film Weekly*, 29 February 1936, pp. 7–8. (*Things to Come*)

*Miscellaneous*

Duncalf, Bill, *The Epic That Never Was*, BBC Television documentary, originally shown 24 December 1965. (*I, Claudius*)

IV. BACKGROUND SOURCES AND REFERENCE WORKS CONSULTED

*Books and pamphlets: non-fiction*

American Film Institute, *The American Film Institute Catalog of Motion Pictures produced in the United States: Feature Films 1921–30*, edited by Kenneth W. Munden, New York and London, Bowker, 1971.

Carrick, Edward, compiler, *Art and Design in the British Film: a pictorial directory of British art directors and their work*, London, Dennis Dobson, 1948.

Dickinson, Thorold, *A Discovery of Cinema*, London, Oxford University Press, 1971.

Durgnat, Raymond, *A Mirror for England: British movies from austerity to affluence*, London, Faber and Faber, 1970.

Eisner, Lotte, *The Haunted Screen*, London, Thames and Hudson, 1969. (Original French edition, 1952.)

Fritz, Walter, *Die Österreichischen Spielfilme der Stummfilmzeit (1907–1930)*, Vienna, Österreichischen Gesellschaft für Filmwissenschaft, 1967.

Gifford, Denis, *British Cinema: an illustrated guide*, London, Zwemmer, 1968.

Guback, Thomas, *The International Film Industry: Western Europe and America since 1945*, Bloomington, Indiana, Indiana University Press, 1969.

Hampton, Benjamin B., *History of the American Film Industry, from its beginnings to 1931*, New York, Dover Publications, 1970. (First published in 1932 as *A History of the Movies*.)

Huntley, John, *British Film Music*, London, Skelton Robinson, 1947.

Kelly, Terence, *A Competitive Cinema*, London, Institute of Economic Affairs, 1966. (I.E.A. Research Report.)

Klingender, F. D., and Legg, Stuart, *Money Behind the Screen: a report prepared on behalf of the Film Council*, London, Lawrence and Wishart, 1937.

Kracauer, Siegfried, *From Caligari to Hitler: a psychological history of the German film*, London, Dennis Dobson, 1947.

Lampe, David, *The Last Ditch*, London, Cassell, 1968.

Lamprecht, Gerhard, *Deutsche Stummfilme 1923–26*, Berlin, Deutsche Kinemathek, 1967.

Low, Rachael, *The History of the British Film, 1918–29*, London, Allen and Unwin, 1971.

Magyar, Bálint, *A Magyar Némafilm Története, 1896–1918*, EM· Epítésugyi Tájékoztatási Kozpont, 1966.

Manvell, Roger, and Fraenkel, Heinrich, *The German Cinema*, London, Dent, 1971.

Pascal, Valerie, *The Disciple and his Devil*, London, Michael Joseph, 1971.

Political and Economic Planning, *The British Film Industry*, London, P.E.P., 1952.

——, *The British Film Industry 1958*, London, P.E.P., 1958.

Rotha, Paul, *The Film Till Now*, London, Vision Press, 1949.

Rotha, Paul, *Documentary Diary*, London, Secker and Warburg, 1973.

Shattuck, Roger, *The Banquet Years*, revised edition, London, Jonathan Cape, 1969.

Spraos, John, *Decline of the Cinema: an economist's report*, London, Allen and Unwin, 1962.

### Fiction

Dell, Jeffrey, *Nobody Ordered Wolves*, London, Heinemann, 1939.

Priestley, J. B., *Bright Day*, London, Heinemann, 1946.

Siepmann, Eric, *Waterloo in Wardour Street*, London, Chatto and Windus, 1936.

*Periodical and newspaper articles*

Bond, Ralph, 'Monopoly: The Future of British Films', London, Association of Cine-Technicians pamphlet, May 1946.

Grierson, John, 'The Fate of British Films', *The Fortnightly*, July 1937.

The Information Department of the British Film Institute has extensive files of press-cuttings on Korda and on London Films. Much information can also be gleaned from the following British and American trade papers and magazines:

> *The Bioscope*
> *Film Daily*
> *Film Weekly*
> *Hollywood Reporter*
> *Kinematograph Weekly*
> *Motion Picture Classic*
> *Picturegoer*
> *Today's Cinema*
> *Variety*

Finally there are various HMSO publications, in particular the Parliamentary Debates of both Houses (Hansard), the Cinematograph Acts 1927–60, and the reports of the Board of Trade Committee on Cinematograph Films.

# Index

Page numbers in **bold** type refer to the filmography.

395